WHO
REALLY
KILLED
KENNEDY?

OTHER WND BOOKS TITLES by JEROME R. CORSI, PH.D.

WHAT WENT WRONG
THE INSIDE STORY OF THE GOP DEBACLE OF 2012 . . . AND HOW IT CAN BE AVOIDED NEXT TIME

WHERE'S THE BIRTH CERTIFICATE?
THE CASE THAT BARACK OBAMA IS NOT ELIGIBLE TO BE PRESIDENT

HOW OBAMA CAN BE DEFEATED IN 2012
A BATTLE PLAN BASED ON POLITICAL STATISTICAL REALITIES

THE LATE GREAT USA
THE COMING MERGER WITH MEXICO AND CANADA

MINUTEMEN (WITH JIM GILCHRIST)
THE BATTLE TO SECURE AMERICA'S BORDERS

ATOMIC IRAN
HOW THE TERRORIST REGIME BOUGHT THE BOMB AND AMERICAN POLITICIANS

BLACK GOLD STRANGLEHOLD (WITH CRAIG R. SMITH)
THE MYTH OF SCARCITY AND THE POLITICS OF OIL

WHO
REALLY
KILLED
KENNEDY?

50 YEARS LATER
STUNNING NEW REVELATIONS ABOUT THE JFK ASSASSINATION

JEROME R. CORSI PH.D.
TWO-TIME #1 NEW YORK TIMES BESTSELLING AUTHOR

 WND Books

FOR JONES HARRIS,

whose knowledge of the JFK assassination and dedication to solving the crime
have inspired and sustained my own research into the enduring enigma —
"Who *Really* Killed Kennedy?"

WHO REALLY KILLED KENNEDY?

WND Books, Inc.
Washington, D.C.

Book designed by Mark Karis.

WND Books are distributed to the trade by:
Midpoint Trade Books
27 West 20th Street, Suite 1102
New York, NY 10011

WND Books are available at special discounts for bulk purchases. WND Books, Inc.,
also publishes books in electronic formats. For more information call (541) 474-1776
or visit www.wndbooks.com.

First Edition

ISBN 13 Digit: 978-1-938067-10-5

Library of Congress information available.

Printed in the United States of America.

CONTENTS

PREFACE

THE END OF CAMELOT

J. Lee Rankin, Chief Counsel, Warren Commission: . . . They [the FBI] have decided that it is Oswald who committed the assassination, they have decided that no one else was involved, they have decided . . .

Sen. Richard Russell: They [the FBI] have tried the case and reached a verdict.

Rep. Hale Boggs: You have put your finger on it.

—Warren Commission Executive session, Jan. 27, 1964[1]

THE ASSASSINATION OF PRESIDENT JOHN FITZGERALD KENNEDY in Dallas on November 22, 1963, is easily the greatest whodunit murder mystery of the twentieth century.

JFK, a young and beloved president, was cruelly and brutally gunned down at half-past noon at his wife's side. The images of his murder, captured that day in Dealey Plaza by dozens of amateur photographers, were so horrific that many, including the Zapruder film—the most important of all the movies taken that day—were suppressed from full public viewing for more than a decade.

The assassination had all the elements of classic Greek tragedy. Camelot, the magic of the JFK administration, was destroyed in the span of less than ten seconds. The presumed assassin, Lee Harvey Oswald, was identified in the first hour after the shooting. At approximately 1:51 p.m., less than an hour and a half later, he was found by Dallas Police hiding in a dark movie theater, sitting alone, with his .38 snub-nose revolver in his belt. But Oswald did not surrender without a struggle. Seeing Dallas patrolman M. N. "Nick" McDonald approach him in the theater, he jumped up, threw his hands in the air as if to surrender, and shouted, "Well, it's over now." Then, when McDonald reached for Oswald's right wrist, Oswald punched McDonald between the eyes with his left fist. McDonald hit him back, and in the ensuing scuffle, Oswald drew the .38 out of his belt. McDonald managed to grab the gun as Oswald pulled the trigger. The gun misfired, and in the course of grappling with Oswald, McDonald suffered a pronounced four-inch scratch, from the corner of his eye down to the corner of his mouth. But fortunately McDonald's life was spared.[2]

No giant, Oswald turned out to be a loner who moved to Russia intending to give up his US citizenship. In Russia, he acquired a Russian bride and became a self-professed Marxist. When he returned from Russia, Oswald brought back his Russian wife, Marina, and their first child, a daughter named June Lee. Even with his family in the United States, Oswald had a history of living alone. At the time of the assassination, Oswald was living in a rooming house, while his wife and daughter were rooming with a Russian speaking acquaintance, Ruth Paine. Back in the United States, Oswald had a difficult time holding a job. At the time of the assassination, he was still living in the rooming house, when he began working as a book clerk in the Texas School Book Depository on October 16, 1963. Four days later, on October 20, 1963, Marina gave birth to their second daughter, Audrey Marina Rachel Oswald, approximately one month before the JFK assassination.

So how was it possible that such an insignificant misfit could bring down the most powerful man in the world at the height of his power and popularity?

Truly, the JFK assassination was a watershed event in United States history. The instant rifle fire broke out on that sunny November day in Dallas, the innocence of the postwar prosperity and optimism of the

Eisenhower years died for good. President Lyndon Baines Johnson was sworn into office before Air Force One departed Dallas that day for Washington. After JFK's death Johnson led the nation into the dark days of Vietnam, proclaiming the necessity of a war JFK had already decided to abandon. The 1960s, after JFK's death, was marked by antiwar protests, urban racial riots, the feminist revolution and the rise of a new sexuality, and an upheaval in economics and politics that questioned whether the United States could and would provide social and economic justice for all US citizens, let alone for peoples of other nations striving to achieve their own freedom in their homelands.

Almost from the first hour after the Warren Commission delivered its final report to President Johnson on September 24, 1964, critics began to raise serious considerations that the Commission was a whitewash. Contrary to the impression given the public, the Warren Commission was not unanimous in its conclusion Lee Harvey Oswald was the lone assassin. US Senator Richard Russell Jr., a Democrat and member of the Warren Commission, in the final session of the Commission on September 18, 1964, led a group of three dissenting members that included himself, Sen. John Sherman Cooper, a Republican from Kentucky with a reputation for his independent views, and Rep. Hale Boggs, a Democrat from Louisiana who was then serving as majority whip of the U.S. House of Representatives. Russell, Cooper, and Boggs wanted to file a separate dissenting opinion stating that the available evidence was incomplete and did not rule out Lee Harvey Oswald being part of a conspiracy to assassinate JFK. Ultimately, the dissenters accepted the final report with minor changes, but only after Supreme Court Justice Earl Warren insisted the final report needed to be unanimous. Later, Russell was shocked to find out that of the thirteen executive sessions held by the Warren Commission, the one where the objections were made was the only session that had not been transcribed. Instead, all that was published were brief minutes of the meeting that left out any mention of the disagreement.[3] On November 20, 1966, in an interview published in *The Atlanta Constitution*, Russell made clear he could not agree with certainty that Oswald had acted alone.[4] In a television interview given on January 19, 1970, less than a year before his death, Russell again proclaimed his doubts about the Warren Commission's conclusion. While conceding he did not have "the slightest doubt" that

Oswald fired the fatal shots, Russell made clear that he "never believed that Lee Harvey Oswald assassinated President Kennedy without at least some encouragement from others." To this, Russell added, "I think someone else worked with him."[5]

Was it possible the Warren Commission was designed from the beginning, not to solve the crime, but to cover up a malignant conspiracy that reached the topmost levels of government, possibly involving even LBJ himself? In a 2003 Gallup poll three-quarters of Americans, fully 75 percent, responded that they believed Lee Harvey Oswald did not act alone.[6]

Was it possible JFK's assassination was not the psychologically disturbed act of a lone gunman, but a sophisticated coup d'état callously orchestrated and professionally accomplished to advance political ambition, changing forever the destiny of the nation?

Now, fifty years after the assassination, despite repeated efforts by the US Congress to force full disclosure, the CIA and other US agencies continue to lock away hundreds of thousands of documents in secret files.

To maintain the shroud of secrecy over the JFK assassination a half-century after the event is a disgrace for a nation that proclaims values of truth and justice. In 2013 the government continues to suppress key documents regarding the JFK assassination, which reinforces the suspicion that there remains some deep, dark, disturbing truth that would be more than the American people could handle. The impression of a cover-up is reinforced even today when critics of the Warren Commission are demonized as "conspiracy theorists."

Truthfully, the innocence of accepting government at face value died along with JFK in the streets of Dallas on November 22, 1963. A nation committed to a robust First Amendment would welcome the challenge of contesting competing versions of history, especially when evidence abounds that Lee Harvey Oswald was not a lone-nut assassin, but a highly complicated young man with tentacles that reached into the KGB, as well as the CIA, the FBI, and Navy Intelligence.

The JFK assassination, as is the case with the Lincoln assassination, may endure as a perpetual mystery of American politics. Each generation sees the trauma through the lens of their particular experience with politics and each remains ever fascinated with the enigma.

This book begins where all good murder investigations should begin, namely, with an investigation of the ballistics evidence. The point of the first chapter is that a careful examination of the ballistics evidence makes clear a lone-assassin cannot account for all the bullet damage that occurred that day.

If there were more than one shooter, then Lee Harvey Oswald, at most, only played a part in the assassination, so the question remains: "Who really killed JFK?"

So who was involved? The KGB or the CIA? The mob? Cuba? Possibly even LBJ himself? Each had a motive; each had the opportunity to be involved.

After fifty years of continuing controversy, no book could possibly cover every aspect of an event as complicated as the JFK assassination. And this book is not different. Instead it seeks to communicate that the investigation of the JFK assassination is more than an attempt to find the shooters. It is an attempt to plumb the motivation of the guilty parties, regardless of how high up the suspicion goes. While finding out who pulled the trigger or triggers involved in shooting JFK is important, the key to the puzzle requires deciphering the motivations of those who wanted JFK dead so LBJ could be placed in the White House. To be successful the inquiry must probe who were the forces higher up that organized the conspiracy and why did they want JFK murdered. The goal of this book is to answer one question: "Who *really* killed JFK?"

ONE

THE SINGLE-BULLET THEORY

But on the *Life* blowups, I saw for the first time enough evidence to prove that Connally had not been hit until at least thirteen frames (or three-quarters of a second) later—too late for it to have been the same bullet, too soon for it to have been a second bullet from the same rifle.

—Josiah Thompson, *Six Seconds in Dallas*, 1967[7]

A WEEK AFTER THE ASSASSINATION, FBI chief J. Edgar Hoover told President Lyndon Johnson in a phone call that three shots were fired, with two hitting JFK and a separate shot hitting Governor John Connally. In accounting for three shots, Hoover did not imagine one shot had missed. More important, Hoover rushed to identify incorrectly the bullet the Warren Commission later was to designate as the single bullet that hit both JFK and Connally. Hoover told LBJ, "one complete bullet rolled out of the President's head," after it destroyed much of JFK's head on impact. "In trying to massage his heart,"

Hoover continued, "on the way to the hospital, they loosened the bullet, which fell on the stretcher and we have that."[8] This Hoover fabricated. But somehow, from the very beginning of the investigation into the assassination, finding a nearly pristine bullet was important in the process of framing Lee Harvey Oswald as the assassin.

Only days after the assassination, *Life Magazine* writer Paul Mandel published an article in the December 6, 1963 issue, in which he asked questions that ultimately led to the conclusion of a conspiracy. Even though the purpose of Mandel's article was to argue that Lee Harvey Oswald was the lone shooter, firing three shots with a mail-order Mannlicher-Carcano rifle in an interval of 6.8 seconds from the sixth floor of the Texas School Book Depository, Mandel raises doubts in his examination of the evidence. Perhaps most important, Mandel makes people aware that JFK's neck wound was an entry wound. "The description of the President's two wounds by a Dallas doctor who tried to save him have added to the rumors," Mandel wrote. "The doctor said one bullet passed from back to front on the right side of the President's head. But the other, the doctor reported, entered the President's throat from the front and then lodged in his body."[9]

Mandel explained what he believed to be the evidence as follows: "Since by this time the limousine was 50 yards past Oswald and the President's back was turned almost directly to the sniper, it has been hard to understand how the bullet could enter the front of his throat. Hence the recurring guess that there was a second sniper somewhere else. But the 8 mm [Zapruder film] shows the President turning his body far around to the right as he waves to someone in the crowd. His throat is exposed – toward the sniper's nest – just before he clutches it." *Life* had purchased the exclusive rights to the Zapruder film and did not make it available to the public, so Mandel's claim had to be taken at face value.

In a special memorial issue that *Life* published in the days after the assassination, the editors chose to show some stills from the film. In the first photograph published JFK is waving to the right just before the shooting began, but his torso is not turned back behind the limo.[10] In Zapruder frame 183, as published in the magazine, JFK's head can be seen turning to the left, as he waves to the left, but his neck continues to face forward, as his back remains full into the seat behind him. Mandel knew the medical evidence at Parkland Hospital conflicted with the theory that all the bullets were fired from the Texas School Book Depository behind the limo as the JFK motorcade headed west on Elm Street.

Mandel also assumed that only three bullets were fired and that a separate bullet hit JFK and Connally. Mandel wrote: "Three shots were fired. Two struck the president, one Governor Connally. All three bullets have been recovered – one deformed, from the floor of the limousine; one from the stretcher that carried the President; one that entered the President's body. All were fired from the 6.5mm Carcano carbine which Lee Oswald bought by mail last March."[11] The truth is that no bullet was found in the limousine and no bullet was recovered from the president's body. The bullet that was found at Parkland Hospital, marked Warren Commission Exhibit 399, was found on a stretcher at Parkland Hospital, but there is no evidence President Kennedy's body was ever placed on that stretcher. Mandel assumed the first bullet struck JFK, the second bullet struck Connally, and the third bullet was the fatal headshot that mortally wounded JFK at Zapruder frame 313.

What was clear from the Mandel article was that in the first days after the JFK assassination, information was being fed to credible journalists like Mandel at *Life* to refute the physical evidence observed by the physicians who treated JFK immediately after the shooting at Parkland Hospital.

A STRAY BULLET

The FBI's official theory remained that three bullets had been fired, with two hitting Kennedy and one hitting Connally, at least until government investigators realized a witness to the assassination, James Tague, had been hit in the cheek by a ricochet from a missed shot. On July 23, 1964, Warren Commission counsel Wesley J. Liebeler took Tague's testimony in Dallas. As the motorcade passed through Dealey Plaza, Tague was standing on the far side of the triple underpass by the bridge abatement. When he realized what he first heard as firecrackers were actually gunshots, he ducked behind the bridge abatement. Tague testified as follows:

> **Mr. Tague**: . . . We walked back down there, and another man joined us who identified himself as the deputy sheriff, who was in civilian clothes, and I guess this was three or four minutes after. I don't know how to gauge time on something like that.

And I says, "Well, you know now, I recall something sting me on the face while I was standing down there."

And he looked up and he said, "Yes, you have blood there on your cheek."

And I reached up and there was a couple of drops of blood. And he said, "Where were you standing?"

And I says, "Right down here." We walked fifteen feet away when this deputy sheriff said, "Look here on the curb." There was a mark, quite obviously was a bullet, and it was very fresh.[12]

The same day, Liebeler took the testimony of Dallas County Deputy Sheriff Eddy Raymond Walthers who confirmed Tague's story. Although Walthers could not remember Tague's name, he remembered a man who claimed he had been struck by something on the face during the shooting in Dealey Plaza. " . . . I started to search in that immediate area and found a place on the curb there in the Main Street lane there close to the underpass where a projectile had struck that curb," Walthers told the Warren Commission.[13]

Tague's confirmed testimony created a problem for the Warren Commission, especially after photographic evidence emerged showing exactly where Tague stood to watch the motorcade, along with a second photo that showed the cut on his cheek after the shooting. Tague was not sure which shot resulted in the ricochet that hit him, but he believed it was the second or third shot, not the first.

Tague's testimony forced the Warren Commission to recalculate. If shots one and three hit JFK and shot two hit Connally, which shot hit Tague? Only three spent cartridges had been found on the floor of the sniper's nest in the Texas School Book Depository. The Zapruder film set a narrow time frame in which the shooting could have happened, somewhere between 4.8 seconds and 7 seconds, according to the final report.[14] Even a top expert using a bolt-action Mannlicher-Carcano rifle would be limited to three shots in that time range, especially with the need to zero in the target with the scope anew for each shot.

The Warren Commission's final report conceded that one shot missed, although the report equivocated over whether the missed shot was the first or the second. In acknowledging a stray shot had hit Tague, the Commission implied that a single bullet had to have been responsible for hitting both JFK and Connally. The alternative was to argue a bullet fragment had hit Tague, most likely from the third shot that hit JFK's head. But the markings the bullet left on the pavement prior to ricocheting to hit Tague made it unlikely that Tague was hit by a bullet fragment. The only room for doubt the Warren Commission's conclusion left was whether the first shot had missed, or the second. But either way, the Warren Commission was stuck attributing all the damage done to JFK and to Connally to two bullets.

The pristine bullet J. Edgar Hoover had discussed with LBJ in the immediate aftermath of the assassination came in handy. Warren Commission junior counsel Arlen Specter cleverly decided he would craft the pristine bullet into the single bullet that hit both JFK and Connally. So if a first shot missed, Specter reasoned that was the shot that ricocheted to hit Tague, with the second shot hitting both JFK and Connally, and the third shot being the head shot that killed JFK at Zapruder frame 313. Or, alternatively, the first shot may have hit both JFK and Connally, with the second shot ricocheting to hit Tague, and the third shot being the head shot that killed JFK at Zapruder frame 313. Either way, the pristine bullet Hoover discussed became the "single bullet" of the Specter theory. Doubters quickly characterized Specter's single bullet as the "magic bullet" that injured two adult men only to emerge from Connally's body in pristine condition—a theory that quickly raised eyebrows from those experienced with firearms.

FINDING THE MAGIC BULLET

Key to the Warren Commission's conclusion that a lone shooter was responsible for killing JFK is what has become known as the "magic bullet," a pristine bullet identified as Commission Exhibit 399, or CE399 for short. The bullet found on a stretcher at Parkland Hospital in the first hour after JFK was admitted for treatment is important because ballistics linked it to having been fired from Oswald's Mannlicher-Carcano rifle. The bullet is controversial in that the precise stretcher on which the bullet was found is not certain, and because the Parkland Hospital employees who found the bullet were unable to identify with certainty that it was the CE399 bullet. As a footnote, without explanation the Warren Commission dropped Hoover's suggestion the pristine bullet had fallen on a stretcher as a result of massaging JFK's heart on the way to the hospital. For one, Jackie Kennedy and a brain dead JFK remained in the back seat of the limo on the way to the hospital; no one massaged JFK's heart. And second, Specter had to dismiss the idea the pristine bullet dropped from JFK's body because if the pristine bullet remained in JFK's body, then it couldn't have been the single bullet that hit both JFK and Connally.

Professor Richard H. Popkin, writing in the *New York Review of Books* on July 28, 1966, summarized succinctly the problem with CE399, when he wrote:

> The [Warren] Commission never seems to have considered the possibility the bullet was planted. Yet in view of evidence concerning No. 399 it is an entirely reasonable hypothesis that the bullet had never been in a human body, and could have been placed on one of the stretchers. If this possibility had been considered, then the Commission might have realized that some of the evidence might be "fake" and could have been deliberately faked. Bullet No. 399 plays a most important role in the case, since it firmly links Oswald's rifle with the assassination. At the time when the planting could have been done, it was not known if any other ballistics evidence survived the shooting. But certainly, the pristine bullet, definitely traceable to Oswald's Carcano, would have started a chase for and pursuit of Oswald if nothing else had, and would have made him the prime suspect.[15]

The story of CE399 begins at about 1:00 p.m. on November 22, 1963, when Darrell C. Tomlinson, a senior engineer at Parkland Hospital then in charge of the hospital power plant pushed a stretcher off a hospital elevator onto the hospital ground floor, placing the stretcher against the wall about two feet away from another stretcher already in the ground floor hall. In the process of arranging the stretchers to allow someone to use a restroom along the wall, Tomlinson bumped the wall with the stretcher he took off the elevator. This caused a bullet on the stretcher already in the hall to roll out. Tomlinson assumed the bullet had been lodged under the edge of a mat on top of the stretcher. In the testimony he gave to the Warren Commission at Parkland Hospital on March 20, 1964,

Tomlinson noted there were two bloody sheets rolled up on the stretcher from which the bullet rolled out, along with a few surgical instruments and a sterile pack or two.[16]

Through two pages of questioning, committee junior counsel Arlen Specter expressed frustration that Tomlinson's story had apparently changed from an earlier account in which Tomlinson supposedly told the Secret Service the bullet was found on the stretcher he rolled off the elevator, not the stretcher that was already in the hall. Repeatedly, Tomlinson made clear he could not remember precisely. The following exchange is typical of how Specter pressed Tomlinson to change his story:

> **Mr. Specter**: What did you tell the Secret Service man about which stretcher you took off the elevator?
>
> **Mr. Tomlinson**: I told him that I was not sure, and I am not—I'm not sure of it, but as I said, I would be going against the oath which I took a while ago, because I am definitely not sure.
>
> **Mr. Specter**: Do you remember if you told the Secret Service man which stretcher you thought you took off the elevator?
>
> **Mr. Tomlinson**: Well, we talked about taking a stretcher off the elevator, but when it comes down on an oath, I wouldn't say for sure, I really don't remember.[17]

Finally, in exasperation, Tomlinson told Specter, "Yes, I'm going to tell you all I can, and I'm not going to tell you something I can't lay down and sleep at night with either."[18] In the very next exchange, Tomlinson explained to Specter that he had no idea where the stretcher in the elevator came from, or who put it there. This is important. The stretcher was on the elevator when Tomlinson got on the elevator. Despite repeated attempts, Specter was unable to establish that the bullet was found on the stretcher Tomlinson rode with in the elevator, or that Tomlinson had any idea where the bullet may have come from. To Specter's obvious frustration, Tomlinson testified the bullet came from the stretcher already in the hall on the ground floor, a stretcher Tomlinson knew even less about than the stretcher he found in the elevator when he entered.

Making Tomlinson's testimony even weaker, at no point while Tomlinson was under oath did Specter show Tomlinson CE399, or a photograph of CE399, to ask him if it was the bullet he found on the stretcher at Parkland Hospital. Just to be clear, the interview under oath ended without Tomlinson making a positive ID of CE399 as the bullet he found.

Tomlinson testified that he handed the bullet over to Mr O. P. Wright, the personnel director of security for the Dallas County Hospital District and a former police detective with the Dallas Police Department. Commission Exhibit 1024, CE1024 for short, is a note from FBI Special Agent E. Johnson, dated 7:30 p.m. on November 22, 1963. Johnson explains how the bullet found by Tomlinson was handed over to the FBI:

> The attached expended bullet was received by me about 5 min. prior to Mrs. Kennedy's departure from the hospital. It was found on one of the stretchers located in the emergency ward of the hospital. Also on this same stretcher was rubber gloves, a stethoscope and other doctor's paraphernalia. It could not be determined who had used this stretcher or if President Kennedy had occupied it. No further information was obtained. Name of person from who I received this bullet: Mr. O. P. Wright.[19]

Again, no photograph of the bullet accompanied CE1024. An exhaustive search of the documentary record failed to produce any photograph of the bullet found on the stretcher before the FBI removed the bullet from Parkland Hospital. FBI Special Agent Johnson made no note of the two bloody sheets Tomlinson noticed on the stretcher he found in the hall on the ground floor.

According to Commission Exhibit 2011 (CE2011), on June 12, 1964, FBI Special Agent Bardwell Odum showed Tomlinson and Wright CE399 and both stated that while the bullet looked like the bullet Tomlinson found on the stretcher, neither of them positively identify CE399 as the bullet.[20] A declassified FBI memo dated June 20, 1964, provides additional evidence, stating without qualification that neither Tomlinson nor Wright could positively identify CE399 as the bullet they found at Parkland Hospital.[21] In subsequent interviews Odum refused to back up CE2011, claiming he never had in his possession any bullet related to the JFK assassination and he never showed CE399 to anyone at Parkland Hospital to get confirmation of the bullet found there on November 22, 1963.[22]

In an interview in November 1966 O. P. Wright told Josiah

Thompson, author of the 1967 book *Six Seconds in Dallas*, that the bullet Tomlinson found on the stretcher on November 22, 1963, had a pointed tip, which obviously did not meet the description of the rounded tip of CE399. Wright reached into his desk and produced for Thompson a pointed .30 caliber round he claimed looked like the bullet Tomlinson found. Thompson was so impressed by the discrepancy that he photographed Wright's pointed-tip round next to a key to give an indication of size. (The photo appears in Thompson's book, *Six Seconds in Dallas*.) Clearly, the pointed .30 caliber round Wright produced is shorter than CE399 and bears a pointed tip distinct from CE399's rounded tip. "As a professional law enforcement officer, Wright has an educated eye for bullet shapes," Thompson noted.[23]

Thompson also researched and ruled out that the stretcher on which Tomlinson found the bullet was the stretcher used for either President Kennedy or Governor Connally. When the presidential limo arrived at Parkland, JFK was taken to Trauma Room 1, where he was pronounced dead at 1:00 p.m., approximately the same time Tomlinson testified he found the bullet. JFK's body remained on his stretcher until 1:45 p.m., when the casket arrived. Connally was taken to Trauma Room 2 on a stretcher and then wheeled into Operating Room 5. The stretcher was wheeled out of Operating Room 5, placed on an elevator, and returned to the ER at approximately 1:00 p.m., as Connally was being placed under anesthesia in Operating Room 5. Again, Tomlinson testified he found the bullet at approximately 1:00 p.m. on a stretcher located on the ground floor that was already in the hall when his elevator door opened.[24]

Yet, the Warren Commission concluded CE399 had to have been found on Connally's stretcher, since it was not found on JFK's stretcher. In the final report, the Warren Commission wrote, "Although Tomlinson was not certain whether the bullet came from the Connally stretcher or the adjacent one, the Commission concluded that the bullet came from the Governor's stretcher. That conclusion is buttressed by evidence which eliminated President Kennedy's stretcher as a source of the bullet."[25] Here the Warren Commission committed a classic error of forcing the evidence to fit a pre-determined theory, rather than presenting the evidence and letting the theory follow from the evidence.

Clearly, the Warren Commission wanted CE399 to have been found on Connally's stretcher because that would support the single-bullet theory that assumes CE399 wounded Connally after wounding JFK in the back and neck. The assumption was that CE399 dropped out of Connally's thigh. Finding CE399 on Connally's stretcher would eliminate the problem that no bullet had been found in either body. The Warren Commission's logic that because CE399 was not found on JFK's stretcher it had to be found on Connally's stretcher is shaky when we realize that four other emergency cases were admitted to Parkland Memorial Hospital in a space of twenty minutes, with two of these patients bleeding profusely. At 12:38 p.m., a woman identified as Helen Guycion was admitted to Parkland Hospital, bleeding from the mouth. Sixteen minutes later, Arnold Fuller, a two-and-a-half-year-old child, was admitted with a deep cut on his chin. "It is possible that this second stretcher belonged to one of these patients," assassination researcher Jerry McKnight commented. "The Commission, however, opted to leave this possibility unexplored."[26]

Yet another possibility remains to explain how CE399 got on the stretcher. Secret Service Agent Andrew Berger, in a memorandum placed into evidence with the Warren Commission's Report as Commission Exhibit 1024, described a bizarre incident where a man claiming to be an FBI agent tried to force his way into the ER trauma room where JFK was being treated. Berger wrote:

> At approximately 1:30 PM, the Chief Supervising nurse, a Mrs. Nelson started to enter the emergency room with an unidentified male (WM, 45yrs, 6'2", 185–190 lbs, grey hair). As the reporting agent and SA Johnsen started to ask his identity he shouted that he was FBI. Just as we began to ask for his credentials, he abruptly attempted to enter the emergency room and had to be forcibly restrained by us. ASAIC Kellerman then appeared and asked this individual to go to the end of the hall.[27]

Josiah Thompson pointed out that two witnesses to the Warren Commission testified to having seen Jack Ruby at Parkland Hospital at about the time JFK's death was announced.[28] Jack Ruby was a colorful character in Dallas. A nightclub owner with connections to the mob, he had a habit of schmoozing with police to make sure his business was not harassed, especially as Ruby's Carousel Club featured burlesque-like strip-tease dancers. It was not unusual to see Ruby milling around the heart of the action anytime the police radio announced something of special interest was happening in the city. Seth Kantor, a Scripps Howard newspaper writer, testified to the Warren Commission on June 2, 1964, that he saw Ruby near the entrance to Parkland Hospital immediately after the JFK shooting. According to Kantor, Ruby and he shook hands and Ruby asked whether he should close his nightclubs because of "this terrible thing." Kantor commented it seemed just perfectly normal to see Jack Ruby standing there, because Ruby was a known "goer to events."[29] A woman, standing outside the ER at Parkland next to Ruby, heard Ruby comment that he would be happy to donate a kidney to save Governor Connally, in response to a rumor that Connally had been shot in the kidney.[30] "A number of people could have had access to that hospital vestibule on November 22," Josiah Thompson commented. "It would have been a task of no great difficulty to plant a bullet on the stretcher where CE399 was found."[31]

The lone assassin theory came to hinge on the Warren Commission proving the near-pristine bullet CE399 struck both JFK and Governor John Connally. However, the Warren Commission's failure to consider the possibility CE399 was planted on the stretcher at Parkland Hospital, possibly by Jack Ruby, suggests the Warren Commission was primarily interested in CE399 because it could be made to fit the predetermined theory that Lee Harvey Oswald was the lone assassin.

GOVERNOR CONNALLY'S WOUNDS

Dr. Robert Roeder Shaw, the chief of thoracic surgery at Parkland Hospital in Dallas, operated on Connally's obvious and serious chest wound. Testifying to the Warren Commission on April 21, 1964, Shaw established that he had personal experience with approximately one thousand cases involving bullet wounds, both at Parkland Hospital and during World War II, when he served as chief of thoracic surgery in Paris, France. Shaw testified that a bullet entered Connally's back just below his right shoulder blade, proceeded to shatter Connally's fifth rib, and exited just below Connally's right nipple. When asked if one or two bullets had caused the injuries to Connally, Shaw testified that he assumed at the time the wounds to Connelly's chest, wrist, and thigh had been caused by the same bullet, although he also considered it possible that a second or even a third bullet might have caused the wrist and thigh wounds. With his focus on making sure Connelly could breathe, Shaw gave Connelly's wrist and thigh wounds only cursory thought or examination.

Warren Commission counsel Arlen Specter then asked Shaw whether he believed CE399, the pristine bullet found on the stretcher at Parkland Hospital, could have caused all three of Connally's wounds. Shaw answered in a way that summarized the medical evidence so as to devastate the single-bullet theory: "I feel that there would be some difficulty in explaining all of the wounds as being inflicted by bullet Exhibit 399 without causing more in the way of loss of substance to the bullet or deformation of the bullet."[32] In other words, a single bullet that caused such extensive wounds including shattering a rib and breaking a wrist, would be expected to have lost substantial mass through fragmenting or would have been seriously deformed, or both. For CE399 to have emerged in near-pristine shape after having inflicted the wounds Shaw observed and treated on Connally was simply not credible.

Dr. Milton Helpern, formerly chief medical examiner of New York City who had conducted autopsies on more than two thousand victims of gunshot wounds and was credited by *The New York Times* as knowing "more about violent death than anyone else in the world," expressed similar doubt when questioned about CE399:

> The original, pristine weight of this bullet before it was fired was approximately 160–161 grains. The Commission reported the weight of the bullet recovered on the stretcher at 158.6 grains in Parkland Hospital. This bullet wasn't distorted in any way. I cannot accept the premise that this bullet thrashed around in all that bony tissue and lost only 1.4 to 2.4 grains of its original weight. I cannot believe either that this bullet is going to emerge miraculously unscathed, without any deformity, and with its lands and groves intact. . . . You must remember that next to bone, the skin offers greater resistance to a bullet in its course through the body than any other kind of tissue. . . . This single-bullet theory asks us to believe that this bullet went through seven layers of skin, tough, elastic, resistant skin. In addition . . . this bullet passed through other layers of soft tissue; and then shattered bones! I just can't believe that this bullet had the force to do what [the

Commission] have demanded of it; and I don't think they have really stopped to think out carefully what they have asked of this bullet, for the simple reason that they still do not understand the resistant nature of human skin to bullets.[33]

More evidence against the single-bullet theory is Dr. Shaw's testimony about his examination of Connally's wrist. X-rays showed that there were more than three grains of metal from the bullet lodged in the wrist, ruling out the possibility that CE399 was the bullet that hit Connelly's wrist.[34] Testifying before the Warren Commission on March 16, 1964, Dr. James Humes, the presiding pathologist at JFK's autopsy at Bethesda Naval Hospital, also hesitated to agree that CE399 was responsible for Connally's injuries. First, Humes rejected the contention that CE399 caused Connally's wrist injuries, saying it was "highly unlikely," explaining, ". . . this missile [CE399] is basically intact," and elaborating, "its jacket appears to me to be intact, and I do not understand how it could possibly have left fragments [in Gov. Connally's wrist]."[35] Then, continuing with his testimony, Humes also rejected the contention CE399 was the bullet that struck Connally's thigh. Referring to X-rays that show "metallic fragments in the bone" apparently not removed from Connally's thigh, Humes testified it was highly unlikely CE399 was the bullet that hit Connally because he could not "conceive of where they [the bullet fragments shown in the X-rays of Connally's thigh] came from in this missile [CE399]."[36] Testifying that same day, Dr. Finck, a US Army physician who served for three years as the chief of the Wound Ballistics Pathology Branch of the Armed Forces Institute of Pathology and participated in the JFK autopsy, rejected the contention that CE399 was the bullet that injured Connally's right wrist, answering, "No; for the reason there are too many fragments described in that wrist."[37]

On May 6, 1964, FBI special agent Robert A. Frazier, then assigned to the FBI Laboratory in Washington, D.C., testified to the Warren Commission that he placed into evidence as Commission Exhibit 842 a metal fragment weighing a half-grain that he was told had been removed from Connally's wrist.[38] At the 1991 Dallas Conference on the Assassination of President Kennedy, Parkland Hospital nurse Audrey Bell drew a life-size picture of five bullet fragments she placed in a vial after physicians removed the fragments from Connally's body. Bell claimed, "Well, we had too much [metal] to go on the 'Magic Bullet'!"[39] Charles A. Crenshaw, M.D., a physician present at Parkland confirmed Bell's testimony. Crenshaw observed Dr. William Osborne hand at least five bullet fragments to Bell that he had removed from Connally's arm. Osborne had assisted Dr. Charles Frances Gregory, who was the lead surgeon operating on Connally's wrist and then a professor of Orthopedic Surgery at the University of Texas Medical School.[40] The only documentation of the fragments collected by nurse Bell is a Dallas Police Department summary of evidence transferred to the FBI, reproduced in Volume 24 of the Warren Commission Report and listed as CE2003 on page 260, stating: "Bullet fragments taken from body of Governor Connally." The notation on the exhibit lists that Mrs. Audrey Bell, operating room nurse, gave the bullet fragments to Bob Dolan of the Dallas Police Department, who gave them to Captain Fritz of the Dallas Police Department, who transferred the fragments to the Dallas Police Department crime lab. From there they were sent to the FBI. The notation does not list the number or the weight of the fragments. Who received the bullet fragments at the FBI and when are not indicated, leaving open the question whether the bullet fragments nurse Bell placed in a vial in the Parkland Hospital operating room are the same fragments that ended up in the FBI crime laboratory in Washington.

The chain of custody of the Connally bullet fragments was so poorly established there was no chance any of these bullet fragments would ever be introduced in court. Assassination researcher Russell Kent has catalogued fifteen different references in the Warren Commission Reports and the House Select Committee on Assassinations that itemize various bullet fragments supposedly taken from Connally's wrist. The references are all vague: "Four lead-like fragments," in one instance; "One large fragment and 2–3 smaller ones," in another reference. Kent concludes, "the confusion over the number of fragments removed from Connally's wrist is remarkable." He goes on to argue, "Such inconsistency would almost certainly result in the exhibit being ruled as inadmissible in a trial because it raises reasonable doubt that the fragments removed during surgery are the ones shown in the exhibit."[41] How did the FBI know for certain that the bullet fragments flown to the FBI Laboratory from Dallas were actually the bullet fragments removed from Connally's wounds? What happened to the bullet fragments a nurse put in a vial as doctors operated on Connally in Dallas?

Were the bullet fragments taken from Connally's wrist marked as evidence, photographed or otherwise documented, and placed in reliable safekeeping so as to prevent substitution or tampering? The answer is a resounding "no." The historical record of the bullet fragments taken from Connally's wrist is woefully inadequate as the type of forensic documentation needed for these various bullet fragments to serve any purpose, including being introduced as evidence into a court proceeding to establish fact.

Were bullet fragments discarded in the operating room or simply lost? Again, the possibility remains open that only some of the bullet fragments removed from Connally's wrist made their way into one or more of the various fifteen different exhibit references Kent catalogued. Were X-rays examined to determine where precisely in Connally's body a particular fragment was found and extracted? The answer is inevitably a resounding "no," judging from the JFK assassination medical record, as documented by the Warren Committee or the House Select Committee on Assassinations.

The doctors at Parkland Hospital were interested first in making sure Connally's life was secure and second in operating on him as quickly and efficiently as possible so as to stabilize his medical condition and increase his chances of healing. But when the victim was the governor of Texas, shot in what turned out to be the assassination of the president of the United States, it is remarkable that medical considerations completely outweighed legal considerations in Connally's emergency medical treatment. Granted, the primary concern of the doctors at Parkland Hospital was the care of Connally as a patient. Yet, in the most important criminal case in twentieth-century US history, the forensic importance of the metal fragments in Connally's body could not have been higher. The record shows that while the Parkland Hospital physicians did their job attending to Connally's wounds, no similar attention was given to the legal implications of the medical evidence they were encountering while operating on their patient.

Even more remarkable was the number of law enforcement personnel Parkland Hospital allowed to be in the operating room as surgeons were treating Connally's wounds. They appear to have been lax regarding the importance of preserving for trial the ballistic evidence extracted from Connally's body during the operation. Once the doctors removed the bullet fragments from Connally's wrist, the chain-of-custody description shows law enforcement procedures—tracking the bullet fragments from the hospital to the Dallas Police Department to the FBI—were sloppy at best. Debate continues today regarding how much lead was removed from Connally's body, where those bullet fragments ended up, and how much lead was left in Connally's body.

So the debate over bullet fragments and the so-called "magic bullet" continues. Logically, those arguing CE399 is the same bullet that hit JFK in the back and neck and hit Connally in the chest, the wrist, and the thigh are bound to assume that all bullet fragments have been identified and measured precisely, so as to conclude the mass missing from CE399 is not exceeded by the bullet fragments that occurred in the shooting. The proof for this, however, is far from certain.

Connally died in 1993, and a frantic effort to get family permission to extract bullet fragments that remained in his body thirty years after the JFK assassination was unsuccessful. The Justice Department refused to intervene, and Connally was buried with bullet fragments from the JFK assassination still in his body.[42] To make matters even worse, in the fifty years intervening since the JFK assassination, the bullet fragments extracted from Connally's chest, wrist, and thigh, had been so poorly handled that since 1963 some bullet fragments have simply disappeared.[43] The inability to examine the bullet fragments remaining in Connally's body, plus the fact that bullet fragments taken from Connally's body are missing, make it impossible for proponents of the single-bullet theory to argue convincingly that the mass of fragments removed from Connally's wrist or known from X-ray analysis to have remained in Connally's body, including bullet fragments in his chest and thigh, do not exceed the minimal loss in mass observed in CE399.[44] Now, fifty years after the crime, there is no way to determine precisely the weight of the fragments from the bullet (or bullets) that hit Connally, unless the Connally family would give permission to have the body exhumed so the bullet fragments remaining in the body could be identified, measured, and weighed.

This problem, to an even larger extent, applies as well to JFK. Since

JFK was pronounced dead in the operating room, the doctors at Parkland Hospital never performed surgery in the attempt to save his life. Therefore, they never removed or measured bullet fragments remaining in JFK's brain and skull. Since the head wound was obviously a fatal wound, they had no reason to find or treat any other wounds. While it is understandable that no precise determination appears to have been made at Parkland Hospital regarding what bullet fragments remained in JFK's body at the time of his death, no precise determination appears to have been made during the subsequent autopsy at Bethesda. Moreover, given the massive nature of JFK's head wounds, bullet fragments were widely scattered throughout the limousine, possibly even causing the fractures observed on the limousine windshield after the shooting had occurred. JFK skull and brain matter splattered out of the limousine, hitting the motorcycle officers trailing the limousine and Secret Service Agent Clint Hill as he jumped onto the limousine from behind. Yet, immediately following the assassination law enforcement officers appear to have made no attempt to precisely gather bullet fragments from the street, from bystanders, from the motorcycle officers, or from Agent Clint Hill. Remarkably, film footage taken at Parkland Hospital after the assassination shows government officials actually cleaning the limousine with a bucket of water and cloth rags to remove the blood, skull parts, and brain debris from the limo's interior, with no apparent regard for the evidence. The JFK limousine was part of the crime scene. Yet, not only was the limousine cleaned at Parkland, the limousine was sent for repairs before forensic experts had a chance to collect evidence.

Another problem with the investigation and ballistic analysis is the lack of deformity observed in CE399. Assassination researcher Josiah Thompson found the lack of deformity in the bullet CE399 to be a major problem. Thompson argued in his 1967 book, *Six Seconds in Dallas,* that he was not convinced the weight loss evidenced in the bullet fragments precluded CE399 from being the bullet that wounded Connally. "What does preclude such a conclusion," Thompson wrote, "is the lack of 'deformation of the bullet' alluded to by Dr. Shaw."[45] Thompson notes the Warren Commission was aware of this problem as early as April 1964. On April 14, 1964, various members of the Warren Commission staff arranged a viewing of the Zapruder film with two autopsy surgeons and two experts from the Army's Wound Ballistics Branch at Edgewood

Arsenal. Thompson recorded that Assistant Counsel Melvin Eisenberg wrote a "Memorandum for the Record," memorializing the meeting, and recording the following conclusions: "Since the bullet removed from the Governor's stretcher does not appear to have penetrated a wrist, if he was hit by this (the first) bullet, he was probably also hit by the second bullet." Such a conclusion, if embraced by the Warren Commission, would have been lethal to the single-bullet theory.[46]

A meeting in April 1964, with wound ballistics experts F. W. Light Jr. and Joseph Dolce, provided the Warren Commission additional argumentation that CE399 would have been deformed had the bullet caused the damage being attributed to it: "Drs. Light and Dolce expressed themselves very strongly that the bullet recovered from Connally's stretcher could not have broken his radius without having suffered more distortion. Dr. Oliver [another wound ballistics specialist] withheld a conclusion until he has had the opportunity to make tests on animal tissue and bone with the actual rifle."[47] Thompson reported that, under Oliver's direction, a slug from Oswald's rifle was fired through a cadaver's wrist to simulate Connally's wrist injury. The impact badly smashed the front end of the resulting bullet, shown in the Warren Commission's report as CE856. Oliver had another bullet fired through an anesthetized goat to simulate 66 percent of the resistance encountered by a bullet through Connally's chest. As a result, the projectile was badly squeezed along a longitudinal axis, as seen in CE853. A third bullet was fired into a skull, with the resulting two pieces of the bullet being scarcely recognizable, as seen in CE857. "None of these bullets looks anything like CE399," Thompson concluded. "The results of Dr. Oliver's experiments validated a principal long accepted in wound ballistics and forensic pathology, namely, that a high-velocity bullet striking bone is always grossly deformed."[48]

Thompson also reported that he showed noted forensic pathologist Dr. Cyril Wecht the X-rays of Connally's chest and wrist together with multiple close-up photographs of CE399. Wecht left no doubt that his conclusion was that the single-bullet theory was nonsense. Wecht said:

I do not think that it could have been possible for the bullet shown as CE399 to have been a bullet that traversed the bodies of both President Kennedy and Governor Connally. I think it's something which I could not accept, that this bullet which is not fragmented, not deformed or mutilated, with just a slight defect at the tail could have inflicted this amount of damage. Particularly the damage I'm talking about to the bony structures, the rib and right radius (just above the junction of the wrist)—I doubt that this bullet could have done it. It just does not seem to fit with any of the cases I've seen of what happens to pellets after they have struck bone.[49]

Vincent Guinn, a chemist at the University of California, Irvine, was asked by the House Select Committee on Assassinations to conduct a neutron activation analysis, or NAA, on the 6.5 mm ammunition for the Western Cartridge Company's Mannlicher-Carcano rifle. Guinn testified to the House Select Committee on Assassinations that the Western Cartridge Company Mannlicher-Carcano bullets were unhardened bullets with the unusual feature that "there seems to be no uniformity within a production lot." He went on to specify, "That is, even when we would take a box of cartridges all from a given production lot, take 1 cartridge out and then another and then another and then another, all out of the same box—boxes of 20, these were—and analyze them, they all in general look different and widely different, particularly in their antimony content."[50] Antimony hardens the lead in commercial bullets. Are we to believe that C399 was one of the bullets where antimony had hardened the bullet to the point where it would have remained pristine despite the wounds the bullet supposedly caused in the two adult men?

Still, despite admitting the ammunition manufactured by Western Cartridge for the Mannlicher-Carcano rifle had no consistency of composition, Guinn insisted fragments allegedly from Connally's wrist (CE842) came from CE399. Assassination researcher Russell Kent points out the problems with Guinn's analysis: "For the HSCA, he [Guinn] tested fragments different from those tested by the FBI for the Warren Commission. Furthermore the FBI fragments are now 'missing' and their weights unknown. They could have been huge pieces weighing tens of grains and thus could not possibly have come from CE399."[51] Professor Ronald White points out that while Guinn concluded the CE842 fragments came from CE399 because they were similar in chemical composition, CE842 contained 2,400 percent more sodium and 1,100 percent more chlorine. Finally, CE842 contained 8.1-ppm aluminum but CE399 contained none.[52] From this White argued, "it was difficult to fathom how Guinn could conclude that

CE842 and CE399 were similar in composition." White also noted that to confirm the single-bullet theory, it is necessary to link CE399 with Kennedy's neck and back wounds. But since no bullet fragments were removed from Kennedy's neck and back wounds even at the autopsy, it is impossible to link CE399 to JFK with certainty, even if CE399 matched precisely the CE842 fragments in chemical composition.[53]

Yet another problem is that the ammunition used in the rifle found on the sixth floor of the Texas Schoolbook Depository was World War II vintage surplus ammunition last manufactured in 1944, and was no longer available. A spokesman for Western Cartridge declared the reliability of such ammunition would be questionable today.[54] This was in direct contradiction to the Warren Commission's conclusion that the ammunition was recently made by Western Cartridge, "which manufactures such ammunition currently."[55]

Two of the more prominent defenders of the single-bullet theory, former Wall Street lawyer Gerald Posner and former prosecutor from the Los Angeles County District Attorney's Office Vincent Bugliosi, have argued CE399 was not deformed because the velocity of the bullet had slowed to a fraction of its original speed after passing through JFK's back, exiting JFK's neck, puncturing Connally's back, exiting Connally's chest, hitting Connally's wrist, and lodging in Connally's thigh.[56] What Posner and Bugliosi fail to explain is how a missile slowed enough so as not to become deformed upon hitting bone, yet was going fast enough to destroy 10 cm of Connally's rib and shatter the radius bone in Connally's wrist.

JFK'S NECK AND BACK WOUNDS

The ER team at Parkland Hospital in Dallas and the autopsy team at Bethesda Naval Hospital produced medical records that describe two completely different views of JFK's wounds. Professor Ronald F. White succinctly summarized the problem as follows:

> Because the ER team [at Parkland Hospital] focused exclusively on stabilizing vital signs, they did not turn over the President's body, and therefore did not notice another bullet wound (or wounds) located in the President's upper back. Hence, we have the makings of one of the most incredible foul-ups in medical history. The Parkland physicians didn't

know of the back wound and the Bethesda autopsy team did not know that the tracheostomy incision concealed a bullet wound. Or, at least, so they have alleged. It is difficult to believe that subsequent controversy over the exact location of the wounds can be attributed solely to an unfortunate communication failure between two groups of physicians.[57]

After realizing JFK had been shot, the motorcade rushed from Dealey Plaza directly to Parkland Hospital. Once the presidential limousine arrived, the ER team at Parkland went into immediate action implementing trauma efforts to resuscitate JFK, despite realizing almost immediately that the president's massive head wounds made their efforts to save his life futile.

Once JFK was pronounced dead, a scuffle arose between the Secret Service and local Dallas authorities who insisted the crime committed in Dallas had to be investigated and prosecuted in Dallas. At issue was whether or not the autopsy should be done in Dallas, supervised by Texas law enforcement personnel under the jurisdiction of Texas criminal law. JFK had been murdered in Dallas. Thus, the jurisdiction for the investigation and prosecution of the crime fell under the jurisdiction of Texas law. In 1963 there was no law making it a federal crime to assassinate the president. Truthfully, Jackie Kennedy and the White House had no authority to remove JFK's body from Dallas. An autopsy should have been performed in Dallas under Texas law and a criminal investigation should have been undertaken in Dallas under Texas law. The FBI had no jurisdiction. Under Texas and federal statutes at the time, JFK's body should have remained in Dallas for autopsy, and the criminal investigation and trial should have been handled locally.

Yet, the White House and the Secret Service won the argument in a confrontation that almost ended up in a fistfight. A casket was ordered to fly JFK's body back to Washington, and the Secret Service quietly took LBJ back to Love Field. Once the casket arrived, the Secret Service made sure JFK's body was whisked from Parkland Hospital and driven directly to Love Field where it was loaded aboard Air Force One.

Chaos would perhaps best describe the way JFK's body left Dallas, and controversy would perhaps best describe the way the JFK autopsy was conducted. The hurriedly assembled autopsy team in Washington was not given the luxury of even a single night to prepare. Typically an autopsy team takes time to research the case and plan the autopsy based on reports of the crime scene so they can produce reliable and comprehensive medical evidence that would be admissible in court. Jackie Kennedy insisted that since JFK was a navy officer, the autopsy should take place at Bethesda Naval Hospital, thus overruling administration officials who scheduled the autopsy to be conducted at the army's Walter Reed Hospital.

In the confusion at both Dallas Parkland Hospital and at Bethesda Naval Hospital, no one imagined junior counsel Arlen Specter would virtually single-handedly take over configuring the medical evidence into a legal argument to frame Lee Harvey Oswald as the victim before the official Warren Commission government inquiry into the assassination. In doing so, Specter concocted his single-bullet theory in order to deflect consideration of a conspiracy, and in the process pinned the blame on the conveniently deceased Lee Harvey Oswald as the sole gunman responsible for shooting the president. Lee Harvey Oswald's murder brought the criminal investigation to a screeching halt and obviated the need for a criminal prosecution. Yet the problem remained that Specter's single-bullet theory depended upon establishing medical proof that CE399 passed from the entrance wound in JFK's back, through JFK's body, to exit in JFK's throat and this theory was never considered or pursued by the medical team at either Dallas Parkland Hospital or Bethesda Naval Hospital.

Here was the crux of the medical dilemma:

- The Parkland Emergency Room doctors identified JFK's throat wound as an entry wound, and never noticed the wound in his back.

- The Parkland medical team enlarged the throat wound with their tracheotomy.

- Once the Parkland medical team realized they had no chance of reviving JFK, they didn't bother searching for an exit wound or the bullet in JFK's body.

- The Parkland medical team assumed JFK had been hit twice from the front: once in the throat and once in the right front forehead.

- Viewing the throat wound as a large gaping hole, the Bethesda autopsy team assumed the throat wound was caused by a tracheotomy, not by a bullet.

- The Bethesda autopsy team assumed the wound in JFK's back to be a superficial entry wound but could not identify the path of the bullet or find the bullet itself.

- Upon learning from Parkland that a pristine bullet had been found on a stretcher, the Bethesda autopsy team assumed it was the bullet they were unable to find.

- The Bethesda autopsy medical team concluded JFK had been hit twice from the back: first, in the back and then by a shot to the back of the head.

The doctors at Parkland assumed JFK had been shot from the front, while the doctors at Bethesda concluded JFK had been shot from the rear. Only after Arlen Specter proposed the single-bullet theory did it become important to prove the bullet that wounded JFK's back and neck was the same bullet that wounded Connally. Both men *had* to have been wounded by the same bullet, or, given the Warren Commission's conclusion only three shots could had been fired by the Mannlicher-Carcano bolt-action rifle in the time available for shooting, there had to have been a second shooter. Moreover, Lee Harvey Oswald was firing from the sixth floor of the Texas School Book Depository, behind JFK when the shooting started. If the throat wound was determined to be an entrance wound, there had to be a second shooter positioned to the front of the motorcade. Specter's entire argument came to rest on the hypothesis the bullet that entered JFK's back exited through his throat and went on to cause all Connally's wounds, despite the fact neither the medical evidence ascertained in the ER at Parkland nor the medical evidence ascertained in the autopsy at Bethesda supported that theory.

Arlen Specter was out of luck once he realized neither the doctors at Parkland nor Bethesda had established a bullet path through JFK's body. That was a lynchpin for the Warren Commission's central conclusion that Oswald was the lone gunman responsible for gunning down JFK, but it did not deter Specter. Lacking the medical evidence to prove the point, Specter resorted to elaborate diagrams of various assassination reconstructions to argue the hypothetical case that a trajectory could be established making it possible for a single bullet to injure both men. Despite medical and ballistics evidence, in the end the Warren Commission resorted to arguing it was possible the bullet entered JFK's back, exited his throat, and then continued on its trajectory to hit Connally in the back, lungs, wrist, and thigh. The Commission had to succeed in their argument otherwise the effort to establish that Lee Harvey Oswald was the lone assassin would fail. If there were more than one shooter, that would mean there was a conspiracy to assassinate JFK, which would instigate a public outcry for an investigation. The Warren Commission sought to avoid that because no one knew how high up and widespread a conspiracy might go. As long as Lee Harvey Oswald remained the only viable suspect, the case could be closed as a horrible accident of history.

No doctor at Parkland or Bethesda ever thought to postulate a single-bullet theory. That took a lawyer like Arlen Specter. And JFK was long buried at Arlington Cemetery before anyone realized the single-bullet theory would depend on medical questions the doctors at Parkland and Bethesda had never thought to ask and on ballistic evidence establishing a bullet path from the back wound to the neck wound that the doctors at Parkland and Bethesda had never thought to look for. The simple truth was the doctors examining JFK at Parkland and at Bethesda never thought to connect the bullet paths through Kennedy's body.

President Lyndon B. Johnson and the Justice Department used the Warren Commission to create an official government narrative explaining why and how JFK was killed. After the nearly yearlong investigation, the Commission interviewed more than 500 witnesses to document nearly 8,000 pages of testimony to produce an 888-page report. The transcripts to the testimony provide insight into the leading nature of the investigation and the desire to force a particular outcome. But if we take a look at the facts, the Warren Commission largely ignored how the doctors at Parkland Hospital, the first to see JFK's wounds, nearly unanimously describe their findings in contradiction to the Warren Commission's conclusions.

According to the doctors at Parkland hospital, JFK suffered an entrance wound in his neck. At a press conference held at Parkland Hospital on November 22, 1963, a newsman asked Dr. Malcolm Perry, the physician who had performed the tracheotomy on JFK, whether or not the wound to JFK's throat was an entrance wound. Perry explained:

The wound appeared to be an entrance wound in the front of the throat; yes, that is correct. The exit wound, I don't know. It could have been the head or there could have been a second wound of the head. There was not time to determine this at the particular instant.[58]

Tom Wicker, reporting for *The New York Times* in an article published two days after the assassination, wrote, "Mr. Kennedy was hit by a bullet in the throat, just below the Adam's apple, [Dr. Malcolm Perry, an attending surgeon at Parkland, and Dr. Kemp Clark, chief of neurosurgery at Parkland] said. This wound had the appearance of the bullet's entry."[59] Wicker also reported JFK had "a massive, gaping wound" in the back and on the right side of his head and that Parkland physicians said immediately after the shooting that it was impossible to tell if JFK's wounds were caused by one or two bullets. "According to the doctors at Parkland Hospital, the President suffered an entrance wound at the Adam's apple and a massive wound at the head," wrote assassination researcher Sylvia Meagher, whose 1967 book, *Accessories After the Fact: The Warren Commission, the Authorities, and the Report,* is considered the definitive guide to the Warren Commission testimony.[60]

In his testimony to the Warren Commission on March 30, 1964, Dr. Charles James Carrico explained why the back wound went unnoticed at Parkland Hospital. Warren Commission counsel Arlen Specter asked Carrico about whether he had noticed a small wound on the right side of JFK's head:

Dr. Carrico: No, sir; at least initially there was no time to examine the president completely for all small wounds. As we said before, this was an acutely ill patient and all we had time to do was to determine what things were life-threatening right then and attempt to resuscitate him and after which a more complete examination would be carried out, and we didn't have time to examine for other wounds.

Mr. Specter: Was such a more complete examination ever carried out by the doctors in Parkland?

Dr. Carrico: No, sir; not in my presence.

Mr. Specter: Why not?

Dr. Carrico: As we said initially, this was an acute emergency situation and there was not time initially and when the cardiac massage was done this prevented any further examination during this time this was being done. After the President was pronounced dead, his wife was there, he was the President, and we felt certainly that complete examination would be carried out and no one had the heart, I believe, to examine him there.[61]

According to notes he wrote on the airplane back to Washington, Secret Service Agent Glen A. Bennett, who had been riding in the follow-up car immediately behind the JFK limousine, wrote that he "saw the shot that hit the President about four inches down from his right shoulder."[62] In his testimony to the Warren Commission on March 9, 1964, Secret Service Agent Roy Kellerman described how he discovered JFK's back wound in the morgue at Bethesda Naval Hospital the evening of the assassination just prior to the start of the autopsy. "Just for the record, I wish to have this down," Kellerman began. "While the President is in the morgue, he is lying flat. And with the part of the skull removed, and the hole in the throat, nobody was aware until they lifted him up that there was a hole in his shoulder. That was the first concrete evidence that they knew that the man was hit in the back first."[63] Interestingly, Kellerman commented here that the doctors conducting the Bethesda autopsy somehow concluded the back wound resulted from the shot that hit JFK "first." Unfortunately, Kellerman did not get questioned on this point and he did not return to explain the comment. But the comment suggests a sequence of shots that would separate JFK's back wound from his throat wound, providing additional support to the hypothesis the back and throat wounds were separate wounds.

During the Bethesda autopsy, Dr. Humes examined the back wound and found it to be a shallow entry wound that had penetrated less than an inch into JFK's back. Navy Commander J. Thornton Boswell, attending the autopsy, found the depth of JFK's back wound could be probed up to only the first or second knuckle of the little finger, a depth of about two inches.[64] No path through JFK's body could be established for the missile, and X-rays failed to detect any bullets yet remaining in JFK's body. A report by FBI agents James W. Silbert and Francis X. O'Neill Jr., who were present during the autopsy, gives the following description of the examination of JFK's back wound:

During the latter stages of this autopsy, Dr. Humes located an opening which appeared to be a bullet hole which was below the shoulders and two inches to the right of the middle line of the spinal column.

This opening was probed by Dr. Humes with the finger, at which time it was determined that the trajectory of the missile entering at this point had entered at a downward position of 45 to 60 degrees. Further probing determined that the distance traveled by this missile was a short distance inasmuch as the end of the opening could be felt with the finger.

Inasmuch as no complete bullet of any size could be located in the brain area and likewise no bullet could be located in the back or any other area of the body as determined by total body X-rays and physical inspection revealing there was no point of exit, the individuals performing the autopsy were at a loss to explain why they could find no bullets.[65]

What seems clear is that prior to the Bethesda autopsy, the evidence strongly suggested there were multiple shooters and that some of the shooters were positioned in front of the motorcade along the grassy knoll. What happened at the Bethesda autopsy that the medical evidence changed?

WHO WAS IN CHARGE?

Claw Shaw was a New Orleans businessman who was the only person brought to trial in connection with the JFK assassination. He was acquitted, but during the trial US Army physician, Lt. Col. Pierre A. Finck, a participant in the JFK autopsy at Bethesda, admitted that military brass present in the Bethesda autopsy room interfered with the doctors conducting the autopsy. He claimed military brass actually stopped the doctors from performing procedures they felt were necessary to determine the exact type and nature of wounds JFK suffered. Alvin Oser, one of the chief prosecutors working on the trial under the direction of District Attorney Jim Garrison, cross-examined Finck. The cross-examination was particularly important because Dr. Finck had testified to the Warren Commission that he was confident that the bullet which hit JFK's back had passed through his neck and continued on to injure Connally, even though he believed a bullet doing this much damage would have fragmented or deformed. Finck told the Warren Commission he was completely confident that JFK's wounds were exit wounds, consistent with JFK being shot from behind.[66] Yet, when pressed by Alvin Oser's aggressive questioning in the Clay Shaw trial, Finck was forced to admit reluctantly that the military brass had interfered with the autopsy:

Mr. Oser: How many other military personnel were present at the autopsy in the autopsy room?

Dr. Finck: The autopsy room was quite crowded. It is a small autopsy room, and when you are called in circumstances like that to look at the wound of the President of the United States who is dead, you don't look around too much to ask people for their names and take notes on who they are and how many there are. I did not do so. The room was crowded with military and civilian personnel and federal agents, Secret Service agents, FBI agents, for part of the autopsy, but I cannot give you a precise breakdown as regards the attendance of the people in that autopsy room at Bethesda Naval Hospital.

Mr. Oser: Colonel, did you feel that you had to take orders from this Army General that was there directing the autopsy?

Dr. Finck: No, because there were others, there were Admirals.

Mr. Oser: There were Admirals?

Dr. Finck: Oh, yes, there were Admirals, and when you are a Lieutenant Colonel in the Army you just follow orders, and at the end of the autopsy we were specifically told – as I recall it, it was by Admiral Kenney, the Surgeon General of the Navy – this is subject to verification – we were specifically told not to discuss the case.

Mr. Oser: You were told not to discuss the case?

Dr. Finck: – to discuss the case without coordination with the Attorney General.[67]

The next sequence is lengthy, but crucial to understanding the apparent political intervention that prevented the autopsy physicians from producing a complete or reliable examination of his wounds:

Mr. Oser: Doctor, speaking of the wound to the throat area of the president as you described it, after this bullet passed through the president's throat in the manner in which you described it, would the president have been able to talk?

Dr. Finck: I don't know.

Mr. Oser: Do you have an opinion?

Dr. Finck: There are many factors influencing the ability to talk or not after a shot.

Mr. Oser: Did you have an occasion to dissect the track of that particular bullet in the victim as it lay on the autopsy table?

Dr. Finck: I did not dissect the track in the neck.

Mr. Oser: Why.

Dr. Finck: This leads us into a disclosure of medical records.

Mr. Oser: Your Honor, I would like an answer from the Colonel and I would ask the Court so to direct.

The Court: That is correct, you should answer, Doctor.

Dr. Finck: We didn't remove the organs of the neck.

Mr. Oser: Why not, doctor?

Dr. Finck: For the reason that we were told to examine the head wounds and that the –

Mr. Oser: Are you saying someone told you not to dissect the track?

The Court: Let him finish his answer.

Dr. Finck: I was told that the family wanted an examination of the head, as I recall, the head and the chest, but the prosecutors in this autopsy didn't remove the organs of the neck, to my recollection.

Mr. Oser: You have said they did not. I want to know why didn't you as an autopsy pathologist attempt to ascertain the track through the body which you had on the autopsy table in trying to ascertain the cause of death? Why?

Dr. Finck: I had the cause of death.

Mr. Oser: Why did you not trace the track of the wound?

Dr. Finck: As I recall I didn't remove these organs from the neck.

Mr. Oser: I didn't hear you.

Dr. Finck: I examined the wounds but I didn't remove the organs of the neck.

Mr. Oser: You said you didn't do this; I am asking you why you didn't do this as a pathologist?

Dr. Finck: From what I recall I looked at the trachea, there was a tracheotomy wound the best I can remember, but I didn't dissect or remove these organs.

Mr. Oser: Your Honor, I would ask Your Honor to direct the witness to answer my question.

Mr. Oser (continued): I will ask you the question one more time: Why did you not dissect the track of the bullet wound that you have described today and you saw at the time of the autopsy at the time you examined the body. Why? I ask you to answer that question.

Dr. Finck: As I recall I was told not to, but I don't remember by whom.

Mr. Oser: You were told not to but you don't remember by whom?

Dr. Finck: Right.

Mr. Oser: Could it have been one of the Admirals or one of the Generals in the room?

Dr. Finck: I don't recall.

Mr. Oser: Do you have any particular reason why you cannot recall at this time?

Dr. Finck: Because we were told to examine the head and the chest cavity, and that doesn't include removal of the organs of the neck.

Mr. Oser: You are one of three autopsy specialists and pathologists at the time, and you saw what you describe as an entrance wound in the neck area of the President of the United States who had just been assassinated, and you were only interested in the other wound but not interested in the track through his neck, is that what you are telling me?

Dr. Finck: I was interested in the track and I had observed the conditions of bruising between the point of entry in the back of the neck and the point of exit at the front of the neck, which is entirely compatible with the bullet path.

Mr. Oser: But you were told not to go into the area of the neck, is that your testimony?

Dr. Finck: From what I recall, yes, but I don't remember by whom.[68]

Finck was perhaps the most highly qualified forensic pathologist to attend the JFK autopsy in Bethesda. If he had been allowed to dissect the back and neck wounds to his satisfaction, it is highly likely Finck would have concluded the neck wound was an entry wound and the back wound was an unconnected entry wound, and he likely would have rejected the lone-gun hypothesis. Had Finck been allowed to complete his work, his conclusions would have been devastating to any attempt to frame Lee Harvey Oswald as the sole assassin. Military brass at the autopsy intervened to stop his work most likely because politics dictated they do so. And Dr. Finck acquiesced to Arlen Specter's hypothetical questions that all the wounds seen in JFK's body could have been caused by shots from the rear because politics dictated him to do so. As a junior military officer Finck did not feel he had the authority to countermand orders.

Three decades later, in 1996, the Assassination Records Review Board asked Dr. J. Thornton Boswell, another of the pathologists attending the JFK autopsy, who was in charge of the autopsy. Dr. Boswell testified that upon entering the autopsy room he thought Dr. Hume was in charge. He said that he changed his mind however after Dr. Finck's testimony at the Clay Shaw trial in New Orleans in 1969. Boswell explained to the review board [Mr. Eardley from the Justice Department] was really upset. He says, 'J., we got to get somebody in New Orleans quick. [Finck] is testifying, and he's really lousing everything up.'" Boswell explained to the Assassinations Records Review Board that the Department of Justice (DOJ) put him on an airplane that day and flew him to New Orleans. The DOJ officials in New Orleans showed Boswell a transcript of Finck's testimony and Boswell spent all night reviewing the testimony. "And when they asked Pierre [Finck] in court who supervised and ran the autopsy, he says, 'Some Army General.'" This was an answer the Justice Department obviously felt could not be allowed to stand on the record without a rebuttal.[69]

That politics controlled the JFK autopsy is devastating to the reliability of the Warren Commission Final Report that relied upon the autopsy findings to pin all the blame on Oswald acting alone. If Oswald was to be framed as the lone-gun assassin, the hypothetical possibility counsel Arlen Specter continually posed to medical witnesses that a path from the back wound to the neck wound could have been established if only it had been examined, had to remain open.

THE MAGIC BULLET TO THE RESCUE

Now, to return to the autopsy, a message from Dallas also changed the course of the examination being undertaken by the physicians in the autopsy room at Bethesda Naval Hospital. While the autopsy was yet in progress on the night of the assassination, Dr. Humes at Bethesda received information that a bullet had been found on a stretcher at Parkland Hospital. That information arrived with the delivery of a portion of JFK's skull that apparently had also been delivered from Dallas.

Silbert and O'Neill continued their report:

> On the basis of the latter two developments, Dr. Humes stated that the pattern was clear that the one bullet had entered the President's back and had worked its way out of the body during external cardiac massage and that a second high-velocity bullet had entered the rear of the skull and had fragmented prior to exit through the top of the skull.[70]

What is clear from Silbert and O'Neill's report is that Dr. Humes had no idea Arlen Specter would later expect him to declare the back wound as an entrance wound and the throat wound as an exit wound. At the autopsy on the night of November 22, 1963, news that a bullet had been found at Parkland Hospital was "a godsend" that "reduced the high stress level taking its toll" on the doctors "who were frantically searching for a missile in Kennedy's body," noted assassination researcher Jerry McKnight. "The discovery of the Parkland Hospital bullet not only reduced the confusion and circus-like atmosphere in the Bethesda morgue, it provided a ready excuse for not dissecting the president's back wound to lay open the track of the bullet in JFK's body. Humes now felt safe concluding the back entrance wound had been so superficial that the bullet just fell out, without having transited through JFK's body."[71] The problem is there was no chain of evidence to link CE399 to JFK's back wound. There is no proof the stretcher on which CE399 was found was a stretcher ever used to hold JFK's body.

Specter would also later argue that the pristine "magic bullet," identified by the Warren Commission as CE399, did fall out nearly unscathed, but only after it exited JFK's throat and passed through Connally's chest, fractured his right wrist, and punctured his thigh, leaving a small fragment in Connally's thigh bone.

Sylvia Meagher pointed out that Humes at the autopsy did not even realize the throat wound involved a bullet wound, thinking the throat wound was a tracheotomy and nothing more. Meagher wrote:

> Clearly, the observers at the autopsy took away the impression that the bullet in the back had penetrated only a short distance, without exiting from the body, and that the surgeons believed that the missile had worked its way out of the body during external cardiac massage. Everything suggests that their impression was correct, and that Dr. Humes did not come to believe the bullet had passed through and exited from the body until at least the next day, when he learned from Dr. Perry at Parkland Hospital that the President had arrived there with a bullet wound at the Adam's apple which had been obliterated during the tracheotomy.[72]

The physicians examining JFK in Parkland determined the throat wound was an entrance wound and physicians at the autopsy at Bethesda had determined the back wound was an entrance wound. That was a problem for Arlen Specter and the Warren Commission, because as we have noted, an entrance wound in the throat and an entrance wound in the back meant there had to be two shooters, one in front of the limousine and the other in back of the limousine.

GOVERNOR CONNALLY SPEAKS

Journalist Martin Agronsky interviewed Governor John Connally from his Parkland Memorial Hospital room on November 27, 1963, five days after the JFK assassination. Governor Connally insisted he was hit by the second shot, not the same shot that hit JFK:

> And then we had just turned the corner [from Houston onto Elm], we heard a shot; I turned to my left—I was sitting in the jump seat. I turned to my left to look in the back seat—the President had slumped. He had said nothing. Almost simultaneously, as I turned, I was hit and I knew I had been hit badly. I knew the President had been hit and I said, "My God, they are going to kill us all." Then there was a third shot and the President was hit again and we thought then very seriously. I had still retained consciousness but the President had slumped in Mrs. Kennedy's lap and when he was hit the second time she said, "Oh, my God, they have killed my husband—Jack, Jack." After the third shot, the next thing that occurred—I was conscious, the Secret Service man, of course, the chauffeur had pulled out of the line, they said, "Get out of here"; on the radios they said, "Get us to a hospital immediately" and we pulled out, of course, immediately, as fast as we could go and got to the hospital. In the space of a few seconds, it is unbelievable what can happen, Martin. We went from great joy, anticipation, wonderful crowds, wonderful throngs, to great tragedy.[73]

On April 21, 1964, Connally testified to the Warren Commission, telling essentially the same story—that he was hit by the second shot. Connally testified:

> **Governor Connally**: We had just made the turn . . . when I heard what I thought was a shot. I heard this noise, which I immediately took to be a rifle shot. I instinctively turned to my right because the sound appeared to come from over my right shoulder, so I turned to

look back over my right shoulder, and I saw nothing unusual except just people in the crowd, but I did catch the President in the corner of my eye, and I was interested, because once I heard the shot in my own mind I identified it as a rifle shot, and I immediately—the only thought that crossed my mind was that this is an assassination attempt.

So I looked, failing to see him, I was turning to look back over my left shoulder into the back seat, but I never got that far in my turn. I got about in the position I am now in facing you, looking a little bit to the left of center, and then I felt like somebody had hit me in the back.

Mr. Specter: What is the best estimate that you have as to the time span between the sound of the first shot and the feeling of someone hitting you in the back, which you just described?

Governor Connally: A very, very brief span of time. Again my trend of thought just happened to be, I suppose along this line. I immediately thought that this—that I had been shot. I knew it when I just looked down and I was covered with blood, and the thought immediately passed through my mind that there were either two or three people involved or more in this or someone was shooting with an automatic rifle. These were just thoughts that went through my mind because of the rapidity of these two, of the first shot plus the blow that I took, and I knew I had been hit, and I immediately assumed, because of the amount of blood, and, in fact, that it had obviously passed through my chest that I had probably been fatally shot.

So, I merely doubled up, and then turned to my right again and began to—I just sat there, and Mrs. Connally pulled me over to her lap. She was sitting, of course, on the jump seat, so I reclined with my head in her lap, conscious all the time, and with my eyes open; and then, of course, the third shot sounded, and I heard the shot very clearly. I heard it hit him [JFK]. I heard the shot hit something, and I assumed again—it never entered my mind that it ever hit anybody but the President. I heard it. It was a very loud noise, just that audible, very clear.[74]

Connally testified that he did not hear the second shot that hit him, but that he estimated he was hit approximately ten to twelve seconds after JFK was hit with the first shot. He was emphatic about the time frame, even when under cross-examination Specter repeatedly asked the same question slightly rephrased each time he asked it. "It is not conceivable to me that I could have been hit by the first bullet, and then I felt the blow from something which was obviously a bullet, which I assumed was a bullet, and I never heard the second shot, didn't hear it," Connally explained to Specter. "I didn't hear but two shots. The first shot and the third shot."[75] Connally further explained he did not know he had been hit in the left wrist and left thigh until he woke up in the hospital and saw his arm bandaged in a sling. In response to a question from Allen Dulles, Connally elaborated once again:

> **Governor Connally**: I turned to the right both to see, because it was an instinctive movement, because that is where the sound came from, but even more important, I thought it was a rifle shot. I immediately thought of an assassination attempt, and I turned to see if I could see the President, if he was all right. Failing to see him over my right shoulder, I turned to look over my left shoulder.

> **Mr. Dulles**: I see.

> **Governor Connally**: Into the back seat, and I never completed that turn. I got no more than substantially looking forward, a little bit to the left of forward when I got hit.[76]

Connally further testified that he had been familiar with the sound of a rifle shot all his life, and that he never thought the first sound he heard was a firecracker or a tire blowout. "I thought it was a rifle shot," he insisted. "I have hunted enough to think that my perception with respect to directions is very, very good, and the shot I heard came from back over my right shoulder, which was in the direction of the School Book Depository, no question about it. I heard one other. The first and third shots came from there."[77] Connally testified he did not hear any shots from the direction of the overpass ahead of the limousine.

Nellie Connally, the governor's wife, testified to the Warren Commission immediately following her husband. She was equally clear that Connally was hit by the second shot:

> **Mrs. Connally**: In fact, the receptions had been so good every place that I had showed much restraint by not mentioning something about it before.
>
> I could resist no longer. When we got past this area [the turn from Main onto Houston] I did turn to the president and said, "Mr. President, you can't say Dallas doesn't love you."

Then I don't know how soon. It seems to me it was very soon, that I heard a noise, and not being an expert rifleman, I was not aware that it was a rifle. It was just a frightening noise, and it came from the right. I turned over my right shoulder and looked back, and saw the President as he had both hands at his neck.

Mr. Specter: And you are indicating with your own hands, two hands crossing over gripping your own neck.

Mrs. Connally: Yes; and it seemed to me there was—he made no utterance, no cry. I saw no blood, no anything. It was just sort of nothing, the expression on his face, and he just sort of slumped down.

Then very soon there was the second shot that hit John. As the first shot was hit, and I turned to look at the same time, I recall John saying, "Oh, no, no, no." Then there was a second shot, and it hit John, and as he recoiled to the right, he said, "My God, they are going to kill us all."[78]

Mrs. Connally explained: "I put my head down over his head so that his head and my head were right together, and all I could see, too, were the people flashing by. I didn't look back any more."[79]

The controversy over which bullet hit Connally intensified in November 1966, when *Life Magazine* arranged to have Connally inspect enlarged frames from the Zapruder film. An article entitled "A Matter of Reasonable Doubt: Amid Heightening Controversy about the Warren Report, Governor Connally Examines for 'Life' the Assassination Film," published by *Life* on November 25, 1966, hit the newsstands on the third anniversary of the assassination. The multiple-page article featured on the magazine's cover, contained a full-page photograph of Connally, shown with a magnifying glass held in both hands, bent over a light table to examine enlarged positives of six frames from the Zapruder film displayed for his examination.[80] This was the first time Connally had made a public comment about the assassination since the Warren Commission presented its report to President Lyndon Johnson on September 24, 1964.

Connally identified for *Life* that he was looking over his right shoulder at frame 193 of the Zapruder film, just before the limousine went behind the highway sign. At frame 222, as the limousine pulls clear of the highway sign, Governor Connally emerges, still turned to his right. When President Kennedy can be seen, a sixth of a second later, at frame

225, President Kennedy emerges from the highway sign and it is clear he has been hit. Beginning at frame 225, Governor Connally turns his head leftward until, in 228, he faces straight ahead through frame 231, the last frame *Life* showed on a page-and-a-half spread featuring frames from the Zapruder film. "You can see my leftward movement clearly," Connally explained to *Life* as he studied the frames. "I had turned to the right when the limousine was behind the sign. Now I'm turning back again. I know that I made that turn to the left before I was hit. You can see the grimace on the President's face. You cannot see it in mine. There is no question about it. I haven't been hit yet." Connally told *Life* he believed, as best he could judge it, that the bullet hit him in frame 234, nine frames and one-half second later than the Warren Commission said he had been hit. "Having looked at frames 233 to 235," he told *Life*, "I can begin to see myself slump in 234. The slump is very pronounced in 235. I am hunched. It looks as if my coat is pulled away from my shirt. My mouth is elongated. I don't think there is any question that my reaction to the shot begins in this time sequence."[81]

In the interview with *Life*, Nellie Connally was equally firm on her testimony. "As far as the shots go," she explained to the magazine, "my memory is divided into four distinct events. First I heard the shot, or a strange loud noise—I'm not that expert on rifles—back behind us. Then next I turned to my right and saw the President gripping at his throat. Then I turned back toward John, and I heard the second shot that hit John. . . . I must have been looking right at him when it hit because I saw him recoil to the right . . . so you see I had time to look at the President after he was already hit, then turn and see John hit by a second shot. Then, of course, he slumped, and I reached to pull him toward me."[82] Governor Connally ended the *Life* interview by insisting he would never change his story. "They talk about the 'one-bullet or two-bullet theory,'" he concluded, "but as far as I'm concerned, there is no 'theory.' There is my absolute knowledge, and Nellie's too, that one bullet caused the President's first wound, that an entirely separate shot struck me." Mrs. Connally added, "No one will ever convince me otherwise." Her husband concurred: "It's a certainty. I'll never change my mind."[83] It turned out exactly that way. To the end of their lives, both John Connally and his wife Nellie held to their original recollections of the tragic sequence of shots on November 22, 1963.

SPECTER'S SINGLE-BULLET THEORY

The Warren Commission chose to disregard the testimony of John and Nellie Connally because the single-bullet theory proposed by counsel Arlen Specter required that JFK and Connally had to have been hit by the same shot. "Governor Connally's testimony supported the view that the first shot missed," the Warren Commission's final report concluded, "because he stated that he heard a shot, turned slightly to his right, and, as he started to turn back to his left, was struck by a second bullet."[84] The Commission rejected this testimony, reasoning instead that: "He [Connally] never saw the President during the shooting sequence, and it is entirely possible that he heard the missed shot and that both men were struck by the second bullet." This directly contradicts the statement by both John and Nellie Connally that they saw JFK react to the neck wound before the shot that hit Connally in the back.

But the key phrase in the Commission's conclusion ends up being the statement: "it is entirely possible." In taking testimony from witnesses, Specter had pressed the medical doctors not trained in the fine points of legal testimony to answer hypothetical questions. But competent lawyers would be expected to coach their clients never to answer such questions in court. Hypothetical questions always propose a fictional possibility, or counterfactual conclusion, in which even the most outrageous outcomes typically cannot be ruled out.

Regarding Nellie Connally's testimony, the Warren Commission grasped the Specter-postulated counter-factual as if it were proven fact. "If the same bullet struck both the President and the governor, it is entirely possible that she saw the President's movements at the same time as she heard the second shot," the Commission concluded, trying desperately to buttress the argument the first shot missed. "Her testimony, therefore, does not preclude the possibility of the first shot having missed."[85] Slipping by hopefully unnoticed, there is a huge logical difference between the hypothetical "does not preclude the possibility" and a statement of fact, proven by testimony and evidence.

Specter hung his single-bullet interpretation on the assumption that Connally had a "delayed reaction" to having been shot, allowing for the possibility Connally misinterpreted that the first shot missed and the second shot might have been the one that hit both JFK and Connally. This is the theory Specter pursued when questioning Dr. Humes:

Mr. Specter: Could that missile have traversed Governor Connally's chest without having him know it immediately or instantaneously?

Commander Humes: I believe so. I have heard reports, and have been told by my professional associates of any number of instances where people received penetrating wounds in various portions of the body and have only the sensation of a slight discomfort or slight slap or some other minor difficulty from such a missile wound. I am sure he would be aware that something happened to him, but that he was shot. I am not certain.

Representative Ford: Would that have been the potential reaction of the President when first hit, as shown in [CE] 385?

Commander Humes: It could very easily be one of some type of an injury—I mean the awareness that he had been struck by a missile. I don't know, but people have been drilled through with a missile and didn't know it.[86]

Dr. Humes in his next answer blew Specter's single-bullet theory out of the water. Humes testified it was "extremely unlikely" the nearly pristine CE399 struck Connally's thigh because X-rays show metallic fragments in the thigh bone. "I cannot conceive of where [the fragments] came from." The Commission conveniently overlooked that comment and focused on the possibility of a delayed reaction to a gunshot wound. The Warren Commission continued:

There was, conceivably, a delayed reaction between the time the bullet struck [Connally] and the time he realized he was hit . . . . The Governor did not even know that he had been struck in the wrist or in the thigh until he regained consciousness in the hospital the next day. Moreover, he testified that he did not hear what he thought was the second shot, although he did hear a subsequent shot, which coincided with the shattering of the President's head. One possibility, therefore, would be a sequence in which the Governor heard the first shot, did not immediately feel the penetration of the bullet, then felt the delayed reaction of the impact on his back, later heard the shot which shattered the President's head, and then lost consciousness without hearing a third shot which might have occurred later.[87]

"It is frustrating and ironic that the Zapruder film does not enable the viewer to pinpoint the exact moment of impact of the bullet in the President's back, or of the bullet (or bullets) that struck the Governor," Sylvia Meagher wrote. "But the film does establish a definite delay between the wounding of the two men—a delay too short for the Carcano rifle to be fired twice by one man, and too long to leave the single-missile hypothesis with credibility."[88]

A further anomaly is that to establish that CE399 traversed JFK's back through his neck Specter would have had to concede an upward trajectory. However, to establish that the same bullet hit Connally, who was sitting in the limousine's jump seat several inches below JFK, he would have to allow a downward trajectory.

Commission Exhibit 385 was a drawing that showed the "magic bullet" CE399 penetrating JFK's back at nearly the base of the neck and exiting through the throat. CE385 is inconsistent with the testimony of the doctors at both Parkland and Bethesda and with autopsy photographs that place JFK's back wound considerably lower on the back, down at least an inch or two from the neck. The drawing was controversial because it showed the bullet trajectory on a downward angle when the natural assumption and the available medical evidence of JFK wounds suggest that a line drawn from a back entrance wound to a neck exit would be on an upward bullet trajectory. However, an upward trajectory through JFK's body would be inconsistent with the assumption that a lone gunman firing from the far corner sixth floor window in the Texas School Book Depository shot both bullets that struck JFK, which would have been on a downward trajectory. To achieve this affect, Specter had the drawing made to show the point where the bullet entered JFK's back higher than where it actually did enter. Specter also drew the attention of the commissioners to photographs showing JFK's suit jacket was bunched up in the back so as to explain why the bullet holes observed in JFK's shirt and suit coat were lower down on the back where he argued the bullet entered.

Three important photographs taken instants before JFK was wounded the first time, supported Specter's argument that JFK's suit jacket was bunched up in back at the time of the shooting. Yet all three photographs show JFK sitting upright, such that a bullet hitting him in the back an inch or more below the neck would have had an upward trajectory to exit JFK's neck. And in none of the three photographs is JFK's head bent down. JFK is clearly seen sitting in a normal posture with his head upright as he observed bystanders along Elm Street on the right side of the limo.

The first photograph, taken by Hugh William Betzner, is a photo of the Dallas motorcade roughly at Zapruder's frame 186, showing the back of JFK's head as the limo approaches the R. L. Thornton Freeway "Keep Right" road sign on Elm Street. Betzner's photo shows JFK sitting upright, with his head held upright and JFK looking right.[89]

The second photograph, taken by Phillip L. Willis, is a color slide labeled by the Warren Commission as "Willis Slide #5."[90] Willis took it at apparently the precise moment the first shot was fired. "As I was about to squeeze my shutter, that is when the first shot rang out and my reflex just took the picture at that moment," Willis later recalled. "I might have waited another full second . . . but being with my war nerves anyway— when that shot rang out, I just flinched and got it."[91] Willis, a World War II Army Air Corp veteran, was at Pearl Harbor the day the Japanese attacked. From his military and hunting experience, Willis immediately recognized the first shot as a gunshot. His photograph, corresponding to Zapruder frame 202, shows Kennedy's limo from the rear, approaching the Stemmons Freeway sign. Kennedy can be seen sitting upright, his head held upright, with his gaze turned slightly to the right as the limo approached the Stemmons Freeway "Keep Right" road sign and JFK looks to his right at the bystanders on Elm Street.

The third photograph is the most important of the three. Robert Earl Croft's photograph, taken a few instants ahead of the Betzner and Willis photographs, shows the limo on Elm Street before reaching the R. L. Thornton "Keep Right" road sign. Croft's photo has the advantage of showing the limo from a side view. In the photo, JFK's head is clearly upright as he looks slightly to the right. There is no doubt Kennedy is sitting upright, with the entry point on his back clearly being lower than where Kennedy's neck wound was found. The photo makes it obvious that any bullet passing through JFK's body from the back to the neck would have had to have been on an upward trajectory.

So, a careful analysis of the Betzner and Willis photographs suggests a shot hitting Kennedy three to four inches down on the right side of his back would have passed through his body on a slightly upward trajectory, not the downward trajectory required by the single-bullet theory. Various documents, including JFK's death certificate, reveal that the back wound was located at the third thoracic vertebrae, which would place the bullet wound some three to four inches from the base of the neck. This evidence, plus the three photographs taken at approximately the instant the first shot was fired, suggests that JFK's suit coat bunched up in back, but not bunched so high as to reverse the bullet trajectory. At most, the angle would have been horizontal instead of downward, and a horizontal angle would have missed altogether the entry point on Connally's back near the angle of the shoulder blade.

The controversy was intensified when researchers discovered handwritten editing that Warren Commission member Congressman Gerald R. Ford had done on the final report. The two key sentences originally read: "The President's hands moved to his neck and he stiffened in his seat. A bullet entered his back at a point slightly above the shoulder to the right of the spine." Ford edited the second sentence to read: "A bullet had entered the back of his neck at a point slightly to the right of the spine." Ford argued he did not alter the language to support the single-bullet theory, but because he felt the changes made the language more precise.[92]

Specter's efforts to establish the single-bullet theory inevitably required moving JFK's back wound higher. Commission Exhibit 903 is a photograph taken on May 24, 1964, the same day as the Warren Commission's re-enactment of the assassination in Dealey Plaza.[93] In the photograph, Arlen Specter can be seen holding a metal rod or pointer at approximately a 17.5 degree angle—the angle the Commission calculated was required for the single bullet to hit both JFK and Connally. Two stand-ins are sitting in the JFK limo, one in JFK's seat and the other in Connally's seat. The person in Connally's seat is wearing the same suit jacket Connally wore when he was shot. This gave Specter an exact location within which to point the tip of his metal rod. Examined closely, it is clear Specter had placed the pointer on JFK's shoulder to make the angle work. Had

Specter placed the pointer four or five inches down on the JFK actor's back—much closer to the actual location in which the bullet hit JFK, the bullet passing through JFK's neck according to this photograph would have had to travel an upward trajectory, making it highly likely the bullet would have missed Connally altogether.

When examining FBI firearms expert Robert A. Frazier, Specter returned to asking hypothetical questions in the attempt to establish a downward trajectory could be established between JFK's back wound and neck wound that would permit the argument that CE399, fired from the sixth floor of the Texas School Book Depository, could have transited JFK to enter Connally. Consider the following exchange:

> **Mr. Specter:** I have one additional question.
> Mr. Frazier, assuming the factors which I have asked you to accept as true for the purposes of expressing an opinion before, as to the flight of the bullet and the straight line penetration through the President's body, considering the point of entry and exit, do you have an opinion as to what probably happened during the interval between [Zapruder] frames 207 and 225 as to whether the bullet which passed through the neck of the President entered the Governor's back?
>
> **Mr. Frazier:** There are a lot of probables in that. First, we have to assume that there is absolutely no deflection in the bullet from the time it left the barrel until the time it exited from the Governor's body. That assumes that it has gone through the President's body and through the Governor's body.
> I feel that physically this would have been possible because of the positions of the Presidential stand-in and the Governor's stand-in [in the FBI reconstruction], it would be entirely possible for this to have occurred.
> However, I myself don't have any technical evidence, which would permit me to say one way or the other. In other words, that would support it as far as my rendering an opinion as an expert. I would certainly say it was possible but I don't say that it probably occurred because I don't have the evidence on which to base a statement like that.
>
> **Mr. Specter:** What evidence is it that you would be missing to assess the possibilities?
>
> **Mr. Frazier:** We are dealing with hypothetical situations here of placing people in cars from photographs which are not absolutely

accurate. They are two-dimensional. They don't give you the third dimension. They are as accurate as you can accurately place the people but it isn't absolute.

Secondly, we are dealing with the fact that we don't know whether, I don't know technically, whether there was any deviation in the bullet which struck the President in the back, and exited from his throat. If there were a few degrees deviation then it may affect my opinion as to whether or not it would have struck the governor.

We are dealing with an assumed fact that the Governor was in front of the President in such a position that he could have taken. So when you say would it probably have occurred, then you are asking me for an opinion, to base my opinion on a whole series of hypothetical facts, which I can't substantiate.[94]

This has been the crux of the argument presented by computer simulations of Dealey Plaza and the JFK limousine popularized by various television shows that attempt to show it was possible for JFK and Connally to have lined up in such a way that a path could be projected back in a straight line to the supposed sniper's nest in the sixth floor far corner window of the Texas School Book Depository Building. Even if that straight-line hypothetically—from (a) the sixth floor corner window to (b) JFK's back wound to (c) JFK's throat wound to (d) Connally's back wound to (e) Connally's wrist wound to (f) Connally's thigh—existed at the moment of the JFK assassination, that still does not prove that a single bullet actually hit both men as speculated.

Specter resorted to asking hypothetical questions in the attempt to convince an American public not trained in legal logic that a lone shooter killed JFK. Specter did so, largely because he had no alternative. The proof Specter needed lay buried with JFK in Arlington Cemetery. As a consequence, the single-bullet theory at best assumes the status of a clever solution to a whodunit parlor game—a possible, but not proven explanation for who committed a crime, and how. As such, the single-bullet theory is not definitive proof Lee Harvey Oswald pulled off the greatest political crime of the twentieth century with an Italian Army World War II surplus rifle he purchased by mail order for a total cost of around twenty dollars, including tax and shipping. The facts that were established leave us with an unexplained entry wound in JFK's neck that, by itself, proves the presence of a second shooter from the front.

We are also left with CE399, a pristine bullet that strains credibility by mysteriously appearing at Parkland Hospital and causing massive damage in two adult men without fragmenting or becoming distorted in the process. With the autopsy failing to establish a bullet path through JFK's body connecting his back wound with his neck wound, there is no proof whatsoever that CE399 is the missile that wounded both JFK and Governor Connally.

TWO

THE GRASSY KNOLL

"The reason I *knew* that Oswald could not have done it, was because *I* could not have done it."

—Craig Roberts, *Kill Zone: A Sniper Looks at Dealey Plaza*, 1994[95]

KEY TO DECIPHERING THE JFK ASSASSINATION is the geography of Dealey Plaza.

In 1986, Craig Roberts, a combat veteran from Vietnam and a trained police sniper, viewed Dealey Plaza from the museum on the sixth floor of the Texas School Book Depository. His first realization was the difficulty of the three shots the Warren Commission concluded Lee Harvey Oswald took in killing JFK. "I knew instantly that Oswald could not have done it," Roberts wrote. "At least not alone." Roberts's analysis was not complicated: "Oswald could not have possibly fired three shots in rapid succession—5.6 seconds according to the museum displays—with a worn-out military surplus Mannlicher-Carcano mounted with a cheap telescopic sight from that particular location to the kill zone I now examined in more detail on the street below. [96]

Roberts compared Oswald, who barely qualified as a "Marksman — the lowest of three shooting grades established by the US Marine Corps— to his own year-long experience in Vietnam where he served as a trained, combat-experienced Marine sniper. During his year in Vietnam, Roberts recalled he had "numerous occasions to line up living, breathing human beings in the crosshairs of my precision Unertl scope and squeeze the trigger of my bolt-action Winchester and send a .30 caliber match-grade round zipping down range." [97]

Roberts concluded that acting alone, even with the precision equipment he used in Vietnam; he doubted he could duplicate the shooting feat the Warren Commission ascribed to Oswald. But in the military, single snipers are rarely used. Normally, Roberts pointed out, the smallest team would consist of two men, a sniper and a spotter who would double as security. Even in police SWAT teams, a spotter equipped with a scope or binoculars typically accompanies a marksman.

ANALYZING THE KILL ZONE

The angle of engagement from the sixth floor of the Texas School Book Depository was entirely wrong. "The wall of the building in which the windows overlooked Dealey Plaza ran east and west," Roberts analyzed. "By looking directly down at the best engagement angle—which was straight out the window facing south—I could see Houston Street. Houston was perpendicular to the wall and ran directly toward my window." This was the street on which the motorcade approached Dealey Plaza and Roberts concluded it was his second choice as a zone of engagement. "My first choice was directly below the window, at a drastic bend in the street that had to be negotiated by Kennedy's limousine. It would have to slow appreciably, almost to a stop, and when it did, the target would be presented moving at its slowest pace." [98] A sniper in the sixth floor of the School Book Depository at the window on the far east of the building would have a direct-on, full-body shot at the president as the limousine wound its way down Houston Street. The sharp angle turn onto Elm meant the limousine would be virtually stopped directly below the sniper's nest window, affording the sniper a close-range full-body shot at JFK as he sat in the back seat closest to the window.

The only other reason not to take a shot as the limo was proceeding down Houston was that from Houston, the driver of the limo had two escape routes: continuing straight past Elm onto North Houston Street or turning right at the intersection of Houston and Elm and escaping east away from the Texas School Book Depository. Once the limousine made the hard left turn from Houston onto Elm, there was no choice but to continue west along Elm until the triple underpass had been reached. Once that left-hand turn was made, an inescapable kill zone stretched from the Texas School Book Depository until the car passed the pergola monument and the picket fence along the grassy knoll, headed past the railroad yard on the right, and disappeared from sight under the triple underpass as the limo exited right onto the Stemmons Freeway. Having additional shooters positioned behind the picket fence on the grassy knoll, or in the three buildings along Houston at Elm—(1) the Dal-Tex building on Houston Street north of Elm across the street from the Texas School Book Depository; (2) the Dallas County Records Building on Houston Street south of Elm; and (3) the Dallas County Criminal Courts Buildings on Houston Street south of Elm immediately next to the Dallas County Records Building—would be the only justification for trading a straight-on full-body shot at close range for the much more difficult shot as the limo traveled through the Elm Street kill zone. The only part of JFK's body likely to be visible from the sixth floor corner window, as the limo receded down Elm Street toward the triple underpass, was a distant shot at JFK's back and shoulders, with the view partly blocked by a tree.

Roberts argued the last zone of engagement he would have picked was the Elm Street kill zone as the limo drove away from the Texas School Book Depository and headed west toward the grassy knoll. "Here, from what I could see, three problems arose that would influence my shots," Roberts pointed out. "First, the target was moving away at a drastic angle to the right from the window, meaning that I would have to position my body to compete with the wall and a set of vertical water pipes on the left frame of the window to get a shot. This would be extremely difficult for a right-handed shooter. Second, I would have to be ready to fire exactly when the target emerged past some tree branches that obscured the kill zone."[99]

Roberts realized that in choosing the Elm Street shot, Oswald was forcing himself to deal with two difficult factors at the same time, generally appreciated only by professional snipers: the curve of the street, and the high-to-low angle formula that Roberts characterized as "a law of physics Oswald would not have known." Imagining himself in Oswald's position, Roberts noted that the "high-low formula," also known as the minute-of-angle rule, demanded a sniper had to aim low at the range selected to avoid missing the target by shooting high by as much as a foot. "No one has told you that because of the effects of gravity, the bullet will not drop an appreciable amount—like it did on the rifle range which was a flat-trajectory shot."[100] What is not obvious from the Zapruder film is that Elm Street declines at approximately 3 degrees, east to west, for about a 1-foot drop per 20 linear feet. The distance from Houston Street to the triple underpass is approximately 495 feet by way of Elm and Commerce Streets. Elm Street at the triple underpass is approximately twenty-four feet lower than Elm Street at the Houston Street level.[101] Also not obvious from watching the Zapruder film is that Elm Street makes a pronounced S-curve as it winds toward the triple underpass, with the result that the angle of the shot from the sixth floor corner window to the back of JFK's head was changing constantly as the limo headed west down Elm Street. By comparison, Houston Street is straight and level, without the shooting complications Elm Street involves.

Also, Roberts realized the Mannlicher-Carcano with its bolt-action complicated the use of the telescopic scope. "You wait for a few seconds as they [JFK and the limo] come into your kill zone, then raise the scope to your eye, taking a second to establish the proper eye-relief between your eyeball and that lens so that 'half moon shadows' don't appear on the edge of the sight picture," Roberts imagined himself having to advise Oswald. "After all, the crosshairs and scope have to be exactly aligned or you will miss the target entirely. And this *has* to be done for every shot."[102] Making the scope work with the awkward touch of the Mannlicher-Carcano bolt-action may have made the rifle more difficult to shoot and possibly even less accurate, because the weapon had a scope, than if all the shooter had to do after chambering a round was to aim along the barrel and fire.

Roberts concluded the shots the Warren Commission reported Oswald took were the farthest and most difficult he could have taken from the sixth floor corner window, given the geography of Dealey Plaza. The third, fatal headshot was the most distant of the available shots, at a range Roberts estimated somewhere between eighty and ninety yards. This is absurd considering that Oswald had a full-body shot only a few yards away when the limo came to a near stop before making the sharply angled left turn from Houston onto Elm, directly below the sniper's window. The only more difficult shot Oswald could have taken would have been to fire an additional last shot as the limo disappeared at an accelerated rate, escaping under the triple underpass.

A sniper who knows weapons, Roberts observed one additional critical fact that made the Mannlicher-Carcano rifle Dallas Police found on the sixth floor unlikely to be involved in the shooting. "Mysteriously," Roberts wrote, "there *is no stripper clip which should have fallen to the floor through the magazine floor plate—and the weapon could not have functioned without it!*"[103] The Mannlicher-Carcano rifle uses a clip to load multiple rounds into the chamber; it was not designed be used as a single-shot rifle loaded without a clip. The clip for a Model 1891 6.5 mm Mannlicher-Carcano rifle holds six cartridges, and is supposed to fall out of the bottom of the magazine after the last round is chambered. When the rifle was discovered in the Texas School Book Depository, the clip was empty and one round was found in the chamber, but the clip remained in the magazine instead of falling out, as it was designed to do.

Furthermore, the Dallas Police Department found the clip in the rifle had been loaded not with original Italian ammunition, but with old surplus bullets considered highly unreliable that had been manufactured in the United States by the Western Cartridge Company decades earlier. "Of all the manually operated military rifles in use since the end of the last century, the one which has the worst reputation and that always has been viewed with approbation is probably the poor Carcano," wrote the now-deceased Canadian firearms expert Finn Nielsen.[104] Was the failure of the clip to fall out an indication Oswald was relying upon a defective weapon as his weapon of choice for assassinating the president of the United States? Or was the fact no clip was found on the floor with the three cartridge shells an indication that the weapon was planted as a decoy.

Remarkably, after finding the Mannlicher-Carcano the Dallas Police Department ran no tests on the Mannlicher-Carcano to determine if the weapon had been fired recently.

What Roberts concluded was that for an amateur like Oswald, Dealey Plaza was far too difficult a kill zone to have any reasonable chance of success. Consider the high school athlete. Of all the thousands of NCAA Division I men's football players, only 1.6 percent make the pros; In men's baseball, it's only 1.3 percent that make the big leagues. Basketball has the highest percentage with 9.7 percent of NCAA Division I players going pro.[105] Even if a player has the required ability, it takes a lot of practice and training to reach the highest ranks of a sport. Sure, a high school baseball player might be able to get lucky and knock a professional's pitch out of the park once, but it is not the way to bet. The curve in all athletics to get the improvement needed to be world class is incredibly steep. Typically the transition to world class involves a transformation where the pro learns to see the game differently than the amateur. Consider the game of chess. Studies have shown chess masters truly see no more moves ahead in a chess game than beginners. The difference is that where beginners see moves, chess masters see patterns.[106]

Roberts's conclusion was that the Dealey Plaza kill zone was no place for a lone amateur sniper. The easy shot from the sixth floor window as the limo came down Houston or turned the corner onto Elm would draw too much attention to the location where the shots originated. Successful sniping requires not only the ability to plan and take the shot so as to hit the target, but also the ability to take the shot undetected and to escape without being captured after the shot has been taken. As Roberts had judged, the perfect shot if the gunman were a lone shooter was as the limo turned onto Elm Street.[107] Waiting until the after limo turned onto Elm made sense only if the kill zone was designed for multiple snipers, each positioned to command a particular view or angle as the limo proceeded down the decline of Elm Street, twisting as it went through the S-curve that defined Elm Street from the Book Depository to the triple underpass. The tree that blocked much of the view complicated the shot from the sixth floor window, to say nothing of the diminishing target as the car went down Elm Street away from Houston Street. If there were multiple shooters, the prime spot for the kill zone was as the car cleared the tree just before the Stemmons Freeway sign. A little further down Elm past the Stemmons Freeway sign, a shooter on the grassy knoll behind the picket fence close to the railroad would have a close distance shot that would include JFK's torso as well as his head. Selecting a spot behind the picket fence too near the Texas School Book Depository would have given the shooter a direct shot into the limo but at an angle that would have risked hitting Jackie Kennedy sitting in the back seat of the limo to the left of JFK. Triangulating the kill shot by positioning additional shooters behind JFK in the buildings along Houston perpendicular to Elm would afford multiple opportunities to hit the target simultaneously from the front and the back, even if all the shots from the rear of the limo were difficult at best.

But for the full advantages of multiple shooting to be gained, the shooting had to be timed perfectly. Random shooting by will from multiple shooters would convey to onlookers the impression of crossfire, making it difficult, if not impossible, to pin the shooting on a fall guy—a "patsy" as Oswald described himself. If Oswald was to be framed as the lone shooter, it was imperative the gunshots had to be timed so that onlookers would assume that one gunman was firing three shots when the reality might be that three gunmen were firing three shots each, for a total of nine shots. To achieve the effect of synchronized shooting, the team had to have a fixed signal or target point for when the shooting was to begin. From the first shot fired, each shooter could count—one one thousand shoot, two one thousand shoot, three one thousand shoot—so that each shooter would have sufficient time to chamber the next round and aim. If the shooters had a spotter, the spotter could receive the signal to shoot by walkie-talkie, to keep the shooter in sequence. Synchronized shooting from multiple concealed locations was a solution that made Dealey Plaza an ideal kill zone, provided each shooter also had an accomplice to assist with communications, sighting, and escape. Professionally planned, Dealey Plaza quickly transformed from a nearly impossible kill zone for an amateur acting alone into a near-sure thing for a team of world-class marksmen.

The one final element needed was experience. This could not be the first kill for any of the shooters or their accomplices. The adrenalin flow in seeing JFK alive and knowing you were about to assassinate the president of the United States required steely nerves only a proven sniper with a track record of success would have. An accurate sniper shot requires a smooth and precise trigger pull. Only shooters with the demonstrated ability to remain dispassionate and calculating—a skill not reliable without a proven track record—could get this particular job done. An amateur could be expected to fumble with the bolt-action loading an old World War II Italian Army rifle. Moreover, a high-powered scope that filled the shooter's vision with a highly magnified vision of a small part of the target's body might make finding and locking on the target more difficult for an amateur. One foul-up and the target might be wounded but not killed, or the shooter might be detected and brought into custody. A professional team would not take amateur risks.

Taking the shots after the limo passed the Stemmons Freeway sign would take advantage of a relaxed entourage. It was the last leg of a long motorcade that began at Love Field and wound through downtown Dallas. The VIPs in the JFK limo would be looking forward to getting out of the sun and into the ample shade under the triple underpass. They were anticipating getting to the Trade Center where JFK was to give a luncheon address and a cool drink and something to eat would be waiting. The crowd was expected to thin as the limo traveled Elm Street as it was assumed spectators would prefer downtown vantage points where the passage of the limo would be slower. After successfully negotiating downtown without an incident, the Secret Service and Dallas police accompanying the motorcade were likely also to be ready to relax their guard. An advantageous aspect of the JFK assassination from a sniper's point of view was that the shooting started when the motorcade was just about finished—at the tail end of the planned route, where security personnel were least likely to suspect danger—especially once the tall buildings back on Houston and Elm, including the School Book Depository—were receding in the distance.

The ballistics evidence supports the multiple shooter assumption. The first shots that hit JFK were obviously the least powerful. The neck wound from the front did not exit JFK's body. The back entrance wound penetrated less than one joint of a doctor's little finger, as measured at the autopsy. Yet, the headshot or headshots shattered JFK's skull and splattered brain tissue in a mist that reached a foot or more in the air and wafted back to bathe the motorcycle police immediately tailing the limo. This difference in ballistic impact on the target would suggest each shooter had a different type of ammunition and very likely a different weapon. It is hard to imagine requiring shooters to change weapons and/ or ammunition as the kill proceeded. But it appears each shot had a different impact. This would imply each shooter could have had in mind or had been assigned a particular kind of shot that required a particular weapon and type of ammunition.

In other words, it is conceivable the various shots taken during the assassination could well have been designed to have different effects. The first two shots to hit JFK—in the neck and the back—may have been set-up shots. JFK was only wounded by these shots and the surprise of being shot was obvious on his face. Security personnel and others in the car could be expected to react relatively slowly, or so it would seem to shooters in the slow-motion bubble that surrounds professional snipers at the moment of their kill. After the first shots hit JFK and Connally, the Secret Service agents in the front seat—driver William Greer and Roy Kellerman—turned around to look back at JFK. Films taken during the assassination, especially the film taken by Orville Nix, show that Greer applied the brakes, slowing down enough to bring the limo to a near halt. It was after the fatal shot when Greer finally turned around to look forward, hunkered down behind the steering wheel, and released the brakes, so he could accelerate the vehicle along the last few yards of Elm Street through the triple underpass.[108] Shots that missed may have been planned to miss, as diversionary shots, or to create confusion so as to facilitate the escape.

Ironically, the therapeutic back-brace that JFK habitually wore was wrapped tightly around his torso under his shirt that day. An experienced sniper designing the assassination may have known the back-brace JFK habitually wore would hold his torso upright and straight, provided the bullets selected to hit his neck and back were a sufficiently low caliber. A wounded JFK was partially immobilized, held upright, and struggling to react—a perfect set-up for the final headshot, or headshots, to end his life. Each shooter on the team could have been given a particular objective, a particular weapon, and a particular shot to achieve a particular effect. Attempting the fatal headshot from the rear was risky because that shot was the most difficult. The only way it made sense for shooters positioned in the buildings behind the limo to attempt a head shot was if their head shots were designed as a back-up to the more sure-fire head shots planned to be taken by the shooters planned at the front of the motorcade.

The first shots that entered JFK's back from behind and his throat from the front involved lower-powered ammunition most likely fired by low-powered weapons. There is no proof either shot exited JFK's body. These two shots might have been aimed as head shots, but a .22 caliber bullet that entered the head might not have sufficient velocity or power to exit the skull. A .22 caliber bullet would have most likely done irreparable damage to JFK's brain, but not nearly as much damage as a higher-caliber bullet or a custom-designed explosive bullet. Consider that the headshot from the back that blew out the head-flap at JFK's forehead or the headshot from the front that blew out the back of JFK's head may have been done with a custom-designed bullet where the point had been hollowed out, or filled with mercury, and sealed with paraffin or some other type of sealant to keep the mercury contained within the shell. A modified hollow-point bullet was the favorite of many assassins because it explodes upon impact and causes massive damage. An exploding, hollow-point bullet could explain the fracture damage seen in the autopsy photos of JFK's skull, as well as the plume of brain tissue and blood that shot out of JFK's head on impact.

THE WITNESSES

In the immediate aftermath of the shooting, witnesses in Dealey Plaza rushed the grassy knoll, searching for the killers. No one rushed the Texas School Book Depository. From the movies and still photographs taken at the time, there is little doubt in-person witnesses to the assassination thought the shots came from behind the picket fence on the grassy knoll or from the railroad yard and parking lot that filled the area behind the grassy knoll, stretching from the railroad yard on the west near the triple underpass to the Texas School Book Depository on the right.

In 1966 attorney Mark Lane's book, *Rush to Judgment,* began a critical re-examination of the Warren Commission's conclusion that Lee Harvey Oswald was the lone gunman who assassinated JFK.[109] Lane created a sensation with his interview with Lee E. Bowers Jr., a Union Terminal Company employee who was working in the north tower in the railroad yard the day of the assassination. From his location on the second floor of the railroad tower, some twelve to fourteen feet above the ground, Bowers had a clear vantage point on all four sides, providing him a commanding view of everything that went on in the railroad yard and in the parking lot that stretched from the railroad yard to the Texas School Book Depository. Lane was extremely critical of the interview the Warren Commission had conducted with Bowers in Dallas on April 2, 1964.[110]

Bowers testified to the Warren Commission that he observed three suspicious automobiles enter the area in the half-hour preceding the assassination. The first car was a 1959 blue-and-white Oldsmobile, with an out-of-state license plate, and a "Goldwater for President" bumper sticker. Bowers testified that around 12:10 p.m., about twenty minutes before the assassination, the car passed down across two or three railroad tracks, and circled to the west of the tower as if the driver "was searching for a way out, or was checking the area." The car exited the way it came in, the only outlet by the school depository.[111] The second car, a 1957 black Ford with a Texas license plate, driven by a white male that was driving with one hand while holding what looked like a microphone with his other hand, entered the area around 12:20 p.m., some ten minutes after the first car. Bowers explained the black Ford came in from the extension of Elm Street in front of the school depository and left after three or four minutes. The third car, a 1961 or 1962 four-door white Chevrolet Impala with an out-of-state license plate and driven by a white male, circled the area and probed one spot right at the tower in an attempt to get out. Failing to find an exit, the car backed out a considerable distance. Bowers was too busy to watch to see if the car left the area, but the last he remembered, the car paused just above the assassination site. Bowers also observed the first and third car were covered with a red mud.

Just prior to the shooting, Bowers observed two men standing behind the picket fence toward the mouth of the underpass. Bowers described one of the men as "middle-aged, or slightly older, fairly heavy set," and wearing a white shirt and fairly dark trousers. The second, younger man was in his mid-twenties, wearing either a plaid shirt or plaid coat or jacket. Bowers observed the two men were within ten or fifteen feet of each other, facing the motorcade as it approached. "These were the only two strangers in the area," Bowers testified. All the others Bowers saw in the area, he knew, including two policemen standing on the overpass, a railroad signal man, two welders, a labor's assistant helping the welders, and a couple of parking lot attendees. Bowers testified he heard three shots: "One, then a slight pause, then two very close together. Also reverberation from the photo,"[112] He further testified, "The sounds came either from up against the School Depository or near the mouth of the triple underpass," but he was not able to tell which.[113]

The critical part of Bower's testimony came when he said at the time of the shooting there seemed to be "some commotion." Warren Commission assistant legal counsel Joseph Ball followed up with a question:

Mr. Ball: When you said there was a commotion, what do you mean by that? What did it look like to you when you were looking at the commotion?

Mr. Bowers: I just am unable to describe rather than it was something out of the ordinary, a sort of milling around, but something occurred in this particular spot which was out of the ordinary, which attracted my eye for some reason, which I could not identify.

Mr. Ball: You couldn't describe it?

Mr. Bowers: Nothing that I could pinpoint as having happened that—[114]

Here attorney Ball cut Bowers off. Mark noted that Ball's interruption prevented Bowers from concluding his most important sentence in which Bowers would have explained what it was in the area behind the fence that caught his attention at the time JFK was shot. Lane corrected this in a filmed interview with Bowers.

Mr. Bowers: At the time of the shooting, in the vicinity of where the two men I have described were, there was a flash of light or, as far as I am concerned, something I could not identify, but there was something I could not identify, but there was something which occurred which caught my eye in this immediate area on the embankment. Now, what this was, I could not state at that time and at this time I could not identify it, other than there was some unusual occurrence—a flash of light or smoke or something which caused me to feel like something out of the ordinary had occurred there.

Lane: In reading your testimony, Mr. Bowers, it appears that just as you were about to make that statement, you were interrupted in the middle of the sentence by the Commission counsel, who then went into another area.

Mr. Bowers: Well, that's correct. I mean. I was simply trying to answer his questions, and he seemed to be satisfied with the answer to that one and did not care for me to elaborate.[115]

Both Vincent Bugliosi and Gerald Posner discount the testimony of Lee Bowers, arguing that echoes in Dealey Plaza made difficult the determination of where shots came from. Bowers had testified he thought the source of the shots was either "up against the School Depository or near the mouth of the triple underpass." He was not able to tell which. Bowers explained: "I had worked this same tower for some ten or twelve years, and was there during the time they were renovating the School Depository Building, and had noticed at that time the similarity of sounds occurring in either of these two locations."[116] Bowers elaborated, "There is a similarity of sound, because there is a reverberation which takes place from either location."[117] Former Los Angeles County prosecutor Bugliosi subtly reframed Bowers' answer to claim Bowers "testified it was difficult to tell where the source of any loud sound was coming from, 'because there is a reverberation that takes place' in the plaza."[118] What Bowers said in his testimony was precisely that it was hard to distinguish whether a sound came from the Depository or from the area of the grassy knoll closest to the underpass, but he did not doubt the shots he heard came from one or the other. Posner was more accurate in his description of Bowers' testimony, but he took Bowers' inability to determine if the shots came from closer to the underpass or the Depository as proof that echoes made "ear-witness" testimony inherently unreliable in Dealey Plaza.[119] Still, neither Bugliosi nor Posner had any explanation for the cars Bowers observed prior to the assassination or for the suspicious behavior of the two men Bowers saw before the shooting behind the picket fence on the grassy knoll.

S. M. Holland, at the time a railroad employee since 1938, who was standing at the bannister of the triple underpass, by the railroad yard, at the time of the shooting, testified he heard four shots fired and saw a puff of smoke emerge from under the trees on the grassy knoll. Holland also supported Governor Connally's recollection, stating JFK was hit by the first shot and Connally by the second shot. In his testimony to the Warren Commission in Dallas on April 8, 1964, Holland remembered of the third and fourth shots: "And a puff of smoke came out about six or eight feet above the ground right from under those trees. And at just about this location from where I was standing you could see that puff of smoke, like someone had thrown a firecracker, or something out, and that is just about the way it sounded."[120] After the shooting, Holland joined the search behind the picket fence on top of the grassy knoll. One station wagon in particular caught his attention. "I remember about the third car down from this fence, there was a station wagon backed up toward the fence, about the third car down, and a spot, I'd say three foot by two foot. It looked to me like somebody had been standing there for a long time," he testified. "I guess if you could count them about a hundred foot tracks in that little spot, and also mud up on the bumper of that station wagon."[121] He felt the mud on the bumper indicated that "someone had cleaned their foot, or stood up on the bumper to see over the fence."[122] Holland further testified that he watched a motorcycle policeman breaking out of the motorcade and stopping his motorcycle, so he could run up the grassy knoll with his gun drawn at approximately the place where Holland had seen the puff of smoke.[123]

Many witnesses who claimed the shots came from the grassy knoll were never called by the Warren Commission to testify. William E. Newman Jr. and his wife Gayle were standing on the north curb of Elm Street with their two children, waving at the president as the limousine passed, some fifteen feet from the president at the time of the head shot. In several different interviews, including an interview he gave to Dallas police in Dealey Plaza at the time of the shooting and an interview on Dallas television immediately after the shooting, Newman insisted that the shots were fired from directly behind where he was standing with his wife and children, from behind the picket fence at the top of the grassy knoll. Newman said it never entered his mind that the shots might be coming from the Texas School Book Depository.[124] Newman and his wife can be seen in several assassination films and photographs lying on the ground, each covering one of their children to protect the child, in the immediate aftermath of the shooting.

The only place Newman's testimony shows up is in his signed affidavit to the Dallas Police Department, dated the day of the assassination, that is contained on page 45 of a long, 209-page report submitted by the Dallas Police Department on the DPD investigation into the JFK assassination and published as Commission Exhibit 2003 in Volume 24 of the Warren Commission report.[125] In his one-paragraph affidavit, Newman described: "We were standing at the edge of the curb looking at the car as it was coming toward us and all of a sudden there was a noise, apparently gunshot." After describing the fatal headshot, Newman swore to the truth of his recollection the shots came from directly behind where he and his family were standing, identifying the shots as having come from behind the picket fence on the grassy knoll. "Then we fell down on the grass as it seemed that we were in direct path of fire," he said in the affidavit. "I thought the shot had come from the garden directly behind me that was on the elevation from where I was as I was right on the curb. I do not recall looking toward the Texas School Book Depository. I looked back in the vicinity of the garden." Had William and Gayle Newman thought the shots came from the Texas School Book Depository, the Warren Commission most likely would have made them star witnesses, especially given their proximity to JFK at the time of the fatal head shot. Very likely, since both believed the shots were fired from behind them on the grassy knoll, their affidavits were ignored by the official inquiry and neither was called to give testimony to the Warren Commission.

OSWALD IN THE SIXTH-FLOOR WINDOW

The Warren Commission relied heavily on the testimony of Howard L. Brennan, a forty-five-year-old steamfitter who watched the motorcade from the retaining wall at the southwest corner of Elm and Houston across the street from the Texas School Book Depository Building. Brennan claimed to have had a clear view of the assassin in the sixth floor corner window of the depository building, directly above his vantage point. Brennan was the only witness to claim to the Warren Commission he saw Lee Harvey Oswald fire a rifle at the JFK motorcade from the sixth floor of the Texas School Book Depository. On March 24, 1964, Brennan testified to the Warren Commission in Washington.[126] Brennan claimed to have gotten a particularly good look at the shooter firing the third shot:

Well, as it appeared to me he was standing up and resting against the left window sill, with gun shouldered to his right shoulder, holding the gun with his left hand and taking positive aim and fired his last shot. As I watched a couple of seconds. He drew the gun back from the window as though he was drawing it back to his side and maybe paused for another second as though to assure himself that he hit his mark, and then he disappeared.[127]

The Warren Commission Report concluded Brennan's description of the man he observed in the sixth floor window was what most probably led to the description of the suspect that was called in by Dallas Police Department inspector J. Herbert Sawyer and broadcast over the radio alert sent to police cars at approximately 12:45 p.m., describing the suspect as white, slender, weighing about 165 pounds, about 5'10" tall, and in his early thirties.[128] The Warren Commission Report considered Brennan's testimony "as probative in reaching the conclusion the shots came from the sixth floor, southeast corner window of the depository building."[129] The Commission further relied on Brennan's testimony "that Lee Harvey Oswald, whom he viewed in a police lineup on the night of the assassination, was the man he saw fire the shots from the sixth-floor window of the Depository Building."[130] The Commission further noted Brennan "was in an excellent position to observe anyone in the window," because he was sitting on a concrete wall on the southwest corner of Elm and Houston Streets, "looking north at the Depository Building which was directly in front of him," such that the sixth floor window was approximately 120 feet away.[131]

At a police lineup the night of the assassination, Brennan evidently was either unable or unwilling to positively identify Oswald as the shooter, a failure that should have badly damaged his credibility. A memo written by Secret Service Agent Robert C. Dish on the evening of the assassination noted: "BRENNAN advised he later viewed LEE OSWALD in a police lineup, Dallas PD, at which time he failed to positively identify him as the person he had observed standing in the window with a rifle, but that of all the persons in the lineup, he most resembled the man he observed with the rifle."[132] In his testimony to the Warren Commission, Brennan admitted that he could not make a positive identification of Oswald at the lineup. Consider the following exchange, with Brennan being questioned by Warren Commission assistant counsel David Belin:

Mr. Belin: All right. Did you see anyone in the lineup you recognized?

Mr. Brennan: Yes.

Mr. Belin: And what did you say?

Mr. Brennan: I told Mr. Sorrels [Secret Service] and Captain Fritz [Dallas Police Department] at that time that Oswald—or the man in the lineup that I identified—looked more like a closest resemblance to the man in the window than anyone in the lineup.

Mr. Belin: Were the other people in the lineup, do you remember— were they all white, or were there some Negroes in there, or what?

Mr. Brennan: I do not remember.

Mr. Belin: As I understand your testimony, then, you said that you told him that this particular person looked the most like the man you saw on the sixth floor of the building there.

Mr. Brennan: Yes, sir.

Mr. Belin: In the meantime, had you seen any pictures of Lee Harvey Oswald on television or in the newspapers?

Mr. Brennan: Yes, on television.

Mr. Belin: About when was that, do you believe?

Mr. Brennan: I believe I reached home quarter to three or something of that, 15 minutes either way, and I saw his picture twice on television before I went down to the police station for the lineup.

Mr. Belin: Now, is there anything else you told the officers at the time of the lineup?

Mr. Brennan: Well, I told them I could not make a positive identi-fication.[133]

Yet, only a few questions later, Brennan insisted he could "with all sincerity" identify Oswald as the man he saw in the sixth floor window, even though he admitted that whether seeing Oswald on television might have affected his identification was "something I do not know." Brennan later said he hesitated to give a positive description of Oswald at the lineup because he was afraid doing so might place him and his family in personal danger of a reprisal, although Brennan did not specify who might do what to him or to his family. "After Oswald was killed, I was relieved quite a bit that as far as pressure on myself of somebody not wanting me to positively identify anybody, there was no longer that immediate danger," he explained to counsel Belin in the questioning before the Warren Commission.[134] Documentary evidence exists supporting Brennan's claim he did not make a positive identification of Oswald in a lineup. Commission Exhibit 2003, the Dallas Police Department report on their investigation into the JFK assassination, lists the names of all witnesses who positively identified Oswald in a DPD lineup, and Brennan's name is not included on the list.[135] If Brennan told Dallas police that Oswald resembled the man he saw in the sixth floor window, he did so unofficially, off the record. Still, in response to Belin's direct questioning, Brennan insisted Oswald was the shooter:

> **Mr. Belin**: Was the man that you saw in the window firing the rifle the same man that you had seen earlier in the window, you said at least a couple of times, first stepping up and then stepping back?
>
> **Mr. Brennan**: Yes, sir.[136]

Despite the inconsistencies in Brennan's testimony, proponents of the lone-assassin theory embrace his testimony. Bugliosi goes so far as to assert in his "Summary of Oswald's Guilt," that what proves the reliability of Brennan's identification of Oswald as the shooter is that "the description of the man in the window that he gave to the authorities right after the shooting—a slender, white male about thirty years old, five feet ten inches—matches Oswald fairly closely, and had to have been the basis for the description of the man sent out over police radio just fifteen minutes after the shooting."[137] Certainly Bugliosi does not expect the reader to assume that Oswald was the only slender white male matching that description in Dallas on November 22, 1963. Nor do the Warren Commission or Bugliosi provide any proof that Brennan's description was the basis for the police radio suspect description. Who wrote the police radio suspect description? Where did that person or persons get their information? Neither the Warren Commission nor Bugliosi provide any testimony or evidence that would resolve the question with certainty. Similarly, Warren Commission apologist Posner excuses Brennan's failure to positively identify Oswald as being justified by his fear, noting the FBI had already given him a twenty-four-hour guard that continued for three weeks after the assassination.[138] But if Oswald was the lone gunman and was already in custody, who was Brennan afraid would harm him or his family? Certainly, Posner's insistence that Oswald acted alone would not allow him to posit the idea of an accomplice who might seek to silence witnesses.

Historian Gerald McKnight has a different explanation. McKnight described Brennan as a "self-promoting bystander" driven by a need to be associated with some great tragedy, who pretends knowledge after the fact of events over which they truly have no information.[139] Reading the Warren Commission testimony closely, there does not seem to be support for McKnight's supposition. In his testimony to the Warren Commission in Dallas on April 8, 1964, Inspector Sawyer makes no mention of Brennan as his source for the description of the suspect believed to have fired shots from the Texas School Book Depository. Sawyer describes how he entered the Book Depository shortly after the shooting:

Mr. Belin: Where did you park your car?

Mr. Sawyer: In front of the Texas School Book Depository.

Mr. Belin: In front of the main entrance there?

Mr. Sawyer: In front of the main entrance.

Mr. Belin: What did you do then?

Mr. Sawyer. Immediately went into—well, talked to some of the officers around there who told me the story that they had thought some shots had come from one of the floors in the building, and I think the fifth floor was mentioned, but nobody seemed to know who the shots were directed at or what had actually happened, except there had been a shooting here at the time the President's motorcade had gone by.[140]

If Brennan was a source of information about the shooter, why was Sawyer so vague about what floor of the School Depository was involved? Brennan claimed to have seen the shooter so that he could describe his physical characteristics and his actions in detail, commenting even that when Oswald had fired his last shot, he paused to contemplate the scene with satisfaction. Why didn't Sawyer have this detailed information if Brennan was his source? Sawyer recalled that the description of the suspect that he called in, the description that was broadcast over the Dallas Police Department radio at 12:45 p.m. came "from one witness who claimed to have seen the rifle barrel in the fifth or sixth floor of the building, and claimed to have been able to see the man up there."[141] Sawyer could not remember the man's name and he could not provide a physical description of the witness, except to say he was around thirty-five years old.

Brennan was forty-five years old on November 22, 1963, and he was wearing a white construction hard hat in Dealey Plaza during the motorcade. Sawyer remembered none of these details about the man who gave him the suspect description. Sawyer testified he never saw the man again, not even at the line-ups the Dallas Police Department held that evening with Oswald. Sawyer further testified that during the entire time he was at the Texas School Book Depository after the shooting "between 25 to 50 people came up with information of one kind or another."[142] Certainly, Sawyer would have focused on and remembered any witness like Brennan who could give a precise physical description of the suspect and could relate the man's physical position at the sixth floor window and the actions he took in shooting.

"A faithful rendition of the evidence should have led the Commission to say, rather, that Brennan almost certainly was not the source of the description and that the witness who really provided the description has remained unidentified," concluded Sylvia Meagher, in her book, *Accessories After the Fact*.[143] Brennan also testified that he gave his story to Secret Service Agent Forrest V. Sorrels, the head of the Dallas Secret Service office. This, Sorrels confirmed, but Brennan spoke to Sorrels only after Sorrels returned to the Texas School Book Depository from Parkland Hospital considerably after the 12:45 p.m. DPD radio broadcast that contained the suspect's physical description.[144]

While Brennan claimed to have an excellent vantage point from which to observe the assassination, the Warren Commission published a photograph as Commission Exhibit 479, which appears to be frame 188 of the Zapruder film, showing Brennan observing the motorcade from the concrete wall at the southwest corner of Houston and Elm as he claimed.[145] The problem is that Commission Exhibit 479 clearly shows Brennan was sitting on the concrete wall facing Houston and Main, such that his back was to the Texas School Book Depository. In Commission Exhibit 479, Brennan is twisted around to his left, supporting his twisted body by bracing his left hand, palm down, on the top of the concrete wall. Brennan has his back still facing Zapruder's camera, watching JFK as the limousine disappears behind the Stemmons Freeway sign. This evidence clearly suggests that as the last shot was being fired, Brennan was watching the motorcade, not looking up at the shooter in sixth floor corner window of the Texas School Book Depository.

Examining the Zapruder film frame by frame, Brennan can be seen in the Zapruder film from frame 133, the first frame of the Zapruder film in which the JFK limo appears after it has turned onto Elm from Houston, through frame 208, when the limo is heading down Elm and JFK's head is all that can be seen above the Stemmons Freeway sign. In this entire sequence, never once does Brennan turn his body around to face the Texas School Book Depository squarely. Never once does Brennan look at the sixth floor window. With his back turned to the book depository throughout the shooting sequence, it is hard to see how Brennan could have observed as much as he claims to have seen. Brennan further testified that at the moment of the third shot, he was "diving off that firewall and to the right for bullet protection of this stone wall that is a little higher on the Houston side."[146] Yet, sitting with his back to the book depository and then diving for cover, Brennan claims to have seen the shooter shoulder the gun, take aim, fire, draw the gun back, move the gun to his side, and pause to make sure he hit his mark.

Further, Brennan said he observed two African-Americans he thought were watching the motorcade from the fifth floor window below the sniper's nest. He also testified that he saw the shooter take his last shot from a standing position, and that he could see the shooter from the belt up, watching as he took his third shot.[147] What Brennan did not appreciate was how low to the floor are the bottoms of the windows in the

Texas School Book Depository. Commission Exhibit 486 shows the two African-Americans from the inside of the building, doing a re-enactment of their positions at the time of the shooting.[148] Both are crouching down on their haunches, knees bent forward, to enable them to look out the windows as seen from the photographs of the Texas School Book Depository taken as the motorcade passed. Commission Exhibit 887 shows a re-enactment shooter kneeling down at the sixth floor window to take shots at the motorcade.[149]

These photos, along with Commission Exhibits 1310, 1311, and 1312 showing a man with a ruler standing and sitting by the sixth floor window, make it clear that the bottom windowsill is only about one foot above the floor.[150] The corner window in the so-called "sniper's nest" was opened only another foot-and-a-half. Shooting through this narrow opening so low to the floor, a standing shooter would have a difficult time getting the angle needed to hit the motorcade as the limo passed the Stemmons Freeway sign on Elm Street. This is illustrated by Commission Exhibit 1312, which shows the man sitting on a box to look out the open window, down at the path of the motorcade along Elm Street. Furthermore, the obviously dirty windows would have made it, difficult if not impossible, to identify a standing man with any clarity from his belt up. The shape of a man might have been visible, but the dirty windows would have obscured any details.

SECRET SERVICE ON THE GRASSY KNOLL

When bystanders rushed the grassy knoll, with many going behind the picket fence to examine the parking lot and railroad yard, several people reported encountering Secret Service agents, even though no Secret Service agents were assigned duty in Dealey Plaza that day. Seymour Weitzman, a Dallas County deputy constable who played a major role in the search of Dealey Plaza immediately after the assassination, was one such bystander. Testifying to the Warren Commission in Dallas on April 1, 1964, Weitzman explained he encountered Secret Service in the railroad yards.[151] Weitzman's recollection of the Secret Service being there is particularly vivid because it involves a fragment of JFK's skull. Responding to questions posed by Warren Commission assistant counsel Joseph A. Ball, Weitzman testified as follows:

Mr. Ball: What did you notice in the railroad yards?

Mr. Weitzman: We noticed numerous kinds of footprints that did not make any sense because they were going different directions.

Mr. Ball: Were there other people there besides you?

Mr. Weitzman. Yes, sir; other officers, Secret Service as well, and somebody started, there was something red in the street and I went back over the wall and somebody brought me a piece of what he thought to be a firecracker and it turned out to be, I believe, I wouldn't quote this, but I turned it over to one of the secret Service men and I told them it should go to the lab because it looked to me like human bone. I later found out it was supposedly a portion of the President's skull.

Mr. Ball: That you picked up off the street?

Mr. Weitzman: Yes.[152]

Note that Weitzman did not testify the Secret Service agents he found in the railroad after the shooting showed him any identification.

Dallas Police Department Sergeant D. V. Harkness went around to the back of the Texas School Book Depository around 12:36 p.m., some six minutes after the shooting, to make sure the building was sealed off. Testifying to the Warren Commission in Dallas on April 9, 1964, Harkness responded to a question from Warren Commission counsel David Belin as follows:

Mr. Belin: Was anyone around in the back [of the Texas School Book Depository] when you got there?

Mr. Harkness: There were some Secret Service agents there. I didn't get them identified. They told me they were Secret Service.[153]

Note once again, Harkness also did not ask the Secret Service agents to show their identification. He, like Weitzman, simply took their word.

Joe Marshall Smith, a Dallas Police Department uniformed officer, gave similar testimony, answering assistant counsel Wesley Liebeler's questions in Dallas on July 23, 1964:

Mr. Smith: Yes, sir; and this woman came up to me and she was just in hysterics. She told me, "They are shooting the President from the bushes." So I immediately proceed up there.

Mr. Liebeler: You proceeded up to an area immediately behind the concrete structure here that is described by Elm Street and the street that runs immediately in front of the Texas School Book Depository, is that right?

Mr. Smith: I was checking all the bushes and I checked all the cars in the parking lot.

Mr. Liebeler: There is a parking lot in behind this grassy area back from Elm Street toward the railroad tracks, and you went down to the parking lot and looked around?

Mr. Smith: Yes, sir; I checked all the cars. I looked into all the cars and checked around the bushes. Of course, I wasn't alone. There was some deputy sheriff with me, and I believe one Secret Service man when I got down there.

I got to make this statement, too. I felt awfully silly, but after the shot and this woman, I pulled my pistol from my holster, and I thought, this is silly. I don't know who I am looking for, and I put it back. Just as I did, he showed me that he was a Secret Service agent.[154]

Sylvia Meagher strongly suspected this man was one of the assassins with false credentials. Meagher went back to Dallas Secret Service records and concluded there were no Secret Service agents in Dealey Plaza or the vicinity until Forrest Sorrels, the head of the Dallas Secret Service office, returned to Elm Street and entered the Book Depository at 12:50 or 12:55 p.m. Sorrels rode in the lead car of the motorcade, and he stayed with the motorcade to Parkland Hospital, at which time he went back to Dealey Plaza to join in the criminal investigation. Who were the men who claimed to be but could not have been Secret Service? Was there any conceivable reason for such impersonation? Meagher felt so strongly about the evidence she wrote two paragraphs castigating the Warren Commission on this issue:

Few mysteries in the case are as important as this one, and it is appalling that the Commission ignored or failed to recognize the grounds here for serious suspicion of a well-planned conspiracy at work. It seems inconceivable that none of the many investigators and lawyers saw the significance of the reports made by these witnesses or realized that assassins positioned on the grassy knoll—behind the fence or trees— might have been armed with forged Secret Service credentials and lost themselves in the crowd that surged into the area.[155]

As noted at the start of the chapter, a professional sniper plans both to shoot undetected and to escape. Dealey Plaza was at the end of the motor-cade route, with the entrance to Stemmons Freeway just beyond the triple underpass. Within minutes of the shooting, the sparse crowd in Dealey Plaza was enlarged by a surge of onlookers who rushed from downtown in the vicinity of Houston and Main to see if they could find out what had happened. The photographs of the Dealey Plaza area immediately after the shooting show large numbers of people climbing the grassy knoll to mill around in the parking lot and railroad yard beyond. An assassin handing off a rifle for deposit in a case or the trunk of a parked car, could easily walk away, mixing in with the crowd.

If a person looked official enough, perhaps dressed in a suit and tie and claimed to be a Secret Service agent, he could have easily slipped away. Nor does it seem even experienced Dallas Police officers took the time or trouble to study credentials even when they were presented. The escape strategy for a professional team of assassins in Dealey Plaza on November 22, 1963, was simple—blend into the crowd and walk away. If stopped and questioned, claim to be a Secret Service agent and flash what looked like credentials.

In the interview with James Tague, the bystander whose cheek was nicked by a bullet that ricocheted in the shooting, Warren Commission Liebeler acknowledged this exact point. Consider the following exchange that closed out Tague's interview:

Mr. Liebeler: Other than that, is there anything that you can think of that you think the Commission should know about of what you heard and saw that day?

Mr. Tague: No; I don't know a thing. The only thing that I saw that I thought was wrong was that there was about 5 or 6 or 7 minutes in there before anybody done anything about anything.

Mr. Liebeler: That was after the shots were fired?

Mr. Tague: That was after the shots were fired.

Mr. Liebeler: What do you mean, "Before they did anything"?

Mr. Tague: There was no action taken except for the one policeman that I could see that stopped his motorcycle, and it fell over on him at first, and he got it standing upright and drew his gun, and he was the only one doing anything about it.

Mr. Liebeler: You didn't see any other policemen around in the area?

Mr. Tague: Not for 4 or 5 minutes. If Oswald was in that building [the Texas School Book Depository], he had all the time in the world to calmly walk out of there.[156]

As soon as the motorcade cleared Elm Street, passing under the triple underpass, Dallas police opened Dealey Plaza to normal traffic. Studying the various videos of the assassination aftermath in Dealey Plaza, it is unclear if the grassy knoll or the parking lot and railroad yard beyond were ever secured as a crime scene. The Texas School Book Depository remained unsealed for a minimum of fifteen minutes and possibly as long as twenty-five minutes or a half hour before Dallas police sealed the building. With the instant flood of onlookers into the kill zone, the value of Dealey Plaza as a crime scene was irreparably lost. Any evidence of the assassination that might have been found and properly identified for use in subsequent criminal proceedings was squandered, as bystanders and police picked up pieces of evidence—even fragments of JFK's skull—from the pavement and handed them over to people they perceived as authorities, or possibly even to pocket as souvenirs. The swarm of people, still in the grip of shock and disbelief, that descended on Dealey Plaza in the aftermath of the shooting is a case study only in how rapidly police can and do lose control of a crime scene in a downtown outdoor venue open to the public.

THE FATAL HEADSHOT

Josiah Thompson conducted an analysis of the Zapruder and the Nix films of the assassination for his 1967 book, *Six Seconds in Dallas*. He concluded the headshot that killed JFK was a double shot, with one bullet hitting him in the back of the head, followed a fraction of a second later by a shot from the front. Viewing the Zapruder film frame by frame to measure the distance between the back of JFK's head and the top of the back seat, Thompson documented JFK's head moved forward violently, beginning in frames 311–312, only to be driven violently back and to the left, beginning in frames 313–314.

These findings suggested crossfire on Elm Street, as the car approached the triple underpass. More than one shooter, by definition, means JFK was assassinated by a conspiracy. Moreover, the trajectory of the shot to the back of the head appears level, as if the shot came from one of the lower floors in the buildings along Houston Street—the Dal-Tex building north of Elm and across the street from the Texas School Book Depository or one of either the County Records Building or the Criminal Courts Building on Houston St. south of Elm. In the sequence starting at frame 313 the Zapruder film shows JFK's head being blasted apart with brain matter jetting out in a cloud through what appears to be an exit wound in the forehead. The Zapruder film then shows JFK's head being thrown violently back and to the left, a motion that suggests a shot came from the front and left side of the limo to the front. The right part of his forehead flaps open and a massive section of JFK's skull in the back is blown out. Bone fragments and brain matter from JFK's skull and brain spew out onto the trunk of the limousine, spraying the Dallas Police Department motorcycle officers riding to the rear left of the limo and Secret Service Agent Clint Hill as he rushes forward to get his foot on the left running board at the back of the limo and grab the left handrail on the limo's trunk.

Thompson argued his findings of a double headshot almost simultaneously hitting JFK from the front and rear explain the contradictory medical testimony from Parkland Hospital that identified JFK's head wounds as entry wounds and the medical testimony from Bethesda Naval Hospital where autopsy photographs show the back of JFK's head appeared virtually intact, except for a small, round bullet hole that appeared to be an entry wound. The puzzle remains that the Bethesda autopsy photos fail to show the large gaping exit wound in the right back of JFK's head that the doctors at Parkland described. That there was a headshot from the front would also explain why Jackie Kennedy climbed out onto the back of the limousine, not to help Secret Service Special Agent Clint Hill to get into the moving vehicle, but to pick up a piece of her husband's skull. And why the "Harper fragment" found in Dealey Plaza the day after the assassination—the largest fragment of JFK's skull to have flown clear of JFK's body in the explosion of his head resulting from the headshots—has been identified as occipital bone, from the back of JFK's skull.

Thompson summarized his findings as follows:

> The pattern that emerges from this study of medical evidence is a dual one. From the Parkland doctors we get the picture of a bullet that struck the right front of the President's head on a tangent, ranged backward causing massive damage to the right brain hemisphere, sprung open the occipital and parietal bones, and exploded out over the rear of the limousine. From the Bethesda surgeons we get the picture of a bullet entering the rear of the President's head and driving forward to the mid-temple region. Putting the two pictures together, we discern the outlines of the double impact. First, a bullet from behind exploding forward, and in that same split second another bullet driving into the exploding mass, forcing tissue and skull in the opposite direction. This is not a pretty picture, but it reconciles the evidence of the Zapruder film, eye- and ear-witness reports, and the curious double dispersion of impact debris. A coincidence certainly, but a coincidence whose reality is confirmed by the overwhelming weight of evidence.[157]

Thompson goes so far as to suggest the explosive impact of two bullets on JFK's skull blew out all traces of the right front entry wound, or that no entry wound is found in the right front of JFK's skull simply because the bullet from the shooter positioned on the grassy knoll entered JFK's head at the point of the exit wound from the rear shot, an instant after the rear-shot exit wound exploded the top right of JFK's head with a gruesome head flap that blew open over the right forehead. Much of the confusion interpreting the ballistics of JFK's headshot involves attempting to explain all the conflicting damage observed by one bullet, either from the front or from the rear. But realizing multiple shooters could be positioned at various places within Dealey Plaza to take advantage of both high and low trajectories as well as both rear and frontal shots, allows the medical and ballistic evidence to be sorted out with a completely different set of assumptions.[158]

A SECRET AUTOPSY?

David S. Lifton's 1980 bestselling book, *Best Evidence: Disguise and Deception in the Assassination of John F. Kennedy*, attempted to explain the discrepancy between the Parkland Hospital's report that the shots came from the front and Bethesda Hospital's report that the shots came from the rear by suggesting JFK's body had been stolen away after Air Force One landed at Andrews Air Force Base the evening of November 22, 1963, in order to be surgically altered in a secret autopsy.[159] The goal, Lifton argued, was to alter JFK's body—the "best evidence" of the crime that had been committed—so the medical examiner would conclude all shots had been fired from the front, a requirement if a patsy like Lee Harvey Oswald was to take the fall as the lone shooter. "Altering the body provided a means of hiding basic facts about the shooting," Lifton argued. "Surgery on the wounds changed the bullet trajectories and concealed the true location of the shooters. Bullet retrieval insured that bullets and bullet fragments from the weapons that actually murdered the President would never reach the FBI Laboratory."[160] The ability to conduct a secret autopsy was the crux of Lifton's attempt to explain how the conspirators that killed JFK planned to get away with the crime: "Alteration of the body suppressed evidence of shots from the front. If the body were altered in accordance with the trajectory-reversal scheme, plotters must have put a rifle and a sniper's nest behind and above the motorcade, but shot Kennedy from the front. Such falsification of the circumstances of death was integral to the crime."[161]

Lifton's point is that a conspiracy to assassinate JFK required a conspiracy to alter or eliminate any medical evidence that contradicted the one-shooter theory. In a sense, this is precisely what the Warren Commission did, even if Lifton's postulated secret autopsy is dismissed as unlikely or impossible. Arlen Specter invented the single-bullet theory to force all the evidence into a conclusion that Lee Harvey Oswald was a lone-nut gunman whose psychological problems led him to plan and commit the JFK assassination without accomplices. Once the ballistic evidence frees us from this conclusion, for instance, simply by a realization that the throat wound was an entry wound or that JFK's back wound was a superficial wound that did not penetrate the body, we are open to a whole new range of possible solutions. Josiah Thompson argues, for instance, that even if ballistic evidence shows bullet fragments found in the limousine after the shooting were fired from the Mannlicher-Carcano, that does not prove Lee Harvey Oswald fired the weapon. What becomes untenable as evidence accumulates, however, is the assumption the Mannlicher-Carcano, or any one particular weapon for that matter, was the only weapon fired. By freeing Oswald from having to be the lone shooter, we free Oswald from having to be a shooter at all—even if we subsequently find Oswald had deep ties to various conspirators who were involved in killing JFK.

One of the key witnesses in Lifton's book was Paul O'Connor, a laboratory technician at Bethesda Naval Hospital who witnessed the autopsy. O'Connor told Lifton that JFK's body arrived at Bethesda in a "simple shipping casket." This shook Lifton, who recalled JFK's body was taken from Parkland Hospital in Dallas in an elaborate casket provided by a private funeral home, "and for which the Government was billed almost $4,000."[162] Lifton pressed O'Connor, but he was adamant. "Well, I used to work in a funeral home as a kid," O'Connor explained to Lifton, "and a shipping casket is nothing but a cheap casket. It was a kind of pinkish gray, and it's used, for example, say a person dies in California and he wants to be buried in New York. They just bring him in a casket like this, and they ship him to New York, and they bury him. It's nothing fancy. It's just a tin box."[163] Even more startling, O'Connor told Lifton the body arrived in a body bag, which he described as "a heavy rubber bag with a zipper." This too startled Lifton because he knew that a sheet of plastic had been used to line the Dallas casket before JFK's body was placed into the casket.

O'Connor's testimony supported Lifton's hypothesis that JFK's body had been taken from Andrews Air Force Base and was transported by helicopter to the Army's Walter Reed Hospital, or one of the outlying hospitals the Army maintains as part of the Walter Reed system where a secret autopsy was performed to remove any bullet fragments or medical evidence that would prove JFK was shot from the front. Lifton believes JFK's body was then delivered to Bethesda Naval Hospital for the official autopsy.

In the report of the autopsy, FBI agents O'Neill and Silbert comment that when JFK's body was placed on the autopsy table, "it was apparent that a tracheotomy had been performed, as well as surgery of the head area, namely, in the top of the skull."[164] The word "surgery" jumped out at Lifton. There was no intermediate stop recorded on the official timetable where any "surgery" on JFK's skull had been done. O'Connor had told Lifton that when JFK's body arrived at Bethesda, he observed a "terrific wound" measuring eight inches by four inches in the occipital-parietal area of the skull that went "clear up around the frontal area of the brain." Moreover, O'Connor said it looked as if the fatal head shot "blew out all of his brains – literally." O'Connor said there were no brains in the skull to remove at the Bethesda autopsy because JFK's cranium was "empty" when the body arrived at the naval hospital.[165]

Lipton's suspicion was that in the time between the assassination at 12:30 a.m. CST in Dallas and the autopsy at Bethesda Naval Hospital beginning at 8:00 p.m. EST in Washington the FBI and LBJ had assumed control over the criminal investigation and the "best evidence of the crime," namely, JFK's body. At approximately 11:45 p.m. on the night of the assassination, FBI agent Vince Drain took possession of the Mannlicher-Carcano rifle and the three empty shell casings found after the shooting on the sixth floor of the Texas School Book Depository. He interrupted the work of Dallas Police crime scene specialist Lieutenant J. C. Day as he was attempting to lift a palm print off the rifle in order to fly both key pieces of evidence back to the FBI Laboratory in Washington that night.[166] With the rifle in the FBI Laboratory in Washington before the Dallas Police Department had time to complete their investigation. There was no way to know how any fingerprint or palm print information gained from the rifle was not planted there. The FBI had taken over the investigation of the crime, despite lacking the legal justification to do so. With control of the case moving to Washington, altering of evidence to fit the official theory of the assassination was a possibility that could no longer be ruled out.

Dr. Earl Rose, a physician and lawyer who became county medical examiner six months before the assassination, stood in the doorway at Parkland Hospital while insisting JFK's body remain in Dallas so he could conduct a proper autopsy, as was required by Texas law. Federal agents threatened Rose with automatic weapons to get him to stand out of the way. "As Mrs. Kennedy emerged from the trauma room beside a gurney carrying the casket, tension mounted," noted *The New York Times* obituary for Dr. Rose. "Roy Kellerman, head of the White House Secret Service detail, squared off against Dr. Rose. Obscenities were shouted. Unconfirmed accounts said Mr. Kellerman had pointed a gun at Dr. Rose. Years later, Dr. Rose said that might have happened but that he was not sure. 'Finally, without saying any more, I simply stood aside,' Dr. Rose said."[167] Until the day he died in Iowa in 2012, at the age of eighty-five, Rose was convinced that many of the controversies surrounding JFK's assassination could have been avoided if he had been allowed to do a careful, thorough, and fully documented autopsy, instead of the hurried-up, sloppy, incomplete, and highly political autopsy conducted that night at Bethesda Naval Hospital in Washington. Medical technician Paul O'Connor agreed with Dr. Rose's assessment of the Bethesda autopsy. Interviewed extensively on film for Nigel Turner's multi-episode television documentary *The Men Who Killed Kennedy*, O'Connor described the autopsy room at Bethesda Naval Hospital as follows:

> "There were mysterious men in civilian clothes at the autopsy. They seemed to command a lot of respect and attention – sinister looking people. They would come up and look over my shoulder or over Dr. [J. Thornton] Boswell's shoulder, then they'd go back and have a little conference in the corner. Then one of them would say, 'Stop what you're doing and go on to another procedure.' We jumped back and forth, back and forth. There was no smooth flow of procedure at all."[168]

In the same documentary two attending ER physicians clearly indicated that the head wound was fired from the front, blowing out the back of his head. Dr. Paul Peters used his right hand to indicate the back of his head behind his right ear to describe JFK's head wound that he saw as having blown out the right occipital-parietal part of JFK's brain and skull. Dr. Robert McClelland said on film that almost a fifth to a quarter to "the right back part of the head" had been blasted out, along with most of the brain tissue in that area while reaching behind his right ear to indicate the back right of JFK's head was where he too saw the massive wound. The JFK autopsy photographs, however, show the back of JFK's head intact, with his hair in place.

DEAD JFK RISING

At the end of the Zapruder film, as the presidential limo is about to go under the triple overpass, a remarkable series of frames shows a frantic Jackie Kennedy in the back seat propping her husband up to a full sitting position, as if he were alive. The sequence of the Zapruder film, rarely watched or studied, begins around frame 454. In the instants after the fatal headshot, Jackie Kennedy reacted with the type of hysteria that some unfortunate victims experience who have lost an appendage or part of an appendage, such as a finger, a hand, or even an arm. Just as those victims will try to jam the severed appendage back in place, in the film Jackie scrambles onto the trunk of the limo trying to grab some part of JFK's skull or brain matter. Once Jackie gets back in the seat, it appears she desperately tries to put Jack back together again to the point of moving the head flap back in place. By frame 464, JFK can be seen in an upright sitting position, looking reasonably well, even though he is completely brain dead from the massive headshot wounds.[169] Jackie Kennedy was in shock. In her testimony to the Warren Commission, Jackie Kennedy was asked if she remembered Secret Service Agent Clint Hill who climbed on the back of the limo to help. "I don't remember anything," she answered honestly, adding a few questions later that she had no recollection whatsoever of climbing out on the back of the car after the shooting.[170]

Secret Service Agent Clint Hill wrote a book, *Mrs. Kennedy and Me*, in 2012 in which he describes his experience during the JFK assassination. "I heard the shot. The third shot," he wrote. "The impact was like the sound of something hard hitting something hollow—like the sound of a melon shattering onto the cement. In the same instant, blood, brain matter, and bone fragments exploded from the back of the president's head. The president's blood, parts of his skull, bits of his brain were splattered all over me—on my face, my clothes, in my hair." The various photographs of the JFK assassination make clear that Hill was running to get on the trunk. For Hill to have seen brain matter explode out of JFK's head meant the wound at the back of JFK's head had to have been an exit wound. "As I peered into the backseat of the car," Hill recalled. "I saw the president's head in [Jackie's] lap. His eyes were fixed, and I could see inside the back of his head. I could see inside the back of the president's head."[171]

The importance of these few frames at the end of the Zapruder film is that we get a fleeting view at the back of JFK's head. The hair around the back head wound is a richer brownish-red color, and the wound adjacent to the right ear is the size of a grapefruit. These are the first frames with a direct view of the back head wound. The exit wound at the back of JFK's skull is confirmation of the near unanimous testimony of the Parkland Hospital medical team that the wound they observed in the occipital range of JFK's head near the right ear, a wound most described as being the size of a grapefruit, was an exit wound and the shot that had killed JFK.

At the Parkland Hospital press conference held one hour and fifteen minutes after JFK had been pronounced dead, Dr. Malcolm Perry, one of the attending physicians in the emergency room, and Dr. Kemp Clark, a neurosurgeon who also attended to JFK in the emergency room, attributed the cause of death to a massive wound at the back of his head.[172] These two physicians knew almost nothing about the facts of the assassination, and were cautious about making deductions from the medical evidence. Dr. Kemp Clark exhibited caution when he told a reporter that "the head wound could have been either the exit wound from the neck or it could have been a tangential wound, as it was simply a large, gaping loss of tissue." Either way, it's clear the two doctors considered the gaping hole at the back of JFK's skull to have been an exit wound and the bullet hole observed in JFK's neck to have been an entrance wound.

Dr. Charles Carrico, a surgeon doing his residency at Parkland Hospital at the time, was the first physician to treat JFK in the emergency room. In his testimony to the Warren Commission, Dr. Carrico described JFK's head wound as follows:

> **Dr. Carrico**: This [JFK's head wound] was a 5- by 51-cm defect in the posterior skull, the occipital region. There was an absence of the calvarium or skull in this area, with shredded tissue, brain tissue present and initially considerable slow oozing. Then after we established some circulation there was more profuse bleeding from the wound.

> **Mr. Specter**: Was any other wound observed on the head in addition to this large opening where the skull was absent?

> **Dr. Carrico**: No other wound on the head.[173]

Again, the head flap at JFK's right forehead was not of immediate interest to the Parkland Hospital physicians in the emergency room, probably because the massive wound at the back of JFK's head was enough to be fatal and saving JFK's life, not performing an autopsy, was the sole focus of the emergency room doctors at Parkland. "All we had time to do was to determine what things were life-threatening right then and there and attempt to resuscitate him and after which a more complete examination would be carried out and we didn't have time to examine for other wounds," Carrico testified to the Warren Commission. "After the President was pronounced dead . . . his wife was there, he was the President, and we felt certainly that complete examination would be carried out and no one had the heart, I believe, to examine him then."[174]

Dr. Robert McClelland, a surgeon on the staff of the University of Texas Southwestern Medical School, was giving a lecture at Parkland Hospital when JFK was brought into the emergency room. Summoned to the emergency room, McClelland arrived after the tracheotomy had been given. Putting on surgical gloves, McClelland also observed a massive wound to the back of JFK's head. He testified to the Warren Commission that through that wound, "you could actually look down into the skull cavity itself and see that possibly a third or so, at least, of the brain tissue, posterior cerebral tissue and some of the cerebellar tissue had been blasted out."[175] McClellan's testimony shows that the emergency room doctors were more concerned with trying to save the president's life than trying to figure out how he had been shot. "The initial impression that we had was that perhaps the wound in the neck, the anterior part of the neck, was an entrance wound and that it had perhaps taken a trajectory off the anterior vertebral body and again into the skull, exiting out the back, to produce the massive injury in the head," he testified. "However, this required some straining of the imagination to imagine that this would happen, and it was much easier to explain the apparent trajectory by means of two bullets."[176]

The basic logic of gunshot wounds applies: entrance wounds tend to be small, bullet-size holes (as the Parkland Hospital emergency room physicians observed in JFK's neck wound before the incision was made for the tracheotomy) while exit wounds tend to be larger, such as the grapefruit-sized, gaping wounds (as the Parkland Hospital emergency room physicians observed in the back of JFK's head). The Warren

Commission, in its effort to portray Lee Harvey Oswald as the lone assassin, had to ignore or otherwise obfuscate the abundant medical evidence and a testimony that confirmed JFK suffered an exit wound in the back of his head.

A MAUSER FOUND

The initial television reports, including one broadcast nationally by CBS, said that the rifle found on the sixth floor of the Texas School Book Depository was a 7.65 Mauser bolt-action equipped with a scope, not a 6.5 Mannlicher-Carcano. Dallas County deputy constable Seymour Weitzman, the same police officer who found a piece of JFK's skull and encountered what he thought was a Secret Service agent in the aftermath of the shooting, was present when the rifle was found. In an affidavit sworn on the day after the assassination, Weitzman described how the rifle was found:

> I immediately ran to the Texas Building and started looking inside. At this time Captain Fritz [Dallas Police Department] arrived and ordered all of the sixth floor sealed off and searched. I was working with Deputy S. Boone of the Sheriff's Department and helping in the search. We were in the northwest corner of the sixth floor when Deputy Boone and myself spotted the rifle about the same time. The rifle was a 7.65 Mauser bolt action equipped with a 4/18 scope, a thick leather brownish-looking sling on it. The rifle was between some boxes near the stairway. The time the rifle was found was 1:22 p.m. Captain Fritz took charge of the rifle and ejected one live round from the chamber. I then went back to the office after this.[177]

In his testimony to the Warren Commission, Weitzman acknowledged he told the FBI the rifle he found was a 7.65 Mauser.[178]

Deputy Eugene Boone, in an investigative report filed with the Dallas County Sheriff's office on the day of the assassination, reports how he found the 7.65 Mauser:

> I proceeded to the sixth floor of the building to search for the rifle. I started on the east end of the building and worked my way to the west end of the building. In the northwest corner of the building approx.

three feet from the east wall of the stairwell and behind a row of cases of books I saw the rifle, what appeared to be a 7.65 Mauser with a telescopic site. The rifle had what appeared to be a brownish-black stock and blue steel, metal parts. Capt. Fritz DPD was called to this location and along with an ID man DPD took charge of the rifle.[179]

In his testimony to the Warren Commission on March 25, 1964, Deputy Boone repeated his claim the rifle he discovered on the sixth floor was a 7.65 Mauser:

Mr. Ball: There is one question. Did you hear anybody refer to this rifle as a Mauser that day?

Mr. Boone: Yes, I did. And at last, not knowing what it was, I thought it was a 7.65 Mauser.

Mr. Ball: Who referred to it as a Mauser that day?

Mr. Boone: I believe Captain Fritz. He had knelt down there to look at it, and before he removed it, not knowing what it was, he said that is what it looks like. This is when Lieutenant Day, I believe his name is, the ID man was getting ready to photograph it.
     We were just discussing it back and forth. And he said it looks like a 7.65 Mauser.[180]

In a press conference after midnight on the day of the assassination, Dallas District Attorney Henry Wade, in response to a reporter's question, described the make of the rifle: "It's a Mauser, I believe."[181]

The story appeared to change on Saturday, November 23, 1963, the day following the assassination, after the FBI tracked the purchase and shipment of an Italian Mannlicher-Carcano carbine to an A. Hidell in Dallas, Texas. That name matched a forged Selective Service card with a photograph of Oswald and the name Alex James Hidell that Dallas police claimed to have found in Oswald's wallet at the time Oswald was arrested. Warren Commission critic Mark Lane, in his 1966 book, *Rush to Judgment*, pointed out as a condition of testifying to the Warren Commission, he obtained permission to examine the rifle. Finding that the words "MADE ITALY" and "CAL 6.5" were stamped on the rifle, Lane found it not credible that any policeman finding the rifle on the sixth floor of the School Depository could possibly mistake the weapon for a German-made 7.65 Mauser.

Lane made this point to the Warren Commission emphatically, when he testified on March 4, 1964:

> That following day, on the 23rd [of November, 1963], when it was announced by the Federal Bureau of Investigation that Oswald had purchased an Italian carbine, 6.5 millimeters, under the assumed name, A. Hidell, then for the first time the district attorney of Dallas [Henry Wade] indicated that the rifle in his possession, the alleged murder weapon, had changed both nationality and size, and had become from a German 7.65 Mauser, an Italian 6.5 carbine.[182]

Lane further indicated his surprise that District Attorney Wade would make such a mistake given that Wade "is a very distinguished prosecuting attorney, has been for some thirteen or fourteen years, and I believe was an agent of the Federal Bureau of Investigation prior to that time."[183] Lane pointedly asked regarding Wade: "I would like to know how he could have been so wrong about something so important."

For the answer, consider CE399, the pristine bullet Warren Commission counsel Arlen Specter used as the foundation for his single-bullet theory. Once the Commission established that CE399 had been fired from the 6.5 Mannlicher-Carcano, Specter felt he had a "lock" on the case, if only he could establish that CE399 was the bullet that hit both JFK and Connally. The problem remained that no authoritative chain of custody could be established for CE399, since the suspicion remained that CE399 might have been planted on the stretcher at Parkland Hospital where it was found by Darrell C. Tomlinson, a senior engineer in charge of the hospital's power plant. Similarly, the 6.5 Mannlicher-Carcano was the government's rifle of choice after the alias A. Hidell established a link between Oswald as the buyer of the weapon and a mail-order shop in Chicago as the seller of the weapon. Again, what happened to the 7.65 Mauser? The German rifle simply disappears from the case once the Commission realizes linking the murder weapon to Oswald becomes a lot easier to establish if the weapon used to assassinate JFK was the 6.5 Mannlicher-Carcano, not a 7.65 Mauser.

The Warren Commission, however, was satisfied: the alias A. Hidell linked Oswald and the Mannlicher-Carcano rifle; ballistics linked CE399 to the Mannlicher-Carcano rifle; CE399 validated the single-bullet theory; hence, Lee Harvey Oswald had to be the lone gunman. Or, to put the chain of deduction more simply, if Oswald was A. Hidell, he had to be the lone gunman, as proved by the Mannlicher-Carcano rifle and CE399. To make the deduction work, all that was required were two assumptions that could not be proven: namely, (1) that CE399 was a bullet used in the assassination and (2) that the Mannlicher-Carcano was really the rifle that was found on the sixth floor of the Texas School Book Depository, not the 7.65 Mauser the police and the Dallas district attorney initially claimed they found. Another problem was linking the key evidence with the crime: CE399 was not found in the body of JFK or Connally, and no bullet or bullet fragment pulled out of JFK or Connally could be traced back to the Mannlicher-Carcano with certainty. Evidently, the Warren Commission hoped the American public would just forget the Mannlicher-Carcano was a notoriously inaccurate weapon to fire and that the ammunition was World War II vintage.

A question that rarely if ever gets asked is this: Why would Lee Harvey Oswald, after shooting JFK, bother to take the time to hide the rifle with a scope among some boxes on the sixth floor near the stairs? Having just murdered the president of the United States, the first and only thought that should have been on Oswald's mind was getting away undetected as fast as possible. Oswald did not bother to pick up the three shell casings that fell on the floor just under the sixth floor window in the so-called "sniper's nest." So why did Oswald take the time to hide the rifle? Why not simply drop the gun at the sixth floor window and run? Surely the shooter must have realized the police were going to search every square inch of the Texas School Book Depository Building. Why bother hiding the weapon among a bunch of boxes near the stairs?

If the shooter had been professional, no shell casings or rifle would ever have been found, unless, of course, the shell casings and rifle were planted, in order that they would be found.

Could the spent shell casings have been dropped precisely because the markings on them would trace back to the weapon? The Mannlicher-Carcano, as we have just seen, was easily traceable back to Lee Harvey Oswald via the mail-order receipt in the name of the alias Alex Hidell. Long before the shooting ever began, the three spent shell casings could have been dropped at the sixth floor window and the rifle stashed among the boxes exactly where the assassination planners meant for them to be found.

Dropping the shell casings and the rifle would serve a dual purpose. Not only would it frame Oswald as the shooter, the three spent shell casings would lead investigators anxious to solve the crime to conclude no more than three shots had been fired, a conclusion that would help rule out multiple shooters organized in a conspiracy. What could possibly have been better for reasons of political expediency if the crime of assassinating JFK, a well-loved president at the height of his popularity, could be solved within minutes of the shooting? What could have been better for reasons of political expediency than if the lone assassin could be paraded before a national televised audience within two hours of the assassination? A Dallas Police Department incompetent enough to have allowed the assassination to have occurred in the first place could clearly attempt redemption by solving the crime this expeditiously. In the worst case scenario, even if the investigation found there were multiple shooters, the evidence left on the scene on the sixth floor of the Texas School Book Depository would frame Oswald as being one of the shooters.

Lost in the rush-to-judgment was any explanation as to why the first law enforcement investigators on the scene identified the rifle as a 7.65 Mauser when they found it. How did experienced Dallas Police detectives mistake a beat-up, Italian-made, second-rate World War II rifle with a defective clip and a misaligned scope for a precision German-made rifle with a reputation for accuracy?

The truth is the Warren Commission simply dismissed any evidence that contradicted the pre-determined, politically acceptable solution to the crime, namely, that Lee Harvey Oswald was the lone-gun assassin. As we have seen, the Warren Commission ignored the testimony of the many eyewitnesses who were convinced the shots had come from the grassy knoll. Similarly, the Warren Commission dismissed any eyewitness who saw more than one person on the sixth floor of the Texas School Book Depository building at the time of the shooting. Carolyn Walthers, for instance, was a spectator who watched the motorcade from Houston Street, some fifty to sixty feet south of the corner of Elm and Houston, from a vantage point in front of the Criminal Courts building. Walthers told the FBI that she observed two men in an upper floor of the Texas School Book Depository.[184] One man, with blond hair and wearing a white shirt, held a rifle that he pointed down toward Houston Street. She thought the rifle might be a machine gun. Next to him was an accomplice wearing a brown suit coat. Walthers was never called to testify before the Warren Commission. Instead, the Warren Commission cited the testimony of sixteen year-old African-American student Amos Lee Euins who said he saw a man with a rifle shooting out of the sixth floor window of the Book Depository window, even though Forrest V. Sorrels, the head of the Dallas Secret Service office, discounted evidence from Euins because Euins had not seen the supposed shooter well enough to tell if he were white or African-American.[185] The Warren Commission seemingly relied upon Euins, even though the Final Report noted Euins' testimony was considered merely probative rather than conclusive regarding the source of the shots, as well as inconclusive regarding the identity of the shooter.[186]

The Warren Commission was equally selective in which witness testimony was considered credible regarding the shots fired. Witnesses claiming the shots were fired from the grassy knoll were discounted in favor of witnesses that thought the shots came from the Texas School Book Depository. Witnesses disagreed regarding how many shots were fired, whether the first and second shots came in rapid sequence, or whether the rapid sequence involved the second and third shots. Some witnesses heard the shots, especially the first shot, as a firecracker, while others reported the shots boomed like a cannon. The Warren Commission did not probe whether more than one weapon may have accounted for the different ways witnesses heard the shots. The Warren Commission typically ignored testimony that did not conveniently fit the theory that Oswald was the lone shooter. Maybe the Warren Commission deemed publishing twenty-six volumes of hearings that included more than two thousand documents as sufficient weight of evidence to silence doubters. The problem from the beginning was that careful doubters took the time and trouble to read and study the twenty-six volumes. Combining this with their own independent research, skeptics were soon able to raise questions the Warren Commission could not easily answer.

But if the goal of the Warren Commission was to solve the crime, it took exactly the wrong approach. Rather than exclude evidence and testimony contrary to its pre-determined conclusion, the Warren Commission should have avoided forming any hypothesis regarding who killed JFK and how, until after all available evidence had been collected and all available testimony had been taken. Instead, LBJ and the Justice Department pushed a political conclusion that demanded dissenters be dismissed as "conspiracy theory" nut cases. By violating the pursuit for truth, the Warren Commission has committed a more serious crime on the nation than was committed in the JFK assassination itself. For fifty years now the Commission has committed violence against our most sacred of freedoms, our First Amendment right to free speech and the ability to dissent respectfully.

OSWALD IN THE LUNCH ROOM

Dallas Police Department motorcycle patrolman Marrion L. Baker testified to the Warren Commission on March 25, 1964, that he was trailing the JFK limo in the motorcade by about a block. He heard the first shot as he was proceeding down Houston, as JFK's limo was heading down Elm toward the triple underpass. Baker said he recognized the first shot as a rifle shot because he had just returned from deer hunting, where he had heard rifle fire for about a week.

> **Mr. Belin**: All right. Did you see or hear or do anything else after you heard the first noise?
>
> **Mr. Baker**: Yes, sir. As I was looking up, all these pigeons began to fly up to the top of the buildings here and I saw those come up and start flying around.
>
> **Mr. Belin**: From what building, if you know, do you think those pigeons came from?
>
> **Mr. Baker**: I wasn't sure, but I am pretty sure they came from the building right on the northwest corner [the Texas School Depository Building].
>
> **Mr. Belin**: Then what did you see or do?

Mr. Baker: Well, I immediately revved that motorcycle up and was going up there to see if I could help anybody or see what was going on because I couldn't see around this bend [at the corner of Elm and Houston].

Mr. Belin: Well, between the time you revved up the motorcycle had you heard any more shots?

Mr. Baker: Yes, sir; I heard—now before I revved up this motorcycle, I heard the, you know, the two extra shots, the three shots.

Mr. Belin: Do you have any time estimate as to the spacing of any of these shots?

Mr. Baker. It seemed to me like they just went bang, bang, bang; they were pretty well even.[187]

Baker estimated the distance to the corner of Elm and Houston from the point where he had heard the first shot was approximately 180 to 200 feet. He parked his motorcycle approximately 45 feet from the doorway of the Texas School Depository Building. He ran into the building, thinking the shots came from the roof. Once inside the lobby, he met Roy Truly, the building manager. Together, they ran to the northwest side of the building and started taking the stairs after they realized waiting for the elevator was going to take too long.

On the second floor, he got a glimpse of a man who later turned out to be Oswald.

Mr. Baker: As I came out to the second floor there, Mr. Truly was ahead of me, and as I came out I was kind of scanning, you know, the rooms, and I caught a glimpse of this man walking away from this—I happened to see him through the window in this door. I don't know how I came to see him, but I had a glimpse of him coming down here.

Mr. Belin: Where was he coming from, do you know?

Mr. Baker: No, sir. All I seen of him was a glimpse of him go away from me.

Mr. Belin: What did you do then?

Mr. Baker: I ran on over there—

Representative Boggs: You mean where he was?

Mr. Baker: Yes, sir. There is a door with a glass, it seemed to me like about a 2 by 2, something like that, and then there is another door which is 6 foot on over there, and there is a hallway over there and a hallway entering into a lunchroom, and when I got to where I could see him he was walking away from me about 20 feet away from me in the lunchroom.[188]

Baker yelled at the man, "Come here," and the man turned and walked toward Baker, as instructed. Baker testified he had his revolver in his hand and the man he observed had nothing in his hands.

Representative Boggs: Right. What did you say to him?

Mr. Baker: I didn't get anything out of him. Mr. Truly had come up my side here, and I turned to Mr. Truly and I says, "Do you know this man, does he work here?" And he said yes, and I turned immediately and went on out up the stairs.

Later that night, when Baker saw Oswald in custody in the homicide office of the Dallas Police Department, he recognized Oswald as the man he saw in the second floor lunchroom within minutes of the shots being fired.

Representative Boggs: When you saw him, was he out of breath, did he appear to have been running or what?

Mr. Baker: It didn't appear that to me. He appeared normal you know.

Representative Boggs: Was he calm and collected?

Mr. Baker: Yes, sir. He never did say a word or nothing. In fact, he didn't change his expression one bit.

Mr. Belin: Did he flinch in any way when you put the gun up in his face?

Mr. Baker: No, sir.

Mr. Dulles: There is no testimony that he put the gun up in his face.

Mr. Baker: I had my gun talking to him like this.

Mr. Dulles: Yes.

Mr. Berlin: How close was your gun to him if it wasn't the face whatever part of the body it was?

Mr. Baker: About as far from me to you.

Mr. Berlin: That would be about how far?

Mr. Baker: Approximately 3 feet.

Mr. Belin: Did you notice, did he say anything or was there any expression after Mr. Truly said he worked here?

Mr. Baker: At that time I never did look back toward him. After he says, "Yes he works here," I turned immediately and run on up, I halfway turned then when I was talking to Mr. Truly.[189]

Truly's testimony corroborated Baker's testimony. Truly told the Warren Commission he and Baker encountered Oswald on the second floor, just inside the lunchroom. Baker had his gun drawn and pointed toward the middle portion of Oswald's body. Once Truly vouched for Oswald as an employee, Baker resumed running up the stairs, determined to search the roof.

Mr. Belin: About how long did Officer Baker stand there with Lee Harvey Oswald after you saw them?

Mr. Truly: He left immediately after I told him—after he asked me, does this man work here. I said, yes. The officer left him immediately.

Mr. Belin: Did you hear Lee Harvey Oswald say anything?

Mr. Truly: Not a thing.

Mr. Belin: Did you see any expression on his face? Or weren't you paying attention?

Mr. Truly. He didn't seem to be excited or overly afraid or anything. He might have been a bit startled, like I might have been if somebody confronted me. But I cannot recall any change in expression of any kind.[190]

Mrs. Robert Reid, a clerical supervisor with an office on the second floor of the Texas School Book Depository Building was the next person to see Oswald. Mrs. Reid had been standing in the street in front of the depository as the motorcade went by. After the shooting, she ran back into the building and went directly to her office.

Mr. Belin: You went into your office?

Mrs. Reid: Yes, sir.

Mr. Belin: And then what did you do?

Mrs. Reid: Well, I kept walking and I looked up and Oswald was coming to the back of the office. I met him by the time I passed my desk several feet and I told him, I said, "Oh, the President has been shot, but maybe they didn't hit him."

He mumbled something to me, I kept walking, he did, too. I didn't pay any attention to what he said because I had no thoughts of anything of him having any connection with it at all because he was very calm. He had gotten a Coke and was holding it in his hands and I guess the reason it impressed me seeing him in there I thought it was a little strange that one of the warehouse boys would be up in the office at that time, not that he had done anything wrong. The only time I had seen him in the office was to come and get change and he already had his Coke in hand so he didn't come for change and I dismissed him. I didn't think anything else.[191]

Mrs. Reid further testified that Oswald's expression was calm and that he was moving "at a very slow pace."[192]

Oswald, in his first police interview with Dallas Police Department Captain Will Fritz, explained he left the Texas School Book Depository by the front door. He stated that as he was leaving, two men intercepted him at the front door, identified themselves as Secret Service agents, and asked for the location of a telephone. Pierce Allman, a newsman with

WFAA-TV in Dallas telephoned the news of the shooting from a phone in the book depository, after a man he could not identify directed him and one of his fellow workers, Terry Ford, to a telephone. Dallas Police did not question Allman regarding whether the man in the book depository who directed him to a telephone was Oswald. Shown pictures of Oswald by the Secret Service, Allman could not state for certain whether Oswald was the person at the book depository he asked for a phone. All Allman could remember was that the man helping him was a white male.[193]

William Manchester, in his 1967 bestselling book, *The Death of a President*, identifies then-NBC reporter Robert MacNeil as the person Oswald paused to direct to a telephone, some three minutes after the first shot was fired, as Oswald left the book depository by the front entrance.[194] MacNeil, who was on his first presidential reporting assignment, had stopped the press bus to get out, once he realized there was a shooting. After running on top of the grassy knoll to look over the concrete barrier at the top of the triple underpass to see into the railroad yard, MacNeil did run to the book depository and did ask someone at the entrance for a phone. MacNeil saw Oswald several times at the jail but he reported nothing clicked in his mind to recognize him. Oswald said the man who asked for the phone was a young blond crew cut Secret Service man, a description to which MacNeil admits fitting at the time. "Well, I was young, blond, short hair, grey suit, press badge," MacNeil admitted later. "And so Manchester says in the book that Oswald mistook me for a Secret Service man. All of that is intriguing. But what intrigues me more is the unconscious activity of having a little daydream that then programmed me unconsciously to do what I actually did when the shots were fired—that is to stop the bus, get out, and chase."[195]

What is even more intriguing is how Lee Harvey Oswald could have fired three shots from the sixth floor of the Texas School Book Depository in a span of ten seconds beginning at approximately 12:30 p.m. local time, then manage to hide his rifle between boxes on the other side of the building away from his sniper's nest in the northwest corner window, and run down four flights of stairs—from the sixth floor to the second-floor lunchroom—only to remain calm, cool, and collected, as a Dallas motorcycle policeman with a drawn weapon, accompanied by the building manager, stopped him for questioning. How could Oswald have done this, plus strolling into

Mrs. Reid's office, with a soft drink in hand that he just purchased from the lunch room vending machine, all in the span of three or four minutes? Then, Oswald walked quietly out the front door, pausing to give directions to what he thought were Secret Service agents as to where they could find a telephone to use inside the building. What nerves of steel it would take after having just assassinated the president of the United States to hang around the building long enough to drink a soda and simply stroll through the building, exiting through the front door. Rather than rushing out of the building through the back exit to escape law enforcement who could be rushing in to seal off the building, he took his time.

The eye-witness testimony of Oswald's behavior in the minutes immediately following the assassination suggest instead that Oswald was either in the second-floor lunchroom or on his way there when the shooting actually happened. In the thousands of pages of sworn testimony the Warren Commission took, there is no testimony whatsoever from anyone who worked in the Texas School Book Depository on November 22, 1963, who claims to have seen Oswald on the sixth floor at the time of the shooting. The truth is, no one in the Texas School Book Depository that day who saw Oswald in the building in the immediate aftermath of the shooting thought to finger him as a suspect.

THE GIRL IN THE STAIRS

Victoria Elizabeth Adams, a twenty-two-year-old employee of textbook publisher Scott Foresman watched the JFK motorcade from the fourth floor of the Texas School Book Depository as it passed by. After seeing the fatal head shot, Adams and her coworker Sandra Styles ran to the stairwell and raced down the stairs to the first floor, determined to get out the back of the building to see what they could find in the railroad yard behind the fence on the grassy knoll. The key aspect of her testimony was that the stairway Adams took was the same stairway Lee Harvey Oswald would have had to have taken to get from the sixth floor to the lunchroom where he was found by Baker and Truly. Yet, Adams testified she saw and heard nobody else on the stairs at that time. She estimated the time between hearing the shots and leaving the window to head for the stairway was between fifteen and twenty seconds. She estimated it took less than a minute to run down the stairs from the fourth floor to the first floor. The problem was that Adams did not see Lee Harvey Oswald passing her on the stairs; see testified she did not hear anyone else on the stairs when she was running down.[196]

Investigative reporter Barry Ernest describes in his book, *The Girl on the Stairs*, his thirty-five-year search to find and interview Victoria Adams.[197] When he finally found her in 2002, Adams repeated for him her story in person. She explained how various government officials, including the Dallas Police Department, had harassed her over her testimony. She produced for Ernest a 1964 letter her attorney had written to J. Lee Rankin, the chief counsel for the Warren Commission, complaining that someone had made changes in her deposition, altering her meaning. She explained to Ernest that she left Dallas after the assassination because she was seeking to disappear. "Remember, though I was a very young woman at the time (twenty-two years old) and believed in my government," she told Ernest. "Because of the strange circumstances and discounting of my statements, my multiple questioning by various government agencies and the Warren Commission's conclusions, I lost my starry-eyed beliefs in the integrity of our government. And I was scared, too. I was a young lady alone with no family or friend support at the time."[198] Reviewing with Ernest her testimony as printed in the Warren Commission volumes, Adams insisted her testimony as printed had been altered. "The freight elevator had not moved, and I did not see anyone on the stairs," she insisted to Ernest.[199] When Ernest asked her why the Warren Commission never called Sandra Styles to testify, Adams speculated, "Looking backwards I think they didn't want to corroborate any evidence."[200]

Yet, the record is clear. There is no photograph showing Lee Harvey Oswald on the sixth floor during the JFK shooting, and there is no testimony from anyone who worked in the building to suggest that he was there either. The Warren Commission dismissed Victoria Adams, saying she must have come down the stairs later than she estimated—enough later that Oswald had already passed by.[201] But absent this strained explanation, the evidence points to the conclusion that Lee Harvey Oswald was in the lunchroom of the Texas School Book Depository when JFK was assassinated, not on the sixth floor in the "sniper's nest" where the Warren Commission insisted he had to have been.

THREE

OSWALD, TIPPIT, AND RUBY

I don't think that they [the Warren Commission] or me or anyone else is always absolutely sure of everything that might have motivated Oswald or others that could have been involved [in the JFK assassination]. But he [Lee Harvey Oswald] was quite a mysterious fellow, and he did have connections that bore examination.

—President Lyndon Baines Johnson, *CBS REPORTS INQUIRY: "The American Assassins, Part II,"* 1975[202]

O N NOVEMBER 22, 1963, within the first hour after the JFK assassination, Dallas Police Department patrolman J. D. Tippit was gunned down in the Oak Cliff section of the city. The Warren Commission identified Lee Harvey Oswald as the murderer. Then, on Sunday, November 24, 1963, two days after the JFK assassination, Dallas nightclub owner Jack Ruby gunned down Lee Harvey Oswald in the basement of Dallas Police headquarters adjacent to Dealey Plaza, on Houston and Main Streets in downtown Dallas, a distance of only about two blocks from where JFK was murdered.

The Warren Commission concluded these were independent events, with no prior connections between Oswald, Tippit, and Ruby. "Investigation has disclosed no evidence that Officer J. D. Tippit was acquainted with either Ruby or Oswald," the Warren Commission Report declared emphatically.[203]

The Warren Commission concluded that Oswald shot Tippit to avoid being taken into custody. According to the Warren Commission's version of events, approximately 1:15 p.m. on the day of the assassination, Tippit was cruising east on 10th Street in Oak Cliff, just past the intersection of 10th and Patton, when he saw someone walking whom he considered suspicious. "About 100 feet past the intersection Tippit stopped a man walking east along the south side of Patton," the Warren Commission Report wrote, assuming Tippit must have heard the description of the suspect broadcast over police radio immediately after the assassination. "The man's general description was similar to the one broadcast over the police radio. Tippit stopped the man and called him to his car. He approached the car and apparently exchanged words with Tippit through the right front or vent window. Tippit got out and started to walk around the front of the car." This is where the Warren Commission assumes Oswald shot Tippit before Tippit could draw his weapon on Oswald. "As Tippit reached the left front wheel the man pulled out a revolver and fired several shots. Four bullets hit Tippit and killed him instantly. The gunman started back toward Patton Avenue, ejecting the empty cartridge cases before reloading with fresh bullets."[204]

While the Warren Commission did not draw any conclusions regarding why Ruby killed Oswald, the Commission explained Ruby's actions by the emotional distress Ruby felt over Kennedy's assassination. "[Ruby] maintained that he had killed Oswald in a temporary fit of depression and rage over the President's death," the Warren Commission Report noted.[205] The Commission was unequivocal that no connection existed between Ruby and Oswald prior to the shooting. "No direct or indirect relationship between Lee Harvey Oswald and Jack Ruby has been discovered by the Commission nor has it been able to find any credible evidence that either knew the other, although a thorough investigation was made of the many rumors and speculations of such a relationship," the Commission concluded. As far as the Warren Commission was concerned,

Lee Harvey Oswald, Jack Ruby, and Dallas policeman J.D. Tippit had nothing to do with one another prior to the assassination. "After careful investigation the Commission has found no credible evidence either that Ruby and Officer Tippit, who was killed by Oswald, knew each other or that Oswald and Tippit knew each other."[206]

Extensive research over the fifty years since the JFK assassination has called into question the assumption that Oswald, Tippit, and Ruby were all independent actors with no connections among or between them. To begin with, Lee Harvey Oswald and Jack Ruby both lived within blocks of the Oak Hill location, 10th and Patton, where officer J. D. Tippit was gunned down.[207]

AFTER SHOOTING JFK, OSWALD GOES HOME?

According to the Warren Commission reconstruction, Oswald left the Texas School Book Depository building approximately three minutes after the assassination. He was headed home, but the question was why? If Oswald had just shot JFK, why wasn't he escaping, as fast as he could?

According to the Warren Commission, Oswald was in no hurry. Leaving the Texas School Book Depository by the front door, the Warren Commission has Oswald walking east on Elm Street for seven blocks, to the corner of Elm and Murphy, where he boarded a bus heading back toward the book depository, on the way to the Oak Cliff section of Dallas. Why Oswald walked away from the book depository to get a bus when he could have easily walked home is not known. In a reconstruction of the bus trip, Secret Service and FBI agents walked the seven blocks from the entrance of the book depository to the corner of Elm and Murphy, averaging six and a half minutes. A bus moving through heavy traffic on Elm from Murphy to Lamar was timed as taking four minutes. The Warren Commission calculated that if Oswald left the Book Depository at 12:33 p.m., and walked seven blocks directly to Elm and Murphy to board a bus that left almost immediately, Oswald would have boarded the bus at approximately 12:40 p.m., and departed it at Lamar at approximately 12:44 p.m. From there, Oswald walked to the Greyhound Bus Terminal at Lamar and Jackson Streets, where he entered a taxicab at 12:47 or 12:48 p.m. The cab ride to Neely and Beckley in Oak Cliff took approximately six minutes, placing Oswald there at approximately 12:54 p.m. Walking from Neely and Beckley to his rooming house, the Warren Commission calculated Oswald arrived there about 12:59 to 1:00 p.m., approximately one half hour after the assassination.²⁰⁸ The Commission noted that about 1:00 p.m., Oswald entered "in unusual haste" 1026 North Berkley, where he rented a room.²⁰⁹

Mrs. Earlene Roberts, the housekeeper at 1026 North Berkeley, testified to the Warren Commission in Dallas on April 8, 1964, that she rented a room on October 14, 1963, to Oswald, who registered under the name "O. H. Lee." Under questioning by Commission assistant counsel Joseph A. Ball, Mrs. Roberts described what happened when Oswald came home on the day of the JFK assassination:

> **Mr. Ball**: Can you tell me what time it was approximately that Oswald came in?
>
> **Mrs. Roberts**: Now, it must have been around 1 o'clock, or maybe a little after, because it was after President Kennedy had been shot—what time I wouldn't want to say because—
>
> **Mr. Ball**: How long did he stay in the room?
>
> **Mrs. Roberts**: Oh, maybe not over three or four minutes—just long enough, I guess, to go in there and get a jacket and put it on and he went out zipping it up.
>
> **Mr. Ball**: You recall he went out zipping it—was he running or walking?
>
> **Mrs. Roberts**: He was walking fast—he was making tracks pretty fast.²¹⁰

Mrs. Roberts testified she couldn't remember the color of the shirt Oswald put on and she couldn't remember if it was long sleeve or short sleeve. Her testimony that she saw Oswald zipping up the jacket as he left was significant because she did not report noticing a gun stuffed in Oswald's pants. Mrs. Roberts testified that she cleaned Oswald's room and she did not recall ever seeing a gun, but she also clarified that it was "against the rules" to go through the belongings of a roomer. She also acknowledged that when police searched Oswald's room, they found a gun holster she had never seen before.[211]

Journalist Joachim Joesten, in conducting the research for his 1964 book, *Oswald: Assassin or Fall Guy?*, personally went and viewed Oswald's room at 1026 North Berkeley. "It would be difficult to hide a revolver in that room, a cubicle *five feet wide and twelve feet long*," he wrote. "I stood in it and surveyed the sparse furniture—a bedstead, an old vanity dresser, and a small clothes-hanger—as I casually asked the landlady standing next to me: 'Where did he keep the gun, Mrs. Johnson?'" Joesten wrote that Mrs. Johnson fairly exploded, answering, "Oswald never had a gun in this room!"[212]

Here is how Joesten described her reaction:

> Her voice was trembling with the indignation of a law-abiding, respect-able landlady who had told the police there had not been a gun in the room only to have her words disregarded. Yet as I stood there it was obvious that *there was absolutely no hiding place in that room* unless there was some elaborate cavity in the floor or in the walls which certainly would have been discovered and would also militate against the account that Oswald ran in and out of his room. There were only a couple of drawers in the room and Mrs. Roberts, in cleaning, had looked into them.[213]

Joesten concluded this discussion by emphasizing the Dallas Police Department presented absolutely no evidence that Oswald was carrying a gun that day, either before he got to the rooming house, or after he abruptly left after changing clothes.

Her testimony also produced something that has yet to be explained. Mrs. Roberts said that in the three or four minutes Oswald was in his room, a police car drove up and stopped in front of the house, with the police in the car tapping the horn, as if signaling Oswald before driving off.

Mr. Ball: Did a police car pass the house there and honk?

Mrs. Roberts: Yes.

Mr. Ball: When was that?

Mrs. Roberts: He came into the house.

Mr. Ball: When he came into the house?

Mrs. Roberts: When he came into the house and went to his room, you know how the sidewalk runs?

Mr. Ball: Yes.

Mrs. Roberts: Right direct in front of that door—there was a police car stopped and honked. I had worked for some policemen and sometimes they come by and tell me something that maybe their wives would want me to know, and I thought it was them, and I just glanced out and saw the number, and I said, "Oh, that's not their car," for I knew their car.

Mr. Ball: You mean, it was not the car of the policemen you knew?

Mrs. Roberts: It wasn't the police car I knew, because their number was 170 and it wasn't 170 and I ignored it.

Mr. Ball: And who was in the car?

Mrs. Roberts: I don't know—I didn't pay any attention to it after I noticed it wasn't them—I didn't.

Mr. Ball: Where was it parked?

Mrs. Roberts: It was parked in front of the house.

Mr. Ball: At 1026 North Beckley?

Mrs. Roberts: And then they just eased on—the way it is—it was the third house off of Zangs and they just went around the corner that way.

Mr. Ball: Went around the corner?

Mrs. Roberts: Went around the corner off of Beckley on Zangs.

Mr. Ball: Going which way—toward town or away from town?

Mrs. Roberts: Toward town.[214]

She said this happened while Oswald was yet in his room and she confirmed there were two uniformed policemen in the car.

After Oswald went out the front door, Mrs. Roberts looked out the window and saw Lee Harvey Oswald standing on the curb at a bus stop. She said she did not know how long Oswald stood there or what direction he went when he left.[215] How long Oswald waited, Mrs. Roberts did not know. Nor did she know whether he took a bus, whether the police car returned to pick him up, or if someone else picked him up. Oswald could have hailed a cab, or simply walked away. Mrs. Roberts did not know. She did not continue watching Oswald long enough to know how much time he spent there waiting, or how precisely he decided to move on. "Exhaustive investigations have virtually established the only police car officially in the vicinity was that of Officer J. D. Tippit," observed experienced journalist Henry Hurt who spent years with a research team sifting through JFK assassination data, cross-checking and corroborating facts, and tracking down participants and witnesses to interview.[216] Possibly, when Mrs. Roberts observed Oswald standing at the bus stop, Oswald was simply waiting for Officer Tippit to come around and pick him up, as had been pre-arranged.

The Warren Commission concluded that if Oswald left his rooming house a few minutes after 1:00 p.m., he needed to have reached 10th and Patton before 1:16 p.m. The timing was important because Tippit's murder was recorded on the police radio tape at 1:16 p.m., when a citizen witness to the shooting went into Tippit's patrol car and used the police radio in Tippit's patrol car to let Dallas Police know Tippit had been shot. The JFK assassination occurred at approximately 12:30 p.m., and in the following forty-six minutes, Oswald had to have had sufficient time to walk leisurely out of the book depository's front door, walk to a bus stop, get stuck in traffic, exit the bus, walk to the bus terminal, grab a cab, ride a short distance to his rooming house, change clothes, walk to the bust stop, stand for a while, and then walk down 10th just as Tippit was driving by—all within the span of no more than forty-six minutes.

The Warren Commission's reconstruction of the Tippit killing on East 10th Street near Patton Avenue in Oak Cliff had Tippit's patrol car pulling up on Oswald, who stopped casually, bended by resting both his elbows on the passenger door so he could see Tippit through the passenger window, and spoke to Tippit through the open window vent. The conversation was not described as heated or strained. For some reason, Tippit decided to get out of his car. Oswald then stepped back from the car and shot Tippit three times in the chest, as Tippit got level with the car windshield on the driver's side of the car, before Tippit ever reached for his gun. After Tippit fell to the pavement, Oswald moved around the front of the car to shoot him in the head, execution style. Only then did Oswald turn to hurriedly leave the scene.

Witnesses gave conflicting testimony over whether Oswald was walking east or west when Tippit's patrol car came up on him. There was also conflicting testimony over whether Tippit's patrol car first passed Oswald, or whether Oswald turned and went the opposite direction when he saw Tippit's patrol car approaching. What was a consensus was that Tippit stopped and Oswald, or whoever the person was, approached the car from the passenger's side to begin what seemed at first to be an amicable conversation. Suddenly, when Tippit got out of the car, everything changed. Again, there was conflicting testimony whether Tippit was reaching for his gun after he got out of the patrol car, but what was clear was that the assailant opened fire suddenly, pumping three shots into Tippit's chest with a revolver held casually at hip level. Once Tippit fell, why didn't the assailant run? Instead, the assailant acted as if he had all the time in the world. Calmly, the assailant pumped one more round into Tippit—a headshot on a severely wounded man lying helpless and bleeding on the pavement—just to make sure he was dead. Then, walking away, the assailant reloaded, casually tossing the spent shells away at the scene of the crime, seemingly unconcerned about witnesses the assailant knew were watching.

What was going on? If Tippit stopped his patrol car because he felt Oswald met the radio description of the suspect in the JFK assassination, why didn't Tippit radio for help, wanting to make sure headquarters knew the danger he might be taking in detaining the man? If Tippit suspected the man was the assassin of JFK, why didn't he pull his weapon immediately, or certainly before he got out of the car? If Tippit's assailant was Oswald, why did Oswald move toward the patrol car in such a friendly manner? Was Oswald clever and cool enough to think if he acted innocent he could lure the officer out of the car without drawing his weapon? Or did Oswald believe he was really innocent and had no idea police were looking for someone who met his description?

Journalist Joachim Joesten thinks there is only one premise that explains the event: "Patrolman Tippit and his killer knew one another!" Here is Joesten's analysis:

> We surely cannot believe that Tippit, presumably alerted that a presidential assassin was on the loose, would have given an unknown suspect the chance to draw first. Would not any competent police officer—and Tippit, a former paratrooper, had been with the police force for nearly 12 years—have drawn his own gun under the circumstances? Would he not, at the first suspicious look or gesture, have followed the old police maxim: "Shoot first, ask questions later"?[217]

In Joesten's analysis, only if Tippit and his killer knew one another can we explain the free and easy way the unknown killer approached the car and struck up a conversation with the policeman, and the way the policeman behaved, getting out of the car with his guard down, to casually walk over as if to continue the conversation face-to-face. But if the two knew one another, what went wrong?

The manner of shooting—three shots to the chest, followed by a shot to the head after the man was already down—bear all the earmarks of a cold-blooded, professional, gangland slaying, not the nervous or impulsive reaction of a person like Oswald who had no prior history of ever having shot or killed anyone.

WAS TIPPIT AN ACCOMPLICE?

Eva Grant, Jack Ruby's sister, told the *New York Herald Tribune* in a telephone interview that her brother and Officer Tippet knew each other well. "Jack knew him and I knew him," Grant said. "He used to come into the Vegas Club and the Carousel Club. He was a fine man. Jack called him 'buddy.'" According to Buchanan, Eva Grant also told the pro-Gaullist weekly *Candide* that Ruby and Tippit were "like two brothers."[218] At the time, Eva Grant ran the Vegas nightclub in Dallas that Jack Ruby owned. In her testimony to the Warren Commission, Grant said that one of her coworkers at the Las Vegas Club, Leo Torti, showed her a magazine photo of Tippit after he was killed and Grant remembered that Tippit had been in the Vegas Club around a month prior to his murder.[219] The *New York Herald Tribune* published a story on December 5, 1963, with the headline, "Ruby Knew Slain Dallas Policeman." The story left no doubt: "Jack Ruby, the strip-joint proprietor who murdered Lee Harvey Oswald . . . knew the dead patrolman, J. D. Tippit, well." Journalist Joachim Joesten also confirmed Ruby knew Tippit as part of Ruby's policy of working with the cops. "The picture of Ruby's relations with the Dallas police—fixing them up with wine, whiskey and girls—and with Tippit—in and out of his clubs all the time—is not an unfamiliar picture in large American cities," he noted. "It is a picture of a half-underworld of shady characters, of men carrying guns illicitly—and using them."[220]

On page 651, the Warren Commission report concluded Oswald and Ruby were total strangers: "Investigation has revealed no evidence that Oswald and Tippit were acquainted, had ever seen each other, or had any mutual acquaintances. Witnesses to the shooting [of Officer Tippit] observed no signs of recognition between the two men."[221] Yet that conclusion is belied by evidence the Warren Commission had, but refused to consider seriously. Commission Exhibit 3001 is an FBI report filed by Special Agent James W. Swinford, dated July 30, 1964, that documented Oswald, Jack Ruby, and Officer Tippit all frequented the same restaurant, Dobbs House Restaurant in Oak Cliff. Here is what Agent Swinford reported concerning Mary Adda Dowling, a waitress who served Oswald and Tippit at the Dobbs House Restaurant:

> She [Mary Adda Dowling] related she recalled the person now recognized as Oswald was last seen by her in the restaurant at about 10:00 AM, Wednesday, November 20, 1963, at which time he was "nasty" and used curse words in connection with his order. She went on to relate Officer J. D. Tippit was in the restaurant as was his habit at about that time each morning and "shot a glance at Oswald." She said there was no indication, however, they knew each other. Miss Dowling professed not to have known Jack Ruby as a customer, but she said she had heard from another employee he was a night customer.[222]

Sylvia Meagher took the Warren Commission to task for what she termed a "well-defined pattern" in the Commission's "fact-finding" in which the Commission first discounted information inimical to its thesis Oswald was the lone assassin, and then followed by proclaiming that such information did not exist. "Time and again, the Commission's own documents give the lie to its Report and outrage the handful of students who have ventured into the neglected pages of exhibits and testimony," she wrote. "In light of Mary Dowling's report and the total deafness with which it was greeted, the Commission's disclaimer of any link between Oswald and Tippit and its apocryphal version of the encounter in which Tippit was shot to death can hardly be regarded as the last word."[223]

One of the first books to appear questioning whether Lee Harvey Oswald was the lone assassin of JFK was a book entitled *Who Killed Kennedy?* that first appeared as a series of articles written in *L'Express* in Paris, authored by Thomas G. Buchanan, an American journalist who was fired in 1948 from the *Washington Evening Star* because of allegations he was a member of the American Communist Party. Buchanan was exploring a hunch that the JFK assassination was carried out "by gangsters with the aid of a corrupt policeman, who was meant to help Oswald get out of town by hiding him in his patrol car, double-crossed him and attempted to arrest him, and was consequently shot by Oswald."[224] The idea is that Tippit, married with a wife and three small children, found "the lure of money was an irresistible temptation," such that Tippit agreed to help someone escape from Dallas who was described to him as merely a member of the underworld, possibly a bank robbery fugitive. But when Tippit realized that JFK had been assassinated and that he had been set up to help the assassin escape, Tippit changed his mind. "Impelled by patriotic indignation, or by mere desire to win himself a medal and promotion, [Tippit] decided he would not help Oswald to escape but would arrest him, single-handedly," Buchanan speculated.[225]

What Buchanan argues is that Oswald was expecting Tippit on 10th Street at Patton that afternoon. Oswald, pleased to find Tippit, was relaxed as he approached Tippit's patrol car, as indicated by Oswald leaning against the passenger door with both forearms and speaking to Tippit though the window vent. What surprised Oswald was that Tippit was not reacting according to how the script had been written. Tippit was being aggressive, acting as if he intended to arrest Oswald—something that took Oswald completely by surprise. "The effect of lunging from the car and rushing after Oswald was precisely what the least experienced policeman on the force could have predicted," Buchanan wrote. "It provoked Lee Oswald to do what he had not yet been doing—to resist arrest. What Tippit did not know, however, is that Oswald would out-draw him."[227]

Buchanan also played with the theory that Oswald was actually headed to Ruby's apartment, and he had almost arrived at that destination when Tippit intercepted him. Buchanan notes Jim Lehrer, then reporting for the *Dallas Times Herald*, wrote on December 20, 1963, that Ruby had made five reservations on a plane leaving for Mexico.[22/] The suggestion here is that Tippit was set up to play the role of Boston Corbett, the Union army soldier who shot John Wilkes Booth to prevent Booth from exposing at trial a highly-placed Confederate government conspiracy to assassinate Abraham Lincoln. "But Policeman Tippit bungled his assignment," Buchanan concluded. When Oswald turned the tables and killed Tippit, the most upset was Oswald. "He had been so close to safety, only to be thwarted by what must have seemed to him to be bad luck, and nothing more than that," Buchanan wrote.[228]

THE TIPPIT MURDER TIMELINE

Mark Lane argued in his book, *Rush to Judgment,* that the timeline established by the Warren Commission for Oswald's movements immediately after the JFK assassination did not permit Oswald enough time to get to the location where Tippit was killed by 1:16 p.m. "Just about eight minutes after Oswald is seen at the bus stop, Tippit was shot to death nearly one mile away," Lane wrote. "As we shall see, the Commission not only neglected to explain how Oswald could have covered such a distance on foot in the time available to him without running all the way but also failed to investigate the minor point of why when last seen Oswald was apparently waiting for a bus that would have taken him in the opposite direction."[229] And, again, Lane wrote: "I believe that the Commission found it imperative to conclude that Oswald chose the shortest possible route between his rooming house and the intersection of East 10th Street and Patton Avenue near where Officer Tippit was shot. If Oswald had approached the scene of the killing by any other route, he might not have arrived in time to see the ambulance taking Tippit's body away."[230]

Lane also noted a witness, never called to testify, whose affidavit placed the Tippit shooting earlier than 1:16 p.m. Bowley, then a thirty-five-year-old Dallas resident, was driving on 10th Street when he noticed Tippit's patrol car and Tippit lying in the street injured. Here is Bowley's sworn statement:

> I traveled about a block and noticed a Dallas police squad car stopped in the traffic lane headed east on 10th Street. I saw a police officer lying next to the left front wheel. I stopped my car and got out to go to the scene. I looked at my watch and it said 1:10 pm. Several people were at the scene. When I got there the first thing I did was try to help the officer. He appeared beyond help to me. A man was trying to use the radio in the squad car but stated he didn't know how to operate it. I knew how and I took the radio from him. I said, "Hello, operator. A police officer has been shot here." The dispatcher asked for the location. I found out the location and told the dispatcher what it was. A few minutes later, an ambulance came to the scene. I helped load the officer onto the stretcher and into the ambulance. As we picked the officer up, I noticed his pistol laying on the ground under him. Someone picked up the pistol and laid it on the hood of the car. When the ambulance left, I took the gun and put it inside the squad car.[231]

When the police arrived, Bowley explained he did not see the shooting. Assuming Bowley's watch was accurate, this would place the Tippit shooting at a few minutes before 1:10 p.m., making it impossible for Oswald to be the shooter. Lane noted that the police radio broadcast log for November 22, 1963, substantiated Bowley's affidavit, with the log showing a citizen call over the police radio to the dispatcher was responsible for notifying the Dallas Police Department that Tippit had been shot.[232] The Warren Commission credited Domingo Benavides, an eyewitness to the Tippit shooting, as being the citizen who used Tippit's radio to call in at 1:16 p.m. the information that Tippit had been shot.[233] Reading Bowley's testimony clearly, Benavides had been having difficulty using the police radio, lending support for Bowley's placement of the shooting at around 1:10 p.m.

Benavides testified to the Warren Commission that he was driving in his 1958 Chevrolet pickup truck on 10th Street about fifteen feet from Officer Tippit's stopped police car when he saw the first shot. Benavides stopped his truck and ducked down to avoid being seen. He heard but did not see two more shots being fired. Benavides testified that after the shooting, he remained in his pickup truck for a few moments:

> **Mr. Belin**: All right, after you saw him [the shooter] turn the corner, what did you do?
>
> **Mr. Benavides**: After that, I set there for just a few minutes to kind of, I thought he [the shooter] went in back of the house or something. At the time, I thought maybe he might have lived in there and I didn't want to get out and rush right up. He might start shooting again.[234]

Benavides testified that a man he did not know helped him call the shooting into police headquarters using Tippit's radio in the squad car:

> **Mr. Benavides**: Then I don't know if I opened the car door back further than what it was or not, but anyway, I went in and pulled the radio and I mashed the button and told them that an officer had been shot, and I didn't get an answer, so I said it again, and this guy asked me whereabouts all of a sudden, and I said on 10th Street. I couldn't remember where it was at the time. So I looked up and I seen this number and I said 410 East 10th Street.
>
> **Mr. Belin**: You saw a number on the house then?
>
> **Mr. Benavides**: Yes.
>
> **Mr. Belin**: All right.
>
> **Mr. Benavides**. Then he started to—then I don't know what he said; but I put the radio back. I mean, the microphone back up, and this other guy was standing there, so I got out of the car, and I don't know, I wasn't sure if he heard me, and the other guy sat down in the car.
>
> **Mr. Belin**: There was another passerby that stopped?
>
> **Mr. Benavides**: Yes, sir.
>
> **Mr. Belin**: Who was he, do you know?

Mr. Benavides: I couldn't tell you. I don't know who he was.

Mr. Belin: Was he driving a car or walking?

Mr. Benavides: I don't know. He was just standing there whenever I looked up. He was standing at the door of the car, and I don't know what he said to the officer or the phone, but the officer told him to keep the line clear, or something, and stay off the phone, or something like that. That he already knew about it.[235]

Again, Mark Lane focused on the timeline. "Although the radio call was recorded on tape between 1:15 and 1:16 p.m., it is certain that several minutes elapsed between the murder and the time when the radio was first used to contact the police, whether by Benavides or Bowley, as the testimony of both clearly indicates." Lane estimated that Earlene Roberts saw Oswald standing at the bus stop at 1:04 p.m. He calculated that the testimony of Benavides and Bowley put the Tippit murder at no later than 1:12 p.m. The distance between the bus stop and the 10th Street Tippit shooting was just under one mile. "The Commission should have concluded that the slaying took place between 1:08 and 1:12 p.m., but biased as I believe the Commission was toward reaching a finding consistent with Oswald's guilt, it set the time of the murder forward to 1:15 or 1:16 p.m."[236]

Sylvia Meagher, in her 1967 book, *Accessories After the Fact*, is also very critical of the Warren Commission regarding the Tippit murder timeline. "If the shooting of Tippit took place at 1:06 or 1:10 p.m., Oswald would have to be exonerated on the grounds that he could not possibly have walked the nine-tenths of a mile from his rooming house, which he departed a few minutes after 1 p.m., in time to reach the scene," she noted. "The Commission has estimated Oswald's other walks (from the Book Depository to the bus and from the bus to the taxi) at one minute per block. At that rate, Oswald would have required 18 minutes to walk from his rooming house to the spot where Tippit was shot."[237] Meagher further noted that no witness had come forward who saw Oswald walk from his rooming house at 1026 North Berkley to the East 10th Street and Patton Avenue location where Tippit was shot. There is no evidence Oswald took the shortest route; Warren Commission counsel David Belin re-enacted the route, with a stopwatch in hand, taking what he described as the "long way around route," finding the walk took 17 minutes and 45 seconds.[238] Meagher also noted the Warren Commission ignored the question where Oswald was going when he left the rooming house. "Indeed, the Commission has ignored the question of where Oswald was heading—if it *was* Oswald—when he was stopped by Tippit," she wrote. "He had no known social or business contacts in that immediate area, but, as many critics of the Report have pointed out, Jack Ruby's apartment was in the direction in which 'Oswald' was walking and only a few short blocks from the scene of the Tippit shooting."[239]

EYEWITNESSES TO THE TIPPIT SHOOTING

Even though he was the closest to the Tippit shooting, Benavides told police he could not identify the shooter; as a result, Benavides was never taken to Dallas Police headquarters to view Oswald in a line-up.[240]

The only other eyewitness was Helen Markham, a waitress on her way to work when she saw the Tippit shooting. Sylvia Meagher pointed out that Markham lacked credibility, noting: "[Helen Markham] said that she was alone with Tippit for twenty minutes before an ambulance arrived, and that Tippit—who is said to have died instantaneously—tried to talk to her; she was in hysterics and somehow managed to leave her shoes on top of Tippit's car; sedatives had to be administered before she was taken to view the line-up at about 4:30 p.m. on Friday."[241] Here is how Markham described the line-up in which she identified Oswald as Tippit's shooter:

Mr. Ball: Did you recognize anyone in the lineup?

Mrs. Markham: No, sir.

Mr. Ball: You did not? Did you see anybody—I have asked you that question before—did you recognize anybody from their face?

Mrs. Markham: From their face, no.

Mr. Ball: Did you identify anybody in these four people?

Mrs. Markham: No. I had never seen none of them, none of these men.

Mr. Ball: No one of all four?

Mrs. Markham: No, sir.

Mr. Ball: Was there a number two man in there?

Mrs. Markham: Number two is the one I picked.

Mr. Ball: I thought you just told me that you hadn't—

Mrs. Markham: I thought you wanted me to describe their clothing.

Mr. Ball: No. I wanted to know if that day when you were in there if you saw anyone in there—

Mrs. Markham: Number two.

Mr. Ball: What did you say when you saw number two?

Mrs. Markham: Well. Let me tell you. I said the second man, and they kept asking me which one, which one. I said, number two. When I said number two, I just got weak.

Mr. Ball: What about number two, what did you mean when you said number two?

Mrs. Markham: Number two was the man I saw shoot the policeman.

Mr. Ball: You recognized him from his appearance?

Mrs. Markham: I asked—I looked at him. When I saw this man I wasn't sure, but I had cold chills just run all over me.[242]

Sylvia Meagher commented that when reading the testimony about the "identification" on which the Commission relied for determining Oswald killed Tippit, she felt a few cold chills too.[243] Still, the Warren Commission report relied on Helen Markham's identification of Oswald, with her vague recognition she was by no means the best witness. On page 167 of the Warren Commission Report, we find the following:

At about 4:30 p.m., Mrs. Markham, who had been greatly upset by her experience, was able to view a lineup of four men handcuffed together at the police station. She identified Lee Harvey Oswald as the man who shot the policeman. Detective L. C. Graves, who had been with Mrs. Markham before the lineup testified that she was "quite hysterical" and was "crying and upset." He said that Mrs. Markham started crying when Oswald walked into the lineup room. In testimony before the Commission, Mrs. Markham confirmed her positive identification of Lee Harvey Oswald as the man she saw kill Officer Tippit.[244]

We should also note that in an affidavit Markham signed on November 22, 1963, she placed the time of the Tippit shooting at 1:06 p.m.—a fact the Warren Commission omitted in the final report.[245] Also, Mark Lane in testifying to the Warren Commission described his interview with Markham. "[Helen Louise Markham] said [the man who shot Officer Tippit] was short, a little on the heavy side, and his hair was somewhat busy," Lane testified. "I think it is fair to state that an accurate description of Oswald would be average height, quite slender, with thin and receding hair."[246] Lane tape-recorded his conversation with Markham, providing documentation that proved important when Markham tried to convince the Warren Commission she had never spoken with attorney Lane.[247]

Taxicab driver William Scoggins, was eating his lunch at the corner of 10th and Patton when Tippit was killed. He cannot truly be considered an eyewitness because his view was obstructed by shrubbery. Scoggins claims to have caught a glimpse of the assailant's face as the assailant looked back over his shoulder while running from the scene through some shrubbery about twelve feet away from where Scoggins was sitting in his cab. Scoggins testified to the Warren Commission that as the man ran by he heard him mutter something like "poor damn cop" or "poor dumb cop."[248] Scoggins picked Oswald from a Dallas Police lineup attended by another cab driver, William Wayne Whaley, the cab driver that took Oswald from the Greyhound bus terminal to North Beckley, as Oswald was trying to get out of downtown after he walked out the front door of the book depository. Whaley's description of the lineup makes clear picking Oswald out was not a difficult task, whether or not a positive identification could be made.

Mr. Whaley: . . . Then they took me down in their room where they have their show-ups, and all, and me and this other taxi driver who was with me, sir, we sat in the room awhile and directly they brought in six men, young teenagers, and they all were handcuffed together. Well, they wanted me to pick out my passenger.

At that time he had a pair of black pants and white T-shirt, that is all he had on. But you could have picked him out without identifying him by just listening to him because he was bawling out the policemen, telling them it wasn't right to put him in line with these teenagers and all of that and they asked me which one and I told them. It was him all right, the same man.

Mr. Ball: They had him in line with men much younger?

Mr. Whaley: Not much younger, but just young kids, they might have got them in jail.

Mr. Ball: Did he look older than those other boys?

Mr. Whaley: Yes.

Mr. Ball: And he was talking, was he?

Mr. Whaley: He showed no respect for the policemen, he told them what he thought about him. They knew what they were doing and they were trying to railroad him and he wanted his lawyer.

Mr. Ball: Did that aid you in the identification of the man?

Mr. Whaley: No, sir; it wouldn't have at all, except that I said anybody who wasn't sure could have picked out the right one just for that. It didn't aid me because I knew he was the right one as soon as I saw him.[249]

Interestingly, Whaley testified that after Oswald got in the front passenger seat of his cab, an elderly lady stuck her head down past Oswald in the door and asked, "Driver, can you call me a cab down here?" Seeing that this woman wanted a cab, Oswald opened the door like he was going to get out and said, "I will let you have this one." The lady declined, happy to catch the next cab. But the interesting point is that Oswald's action in offering to give up the cab is not consistent with the behavior that might be expected from a vicious criminal who had just assassinated the president of the United States and was desperate to escape capture.[250]

The Warren Commission never interviewed two neighbors who told private investigators two men were involved in the Tippit shooting. Mrs. Acquilla Clemons claimed to have seen two assailants flee the scene after the shooting. Mrs. Clemons described the shooter as short and stocky. She saw a second taller thinner man across the street who looked like he was giving a "go-ahead" sign to the shooter. After the shooting, the taller-thinner man went in one direction while the shorter-stocky man went in the other. Frank Wright, who lived nearby, went to his front porch on hearing the shooting. He described the shooter as being of medium height and wearing a long coat. Wright claimed the shooter made a fast getaway in a 1950 or 1951 gray car that he thought might have been a Plymouth coupé.[251]

In 1978, Anthony Summers, a former investigative journalist for the BBC, had William Alexander, an assistant Dallas district attorney in 1963, drive him around the area of the Tippit shooting. Alexander told Summers that Dallas police had measured the routes Oswald might have taken, interrogated bus drivers, and examined taxicab records, but still were unable to determine how precisely Oswald got to the scene of the Tippit shooting or what he was doing there. "I feel like if we could ever find out why he was there, then maybe some of the other mysteries would be solved," Alexander said. "Was he supposed to meet someone? Was he trying to make a getaway? Did he miss a connection? Was there a connection? If you look at Oswald's behavior, he made very few non-purposeful motions, very seldom did he do anything that did not serve a purpose." Summers reported Alexander slapped the dashboard and repeated, "Oswald's movements don't add up then, and they don't add up now. No way. Certainly he must have had accomplices."[252]

MARITAL PROBLEMS

In 1968, during the criminal investigation into the JFK assassination conducted by New Orleans District Attorney Jim Garrison, an anonymous letter surfaced with information that ended up proving Officer Tippit was not the long-time good cop and family man just doing his job that the

Warren Commission assumed in 1964. The letter indicated that Tippit had been having an affair with a "small blonde waitress" who worked at Austin's Barbecue Drive-in, a Dallas restaurant where Tippit moonlighted as a security officer on weekends. The anonymous letter continued: "[A friend] told me of a friend telling her the story that on the morning Officer Tippets (sic) was killed and on the day of the assassination, Mrs. Tippets (sic) had coffee with a neighbor and was crying because on that morning Officer Tippets (sic) had told her he wanted a divorce to marry someone else."[253]

On November 22, 1963, Tippit evidently knew the waitress was pregnant with his child. On August 6, 1963, the former waitress was granted a divorce by the court, giving her custody of her four children; the woman's husband evidently did not show up at court to contest the divorce. Assassination researcher Dale Myers, in a 702-page investigation into the Tippit murder in 1998, noted the husband of the waitress, divorced again in 1968, continued to believe that the child born in 1964 was fathered by J. D. Tippit.[254] Marital problems and the prospect of a divorce could easily have created for J. D. Tippit the type of financial problems that could send him in the direction of Jack Ruby and the Dallas underworld, making Tippit a candidate for the role of "corrupt policeman" who author Thomas Buchanan speculated was involved with gangsters attempting to get Oswald out of town following the assassination.

On the morning of November 22, 1963, Tippit hugged his oldest son, Allen, and said, "No matter what happens today, I want you to know I love you."[255] The cryptic remark may have been less a premonition of the JFK assassination than the fallout from asking his wife for a divorce. Another issue may have been that the former husband of the waitress evidently had a history of stalking Tippit and his wife when they went out together, leading some to speculate the Tippit murder may have been simply an act of revenge by a jealous husband.[256]

Tippit's movements in Oak Cliff on November 22, 1963, are also suspicious. At approximately 12:45 p.m., about a half hour before he was killed, Tippit was observed in his police car on the Oak Cliff side of the Houston Street viaduct. He sat in his car at a GLOCO gas station and observed traffic crossing the bridge for about ten minutes. There are no police dispatches sending Tippit to this location. Tippit suddenly sped out of the gas station and headed south on Lancaster. At 12:54 p.m., Tippit answered his dispatcher and said he was at "8th and Lancaster," about a mile south of the GLOCO gas station. He then turned right on Jefferson Boulevard and stopped around 1:11 p.m. at the Top Ten Record store at Jefferson and Bishop and ran inside.

According to storeowner J. W. "Dub" Stark and his clerk, Louis Cortinas, Tippit asked several customers to step aside as he made his way to a telephone mounted on the end of the sales counter. Tippet let the number he dialed ring seven or eight times, and hung up without saying a word. Without speaking to Stark or Cortinas, Tippit rushed out of the store, jumped in his squad car, and sped north across Jefferson Boulevard, where he ran a stop sign, turned right on Sunset, and was last seen by multiple witnesses speeding east, one block from North Beckley, the location of Oswald's rooming house.[257]

The story takes another weird twist when a person identified as John D. Whitten called the Dallas FBI office twelve days after the assassination and reported that Oswald had also been in the Top Ten Record store the day of the assassination. The FBI disregarded the story because Oswald was supposed to have been at work in the book depository all day on November 22, 1963. The story also conflicts with the Warren Commission narrative that had Oswald spending the night of the twenty-first in Irving, Texas, with his wife and daughters, who were then living with Ruth Paine. The Commission had reported that Oswald returned to the Paine home on Thursday night, November 21, 1963, to pick up "curtain rods," a cover story for what the Commission maintained was in reality the Mannlicher-Carcano rifle hidden in a crudely constructed paper bag container. When Oswald left the Paine residence at 7:15 a.m. the morning of the assassination, his wife, Marina Oswald, was still in bed. The Commission reported Oswald was driven to work on November 22, 1963, by Buell Wesley Frazier, a neighbor of Ruth Paine.[258] But in 1997, former storeowner J. W. Stark confirmed that Oswald was waiting at the store around 7:30 a.m. when Stark arrived the day of the assassination. Stark recalled that Oswald bought a ticket to the *Dick Clark Show* and left by bus. Stark did not know anyone by the name of Whitten and did not believe there was a Whitten who had a connection to the store.[259] As we shall see at the end of this chapter, credible evidence exists establishing that "the Oswald identity" was being used by two different people, one of whom was known as "Lee" and the other as "Harvey."

No one has established the identity of the person Tippit called from the record store moments before he was shot to death. Nor is it clear why police dispatch assigned Tippit to patrol Oak Cliff, an area Tippit did not normally patrol, when police units around the city were being called downtown to assist in the assassination investigation. Dallas Police dispatch records show that when Tippit called at 8th Street and Lancaster, he was told to stay at large for any emergency that came in. But then, around 1:06 p.m., when Tippit was at either the GLACO gas station or the Top Ten Record store, police dispatch called for Tippit but received no answer.[260] This may have been the time when Tippit stepped into the record store to make the phone call. Tippit had stepped away from his patrol car without notifying the dispatcher, a habit Tippit evidently had developed over the last few years.[261] The next mention of Tippit in the Dallas Police dispatch records is when a citizen calls in saying, "We've had a shooting out here," at what appears to be 1:16 p.m.[262]

THE JACKET

The Warren Commission knew the testimony of Helen Markham, the only eyewitness who had actually seen the Tippit shooting and identified Oswald as the shooter, was too shaky to build a case that could have been expected to stand up at trial. In this regard, consider the following Warren Commission statement: "Addressing itself solely to the probative value of Mrs. Markham's contemporaneous description of the gunman and her positive identification of Oswald at a police lineup, the Commission considers her testimony reliable. However, even in the absence of Mrs. Markham's testimony, there is ample evidence to identify Oswald as the killer of Tippit."[263]

While not abandoning Markham, the Commission clearly downplayed her testimony in favor of what the Commission considered hard evidence, namely, Oswald's jacket that the Commission argues Oswald discarded after shooting Tippit, the shell casings found at the Tippit murder scene, and the revolver Oswald had on his person when he was apprehended later in the day at the Texas Theater.

Dallas Police found a light-gray Eisenhower-style zipper jacket evidently abandoned under a two-door Oldsmobile parked at Ballew's Texaco service station at Crawford and Jefferson.[264] The Warren Commission concluded as follows regarding the discarded jacket: "There is no doubt, however, that Oswald was seen leaving his rooming house at about 1 p.m. wearing a zipper jacket, that the man who killed Tippit was wearing a light-colored jacket, that he was seen running along Jefferson Boulevard, that a jacket was found under a car in a lot adjoining Jefferson Boulevard, that the jacket belonged to Lee Harvey Oswald, and that when he was arrested at approximately 1:50 p.m., he was in shirt sleeves."[265] The Commission felt these facts warranted the finding that Lee Harvey Oswald disposed of his jacket as he fled from the scene of the Tippit shooting. The assumption appeared to be that Oswald must have felt he would be less recognizable if he changed his appearance by discarding the jacket.

Even witnesses who testified Oswald was wearing a jacket when he left the rooming house disagree when describing the jacket. The Commission even admitted, "The eyewitnesses vary in their identification of the jacket."[266] Mrs. Earlene Roberts, the housekeeper at Oswald's rooming house, said the jacket Oswald wore as he ran out onto the street was darker than Commission Exhibit No. 162, the discarded jacket the Commission claimed belonged to Oswald. Others claimed the jacket they saw Oswald wear was more "tan" in color. One witness, William Arthur Smith, who was a block away when Tippit was shot and claimed to see Oswald running, even claimed the zipper jacket as seen in Commission Exhibit 162 was identical to the "sports coat" he believed Oswald was wearing when he shot Tippit. Here is the exact exchange:

> **Mr. Ball**: What kind of clothes did [the man who shot Tippit] have on when he shot the officer?
>
> **Mr. Smith**: He had on dark pants—just a minute. He had on dark pants and a sport coat of some kind. I can't really remember very well.
>
> **Mr. Ball**: I will show you a coat—
>
> **Mr. Smith**: This looks like it.

Mr. Ball: This is Commission's Exhibit 162, a grey, zippered jacket. Have you ever seen this before?

Mr. Smith: Yes, sir; that looks like what he had on. A jacket.

Mr. Ball: That is the jacket he had on.

Mr. Smith: Yes.[267]

With a very few, short questions, Warren Commission Ball led the witness from "I can't really remember very well" to a positive identification of a zipper jacket that looks nothing like a sports coat.[268]

Moreover, a careful examination of the Warren Commission record reveals that while there is confusion about which Dallas Police officer actually found the jacket, the initials of the officers at the scene who could have found the jacket are missing from Commission Exhibit 162. The Warren Commission Report notes on page 175: "At 1:24 p.m., the police radio reported, 'The suspect last seen running west on Jefferson from 400 East Jefferson.' Police Capt. W. R. Westbrook, the senior Dallas Police officer on the scene of the Tippit shooting, and several other officers concentrated their search along Jefferson Boulevard. Westbrook walked through the parking lot behind the service station and found a light-colored jacket which he discovered underneath an automobile."[269]

Westbrook, in his testimony to the Warren Commission, actually denied finding the jacket:

> **Mr. Westbrook**: Actually, I didn't find it [the jacket]—it was pointed out to me by either some officer that—that was while we were going over the scene in the close area where the shooting was concerned, someone pointed out a jacket to me that was laying under a car and I got the jacket and told the officer to take the license number.[270]

A short time later, Westbrook testified that he could not be positive who found the jacket:

> **Mr. Westbrook**: Yes; behind the Texaco service station, and some officer, I feel sure it was an officer, I still can't be positive—pointed this jacket out to me and it was laying slightly under the rear of one of the cars.

Mr. Ball: What kind of car was it?

Mr. Westbrook: That, I couldn't tell you. I told the officer to take the number and the first number.

Mr. Ball: Did you take the number yourself?

Mr. Westbrook: No.

Mr. Ball: What was the name of the officer?

Mr. Westbrook: I couldn't tell you that, sir.[271]

Westbrook could not even remember the name of the officer that took custody of the jacket at the Texaco station where it was found:

Mr. Ball: I show you Commission Exhibit 162, do you recognize that?

Mr. Westbrook: That is exactly the jacket we found.

Mr. Ball: That is the jacket you found?

Mr. Westbrook: Yes, sir.

Mr. Ball: And you turned it over to whom?

Mr. Westbrook: Now, it was to this officer—that got the name.

Mr. Ball: Does your report show the name of the officer?

Mr. Westbrook: No, sir; it doesn't. When things like this happen—it was happening so fast you don't remember these things. [272]

Westbrook's testimony under oath would have been a gift to a competent defense lawyer representing Oswald at trial. What Westbrook established under friendly questioning from counsel was that the Dallas Police Department at the scene failed to establish a chain of custody for the jacket seen in Commission Exhibit 162. The initials on the jacket belong to Dallas Police Department Capt. George Doughty, the DPD crime lab's senior officer; W. E. "Pete" Barnes, the Dallas Police Department crime scene photographer; FBI hair and fiber expert, Paul M. Stombaugh; FBI spectrographic expert John K. Gallagher; a "K42" designation for FBI use; and the initials of FBI firearms experts Charles Killion and Cortland Cunningham. The problem is that Westbrook, the Dallas Police officer credited with finding the jacket, did not initial the jacket as required by Dallas Police Department policy to establish a chain of custody that could be utilized in court if necessary.[273]

The result in any criminal trial would have been that Commission Exhibit 162 would be worthless as evidence against Oswald. Without Westbrook's initials on the jacket, a prosecutor would have difficulty proving Commission Exhibit 162 was the jacket found on the scene. Even if CE162 was the jacket found at the scene of the Tippit killing, tying that jacket to Oswald would be difficult. Eyewitnesses may have agreed Oswald was wearing a jacket when he left his rooming house, but they disagreed over the description of the jacket.

THE AMMUNITION AND THE REVOLVER

Much as the Mannlicher-Carcano rifle found in the Texas School Book Depository, the weapon Oswald had in the Texas Theater when he was arrested was a .38 Special Smith & Wesson Victory Model snub-nose revolver, purchased by A. J. Hidell for $29.95 from a mail-order house in Los Angeles. In both cases, handwriting experts established that the signature and other writing on the mail order applications belonged to Oswald. This was evidently sufficient for the Warren Commission to dismiss the possibility an expert forger may have completed the mail-order application without Oswald's knowledge.

The Warren Commission established that four bullets were removed from the body of Officer Tippit. Of the four recovered bullets, three were copper-coated lead bullets of Western-Winchester manufacture, and the fourth was a lead bullet of Remington-Peters manufacture. But of the four cartridge cases recovered at the scene of the Tippit shooting, two were Western-Winchester and two were Remington-Peters. Granted, the weapon, a .38 Special Smith & Wesson Victory Model snub-nose revolver could fire a wide range of ammunition, but the problem was the recovered bullets did not match the make of the cartridge cases recovered at the crime scene. How was this possible, unless the killer fired five bullets—three Western-Winchester and two Remington-Peters—and one Remington-Peters bullet missed Tippit and one Western-Winchester cartridge case was simply not found?[274]

The mix-and-match problems continued: of the six cartridges found in the revolver when Oswald was arrested, three were Western .38 Specials and three were Remington-Peters .38s. Oswald had in his pocket five live cartridges, all Western-Winchester .38s.[275]

"Again we are presented with the paradox that Oswald must have exhausted his supply of both brands of ammunition except for eleven bullets of one brand and four of the other at the time of the Tippit killing,"[276] Silvia Meagher noted in her book, *Accessories After the Fact*, finding the ammunition raised more questions than were answered.

Perhaps most important, no bullets of either kind were found in Oswald's rooming house in Oak Cliff or in the Paine home in Irving, Texas, where his wife and daughters were living. Meagher stressed that Oswald's purchase of this ammunition was never established.

How could he have used up most of two boxes of ammunition? There is nothing whatsoever to suggest that he ever fired the .38 Smith & Wesson revolver at any time before November 22, 1963. If he did not purchase two boxes of ammunition, how did he acquire the eleven Western and the four Remington-Peters .38s? If he did purchase supplies of each brand, there is no evidence of the transaction, no evidence of use, and no left-over ammunition among his possessions.[277]

Remarkably, at the scene of the Tippit shooting, Dallas Police Department patrolman Joe M. Poe accepted two expended cartridge cases placed in a used Winston cigarette package from witness Domingo Benavides, the same person who used the police radio in Tippit's police car to call Dallas Police dispatch. Benavides explained he watched as the shooter emptied the spent shell cases and tossed them into some shrubs. Still, he did not pick up the cases until some twenty minutes after the shooting had taken place. Neighbors Barbara and Virginia Davis found two other spent shell casings outside their apartment. Poe, who gathered all four of the spent shell casings found at the scene of the Tippit shooting, neglected to place his initials on any of them. Finally, former Dallas Police crime lab lieutenant, J. C. Day, confirmed the Dallas Police in 1963 did not consistently follow rules for the marking of evidence, with the result that no reliable chain of custody could be established for any of the expended shell cases found at the site of the Tippit murder, just as no reliable chain of custody could be established for the discarded jacket found by Dallas Police Capt. W. R. Westbrook.[278]

Someone who murdered a police officer in daylight in a residential neighborhood that included businesses such as a used car lot runs the obvious risk of being observed. That the murderer would reload the weapon on the scene, throwing the spent shell cartridges in some bushes, strains credibility, unless the person wanted the shell cartridges to be found. Given that the weapon was just used to kill a policeman, the discarded spent cartridges would obviously provide a positive identification of the murder weapon. The strange mix of Western-Winchester and Remington-Peters bullets would reinforce this identification. There is no proof Oswald kept a .38 weapon in his rooming house or that he left the rooming house the afternoon of the assassination with a .38 weapon. When he was apprehended at the Texas Theater, Oswald was in possession of a .38 handgun loaded with that particular strange mix of bullets. The person who shot Tippit was observed leaving the scene, but no one reported observing where Tippit's murderer was headed. Oswald was observed leaving the rooming house, but was not identified with certainty until he was apprehended at the Texas Theater. There is nothing in the record of the case to rule out that Tippit's murderer might have been someone different who met up with Oswald and gave him the .38 pistol that was in his possession when he was apprehended at the Texas Theater.

As noted in the preface, during Oswald's arrest in the Texas Theater, Oswald managed to pull the .38 revolver out from his belt and attempt a shot at Dallas Patrolman M. N. "Nick" McDonald. "I finally got my right hand on the butt of the pistol," McDonald recalled. "I jerked the pistol and as it was clearing the suspect's clothing and grip, I heard the snap of the hammer and the pistol crossed over my left cheek, causing a four-inch scratch. I put the pistol all the way out to the aisle, holding it by the butt. I gave it to Detective Bob Carroll at that point."[279] FBI agent Robert M. Barrett confirmed with McDonald that one of the cartridges in the .38 when Oswald was captured displayed a primer indentation, confirming that Oswald had pulled the trigger in the theater, but the gun did not fire.[280] Was the .38 revolver that misfired in the theater scuffle the same .38 revolver that successfully fired four rounds into Officer Tippit's body? Again, the Warren Commission merely assumed that the two weapons were the same, ignoring the need to conduct ballistic tests to establish the fact, and ignoring the inconsistency that a revolver that tried to murder Tippit had misfired in the scuffle with McDonald. Nor is there any indication any of the officers arresting Oswald smelled the muzzle of the weapon to see if the weapon had been fired recently, the same mistake that appears to have been made when the sniper's rifle was found on the sixth floor of the Texas School Book Depository earlier that day.

THE WALLET

In one of the more bizarre aspects of the Tippit shooting, there is credible evidence that a wallet belonging to Lee Harvey Oswald was found by police at the scene of the Tippit shooting. Near the puddle of blood in the street where Officer Tippit lay slain, Dallas Police Captain Westbrook found a man's wallet that contained IDs. What murderer is so careless as to drop their wallet at the scene of the crime? If any clue suggests the Tippit murder was done in a fashion so as to frame Lee Harvey Oswald for the shooting, that detail was the wallet found on the scene. This "evidence" is so preposterous, we must ask additional questions. What exactly is the sequence of events in which Dallas police found the wallet? What was the chain of evidence for the wallet? What is the proof the wallet left at the scene of the Tippit shooting belonged to Oswald? And finally, what was the proof Oswald was the person who dropped the wallet?

FBI Special Agent Bob Barrett and Dallas Police Captain Westbrook were investigating at the Texas School Book Depository when word came on the police radio that a police officer had been shot in Oak Cliff. They both raced to the scene at 10th and Patton. Westbrook called Barrett over to talk with him. "It hadn't been very long [after arriving at 10th and Patton] when Westbrook looked up and saw me and called me over," Barrett recalled. "He had this wallet in his hand. Now, I don't know where he found it, but he had the wallet in his hand. I presumed that they had found it on or near Tippit. Westbrook asked me, 'Do you know who Lee Harvey Oswald is?' And, 'Do you know who Alex Hidell is?' And I said,

'No, I never heard of them.'"[281]

Had the FBI agent on the scene of the Tippit murder been James P. Hosty, Jr., instead of Bob Barrett, Westbrook might have learned about Lee Harvey Oswald immediately. Hosty, the FBI agent assigned by Washington to keep track of Oswald in Dallas, had held repeated meetings with Oswald prior to the assassination. Hosty discussed the wallet incident in his 1995 book, *Assignment: Oswald*, saying:

> Near the puddle of blood where Tippit's body had lain, Westbrook had found a man's leather wallet. In it, he discovered identification for Lee Oswald, as well as other identifications for Alek J. Hidell. Westbrook called Barrett over and showed him the wallet and identifications. Westbrook asked Barrett if the FBI knew anything about Oswald or Hidell. Barrett shook his head. Westbrook took the wallet into his custody so that it could be placed into police property later. Barrett told me that if I had been at the scene with Westbrook, I would have immediately known who Oswald was.
>
> Although official police reports would later state that Oswald's wallet and identification were found on Oswald's person when he was arrested in the movie theater, Barrett insists that Westbrook found them near where Tippit was slain. I have to speculate that at the theater, Westbrook had handed the wallet to a lower-ranking officer, and in the confusion it was assumed that wallet had been retrieved from Oswald's person. The FBI decided to go with the official police version, even though Barrett's version was further proof Oswald had in fact gunned Officer Tippit down. As Barrett said, the case against Oswald was a "slam-dunk."[282]

Photographer Ron Reiland of WFAA-TV was on the Tippit murder scene as police were investigating. In news footage Reiland took immediately after the Tippit shooting, Dallas Police Sargent Calvin "Bud" Owens is seen holding Tippit's service revolver in his left hand and a man's leather wallet in his right. Owens then shows the wallet to Dallas Police Captain George Doughty, who is standing to his left. As Owens holds open the wallet and Doughty examines an item in the wallet in a plastic sleeve, a third person approaches Owens and Doughty. Presumably this third person is Westbrook in plainclothes. Reiland narrated the film sequence during its first showing on television. When the close-up of Tippit's revolver and the wallet were shown, Reiland reported, "This gun you see in the background here in [Officer Owens's] hand is the one that was allegedly used to shoot the police officer. This is the officer's billfold that was found lying on the ground right alongside the car."[283] Reiland was helpful in documenting that a wallet was picked up at the crime scene but he was wrong in his identification of both the weapon and the billfold. The weapon turned out to be Tippit's weapon, and although the wallet was positively identified as Oswald's, its origins are questionable. If Owens found the wallet himself or whether the wallet was handed to Owens by a bystander has never been determined. In his sworn testimony to the Warren Commission, Westbrook said nothing about finding a wallet belonging to Oswald at the scene, although Westbrook gives extensive testimony about finding a jacket.

At the Tippit murder scene, Tippit's service revolver was reported to be found, but no mention was made in the police reports of finding a wallet belonging to Oswald. Ambulance attendants Eddie Kinsley and J. C. Butler confirmed that a police service revolver was found near Tippit's body. All Tippit's personal items, including his wallet, were removed from his pockets at Methodist Hospital after his death. A list of Tippit's personal effects prepared by the Dallas Police Crime Scene Search Section lists one "black billfold" as among Tippit's personal effects at the time of his death. The only item brought to the Methodist Hospital and added to Tippit's personal effects after his death was his service revolver, which by all accounts was left behind at the murder scene, most likely in the possession of Captain Westbrook. The wallet found loose at the crime scene was believed to have belonged to Oswald.[284]

A wallet planted by the assailant was certain to end up identifying Oswald as the shooter and establishing Hidell as an Oswald alias, linking the mail-order purchase of the weapon to Oswald. At the Texas Theater, it is debatable whether or not Oswald paid for a ticket prior to entering the theater, but it is well established that Oswald bought popcorn before sitting down. If Oswald lost his wallet at the scene of the Tippit murder, how did he pay for the popcorn? After apprehending Oswald, Dallas Police reported he had $13.87 on his person at the time of arrest. It strains credibility that Oswald bought refreshments at the Texas Theater with loose change, not realizing he lost his wallet. Ultimately, the FBI catalogued three wallets for Oswald: a brown billfold (FBI Exhibit 114), a red billfold (FBI Exhibit 382), and Oswald's arrest wallet (FBI Exhibit B1).[285]

If an assailant planted a wallet containing identity information for Oswald at the scene of the Tippit murder, the intended goal appears to have been accomplished. The police on the scene began looking for Oswald as a cop-killer. Once Oswald's employment at the book depository was established, police would naturally link Oswald to the JFK assassination. The Tippit shooting then would be the key to establishing Oswald's guilt. Whoever planned the JFK assassination knew the police would immediately conclude Oswald killed Tippit because he was on the run and he wanted to avoid arrest. The Tippit killing could not have been scripted better. But the script only worked if Tippit had not read it in advance. If Tippit had stopped Oswald, he did not follow Dallas Police Department procedure. Tippit did not radio to the police dispatcher that he had identified a suspect. Tippit did not draw his weapon before getting out of the car. Why would Tippit do these things unless he felt safe taking steps to talk with the man more directly? If Tippit had suspected the man he encountered had a weapon and that his life was in danger, he did not act like it.

David Belin, assistant counsel to the Warren Commission, characterized the Tippit killing as the Rosetta Stone to the JFK assassination. Belin is right, but not because the Tippit murder proves Oswald was JFK's assassin. The Tippit killing is the Rosetta Stone to the JFK assassination, because it proves the gunman who killed Tippit set Oswald up as the killer. In the ballistic evidence, the JFK entrance wound in the neck was sufficient evidence to prove JFK was killed by a conspiracy, every bit as much as finding Oswald's wallet at the scene of the Tippit murder proves there was a gunman complicit in the plot who got away. However, it is hard, if not impossible, to shake the suspicious nature of the evidence. The Oswald wallet was one of three Oswald wallets positively identified in the case. The wallet was dropped in the lap of the Dallas police and the FBI and conveniently contained documents linking "Lee Harvey Oswald" to "Alex James Hiddel," the alias used to purchase via mail order the Mannlicher-Carcano rifle identified as the assassin's weapon. The only problem was there was no evidence to establish that Lee Harvey Oswald had ever owned this wallet or created the ID papers found in the wallet. Like much of the evidence in the case against Lee Harvey Oswald, the wallet was just too good and too conveniently found to be believable.

AT THE MOVIES?

Julia Postal was the Texas Theater ticket taker the afternoon that JFK was murdered. In her testimony to the Warren Commission, Postal explained that from 1:00 p.m. on November 22, 1963, the time the movie theater ticket box opened, until 1:15 p.m., a total of twenty-four persons bought tickets and were in the theater.[286] When Postal was asked if Oswald bought a ticket, she explained that Oswald had "ducked into" the ticket box office when he saw a police car go by with its siren on. Postal was not certain the man had paid before entering the theater. Postal had testified to the Warren Commission that both she and Warren "Butch" Burroughs, the ticket taker who also worked the concession stand inside the movie theater, were both preoccupied, listening on a transistor radio to early news report about the JFK shooting.

Objectively viewed, we have to ask why Oswald decided to go to the movies. Was he hiding from police? Or, was he following instructions to head to this movie theater after the assassination to meet a contact that would provide him money, his next instructions, and possibly a plan to get out of Dallas. Going to the movies has to be seen as reflecting a desire to drop from public view, at a time when Oswald had to know police all over the city were looking for JFK's killer. Whatever Oswald's motivation to go to the movies may have been, it is hard to understand why he would have wanted to draw attention to himself by sneaking into the movie theater without paying the ninety cents for a ticket when he had nearly $15.00 with him.

Once inside the theater Oswald first sat next to Dallas Evangelist Jack Davis, during the opening credits for the first movie of a double feature, the 1963 Korean War movie, *War is Hell*, narrated by World War II Congressional Medal of Honor veteran Audie Murphy.[287] Shortly thereafter, at approximately 1:15 p.m., Oswald got up and went to the lobby where he bought some popcorn. Butch Burroughs sold Oswald the popcorn without confronting Oswald about not paying for a movie ticket. Returning to the theater, Oswald picked a different seat and sat next to a pregnant woman sitting alone in the mid-seat section of the movie theater's lower floor. Minutes before the police arrived, this woman got up and moved to a seat in the balcony, and Oswald moved to a seat alone in the center section three rows from the back, in the second seat from the aisle. This is where Oswald was found when a small army of Dallas police and sheriff's deputies stormed the Texas Theater.

What was Oswald doing moving from seat-to-seat sitting next to people he apparently did not know in a largely empty movie theater? One possible explanation is that Oswald had been instructed that after the assassination he would meet a person who would give him an airplane ticket or a car ride out of Dallas, some much needed cash, and instructions regarding what he should do next. Very likely, Oswald had nothing to do with the Tippit murder and was never at the Tippit murder scene. The Dallas police made a complete list of everyone who was in the Texas Theater at the time. That list, however, had disappeared by the time the Warren Commission began taking testimony in 1964. Note also that Oswald had been in the Texas Theater for some fifty minutes before police apprehended him at approximately 1:51 p.m., less than an hour-and-a-half after JFK's fatal shooting.

FBI Agent Barrett and Dallas Police Captain Westbrook both rushed to the Texas Theater when the Dallas police radio call went out, and were both in the theater standing in the aisle when a police rush subdued Oswald following the scuffle with Dallas policeman McDonald. Having examined the photographs of Lee Harvey Oswald on the identification papers found in the wallet at the Tippit murder, Barrett and Westbrook immediately identified the man apprehended in the Texas Theater as Oswald. When Oswald screamed "police brutality," Westbrook had a ready response: "You just had an officer killed in cold blood without even getting his gun out," Westbrook shot back to Oswald. "I don't think there could be any such thing as police brutality to a mad dog like that!"[288] Interestingly, in that moment when emotions were running raw, Westbrook accused Oswald of "having Tippit killed," not precisely of killing Tippit himself.

It is interesting to surmise that the possibility that one or more of the officers had missed an assignment. Was the assassination a success right up until the moment Oswald was taken into police custody alive? Had the plan been for Officer Tippit to swing by Oswald's rooming house after the assassination to arrest Oswald and then shoot him, claiming Oswald resisted arrest?

Oswald had to have been startled in the Texas Theater when the movie stopped and the house lights went on. Seeing police move into the seating area from various directions, Oswald must have quickly figured out the police were after him. Drawing a gun on officer McDonald, Oswald had to have been prepared for his life to end, right then and there. If it had, the course of history would have changed—at least for Jack Ruby. With Oswald dead, there would have been no need for Jack Ruby to kill him. With Oswald alive, Jack Ruby could no longer sit on the sidelines.

RUBY AND OSWALD

One of the first indications that Ruby knew Oswald prior to the assassination came at a press conference given by District Attorney Henry Wade in the Dallas Courts Building on Saturday, November 23, 1963, at 12:30 a.m., almost precisely twelve hours after the assassination. Remarkably, the suspect for both the Tippit murder and the JFK assassination, Lee Harvey Oswald, had been in police custody since approximately 2:00 p.m., within an hour and a half of the shooting. Jack Ruby attended Wade's midnight press conference. News film footage shot within the Dallas Police Department offices showed Jack Ruby, the owner of a well-known downtown strip joint and nightclub named The Carousel, had been present in Dallas Police headquarters continuously since shortly after the assassination, mixing freely with the news reporters and Dallas police as if he had an official purpose being present. At the press conference, Wade was asked about Oswald's motive, whether he belonged to any Communist organizations. Wade answered, "Well, he was a member of the Free Cuba movement." From the back of the Assembly Room, standing among the press, Ruby corrected Wade, shouting, "No, Henry, that's the Fair Play for Cuba Committee."[289]

Beverly Oliver, a performer in Jack Ruby's Carousel Club who also turned out to be the long-unidentified "Babushka Lady," an eyewitness to the JFK assassination taking photographs of the JFK limo as it traveled along Elm Street in Dealey Plaza, described in her 1994 book, *Nightmare in Dallas,* an occasion in 1963 when Jack Ruby brought Oswald into the Carousel Club. Here is how Oliver described the encounter, writing in the third person:

"Beverly. This is my friend Lee Oswald. He's with the CIA." Jack [Ruby] said, nodding his head toward the man on his right, who was sitting at the table in his own cloud of detachment. Beverly tried to extend a simple hello to acknowledge Jack's friend but he seemed as if he could care less about meeting anyone. She quickly assessed that he wasn't worth the bother—to her anyway. He was a "dark" person. When Beverly met people she saw them as having either light or dark personalities, and this man disturbed her. Not that he said anything to warrant that impression, it was an unsolicited gut-feeling she had. Oswald was dressed in casual drab; he was slouched in his chair, his arms folded defiantly across his chest. His eyes were narrow and fixed on Jack as though he was not pleased. Jack, however, was spirited when he introduced Oswald as if he was proud to know someone with the CIA. Beverly didn't know what the CIA was but she thought it must be important or Jack wouldn't have brought it up. She wondered if Lee Oswald really was a friend, or if Jack was once again a little loose with his terminology.[290]

She also described an incident a few days later when Oswald stood up in the club and verbally assaulted a comic named Wally. As Beverly described the incident, Ruby became incensed at the commotion and he unceremoniously threw Oswald out of the club, saying, "I told you little creep—don't ever come back to my club again."[291] Oliver was also suspicious when a dancer at the Carousel Club named "Jada" disappeared after telling reporters that Ruby had introduced her to Oswald at the club a couple of weeks before the assassination. Oliver was doubly suspicious when she found out Jada had disappeared leaving part of her wardrobe at the club. "Beverly was immediately suspicious that the lack of Jada's presence might have something to do with her statement about Jack and Oswald knowing each other," she related in her book.[292]

The FBI turned over to the Warren Commission an eight-page letter that Dallas attorney Carroll Jarnagin wrote to document a conversation he overheard on October 4, 1963, at the Carousel Club where a man using the name "H. L. Lee" was talking with Jack Ruby about plans to kill the governor of Texas, John Connally. When Jarnagin saw Oswald's picture in the newspaper after the JFK assassination, he realized that "H. L. Lee" was Lee Harvey Oswald. Jarnagin, in his cover letter to FBI Director J. Edgar Hoover, noted he had passed this information on to the Texas Department of Public Safety on October 5, 1963, by telephone. Jarnagin related that he heard Oswald ask Ruby for money because he just returned from New Orleans where he got put in jail over a street fight. This appeared to coincide with Oswald's arrest in New Orleans on August 16, 1963, when Oswald was arrested for disturbing the peace in an incident that developed out of his distributing leaflets for the Fair Play for Cuba Committee. "You'll get the money after the job is done," Jarnagin wrote he heard Ruby say. FBI Special Agents Ralph Rawlings and Bardwell Odum interviewed Jarnagin and filed a report on December 19, 1963.

The FBI report documents that Jarnagin, interviewed at the Dallas office of the FBI, related once again the same details of the conversation he overheard between Ruby and Oswald on October 4, 1963, at the Carousel Club when Jarnagin was in the company of a striptease dancer he identified as Robin Hood, plotting to kill the governor of Texas. The FBI report noted the Texas Department of Public Safety had no record of any call being received from Jarnagin or anyone else regarding an alleged attempt to assassinate Governor Connally; the report also indicates the FBI tracked down Shirley Ann Mauldin, the dancer known as Robin Hood. She admitted to being at the Carousel Club with Jarnagin and meeting Jack Ruby there, but denied overhearing any conversation about a plan to assassinate the governor.[293]

JULIA ANN MERCER AND THE PICK-UP TRUCK

One additional witness provided an important testimony that Oswald and Ruby knew each other before the assassination. At approximately 11:00 a.m. on the day of the assassination, Julia Ann Mercer claimed she was driving west on Elm Street when she was brought to a stop just beyond the triple underpass because a green Ford pickup truck, with a Texas license plate and the words "Air Conditioning" painted on the side, was parked and blocking her lane, sitting partly on the curb. She noticed the pickup was driven by a heavyset middle-aged man. She waited approximately three minutes as a younger man in a plaid shirt got out of the passenger side of the truck and went around to the rear. From the tailgate of the pickup truck, the younger man opened a long tool compartment in the back of the truck and removed a package she believed was a rifle case. The young man walked up the embankment with the package in the direction of the grassy knoll area. This was the last time she saw the young man. As she moved her car to get around the green truck, her eyes locked with those of the man driving the truck. Miss Mercer said she was able to see him very clearly, identifying him as heavy built with a round face.

Officers from the Dallas Sheriff's office and the FBI interviewed Mercer the night of the assassination. On November 22, 1963, Mercer signed an affidavit at the Dallas County Sheriff's office that described her sighting of the green Ford pickup truck. In the deposition she said, "A man was sitting under the wheel of the car and slouched over the wheel. This man had on a green jacket, was a white male and about in his 40's and was heavy-set. I did not see him too clearly."[294] She also described what the younger man took out of the back of the truck as a "gun case." On Sunday morning after the assassination, she was watching television with friends and saw Ruby shoot Oswald. Instantly, she recognized these two men as the ones she had identified for the FBI on Friday. She realized she had seen Ruby as the driver and Oswald as the young man with the rifle.[295]

Investigative journalist Henry Hurt tracked down and interviewed Julia Ann Mercer in 1983, after the House Select Committee on Assassinations had attempted but failed to find her. When Hurt showed Mercer a copy of her FBI affidavit, she was "aghast." She could not believe it included a statement attributed to her that said she did not see the driver clearly enough to identify him. "Miss Mercer adamantly denounces the reports as corruptions and fabrications by the FBI and the sheriff's department of her actual experiences," Hurt wrote in his 1985 book, *Reasonable Doubt*. "Perhaps Mercer forgot that her affidavit given to Dallas police on the night of the assassination described only the physical appearance of the two men she observed in the green Ford pickup truck earlier that day but that her recognition of them as Ruby and Oswald did not occur until she was watching television on that Sunday and saw Ruby shoot Oswald. Miss Mercer is one of many other witnesses who claim discrepancies between what was told to the authorities and what later appeared in the official reports."[296]

The House Select Committee on Assassinations was much less convinced than the Warren Commission that Oswald, Tippit, and Ruby had no prior connections to one another. In sharp contrast to the Warren Commission, the House Select Committee's final report noted:

The scientific evidence available to the committee indicated that it is probable that more than one person was involved in the President's murder. That fact compels acceptance. And it demands a re-exam-ination of all that was thought to be true in the past. Further, the committee's investigation of Oswald and Ruby showed a variety of relationships that may have matured into an assassination conspiracy. Neither Oswald nor Ruby turned out to be the "loners," as they had been painted in the 1964 investigation. Nevertheless, the committee frankly acknowledged that it was unable firmly to identify the other gunman or the nature of the conspiracy.[297]

The scientific evidence mentioned in the above quote involved acoustics evidence obtained from a police dictabelt believed to contain sounds of the shooting recorded in Dealey Plaza that recorded a channel of police transmissions due to a microphone switch stuck open on a motorcycle in JFK's police escort. The point is that the House Select Committee on Assassinations realized the minute scientific evidence challenged the assumption Lee Harvey Oswald acted alone. As noted in chapter 1, if all the damage done to JFK, Governor Connally, and witness James Tague could not be done by three shots from a bolt-action Mannlicher-Carcano rifle in the time span available for the shooting, then one or more additional gunmen were involved. If Oswald did not act alone, JFK's assassination was a conspiracy. If there was a conspiracy to shoot JFK, was there also a conspiracy to silence Oswald? If Oswald was merely the fall guy or the patsy he insisted he was, Oswald had to be silenced. The risk was that if Oswald began talking, he knew enough to implicate those in the conspiracy above him. If Oswald, Ruby, and Tippit all knew one another, then why and how precisely was each involved in the conspiracy to assassinate JFK? As important as that question is, the bigger question remains: Who at the higher levels were conspiring to assassinate JFK?

THE NEED TO SILENCE OSWALD

As much as the Tippit murder looks like a gangland slaying, the Oswald murder looks even more so. From the moment Oswald was captured on Friday, November 22, 1963, Jack Ruby began stalking him in the halls of the Dallas Police and Courts Building. News film taken within the Dallas Police Department shows numerous clear and unmistakable views of Ruby mixed in with police and reporters. While in polite Dallas society, the Carousel Club might have been called a nightclub, a more correct designation would have been to characterize the establishment as a strip joint. A holdover from the 1930s and 1940s burlesque theater, strip joints in America in the 1960s were typically connected to the underworld. Second-rate comics mixed openly with striptease dancers, a free flow of alcohol, and relatively cheap but passable food. Police mixed with businessmen, lawyers, and laborers in a smoke-filled atmosphere of live entertainment that for the day was considered risqué. If Jack Ruby had lacked underworld connections, it is unlikely he would have been the proprietor of the Carousel Club in downtown Dallas in the 1960s.

Once in police custody, Oswald was subjected to a rigorous schedule of questioning by seasoned police detectives accompanied by FBI, all without legal representation. When Dallas police apprehended Oswald at the Texas Theater, Oswald had $13.87 in cash on his person, a paltry sum for a man who planned in advance to make a run for it. How was Oswald going to evade police captivity for any length of time with only $13.87 in his pocket? In custody, Oswald called for "someone to come forward," suggesting he expected that possibly a lawyer or maybe even some official in the government would come forward to explain he was not an assassin. When Oswald was told by reporters at a press conference held in the Dallas Police Department that he had been charged with the JFK assassination as well as the Tippit shooting, Oswald appeared shocked. That's when he protested that he was just a patsy.

Clearly, the post-assassination get-away was not going as planned, at least not as far as Oswald was concerned. Once Oswald realized fully that he had been set up as the fall guy, his silence was not likely to last. Under police questioning, Oswald displayed a calculating intelligence and a wry wit. In his few brief televised press conferences or in his off-the-cuff responses to questions reporters threw him in the halls of the Dallas Police Department, Oswald was clearly continuing to think and calculate. Oswald appeared after his arrest to be a highly intelligent individual who was doing his best to cope with a near impossible situation. His face showed signs of having been beaten, a fact he confirmed when answering a reporter's question: "A policeman hit me." Observed closely, Oswald's patience appeared to be running thin in the short time he was held under arrest before he was murdered. How much longer would he continue to parry off law enforcement questions before he broke down and began explaining what had really happened?

Viewed from an underworld or intelligence agency perspective, the only way to protect other conspirators higher up was to silence Oswald permanently. This assignment fell to Ruby.

THE STRANGE CASE OF ROSE CHERAMIE

A bizarre incident ties Jack Ruby and New Orleans mob boss Carlos Marcello to the Marseilles heroin trade through New Orleans and Texas that in the 1960s was known as the "French Connection." On Wednesday, November 20, 1963, a woman named Cheramie was brought to a local hospital by one Frank Odum after he hit her on Highway 190 near Eunice, Louisiana. When sedated in the hospital, Cheramie predicted that JFK would be assassinated in Dallas that coming Friday.

Rose Cherami, or Cheramie, was one of some thirty aliases used by Melba Christine Marcades, born Melba Christine Youngblood. She was a thirty-four-year-old drug and substance abuser with a long list of prostitution and other arrests since she turned eighteen. She had worked as a B-girl for Jack Ruby in his Carousel Club in Dallas and had been mainlining heroin for nine years. According to a Louisiana State Police report in mid-November 1963, she worked "as a dope runner for Jack Ruby," and had "worked in the night club for Ruby and that she was forced to go to Florida with another man whom she did not name to pick up a shipment of dope to take back to Dallas and that she didn't want to do this thing but she had a young child and that they would hurt her child if she didn't."[298] She was thrown out of a brothel after a quarrel ensued with the two men participating in the dope run. A staff report compiled by the House Special Committee on Assassinations reported Cheramie had taken her last injection of heroin around 2:00 pm on Nov. 20, 1963.[299]

Lt. Francis Fruge of the Louisiana State Police was the first to interview Cheramie at Moosa Memorial Hospital in Eunice, Louisiana. Because the hospital was a private hospital and Cheramie had no funds or insurance, Fruge placed Cheramie in the Eunice City Jail. Fruge then called Dr. Derouin, a local doctor from the coroner's office, who administered a sedative to calm her from the effects of drug withdrawal.[300] Dr. Derouin made the decision to commit her to the state hospital in Jackson, Louisiana. On route to the hospital in Jackson, Cheramie talked to Fruge. According to a deposition Fruge gave the House Select Committee on Assassinations, Cheramie told him that "she was coming from Florida to Dallas with two men who were Italians or resembled Italians. They stopped at this lounge . . . and they'd had a few drinks and got into an argument or something. The manager of the lounge threw her out and she got on the road and hitchhiked to catch a ride, and this is when she got hit by a vehicle."[301] Fruge said the lounge was a house of prostitution called the Silver Slipper. He told the committee that he asked Cheramie what she was going to do in Dallas: "She said she was going to, number one, pick up some money, pick up her baby, and kill Kennedy."[302] Fruge claimed Cheramie was lucid making these statements. He had her admitted to the hospital late on November 20, 1963. With further investigation, Fruge found Cheramie's farfetched story had a basis in fact. Fruge tracked down the owner of the Silver Slipper Lounge, Mr. Mac Manual, who told him Cheramie had come into the bar with two men who were pimps engaged in the business of hauling prostitutes in from Florida. When Cheramie became intoxicated and rowdy, one of these men supposedly "slapped her around" and threw her outside.[303]

Fruge further claimed he showed the owner of the Silver Slipper bar a stack of mug shots from which the bar owner identified a Cuban exile named Sergio Aracha Smith as one of Cheramie's traveling companions. Assassination researchers have identified Aracha Smith as an anti-Castro refugee who was active in 1961 as head of the New Orleans Cuban Revolutionary Front. At that time, Aracha Smith befriended anti-Castro activist and commercial pilot David Ferrie, a shadowy New Orleans figure who figured prominently in the investigation of New Orleans prosecutor Jim Garrison. In the investigation of the Cheramie case, there is a suggestion Louisiana state police found diagrams of the sewer system in Dealey Plaza among the contents of Aracha Smith's apartment in Dallas. Increasingly, assassination researchers have concluded Aracha Smith must be listed among the Cuban exiles that are strongly suspected of having played an operational role in the JFK assassination.[304]

After the assassination, Fruge immediately called the hospital and told them not to release Cheramie until he had a chance to speak with her. The following morning, Cheramie told Fruge the two men traveling with her from Miami were going to Dallas to assassinate the president. Cheramie claimed her role was to obtain $8,000 from an unidentified source in Dallas, who was evidently holding her child, and proceed to Houston with the two men to complete a drug deal. Reservations had been made at the Rice Hotel in Houston. She said the trio was to meet a seaman who was bringing in eight kilos of heroin to Galveston by boat. From Galveston, once the drug transaction was completed, the trio expected to head to Mexico. Fruge took Cheramie into custody after customs chief in Galveston verified the scheduled docking of the boat and the name of the seaman. During a flight from Houston, according to Fruge, Cheramie noticed a newspaper with headlines suggesting investigators were trying to establish a link between Ruby and Oswald. According to the deposition Fruge gave the House Select Committee, Cheramie laughed at the newspaper article. She explained to Fruge that she had worked for Ruby, or Pinky as she knew him, at his nightclub in Dallas, and she claimed Ruby and Oswald "had been shacking up for years" as homosexual lovers. Fruge had his superior call Captain Will Frit of the Dallas Police Department with this information, only to find Fritz responded that he was not interested. Other reports indicated that at the state hospital on November 22, 1963, several nurses were watching television with Cheramie when she again predicted the JFK assassination. According to the hospital witnesses, "during the telecast moments before Kennedy was shot Rose Cheramie stated to them, 'This is when it is going to happen' and at that moment Kennedy was assassinated. The nurses in turn, told others of Cheramie's prognostication." Dr. Victor Weis, a psychiatrist at the hospital, also confirmed that Cheramie told him she knew both Ruby and Oswald and had seen them sitting together on several different occasions in Ruby's club.[305] The word spread throughout the state hospital that Cheramie had predicted the JFK assassination and amazingly Cheramie even predicted the involvement of her former boss Jack Ruby. Dr. Wayne Owen, who had been interning from LSU, later told the *Madison Capital Times* that Cheramie had warned him and other interns that the plot involved a man named Jack Rubenstein. Owen said he and the other interns shrugged it off at the time but were shocked when they saw Ruby kill Oswald and found out that Jack Ruby was born Jack Rubenstein.[306] While there remain many unanswered questions about Rose Cheramie's strange story, the public record fully attests to her knowledge of the JFK assassination plot in Dallas, as well as her testimony that Ruby and Oswald knew each other before the event.

LEE OR HARVEY?

In one of the most intriguing studies conducted on the JFK assassination, researcher John Armstrong has argued that "Lee Harvey Oswald" was a case of double identity created by the intelligence community from the time Oswald was thirteen years old. "One boy, named by some as Harvey Lee Oswald, was from New York," Armstrong wrote. "And another boy, Lee Harvey Oswald, was born in New Orleans and grew up in Texas."[307] Armstrong argued that Lee Oswald was the tall southern boy who moved to New York in 1952 and "was teased by his classmates for his southern accent and for wearing jeans." While Harvey Oswald was in New Orleans and "was teased by his New Orleans classmates for his New York accent."[308] Armstrong's argument is that two different people were using the name "Lee Harvey Oswald." Here is the crux of Armstrong's analysis:

> Two young boys, Lee Harvey Oswald and an eastern European refuge who spoke Russian and was given the name "Harvey Oswald," were selected by the CIA for inclusion in a super-secret project known as MK-ULTRA. The plan was to merge the identity of a Russian-speaking refugee with that of American born Lee Harvey Oswald over a period of many years. If the merging of the identities was successful the CIA could then place a native Russian-speaking young man, with an American identity, in the Soviet Union as a spy.
>
> The young man known to the world as "Lee Harvey Oswald" successfully "defected" to the Soviet Union in 1959 and returned to the United States with a Russian wife in 1962. A year and a half later this young man was set-up as the "patsy" in an elaborate scheme engineered by career CIA officials to assassinate John F. Kennedy.
>
> Following the assassination the FBI and Warren Commission collected and pieced together background information from the Russian-speaking refugee and the American born Lee Harvey Oswald

that was used to create a fictionalized person we know as "Lee Harvey Oswald." Two days after the assassination of President Kennedy the Russian-speaking refugee, Harvey Oswald, was shot and killed by Dallas night-club owner/CIA gunrunner, Jack Ruby, American born Lee Oswald was, and may still be, very much alive.[309]

Armstrong further describes that Harvey Oswald and Lee Oswald were two distinct people with two very distinct personalities: "'Harvey' was the Russian speaking, Communist-promoting Oswald—the person killed by Jack Ruby. People's descriptions of 'Lee Harvey Oswald' often vary widely with respect to eye color, height, weight, hair color, and physical characteristics. Lee often got drunk, got into fights and never spoke or read Russian or supported communism. Harvey rarely drank, was never known to get into a fight; he spoke, read, and wrote Russian, and supported communism. The character profiles of these two people, as described by dozens of witnesses, are quite different and distinct."[310]

Armstrong further argued the double identity was key to intelligence efforts to set up the composite "Lee Harvey Oswald" as the patsy responsible for shooting JFK. "In late October and early November [1963], someone matching the description of Lee Oswald was used again and again to set up Harvey Oswald as 'the patsy,'" Armstrong wrote. "In late October, an Oswald drove to the Sports Drome rifle range where he practiced shooting. On October 31, an Oswald applied for a job at the multistory Statler Hilton in downtown Dallas. On November 1, an Oswald purchased ammunition at Morgan's Gun Shop. On November 4, an Oswald visited Dial Ryder's gun shop to have a scope mounted on his rifle—even though Mr. Davis had sighted in Oswald's scope, at the Sports Drome Rifle Range a month earlier."[311] In a convincing manner, Armstrong wrote a one-thousand-page book published with a comprehensive CD-ROM of backup photographs and other documenting material, going through Oswald's life history, demonstrating many instances where biographical discrepancies almost demand a concept of double identity to be explained.[312] Armstrong's argument is that Oswald was not created by the Mafia, the Cubans, the Russians, or the Dallas Police, but instead Lee Harvey Oswald was a creation of the CIA, years before the assassination.

Armstrong's theory does help explain a lot of inconsistent Oswald descriptions and sightings, such as the sworn testimony of Dallas County

Sheriff's Department officer Roger Craig to the Warren Commission. On April 1, 1965, Craig testified that about fifteen minutes after the JFK shooting, he heard someone whistle and he looked up to see a man running down the grassy knoll by the Texas School Book Depository, trying to catch up with a Nash Rambler station wagon that was stopped along Elm Street waiting for the man. Craig testified the driver of the car struck him "as being a colored male," whom he described as "very dark complected, had real dark short hair, and was wearing a thin white-looking jacket—uh, it looked like the short windbreaker type, you know, because it was real thin and had the collar that came out the shoulder (indicating with hands) like that—a short jacket."[313] Craig tried to get across the street to question the subjects, but the traffic was too heavy, so he could not make it before the car pulled away.[314]

Yet many questions remain unanswered, including whether or not the two Oswalds were aware of each other, or whether the CIA manipulated each to believe he was the only Oswald. Even Armstrong's book is insufficient to sort out all the complications involved in a two-Oswald double-identity theory. Importantly, Armstrong pointed out the use of doubles has traditionally offered the intelligence community endless opportunities for deception. Armstrong also admits prying apart the two lives creates a story that becomes very difficult, if not impossible to follow, with twists that are hard to comprehend and results that may seem bizarre at best.

The JFK assassination record contains many documented but inconsistent or conflicting stories of who exactly Lee Harvey Oswald was, stretching back at least to 1956 when Lee Harvey Oswald joined the marines. We have already seen the difficulty of reconciling how Lee Harvey Oswald could have been seen at the Tip Top Record Store on the morning of the assassination when credible witnesses also testify that Oswald spent the night before the assassination with his wife at the Paine residence in Irving, Texas, and was driven to work that morning at the Texas School Book Depository building by Mrs. Paine's neighbor Buell Wesley Frazier. It would be easy to argue the identification of Lee Harvey Oswald at the Tip Top Record Store as a case of mistaken identity, except the massive JFK record compiled in the fifty years since the assassination have scores of similar conflicts in sorting out the complex and often contradictory Lee Harvey Oswald life story.

Later, around 5:00 or 5:30 p.m., Craig was invited to Dallas Police Capt. Will Fritz's office to see the suspect who had been apprehended for the murder of Dallas police officer Tippit. Seeing Oswald, Craig gave a positive identification that Oswald was the man he had seen running down the grassy knoll to get into the Nash Rambler being driven by the dark-complected man. Evidently, Craig was already headed well along the path of assuming that the person who killed Tippit might also have been the person who killed JFK.

On hearing Craig's comment, Fritz asked Oswald, "What about this station wagon?" According to Craig's testimony, Oswald, on hearing how this discussion was proceeding, interrupted and said to Craig pointedly, "That station wagon belongs to Ruth Paine. Don't try to tie her into this. She has nothing to do with it." As noted earlier, at the time of the JFK assassination, Marina Oswald, Lee Harvey Oswald's wife, was rooming with Ruth Paine in Irving, Texas, a suburb within the greater Dallas metropolitan area.

According to Craig's testimony, Captain Fritz explained to Oswald, "All we're trying to do is find out what happened, and this man saw you leave from the scene." Oswald interrupted Fritz: "I told you people I did," Oswald said, seemingly suggesting he had previously described for the police that he left the Texas School Book Depository building after the shooting. Then Oswald added a cryptic comment, saying, "Everybody will know who I am now."[315]

The comment somehow suggested the information about the Nash Rambler would blow his cover. Was Oswald suggesting that now everyone would realize he was an intelligence officer, or a government agent operating undercover? This is what Armstrong apparently believed, although we can only speculate what Oswald meant, as he did not expand on the comment.

Clearly, this version of how Oswald left the Texas School Book Depository contradicts the official version related by the Warren Commission, as explained earlier in this chapter. Lending support to Craig's testimony, a photograph taken by freelance photographer Jim Murray shows a Nash Rambler passing in front of the Texas School Book Depository, exactly as Craig described in his Warren Commission testimony. In Murray's photograph of the Nash Rambler, the Hertz rent-a-car sign on top of the School Depository building records the time as being 12:40 p.m., approximately ten minutes after the shooting.[316]

Just like walking home, hopping into the Nash Rambler heading west on Elm Street would have been a much more direct escape route for Oswald. After entering the Nash Rambler, Oswald and the driver needed only to drive a few blocks on Elm to arrive at Elm and Beckley, a short distance from Oswald's rooming house at 1026 North Beckley. The problem was that if the Warren Commission accepted Officer Roger Craig's testimony, then Oswald had an accomplice. Ruth Paine, it turned out at the time of the assassination, owned a Nash Rambler that Craig described.[317]

Although the Warren Commission did not ask Craig to identify the make of the rifle found on the sixth floor, he recalled deputy constable Seymour Weitzman declaring the weapon to be a 7.65 German Mauser and he remembered Captain Fritz agreeing.[318] Until the end of his life, Craig never changed his story, always insisting he saw Lee Harvey Oswald fleeing the Texas School Book Depository immediately after the shooting by running down the grassy knoll and jumping into a waiting Nash Rambler. Craig's testimony was also at odds with the testimony of fellow workers in the book depository that insisted Oswald was seen in the lunchroom in the immediate aftermath of the shooting, calmly drinking a soda. How could the witnesses that saw Oswald in the lunchroom and Craig who saw Oswald running down the grassy knoll both be right? The first inclination would be that both could not be right, or that the witnesses in the book depository and Craig were describing two completely different people that resembled one another. Is it possible that Oswald somehow had a double in Dealey Plaza that day?

Craig was fired from the Sheriff's office on July 4, 1967 and afterward had difficulty finding steady work. After multiple documented but unsolved attempts made on his life that Craig suspected were attempts to silence him, Craig was alleged to have committed suicide on May 15, 1975.

In the next chapter, we will look at the involvement of intelligence agencies in the JFK assassination. In chapter 5, we will consider the creation by the CIA of an assassination model plan that dates back to Guatemala in the 1950s, involving the creation of a patsy to take the blame.

FOUR

OSWALD, THE KGB, AND THE PLOTS TO ASSASSINATE JFK IN CHICAGO AND TAMPA

"Former marine, Lee Harvey Oswald gave up his American citizenship and moved to Russia."

—Ronald Reagan, Radio Broadcast, 1979[319]

"All I know is that my son is an agent, and that he deserves to be buried in Arlington Cemetery."

—Mrs. Marguerite Oswald, mother of Lee Harvey Oswald, Testimony to the Warren Commission, February 10, 1964[320]

WHEN LYNDON BAINES JOHNSON was sworn in as president in Dallas on the afternoon JFK was murdered, the knee-jerk reaction of the new administration was to convene a public investigation to pin the blame on Lee Harvey Oswald acting as a lone-nut assassin, disavowing any involvement from either the CIA or the KGB.

But what was LBJ's concern? Was he worried that an honest investigation would lead to war with the Soviet Union? Or was he worried that an honest investigation would disclose the CIA had gone rogue and participated in the assassination, if not masterminded it? Was it possible the

CIA had compromised Oswald, taking advantage of his role as a double agent to position him as the fall guy—the patsy—who would take the blame for a presidential assassination Oswald did not commit?

All these possibilities frightened LBJ. He realized KGB involvement in the assassination, if proved, could well lead to a nuclear war with Russia. If the CIA were involved, LBJ realized immediately the JFK assassination amounted to nothing less than a coup d'état. But an official blue-ribbon commission packed with respected government officials with distinguished histories of service to the United States could put an end to the speculation, provided the commission concluded Lee Harvey Oswald was the assassin and that Lee Harvey Oswald had no accomplices in committing his crime. This was an especially convenient solution because Lee Harvey Oswald was dead. With Oswald already framed as the assassin, no trial would ever challenge a verdict already reached in the court of public opinion.

On November 25, 1963, the Monday following Friday's assassination, Deputy Attorney General Nicholas deB. Katzenbach wrote LBJ presidential assistant Moyers a famous memo stating, "The public must be satisfied that Oswald was the assassin; that he did not have confederates who are still at large; and that the evidence was such that he would have been convicted at trial." Katzenbach's second point was aimed at the possibility Moscow was responsible:

> Speculation about Oswald's motivation ought to be cut off, and we should have some basis for rebutting thought that this was a Communist conspiracy or (as the Iron Curtin press is saying) a right-wing conspiracy to blame it on the Communists. Unfortunately the facts on Oswald seem about too pat—too obvious (Marxist, Cuba, Russian wife, etc.). The Dallas police have put out statements on the Communist conspiracy theory, and it was they who were in charge when he was shot and thus silenced.[321]

The world of Cold War espionage was a world of smoke and mirrors. While there is credible evidence Oswald was a KGB agent, strong arguments can be made that Oswald was a double agent, actually working for a combination of naval intelligence and the CIA when he defected to the Soviet Union, a cover that permitted Oswald to penetrate Soviet intelligence. The problem with Oswald is determining whether he was a committed Marxist or whether he was just pretending to be a committed Marxist. Was Oswald's openly expressed support for Castro's Cuba genuine, or was it merely a cleverly crafted cover story designed to permit Oswald to gain KGB acceptance and an invitation to the Soviet Union? After Oswald returned to the United States, how did he avoid CIA scrutiny? Or, once back in the United States, did Oswald resume working directly with the CIA, just as he did before he defected? Was Oswald's defection to the Soviet Union a CIA plan from the beginning?

To complicate the matter even more, assassination researchers in recent years have discovered credible evidence to suggest that the assassination in Dallas was the third in a series of "trials," the other two being in Chicago on November 2, 1963, and Tampa on November 18, 1963, which I discuss later. The similarities between the three plots leaves no doubt it was a conspiracy that involved the KGB, the CIA, the mob, or some combination of all three. That the assassination of JFK was a conspiracy becomes inevitable once we realize two counterparts with remarkable parallels to Lee Harvey Oswald had been setup equally as patsies, one positioned in Chicago and the other in Tampa. Dallas, then, was not a unique event.

RECRUITED BY THE KGB

Ian Mihai Pacepa, the highest ranking Soviet Bloc intelligence officer ever to defect to the United States, has provided highly credible evidence and arguments that Lee Harvey Oswald was a KGB operative sent back to the United States with a mission to assassinate JFK. Pacepa, one of three deputy chiefs of the *Departamentul de Informatii Externe* (DIE), Romania's Department of Foreign Intelligence, was living in his native Bucharest when JFK was assassinated. At that time the DIE was a subsidiary of the Soviet espionage service, the *Pervoye Glavnoye Upravleniye* (PGU), the First Chief Directorate of the KGB. (As a side note, I began communicating with Pacepa by e-mail in November 2011 regarding intelligence activities and intelligence disinformation for various articles I was writing. In January 2013, I e-mailed Pacepa specifically regarding his direct experience in Romania's intelligence operations. Much of the information in this section comes from either the books Pacepa has authored or from my e-mail exchange with Pacepa.)

In his 2007 book, *Programmed to Kill: Lee Harvey Oswald, the Soviet KGB, and the Kennedy Assassination*, Pacepa makes a convincing argument that Oswald was a KGB agent.[322] In one of my e-mail exchanges, Pacepa told me that "during the years when [he] was the chief of Romania's espionage station in West Germany, going back to the late 1950s, [he] became involved in a joint Soviet KGB-Romanian DIE operation that would, eventually, crack open the dark window concealing the super-secret web of connections between Oswald and the KGB."[323] In 1990, after he became a US citizen, Pacepa began examining the documents on the JFK assassination published by the US government. He was impressed with the wealth of Soviet operational patterns visible throughout the material on Oswald that had been turned up by US investigators who lacked the experience and familiarity with Soviet intelligence operations to recognize the telltale patterns that Oswald was a KGB agent.

"Eventually I developed an approach that has never before been used in any of the many studies of the Kennedy assassination," Pacepa wrote in his book, describing his investigative methodology. "Taking the factual material on Oswald developed by official and private U.S. investigators, I stacked it up against the operational patterns used in Soviet espionage—patterns little known to outsiders because of the utter secrecy endemic to that community."[324] After many years of studying evidence on the JFK assassination, Pacepa found a wealth of information that dovetailed with Soviet operational patterns. He became convinced Oswald was recruited by the Soviets when he was a Marine stationed in Atsugi, Japan, outside Tokyo.

Edward Jay Epstein, for his 1978 bestselling book, *Legend: The Secret War of Lee Harvey Oswald*, interviewed some four hundred people who knew Oswald, including Zack Stout, a Marine stationed with Oswald at the top secret U-2 Navy base at Atsugi, Japan. Stout told Lipton that Oswald was spending time with an attractive girl who "worked" at the Queen Bee, one of the three most expensive nightclubs in Tokyo, and one that catered to American senior air officers and U-2 pilots. The Queen Bee, Stout noted, had more than one hundred strikingly beautiful Japanese hostesses. It was expensive. To take a hostess out of a nightclub required paying not only for the girl and for a hotel room, but also compensating the nightclub for the bar business lost during her absence. A "date" at the Queen Bee could cost anywhere from sixty to eighty dollars a night, at a time when Oswald was earning less than eighty-five dollars a month. Still, Oswald saw her regularly, reportedly even bringing her back to the base area several times. "He was really crazy about her," Stout told Lipton, commenting he met the woman with Oswald at local bars around the base. Other Marines less friendly to Oswald were astonished someone of her "class" would go out with Oswald at all.[325]

Pacepa credits Lipton's 1978 book with being well-documented; he only faults Lipton for "lacking the inside background knowledge that would have helped him to fit his bits and pieces together into one whole, and to reach a firm conclusion.[326] Pacepa noted the Soviet PGU (*Pervoye Glavnoye Upravleniye*), the First Chief Directorate of the KGB, would clearly have had an interest in Oswald if only because he was a marine assigned to a super-secret U-2 Navy base in Japan at a time the U-2 was the most advanced spy airplane technology in the world. "Could it really have been possible for a US serviceman who often spent his evenings socializing in bars around his base and loudly proclaiming his sympathy for Marxism to escape the spider's web stretched across such target areas by the Soviet-bloc espionage community?" Pacepa asked. "Possibly, but not likely. Based on my twenty-seven years' experience with Soviet intelligence, I am convinced that the PGU's eye fell on Oswald soon after he began frequenting the bars around the base. There, after a couple of drinks, he would almost certainly have launched into his favorite subject, the virtues of theoretical Marxism."[327]

Pacepa insists the KGB must have been financing Oswald and manipulating the Queen Bee hostess who began spending her days and nights with Oswald. It was only a matter of time before the KGB recruited Oswald. "With the help of that Queen Bee girl, the PGU officer responsible for that night spot could assess Oswald for vulnerabilities and simultaneously smooth the way for his recruitment by making him the envy of his admiring fellow marines, with free sex with a beautiful Japanese girl thrown into the bargain," Pacepa observed. "The scenario follows the usual KGB pattern."[328]

OSWALD AND THE U-2

On May 1, 1960, Gary Powers, a former air force pilot recruited by the CIA, was shot down over the Soviet Union in a U-2 spy flight that took off from Peshawar, Pakistan. The incident was a severe embarrassment to the Eisenhower administration that was forced to admit the operation of the secret US spy planes over Russia after the Soviet Union produced intact pieces of the U-2 airplane as well as Gary Powers, the surviving pilot, for the world press. Edward Jay Lipton wrote that after Powers was returned to the United States he suggested it might have been Oswald who provided the Soviets with the secret information about his flight.[329] Pacepa agreed that Oswald's specific knowledge about the altitude at which the U-2 flew would have more than qualified as Oswald's ticket to defect to the Soviet Union, since in 1959, when Oswald defected, information about the U-2's flying altitude was "the number one Soviet intelligence priority."[330]

After he served in Japan, Oswald was assigned to Marine Air Squadron No. 9 at El Toro Air Base in Santa Ana, California, where he had access to U-2 radar and radio codes, as well as the then-new MPS-16 height finding radar gear.[331] Pacepa also noted that during the summer of 1959, one year before the U-2 was shot down, Petr Semenovich Popov, a Soviet intelligence officer who was cooperating with the CIA, passed the CIA a message indicating the Soviets had "definite knowledge of the specifics of the U-2 program."[332] In a visit to the US embassy in Moscow on October 31, 1959, Oswald said he would tell the Soviets all the information he possessed concerning the Marine Corps and his radar operation specialty. When Pacepa was an intelligence officer for Romania, the KGB in the summer of 1959 pressed him for confirmation that the U-2 spy plane could fly at altitudes of about thirty thousand meters, approximately ninety thousand feet. Pacepa's intelligence station in Romania was asked to make a special effort to check out that information and expedite to headquarters any confirmation or expansion of that information.

Pacepa has no doubt Oswald was the source of the Soviet's U-2 intelligence. In exchange for providing the intelligence needed, the Soviet government richly rewarded Oswald. Pacepa wrote that the moment the U-2 was shot down, "Oswald must have been praised and feted beyond his wildest dreams." On that triumphant Moscow May Day, the U-2 became what Pacepa considered the crowning foreign policy success of Khrushchev's career. However, the commonly accepted version of Oswald's helping the Russians know the U-2 altitude because of his specialized knowledge has been questioned. Jack Swike, an intelligence officer in the US Marine Corps, who was also stationed in Atsugi, Japan with Marine Air Group 11 during the same period as Oswald, in his 2008 book, *The Missing Chapter: Lee Harvey Oswald in the Far East,* claims the Soviets had been tracking all U-2 flights from Atsugi. The extensive Soviet tracking of U-2 flights should have given them sufficient knowledge of the altitude at which the flights flew. Swike was confident Oswald's appeal to the Soviets involved not specialized U-2 knowledge, but Oswald's awareness of the nuclear possibilities the US government was considering for U-2 flights. Swike documented the presence of a Nuclear Weapons Assembly team on base at Atsugi, in addition to the U-2 program. Swike directly questioned how much detailed technical information Oswald obtained at Atsugi concerning the U-2 program. "Lee Harvey Oswald did see U-2 takeoffs and landings during 1957–1958, when his MACS-1 unit was stationed very close to the U-2 hanger," Swike wrote. "Oswald was a plotting board crew member in the radar bubble. He didn't speak with U-2 pilots and did not have anything to do with U-2 operations."[333]

Swike speculated that prior to China successfully testing a nuclear weapon in 1964, while Oswald was yet at the base, there was discussion of modifying a U-2 to carry and drop an atomic weapon over China. He also suggests that Oswald's interest to the Russians may have been because of Oswald's knowledge of the marine's secret atomic weapons facilities at Atsugi. In those years, the Soviets were intensely interested in tracking any and all US nuclear facilities that may have violated international agreements at the end of World War II to keep Japan nuclear free. This was an important subset of the larger interest the Soviets had in the 1950s in identifying and inventorying all US nuclear facilities wherever they might be found.

THE CHINA ANGLE

Little known even today, the United States foreign policy in 1963 was obsessed not only with Cuba and the threat of Soviet nuclear weapons being deployed only ninety miles from US soil, but also with the mounting concern that Mao Tse-Tung and the Communist Chinese were on the fast track to testing an atomic weapon. As documented by historian Gordon H. Chang, "the liberal president John F. Kennedy and his closest advisors, in their quest with a nuclear test ban, not only seriously discussed but also actively pursued the possibility of taking military action *with the Soviet Union* against China's nuclear facilities."[334] By January 1963, Sino-Soviet relations had reached a "new crisis" in which ideological and national differences between Russia and China caused the CIA to warn the White House a separate Asian Communist Bloc under Beijing would have grave implications for the United States in the Far East.[335] JFK also realized the test ban treaty he was contemplating with the Soviets would not stop China from developing a nuclear weapon if China refused to sign the treaty. Finally, JFK selected veteran US diplomat and Soviet expert W. Averell Harriman to push forward with Moscow the idea the United States and the USSR would jointly launch a military attack on China's atomic facilities to prevent or at least to slow China from advancing with atomic weapons. According to Assistant Secretary of State Benjamin H. Read, who was responsible for communications during the Moscow talks, Kennedy "required unusual precautions to ensure complete secrecy in the communications between Washington and Harriman," and he "followed the negotiations with 'a devouring interest'," Chang wrote.[336]

While JFK ruled out attacking China unilaterally, a joint American-Soviet preemptive nuclear attack on China was actively discussed at the top levels of the Kennedy administration. "One idea was to have a Soviet and an American bomber fly over the [Chinese] nuclear facilities at Lop Nor, with each dropping a bomb, only one of which would go off," Chang noted.[337] These discussions were going on at the US base in Atsugi, Japan, while Oswald was stationed there. At the time the United States was flying clandestine U-2 flights from Japan over China, so how difficult would it have been to have one of the high-altitude U-2 spy planes drop an atomic bomb on a key Chinese atomic weapons facility? Chang documented that discussions continued within the White House even as LBJ assumed the presidency.

This puts an entirely different spin on what the CIA possibly may have had in mind for Lee Harvey Oswald. First, it is important to recall that on August 16, 1963, just a few months prior to the JFK assassination, Oswald was filmed on the street in New Orleans handing out leaflets for the Fair Play for Cuba Committee. In 1963, the Progressive Labor Party, an American communist organization, began backing China in the Sino-Soviet split, believing that Moaist principles more precisely articulated the proper role the Cuban revolution had played in the international class struggle.[338] Following up on the efforts of the Fair Play for Cuba Committee, the Progressive Labor Party had announced in late 1962 its intention to organize groups of US students to travel to Cuba, despite the State Department's ban on US citizens traveling to Cuba. By traveling to Cuba the students risked losing their passports, facing long court battles in the United States, and facing fines up to $5,000 plus five years in jail.[339] In 1963 Oswald began corresponding with Vincent T. Lee, the national director of the Fair Play for Cuba Committee who was also a member of the Progressive Labor Party, by then fully recognized as a Maoist organization. In his testimony to the Warren Commission, Lee tried to deny any knowledge of Oswald, claiming many people wrote letters to him that he did not personally know.[340] Yet, when shown the letters Oswald had mailed to Lee as head of the Fair Play for Cuba Committee, Lee finally was forced in an affidavit prepared for the Warren Commission to admit Oswald's membership card was authentic and was sent to Oswald on or about May 29, 1963.[341]

It is possible that had Lee Harvey Oswald been killed immediately after the assassination, either by Officer J. D. Tippit or an officer that apprehended Oswald at the Texas Theater, the CIA might have claimed that Oswald was not specifically a KGB agent, but a KGB agent who had evolved into a Maoist, following the Progressive Labor movement's decision to embrace Chinese Communism in their support of Castro's revolution in Cuba. The storyline could have been that Oswald was a Marxist who became a KGB agent after he defected to Russia, but once in Russia, Oswald became disillusioned with Russian Communism, as he sided ideologically increasingly with China.

Realizing JFK was not going to launch a unilateral atomic attack on China's nuclear facilities, the CIA's goal could have been to cause the American people to rise up, not just against Castro's Cuba for being responsible for JFK's assassination, but also against Communist China. Identifying Oswald as a Maoist would have focused public anger on China, allowing the CIA and State Department to leverage the US resentment against China as a means of widening the Sino-Soviet split and possibly pressuring LBJ into launching a nuclear attack on China and maybe even invading Cuba just as the uprising after 9/11 allowed President George W. Bush to invade Afghanistan and Iraq.

However, the CIA could not spread the disinformation that Oswald was a Maoist if Oswald remained alive. Sooner or later, Oswald was likely to break his cover and pronounce that his support for the Fair Play for Cuba Committee had been a strategy dictated by someone from within the government, most likely from the CIA. With a lawyer's assistance, Oswald might have exposed an intelligence operation that extended back into the 1950s, and likely with culpability of both the USSR and the United States. But with Oswald dead before being arrested, the press would have had no chance to hear anything Oswald may have wanted to say.

Oswald never got the chance to make his criminal defense, or to give his explanation of how he had been manipulated in the run-up to the assassination. Clearly, he appeared surprised, if not also disgusted, when a reporter shouted out to him the fact that he had been charged not only with the shooting of Officer Tippit but also the murder of the President of the United States. Oswald had been set up. The Mannlicher-Carcano mail-order rifle and pistol could easily have been ordered in the name of A. Hidell without Oswald's knowledge, and the rifle could have been planted on the sixth floor of the Texas School Book Depository. CE399, the "magic bullet," which likely was planted on the stretcher, could have been linked to the Mannlicher-Carcano rifle. With the likelihood the wallet found at the Tippit murder scene was planted there, the evidence against Lee Harvey Oswald was circumstantial at best. The only eyewitness that positively identified Oswald was Howard L. Brennan and, as we saw in chapter 2, Brennan's testimony would have been easy to challenge in court. There was not proof beyond a reasonable doubt that Oswald shot anyone on November 22, 1963, and there never was a criminal trial at which Oswald had an opportunity to defend himself.

At any rate, if the plan was to gain public support against Cuba and China, once Oswald survived the post-assassination chaos and was in police custody, the CIA had to back off all attempts to leverage the assassination against China. With the huge success of JFK's assassination turning into a huge disaster with Oswald arrested, the CIA masterminds had no alternative but to frame Oswald as the lone-gun assassin, while simultaneously implementing the back-up plan to silence Oswald. Jack Ruby would silence Oswald once and for all. Not accidentally, Ruby had a history of working with both the mob as a young man in Chicago and then as a Dallas nightclub manager who ran a strip joint, as well as with the CIA as a gunrunner to Cuba. While Ruby burst into the JFK assassination drama as if he were acting on his own, perhaps out of sympathy with JFK's widow and children, one look at Ruby's background quickly cast that myth into doubt.

Researcher Jones Harris has noticed a largely overlooked and seemingly out of context statement former CIA director Allen Dulles made during the Warren Commission hearings. The date was June 9, 1964, and the witness was Abram Chaynes, a legal advisor to the State Department. The issue before the Warren Commission was whether or not Oswald's 1959-issued US passport should have been returned to him in July 1961 for the purpose of returning to the United States, and even more specifically, whether Oswald should have been re-issued his US passport in 1963, when Oswald applied to renew it on June 24. Chayes had just testified as follows: "[Lee Harvey Oswald] applied for the passport in June of 1963. He got it in June of 1963, and he made no effort to use the passport, nor did he have any occasion to use it, until he died." This prompted Allen Dulles to respond as follows: "It would have been a blessing for us if [Lee Harvey Oswald] had used it, say, in the sense that the assassination might not have taken place, if he had taken the passport and gone to China as he may have contemplated."[342] The problem is nothing in the Warren Commission's extensive twenty-six volume records indicates Oswald ever planned to visit China. Yet, the record clearly shows Allen Dulles was thinking about the possibility and had no problem pointing out the possibility to the Committee.

In 1994 an FBI memorandum dated November 26, 1963, four days after the JFK assassination, surfaced.[343] The memo was written by FBI agent W. R. Wannell and addressed to William C. Sullivan, then the head of FBI intelligence operations. It referenced information provided by Bernard Weisman, an employee of the United States Information Agency, or USIA, that suggested the Communist Chinese were behind the JFK assassination. The first paragraph of the memo read as follows.

> "On 11/22/63 a U.S. Information Agency (USIA) employee, Bernard Weisman, furnished the Bureau a four-page memorandum concerning the Fair Play for Cuba Committee (FPCC) in which Weisman raised a question as to whether Communist China was possibly involved indirectly in the assassination of President Kennedy by Lee Harvey Oswald. Weisman indicated he was making copies of his memorandum available to USIA and State Department."[344]

The body of the memorandum referenced Oswald's connection with Vincent Theodore Lee, the national director of the FPCC, as well as several other prominent US citizens who had supported Communist Chinese ideologies. The third paragraph of the memo indicated that "Oswald's disillusionment with the Soviet Union, his recent activities in connection with the FPCC and the fact that he still reportedly held Marxist ideas" indicated that President Kennedy's assassination could have at least advanced the interests of Communist China. The memo leaves little doubt about the Communist China angle. Assassination researcher Jerry Rose characterized William Sullivan as "J. Edgar Hoover's chief red-hunter" and he described W. R. Wannell as a "diehard Hoover loyalist, who was one of the few FBI agents who "handled the Oswald case." As assassination researcher Rose pointed out, J. Edgar Hoover enjoyed juggling both the "lone nut" and "communist conspiracy" angles of the assassination.[345]

OSWALD'S KGB MISSION: ASSASSINATE JFK

"For the last ten years of my military intelligence career I also supervised Romania's ultra-secret equivalent of the U.S. National Security Agency, thus becoming familiar with Soviet ciphers and codes," Pacepa wrote.[346] Analyzing the innocuous-sounding letters from Oswald and his wife to the Soviet embassy, Pacepa recognized the letters as veiled intelligence messages. Pacepa is convinced Oswald's mission upon his return to the United States was to assassinate President Kennedy in retaliation for his forcing Russia to erect the Berlin Wall in 1961 and withdraw their missiles from Cuba in 1962. Pacepa believes Oswald had been dispatched to the United States on a temporary mission and that Oswald planned to return to the Soviet Union once he had accomplished his task of assassinating JFK.

The analysis starts with former Soviet Premier Nikita Khrushchev. Pacepa saw Khrushchev as a crude politician. "Khrushchev belonged to the meanwhile heroicized proletariat, an insignificant social category made up of urbanized Russian peasants—the most backward peasantry in all of Europe," Pacepa wrote. "The grandchild of a serf and the son of an indigent miner, Khrushchev grew up in a deeply ignorant peasant environment and started his working life as an unskilled manual laborer."[347] Unlike Lenin, who was a lawyer, and Stalin, who had studied at a theological seminary, Khrushchev had no formal education whatsoever. He was violently destructive. "Khrushchev had an eminently destructive nature," Pacepa explained. "He smashed Stalin's statues, shattered the Soviet Union's image as the workers' paradise, and broke up the Sino-Soviet alliance all without building anything new to fill the vacuum he had created." Khrushchev was Pacepa's supreme boss for nine years, as he was promoted up to the top of the Soviet bloc intelligence community. His final assessment was that Khrushchev was "brutal, brash and extroverted," noting that Khrushchev "tended to destroy every project he got his hands on, and ended up with an even more personal hatred for what he called the 'Western bourgeoisie' than Stalin had." Pacepa commented that Khrushchev died in ignominy on September 11, 1971, "but not before seeing his memoirs published in the West giving his version of history."[348]

During the Cuban missile crisis "Khrushchev flew into a rage, yelling, cursing, and issuing an avalanche of conflicting orders," Pacepa wrote, describing the moment when Soviet electronic monitoring confirmed the Pentagon was planning a naval blockade of Cuba. "During a state luncheon, Khrushchev swore at Washington, threatening to 'nuke' the White House, and cursed loudly every time anyone pronounced the words *America* or *American*." The next morning Romanian head of state Gheorghiu-Dej was having breakfast with Khrushchev when General Vladimir Yefimovich Semichansky, the new chairman of the KGB, presented the

Soviet leader with a cable Soviet intelligence sent from Washington informing the Kremlin that Kennedy had canceled an eighteen-day trip to Brazil so he could personally manage a naval quarantine designed to block Russian cargo ships from reaching Cuba. Pacepa recounted Dej's astonishment when Khrushchev turned purple reading the cable. Khrushchev cursed violently as he threw the cable on the floor and ground his heel into it. "That's how I'm going to kill that viper." Khrushchev declared.

On Sunday, October 28, 1962, Pacepa was with Dej in Bucharest when Khrushchev decided to recall the Russian ships, avoiding a challenge to the US naval blockade and bringing an end to the Cuban missile crisis. "That's the greatest defeat in Soviet peacetime history," Dej told Pacepa. The day also happened to be Pacepa's birthday. He and Dej celebrated both events with caviar and champagne. Pacepa commented that Dej's reaction was that while Kennedy had won this standoff, his life was now in danger. "Kennedy won't die in his bed," Dej predicted to Pacepa. While Dej appeared to enjoy witnessing Khrushchev's humiliation, he was also troubled. "The lunatic could easily fly off the handle and start a nuclear war," Dej warned Pacepa.[349] The defeat Kennedy handed Khrushchev during the Cuban missile crisis would have confirmed the KGB decision to order Oswald to return to the USA, after having programmed Oswald to assassinate Kennedy.

The Soviet espionage service PGU under General Sakharovsky had a distinct methodology in training an assassin. The first requirement, Sakharovsky explained to Romanian intelligence, was that the officer working behind enemy lines must despise the "bourgeoisie" and regard its leaders as "rabid dogs." Pacepa recalled distinctly how Sakharovsky described the programming process: "Even now my skin crawls when I remember Sakharovsky proclaiming in his soft, melodious voice: 'There is just one way to deal with a rabid dog—shoot it!' The next step was solidly to imprint in the officer's mind a future vision of the wonderful life he would have in the 'proletarian paradise' after completing his mission abroad. Finally, we had to instill in him the firm idea that the very future of Communism depended on the success of his mission."[350] The Thirteenth Department of the KGB, the unit assigned the responsibility of preparing and implementing foreign execution operations, prepared a cover story for Oswald, creating a life for him working at a radio factory in Mimsk. It tested the waters by having

Oswald write a letter to the US embassy in Moscow, asking to return to the United States as a US citizen since he had become disillusioned with his experience in the USSR and had never become a Soviet citizen. The US embassy gave Oswald his passport back and initiated immigration procedures for his Soviet wife, Marina.[351]

ENTER GEORGE DEMOHRENSCHILDT

One of the more enigmatic characters in the JFK assassination saga is George DeMohrenschildt, who together with his wife, Jeanne, befriended Lee Harvey Oswald and Oswald's wife, Marina, when the couple returned to the United States and settled in the Dallas-Ft. Worth area. Both Pacepa and assassination researcher and author Edward Jay Epstein concluded DeMohrenschildt was Oswald's KGB "handler," the person Russian intelligence assigned to watch over and monitor Lee Harvey Oswald in the United States.

Epstein, in his 1978 book, *Legend: The Secret World of Lee Harvey Oswald*, reported that DeMohrenschildt remained a mystery to the FBI, CIA, and Office of Naval Intelligence that had investigated his activities since 1941. According to Epstein all that was known for certain about DeMohrenschildt was that he had arrived in the United States in May 1938 on the SS *Manhattan*, traveling under a Russian passport issued in Belgium.[352] Pacepa catalogued that DeMohrenschildt became an American citizen in the 1930s, when he was Baron George von Mohrenschildt, son of a German director of the Swedish "Nobel interests" in the Baku oilfields. Toward the end of World War II, when it was clear the Nazis were going to be defeated, the German baron became the French DeMohrenschildt who claimed to have attended a commercial school in Belgium founded by Napoleon. After World War II, he claimed his father had been a Russian engineer in the Romanian Ploiesti oilfields where he was captured by the Soviet Army and executed. Epstein claims DeMohrenschildt worked first for Polish intelligence and then for French counter-intelligence in New York after arriving in the United States. Claiming to be a "petroleum" engineer, DeMohrenschildt worked for a series of American oil companies in Cuba and Venezuela.

In testifying to the Warren Commission, DeMohrenschildt was

remarkably vague about how he and his wife, Jeanne, met the Oswalds. "I tried, both my wife and I, hundreds of times to recall how exactly we met the Oswalds," he testified under oath. "But they were out of our mind completely, because so many things happened in the meantime. So please do not take it for sure how I first met them. [353] Jeanne was equally vague in her testimony. "All of a sudden they arrived on the horizon," Jeanne DeMohrenschildt told the Warren Commission. Her vagueness on recalling how she and her husband first met Lee and Marina Oswald strains their credibility to the breaking point. "I cannot even tell," she said finally. "I would like to know myself, now, how it came about."[354] Then George and Jeanne DeMohrenschildt explained they were part of a Russian immigrant community in Dallas that tried to meet all new Russians coming into the area.

The vagueness may have been designed to hide a CIA connection. Attorney Bill Simpich has documented that DeMohrenschildts's relationship to the CIA traces back to the 1950s when DeMohrenschildt was identified as part of an anti-Soviet movement known by its Russian initials "NTS," standing for the National Alliance of Russian Solidarists, a group founded in the 1930s by second generation Russian émigrés. In the 1950s, the CIA included NTS within the Radio Free Europe/Radio Liberty organization, a pet project of Cord Meyer, the CIA International Organization's head who had a background of being a World War II hero with excellent connections in Boston society. Meyers reported directly to CIA Director Allen Dulles and his best friend in the CIA was Counterintelligence chief James Angleton.[355] Curiously, DeMohrenschildt knew Jackie Kennedy's father, John Vernou "Black Jack" Bouvier III, when he was getting a divorce from Jackie Kennedy's mother; in his associations with the Bouvier family, DeMohrenschildt met Jackie Bouvier, the future Jackie Kennedy, when she was a young girl. DeMohrenschildt got in touch with Oswald as a result of a request from Dallas CIA station chief J. Walton Moore.[356]

DeMohrenschildt admitted to Edward Jay Epstein that he had been "dealing with" the CIA from the 1950s.[357] DeMohrenschildt had a tendency for showing up just where the CIA might have needed him, such as in Haiti just before a CIA-engineered effort by Cuban exiles to topple Duvalier and later in CIA training camps set up in Guatemala for Cuban exiles just before the Bay of Pigs invasion.[358] When Warren Commission attorney Wesley Liebeler asked Ruth Paine if Marina Oswald ever mentioned George DeMohrenschildt to her, Ruth Paine answered, "Well, that's how I met her."[359] In February 1963 Ruth Paine attended a party in Dallas especially to meet Marina supposedly because Ruth was looking for someone with whom to practice her Russian. Marina Oswald subsequently moved into Ruth Paine's home as a roomer, as noted earlier, and was living there at the time of the assassination. Later, Ruth Paine's testimony would be particularly damaging to Lee Harvey Oswald, describing him as being a deeply disturbed individual, extremely unhappy with his life in the United States, and always potentially violent to his wife. The evidence that DeMohrenschildt's CIA connections were the magnet that drew him to Oswald is a strong and important counterweight to Pacepa's suggestion that DeMohrenschildt was a KGB agent assigned to be Oswald's handler in Dallas.

THE SHOT TAKEN AT GENERAL WALKER

DeMohrenschildt is an important link to several pieces of evidence the Warren Committee used to conclude Oswald killed JFK. Oswald posed in two backyard photographs holding a rifle, which the Warren Commission assumed was the Mannlicher-Carcano rifle Oswald bought by mail order, and wearing a holster containing a handgun that the Warren Commission assumed was the mail-order weapon used to kill Officer Tippit. In the photographs, Oswald was holding up a March 24, 1963, issue of the newspaper *The Worker* and the March 11, 1963, issue of *The Militant*, two Communist publications to which Oswald subscribed.

The Militant was published by the Socialist Workers Party and was clearly viewed as a Trotskyite publication. In contrast, *The Worker* was considered a Stalinist publication. By holding these two papers, Oswald made a statement that he supported the Trotskyite/Maoist side of the Sino-Soviet. Had Oswald been killed in the process of being apprehended, it could have been argued that Oswald was a Trotskyist/Maoist revolutionary, in line with the Progressive Labor Party support for Cuba. However, during his interrogation after being arrested by the Dallas police, Oswald claimed the photographs were doctored, with his head placed on someone else's body. Curiously, Marina gave DeMohrenschildt a copy of the photograph, which was signed "For George, Lee Harvey Oswald" and dated April 5, 1963. Marina had scribbled on the photograph in Russian, "Hunter of Fascists. Ha. Ha." The joke became more serious when on April 10, 1963, DeMohrenschildt heard on the radio that a sniper had taken a shot at the conservative firebrand General Edwin Walker.[360]

On Sunday, March 10, 1963, Oswald photographed the alley behind Walker's home in the wealthy Turtle Creek suburb of Dallas. Oswald also took careful measurements of various points around the house, using a nine-power hand telescope. Oswald collected bus timetables from the area, putting the photographs and other information into a journal he kept in his study. Epstein further reported it was two days after Oswald's reconnaissance of Walker's home that he ordered the Mannlicher-Carcano rifle with a scope from Klein's Sporting Goods Store in Chicago, using the alias A. Hidell and his post office box in Dallas. Then, on April 10, 1963, Oswald left Marina a note in Russian instructing her to contact the Red Cross for help if he was apprehended by police, he was killed, or he had to flee. Marina, while largely kept in the dark about most of Lee Harvey Oswald's activities when he was away from her, certainly had knowledge of her husband's intelligence agency connections, especially with regard to the Soviet Union. At 9:00 p.m. that evening, Walker was working on his income taxes when a bullet penetrated the window and slammed into the wall, narrowly missing his head. According to the story as told by Epstein, Oswald got home around 11:30 p.m., breathing hard and appearing extremely tense. Oswald evidently told his wife he had just attempted to kill Walker.[361]

In his testimony to the Warren Commission, DeMohrenschildt recalled that he had seen the rifle in a closet at the home Oswald was renting from Ruth Paine, when George and Jeanne DeMohrenschildt stopped by on Orthodox Easter Sunday 1963 to leave off a rabbit toy for their young daughter. When DeMohrenschildt confronted Oswald as to why he had the gun, Oswald explained it was for target shooting. For some unexplained reason, DeMohrenschildt associated this rifle with the attempt on General Walker. Consider this testimony to the Warren Commission, under questioning from Warren Commission assistant counsel Albert Jenner:

Mr. DeMohrenschildt: He [Oswald] said, "I go out and go target shooting. I like target shooting." So out of the pure, really jokingly I told him, "Are you then the guy who took a pot shot at General Walker?" And he smiled to that, because just a few days before there was an attempt at General Walker's life, and it was very highly publicized in the papers, and I knew that Oswald disliked General Walker, you see. So I took a chance and I asked him this question, you see, and I can clearly see his face, you know.

He sort of shriveled, you see, when I asked this question.

Mr. Jenner: He became tense?

Mr. DeMohrenschildt: Became tense, you see, and didn't answer anything, smiled, you know, made a sarcastic—not sarcastic, made a peculiar face.

Mr. Jenner: The expression on his face?

Mr. DeMohrenschildt: That is right, changed the expression on his face.

Mr. Jenner: You saw that your remark to him—

Mr. DeMohrenschildt: Yes.

Mr. Jenner: Had an effect on him.

Mr. DeMohrenschildt: Had an effect on him. But naturally he did not say yes or no, but that was it. That is the whole incident. I remember after that we were leaving. Marina went in the garden and picked up a large bouquet of roses for us. They have nice roses downstairs and gave us the roses to thank for the gift of the rabbit.[362]

Pacepa takes these statements as further evidence Oswald was proceeding with his plan to assassinate Kennedy, despite Khrushchev's change of heart, deciding the possible adverse consequences of assassinating JFK should the United States attribute guilt to Russia and decide to retaliate, were not the risk. "The fact that DeMohrenschildt was the only known individual to whom Oswald gave an autographed copy of one of his now-famous photographs showing him with a holstered pistol strapped to his waist, holding a rifle in one hand, and in the other copies of Communist publications, provides one more reason to believe that George DeMohrenschildt knew a lot more about that rifle and the attempt to kill General Walker than he ever admitted," Pacepa wrote. [363]

Pacepa also found telltale clues in Oswald's note to Marina providing evidence Oswald was a KGB agent. Pacepa explains:

> In an April 10, 1963, note Oswald left for his wife, Marina, before he tried to kill American General Edwin Walker in a dry run before going on to assassinate President Kennedy, I found two KGB codes of that time: *friends* (code for support officer) and *Red Cross* (code for financial help). . . . In this note, Oswald tells Marina what to do in case he is arrested. He stresses that she should contact the (Soviet) "embassy," and that they have "friends here," and that the "Red Cross" (written in English, so that she will know how to ask for it) will help her financially. Particularly significant is Oswald's instruction for her to "send the [Soviet] embassy the information about what happened to me." At that time, the code for embassy was "office," but it seems Oswald wanted to be sure Marina would understand what she should immediately inform the Soviet embassy. [364]

Pacepa also found it noteworthy that Marina did not mention this note to US authorities after Oswald's arrest. The note was found at the home of Ruth Paine.

The ace in the hole for Pacepa involves his personal experience operating in the upper ranks of the Soviet's Eastern Bloc intelligence network. What makes Pacepa's claims about Oswald and DeMohrenschildt so credible is that Pacepa was there. What he reported, he knew from what he saw and heard in person operating as a Soviet Bloc intelligence operative. For instance, he knew for a fact that DeMohrenschildt was in contact with the KGB in 1957. Pacepa further concluded that de Mohrenshildt's efforts to minimize and distort his contact with Oswald suggest DeMohrenschildt was still acting under PGU guidance during the time he was in contact with Oswald in Texas. [365] Seen through Pacepa's eyes, the involvement of DeMohrenschildt in Oswald's life confirms both were Soviet intelligence operatives.

The attempt on General Walker played an important role in the Warren Commission's conclusion that Oswald was the sole shooter in the

JFK assassination, not only because of the physical evidence involved, but also because it provided insights into Oswald's motivation. That Oswald left the photographs of him with the rifle and Communist papers at home when he made his attack on Walker suggests the he may have been concerned about his place in history. If the attack had succeeded and Oswald had been caught, the photos would probably have appeared on the front pages of newspapers and magazines all over the country. The Warren Commission concluded: "The circumstances of the attack on Walker, coupled with other indications that Oswald was concerned about his place in history and with the circumstances surrounding the assassination, have led the Commission to believe that such concern is an important factor to consider in assessing possible motivation for the assassination."[366] But the linchpin in the Walker shooting case was DeMohrenschildt's testimony that he saw the rifle and confronted Oswald about shooting at Walker.

A serious problem remains is trying to reconcile why Oswald would have been equally enthusiastic to murder General Walker, a right-wing member of the John Birch Society, and President John F. Kennedy, a moderate Democrat who right-wing extremists in Dallas at the time tended to view as being virtually a Communist himself. The Warren Commission's determination to use the attempt on Walker as proof that Oswald was the JFK assassin demands we accept Oswald as an equal opportunity murderer.

OSWALD, A "BAD MAN"

Unless the Warren Commission could establish motivation for Oswald, the question remained: why would a loser, as the Commission had painted Oswald to be, care enough to assassinate JFK? The Commission had the final piece when Marina Oswald testified her husband claimed that Walker "was a very bad man, that he was a fascist, that he was the leader of a fascist organization, and when I said that even though all of that might be true, just the same he had no right to take his life, he said if someone had killed Hitler in time it would have saved many lives."[367]

Still, the question remains as to how Lee Harvey Oswald was such an expert marksman that he assassinated JFK with a shot to the back of his head in a limo heading down a declining, twisting road receding into the distance, and yet, he failed to hit General Walker, taking a shot from the alley with ample time to position himself and aim. Even if Oswald were an expert shot, he never had any military sniper experience. An expert sniper is more than an expert shot. An expert sniper understands how to succeed, choosing a high probability shot that takes the best advantage of the physical circumstances of the setting. Obviously Oswald was no expert, having missed an unsuspecting older man sitting largely stationary in a chair with all the time in the world. Further, an expert sniper not only would have no trouble hitting such an easy target, he wouldn't brag about having taken it. If anything, the conclusion from hearing that Oswald shot at General Walker but missed would have been to assume JFK had nothing to worry about.

That DeMohrenschildt's testimony before the Warren Commission was one of the most extensive sworn testimonies taken indicates the importance the Commission believed it was to providing insight into Oswald's psychological state and motivations at the time of the assassination. Although DeMohrenschildt was questioned by the Warren Commission about his complex life history, there is no suggestion in the record that the Commission considered him to be an intelligence asset with connections to the CIA or the KGB. Subtly, DeMohrenschildt's testimony supplied the basis for the Warren Commission to conclude Oswald was a lone loser. "His mind was of a man with exceedingly poor background, who read rather advanced books, and did not understand even the words in them," DeMohrenschildt testified to the Warren Commission describing Oswald.[368] He described Oswald as "an unstable individual, mixed-up individual, uneducated individual, without background."[369] He claimed no government would be stupid enough to trust Oswald with anything important. DeMohrenschildt told the Warren Commission that Oswald was unhappy in his marriage. "There was bickering all the time," he testified. "But as I said before, the bickering was mainly because Marina smoked and he didn't approve of it, that she liked to drink and he did not approve of it. I think she liked to put the makeup on and he didn't let her use the makeup."[370]

Jeanne DeMohrenschildt advanced the same themes, claiming Oswald was "cruel" to his wife. "Any little argument or something—like once something—she didn't fill his bathtub, he beat her for it."[371] This, after

George DeMohrenschildt testified that in their arguments Marina became so enraged she scratched Oswald with her fingernails. Jeanne DeMohren-schildt told the Warren Commission that Marina found Oswald sexually unsatisfying, adding shocking details that Marina had a wild past in Minsk, enjoying sexual orgies before meeting and marrying Oswald.[372] In contrast, she reinforced the stories that Lee Harvey Oswald beat his wife, and she painted him as a small man, filled with envy and resentment. "Everything went wrong for Lee," she testified, "starting with his childhood." Every-thing he did ended up in failure, and Jeanne contrasted Oswald's life with JFK's. "Anything that seems to be President Kennedy was turning into gold, he was so successful in his marriage." She suggested that Oswald could have been jealous of the President.[373]

To an expert like Pacepa, the DeMohrenschildts were building the case that Oswald was an intelligence operative who was given his wife Marina in an arranged marriage that was part of a cover story. For the Warren Commission, the testimony George and Jeanne gave reinforced their impression of Lee Harvey Oswald as a misfit, a loner, a loser who made a pathetic husband to his young, attractive but neglected Rus-sian wife. Reading the extensive testimony given by George and Jeanne DeMohrenschildt conveys the impression the pair were engaged in a classic example of intelligence disinformation, as if their goal was to build a story that would frame Oswald as being a confused, Communist-sympathizing misfit who was capable of a violent act, such as killing the President. If this was the assignment the KGB gave George and Jeanne DeMohrenschildt, the husband-wife pair did an excellent job befriending the Oswalds from out of nowhere and getting to know them well enough that their testimony to the Warren Commission would convey at least surface credibility.

KHRUSHCHEV CHANGES HIS MIND

In a political trial at the end of 1962, the West German Supreme Court mounted a public trial of Bogdan Stashinsky, a Soviet intelligence officer who had been decorated by Khrushchev for assassinating two enemies of the Soviet Union living in the West. By 1963, Khrushchev was no longer in firm control of Russia, such that Pacepa judged the "slightest whiff of Soviet involvement in the Kennedy assassination would have been fatal to Khrushchev."[374] All Khrushchev's political enemies needed to secure Khrushchev's demise would have been proof Khrushchev had supported or promoted an assassination attempt on the US president. Having backed down in the Cuban missile crisis, the last thing top Soviet officials wanted was to cause another provocation that could bring the United States and the Soviet Union into direct confrontation.

Shortly after the attempt on Walker, on April 19, 1963, DeMohrenschildt and his wife abruptly left Dallas for Haiti. Papeca attributes this to a decision Khrushchev made that he was no longer interested in having Kennedy assassinated. Papeca concluded the DeMohrenschildts's decision to leave Dallas was prompted by an order from the Thirteenth Department, writing, "The PGU should also have arranged an emergency contact with DeMohrenschildt and ordered him immediately to break off all relations with Oswald and return to Haiti." The DeMohrenschildts returned to Dallas only briefly, at the end of May, to pack up their household belongings in two days and leave again, without saying good-bye to the Oswalds. From Dallas, the DeMohrenschildts drove to Miami, to fly on to Haiti, where they arrived on June 2, 1963. They remained in Haiti until April 1964, when the Warren Commission called them to testify.

Pacepa reported that a short time after the Kennedy assassination, a "substantial" sum of money, in the range of $200,000 to $250,000 had been deposited in the DeMohrenschildts's account in a Port-au-Prince bank. After the money was withdrawn the DeMohrenschildts left Haiti. Pacepa considered the information credible because it made "operational sense," in that it "tallies with the PGU concept of keeping a close hold on those illegals who were no longer useful, in order to prevent them from 'betraying' what they knew and later to be able to refer to their cases as examples for others."[375] After the Warren Commission absolved George DeMohrenschildt of any subversive or disloyal activity in his interactions with Lee Harvey Oswald, the KGB put together a retirement package for George and Jeanne, Pacepa concluded. "Because for operational and security reasons neither of them would ever be able to retire to the Soviet Union, the PGU must have put together a retirement package for them in the West," Pacepa wrote. "To be on the safe side, the PGU waited a couple of years, keeping the DeMohrenschildts on the sidelines in Haiti. Then the PGU maneuvered to transfer 'laundered' funds into the DeMohrenschildt's account(s) and instructed the couple to leave the small world of Haiti where they were too well known."

Yet, all did not end well for DeMohrenschildt. Epstein, evidently determined to confront DeMohrenschildt about serving as Oswald's KGB handler, was in the process of interviewing DeMohrenschildt at the Breakers Hotel in Palm Beach, Florida, on March 29, 1977, when they broke for lunch. Planning to meet again at 3:00 p.m., DeMohrenschildt returned to the Palm Beach where he was staying. He found a card informing him that he had been subpoenaed to testify before the House Select Committee on Assassinations. A few hours later, DeMohrenschildt was dead. Allegedly, he killed himself with a shotgun blast to the head. Even though shotguns are not typically used in suicides, the death was ruled a suicide and never investigated. "What terrible secret was DeMohrenschildt so eager to protect?" Pacepa asked.[376] Jeanne DeMohrenschildt could not accept that her husband had committed suicide, and for the rest of her life she believed Lee Harvey Oswald was a CIA agent who was set up as a patsy and had no direct role in assassinating JFK.

OSWALD'S TRIP TO MEXICO

Pacepa is convinced Moscow tried to deprogram Oswald to no avail and that despite Moscow's instruction that Oswald should not assassinate JFK, Oswald proceeded with his original plans, convinced he was fulfilling his "historic" task. This would have meant Oswald had to find a way to convince the KGB that allowing him to go ahead with the original plan remained a good idea.

But first, Pacepa believes Oswald took a secret trip to Mexico in April 1963 to meet with the KGB in an effort to convince the Russians he was able to carry out the mission without adverse consequences to the Soviet Union. "In the dry run against Walker, [Oswald] had proved he could both shoot straight and escape cleanly, and Oswald was probably confident he could repeat this performance when Kennedy came to Dallas," Pacepa wrote.[377] During the weekend of November 9–11, 1963, Oswald drafted a letter for the Soviet embassy in Washington, in which he described a meeting he had just had with "comrade Kostin" in Mexico City, who he names elsewhere as Comrade Kostikov. The CIA identified Comrade

Kostin, a.k.a. Comrade Kostikov, as Valery Kostikov, an officer of the KGB's Thirteenth Department responsible for foreign assassinations. Kostikov was assigned under diplomatic cover to the Soviet embassy in Mexico.

Pacepa notes that after the assassination, Oswald's handwritten draft of the letter to the Soviet embassy was found among Oswald's effects in the garage of Ruth Paine's home. Oswald had re-written the letter several times before typing it. Pacepa quoted from the letter, putting earlier versions in italics within brackets:

> This is to inform you of recent events since my meetings with Comrade Kostin [*of new events since my interviews with comrade Kostine*] in the Embassy of the Soviet Union, Mexico City, Mexico. I was unable to remain in Mexico [crossed out in draft: *because I considered useless*] indefinitely because of my Mexican visa restrictions which was for 15 days only. I could not take a chance on requesting a new visa [*applying for an extension*] unless I used my real name, so I returned to the United States.[378]

"The fact that Oswald used an operational codename for Kostikov confirms to me both his meeting with Kostikov in Mexico City and his correspondence with the Soviet embassy in Washington were conducted in a KGB operational context," Pacepa concluded. "The fact that Oswald did not use his real name to obtain his Mexican travel permit confirms this conclusion."[379] A CIA memo dated January 31, 1964, confirmed Pacepa's conclusions that Oswald had met with Kostikov in Mexico City and confirmed Oswald's letter to the Soviet embassy in Moscow, in which Oswald concluded cryptically, "had I been able to reach the Soviet embassy in Havana as planned, the embassy there would have had time to complete our business."[380]

The disclosure of the Kostikov connection caused panic at the upper reaches of the US government. On November 29, 1963, in a taped telephone call convincing his old Senate mentor Richard Russell to join the Warren Commission, President Lyndon Johnson said, "And we've got to take this out of the arena where they're testifying Khrushchev and Castro did this and did that and kicking us into a war that can kill forty million Americans an hour."[381]

While the Warren Commission had no knowledge of a meeting

Oswald may have had with Kostikov in April 1963, the Commission managed to deepen the mystery over Oswald's subsequent trip to Mexico that Oswald took in September 1963, arriving in Mexico City on September 27. The Warren Commission reported Oswald went almost directly to the Cuban embassy and applied for a visa to Cuba in transit to Russia. Representing himself as the head of the New Orleans branch of the pro-Castro organization Fair Play for Cuba, Oswald noted his previous residence in the Soviet Union and indicated his desire to return there to live. The Cubans would not give Oswald a visa until he received one from the Russians, which would take several months. The Warren Commission reported that Oswald became agitated at being given the runaround, and that he left Mexico City on October 2, 1963, after having been rebuffed by both the Cuban and the Soviet embassies.[382]

US surveillance cameras outside foreign embassies in Mexico City photographed the person who was supposed to be Oswald.[383] This Mystery Man photo was rushed to Dallas the evening of the assassination on a special Naval Attaché flight and shown to Oswald's mother, Marguerite Oswald, who said the photograph was of Jack Ruby before Ruby killed her son. The Warren Commission was forced to publish the photo in order to quash her allegations. To this day, the person photographed by the CIA in Mexico has not been identified, but the person in the photograph is clearly neither Oswald nor Ruby.[384]

The possibility remains that someone was trying to frame Oswald given evidence that Oswald was impersonated in his September–October 1963 visit to Mexico. FBI Director J. Edgar Hoover sent a memo to the White House and the Secret Service on November 23, 1963, the day following the JFK assassination, containing the following explosive paragraph:

> The CIA advised that on October 1, 1963, an extremely sensitive source had reported that an individual identified himself as Lee Harvey Oswald, who contacted the Soviet Embassy in Mexico City inquiring as to any messages. Special Agents of this Bureau, who have conversed with Oswald in Dallas, Texas, have observed photographs of the individual referred to above, and have listened to a recording of his voice. These special agents are of the opinion that the above-referred-to individual was not Lee Harvey Oswald.[385]

The US government has never produced any authenticated photograph of Oswald in Mexico City in the supposed September–October 1963 trip, despite the extensive use of surveillance cameras to document all entrance and exit activity at Mexico City embassies. Whether or not Oswald visited Mexico in 1963 remains one of the most hotly debated issues in the JFK assassination mystery. The person in the photograph the CIA released bears no resemblance whatsoever to Lee Harvey Oswald. The person in the photograph the CIA released has never been identified.

A MEETING WITH THE KGB?

Still, Pacepa remains convinced that Oswald did connect with Kostikov in Mexico City. Pacepa focused on a Mexico City guidebook for the week September 28–October 4, 1963, found among Oswald's effects, as well as a Spanish-English directory. The guidebook had the Soviet embassy's telephone number underlined in pencil, with the names *Kosten* and *Osvald* written in Cyrillic on the page listing Diplomats in Mexico, as well as checkmarks next to five movie theaters listed on the previous page. In the back of the Spanish-English dictionary, Oswald wrote: "buy tickets for bull fight," and the Plaza México bullring is circled on his map. Also marked on the map is the Palace of Fine Arts, a place Pacepa notes was a favorite place for tourists to assemble on Sunday mornings to watch the Ballet Folklórico.

All this suggested to Pacepa that Oswald and Kostikov had a secret "iron meeting" in Mexico City. Iron meetings, or invariable meetings, were meetings the KGB used as standard procedure for emergency situations. "In my day, I approved quite a few 'iron meetings' in Mexico City—a favorite place for contacting our important agents living in the U.S.—and Oswald's 'iron meeting' looks to me like a typical one," Pacepa wrote. "This means: a brief encounter at a movie house to arrange a meeting for the following day at the bullfights [in Mexico City they were held at 4:30 every Sunday afternoon]; a brief encounter in front of the Palace of Fine Arts to pass Kostikov one of the bullfight tickets Oswald had bought; and a long meeting for discussions at the Sunday bullfight."[386] Pacepa, in a backhanded way, did not blame the Warren Commission for missing these clues, noting that none of the Warren Commission members had any experience in the techniques of professional counter-intelligence.

Since Oswald knew too much about the original KGB plan, Moscow arranged for him to be silenced forever, fearing that sooner or later Oswald would break down and begin talking to the police more openly and honestly. "That was another Soviet pattern," Pacepa pointed out, noting seven of the eight first chiefs of the Soviet political police were secretly or openly assassinated to prevent them from incriminating the Kremlin.[387] Inevitably, the KGB had no choice but to silence Oswald, or so Pacepa would argue. Pacepa believes that by the time of the September–October 1963 meeting in Mexico City, the KGB had realized there was no way to dissuade Oswald from going forward with his mission to assassinate JFK. "By this time the PGU had evidently realized there was no way the obsessive Oswald could be dissuaded from attempting to kill Kennedy, so to be on the safe side, it had already set in motion measures to 'neutralize' him," Pacepa concluded. "Meanwhile the PGU's only course would have been to keep Oswald believing that the Soviets were his friends, in order to ensure that no matter what happened, he would not compromise the PGU's connection with him."[388]

Pacepa insists Oswald acted alone. "The Soviets may have used assassination gangs inside the Soviet bloc, but they used only lone assassins in the West," he wrote in an e-mail to encourage the single-gunman theory.[389] Most likely, Pacepa is correct that Oswald was on a mission only he truly understood. Even if Oswald were a double agent compromised by the CIA before he defected to Russia, Pacepa is correct that "connecting the dots from the mountain of evidence that has accumulated proves KGB involvement."[390]

Besides, even if Pacepa is right that Oswald was a lone assassin, Pacepa does not necessarily identify with the Warren Commission theory that characterized Oswald as a psychologically weak ex-Marine who acted out his own hateful motives by assassinating JFK. Pacepa continues to believe Oswald was a well-trained and highly committed KGB agent who was determined to carry out his mission to assassinate JFK. For all Oswald knew, as Pacepa argues, the information that Khrushchev had lost his nerve and called off the JFK assassination might just be disinformation best disregarded. Even if Pacepa is right in arguing that Oswald followed the KGB methodology of acting alone, we must draw a distinction between what Pacepa means by "lone-gun assassin" and what the Warren Commission meant by using the same term. The Warren Commission clearly intended to dismiss the idea Oswald had accomplices in order to rule out the possibility of a conspiracy. Pacepa understands that Oswald was carrying out a KGB-ordered foreign assassination that by definition involved an international conspiracy tracing back to Moscow.

Still, nothing about unraveling the mystery surrounding the JFK assassination is so easy as to lay all the blame on the KGB alone. Not unless we want to make the KGB responsible for launching multiple look-alike plans to assassinate JFK, and we are willing to turn a blind eye to the recently discovered evidence of the involvement of the mob and the CIA in the assassination plots.

In their ground-breaking 2005 book, *Ultimate Sacrifice: John and Robert Kennedy, the Plan for a Coup in Cuba, and the Murder of JFK*, assassination researcher Lamar Waldron and syndicated radio talk-show host Thom Hartmann documented that in addition to the plan to assassinate JFK in Dallas, two earlier plots were thwarted: one in Chicago on November 2 and one in Tampa on November 18.[391] The three plans to assassinate JFK were remarkably similar in design.

THE PLOT TO ASSASSINATE JFK IN CHICAGO

The assassination attempt in Chicago was scheduled for Saturday, November 2, 1963. JFK was scheduled to proceed from Chicago's O'Hare Airport via motorcade to Soldier Field, where he was to watch the Army-Air Force football game with Mayor Daley. The eleven-mile motorcade was planned to proceed down what was then known as the Northwester Expressway to the Loop in downtown Chicago. At Jackson Street, the motorcade would make a difficult left-hand turn off the exit ramp onto the street to the stadium. The Jackson Street turn, like the turn from Houston onto Elm, involved a ninety-degree turn that would bring the presidential limousine to a virtual standstill. From there, the limo would travel through the warehouse district where numerous warehouses had empty or near-empty floors similar to the Texas School Book Depository. According to Secret Service agent Abraham Bolden, the FBI sent a teletype message on October 30, 1963, to the Secret Service in Chicago, stating that an attempt to assassinate JFK would be made on November 2, by a four-man team using high-powered rifles.[392]

The shooters in Chicago consisted of a four-man team equipped with military M-1 rifles, staying in a Chicago rooming house until the day planned for the assassination attempt. On November 2, Secret Service agents in an unmarked car tailed two of the four men after they left the rooming house together. The two men being tailed caught onto the surveillance after they doubled back and overheard the agent's radio. With their cover blown, the Secret Service agents apprehended the two men, bringing them to the Chicago Secret Service office for questioning. When no weapons were found in their possession or back at the rooming house, they were ultimately released. "The fact that the two men detained by the Secret Service had nothing illegal on them— or in their rooming house—like illegal weapons, traceable stolen cash or property, drugs, etc.—shows that they were experienced professionals," concluded Waldron and Hartmann.[393]

The patsy in the Chicago assassination plot was Thomas Arthur Vallee, a Chicago resident who, like Oswald, was an ex-marine. Vallee was awarded the Purple Heart for wounds he suffered in the Vietnam War. A member of the John Birch Society at the group's zenith, Vallee was known in Chicago for his outspoken criticism of JFK's foreign policy views. Vallee worked for a printing company located in a warehouse building along the JFK motorcade route. "The view from 625 Jackson Street was strikingly similar to the view . . . from the Texas School Book Depository."[394]

The final report of the House Select Committee on Assassinations notes that Vallee was placed under surveillance by Chicago police and arrested on the morning of the day JFK was scheduled to arrive in Chicago. When arrested, Vallee had in his automobile an M-1 rifle, a handgun, and three thousand rounds of ammunition.[395] The House Select Committee on Assassinations described Vallee in terms reminiscent of Oswald: "The committee found that the Secret Service learned more about Vallee prior to the President's trip to Dallas on November 22: he was a Marine Corps veteran with a history of mental illness while on duty; he was a member of the John Birch Society and an extremist in his criticism of the Kennedy administration; and he claimed to be an expert marksman. Further, he remained a threat after November 2, because he had been released from jail."[396]

Waldron and Hartmann believe those who planned the Chicago assassination attempt set up Vallee, like Oswald, to be the patsy who would take the fall for shooting JFK, even though professional assassins were recruited to do the shooting. "Our analysis of all the available government reports and of Vallee's statements indicates that he was not on his way to murder JFK, or anyone else that morning," Waldron and Hartmann wrote, concluding Vallee could easily have been on his way to meet a supposed weapons buyer who arranged to meet Valle that morning, saying he wanted to buy Vallee's M 1 rifle and his three thousand rounds of ammunition. Vallee's meeting could have been scheduled for a secluded spot or warehouse near Vallee's place of work on Jackson, along the route of the JFK motorcade. "Everyone's attention would be focused on the imminent arrival of JFK's motorcade, not on Vallee as he waited for his contact to show up," Waldron and Hartmann continued. "However, the contact would never appear, because it was all a setup to get Vallee in the right place at the right time with the right weapons and appearance."[397] If the plot had not been disrupted, JFK would have been shot by the professional assassins using M-1s and the same type of ammunition as in the trunk of Vallee's automobile; a bulletin to apprehend an assassination suspect would have been broadcast by Chicago police radio, describing someone similar in appearance to Vallee; very quickly, Vallee would have been found and apprehended.

"If President Kennedy had been assassinated in Chicago on November 2, rather than Dallas on November 22, Lee Harvey Oswald would probably be unknown to us today," assassination researcher and peace activist James W. Douglass wrote in his 2008 bestselling book, *JFK and the Unspeakable: Why He Died & Why It Matters.* "Instead Thomas Arthur Vallee would have likely become notorious as the president's presumed assassin."[398] Still, Douglass found the parallels between Vallee and Oswald startling. Vallee had worked at a secret U-2 base commanded by the CIA at Camp Otsu, Japan; Vallee later worked with the CIA at a camp near Levittown, Long Island, helping to train Cuban exiles to assassinate Fidel Castro, much as Oswald participated in a CIA training camp with Cuban exiles near Lake Pontchartrain near New Orleans.[399]

Chicago corruption investigator Sherman Skolnick researched the New York license plate of Vallee's car and found that the plate was registered to Lee Harvey Oswald.[400] When Jim Douglass looked into it, a retired New York Police Department officer told him that the license plate number in question was "frozen," suggesting Skolnick had to have gotten his information from the FBI. "The registration for the license plate on the car Thomas Arthur Vallee was driving at the time of his arrest was classified—restricted to U.S. intelligence agencies," Douglass wrote.[401]

Kennedy's trip to Chicago on November 2, 1963, was unexpectedly canceled that day at 10:10 a.m. Eastern Time, without explanation. The final report of the House Select Committee on Assassinations noted the committee was "unable to determine specifically why the President's trip to Chicago was canceled."[402] The final report also noted the committee was "unable to document the existence of the alleged assassination team." It also noted that Vallee, while being released from Chicago police custody on the evening of November 2, 1963, remained under "extensive, continued investigation" until 1968.[403]

THE PLOT TO ASSASSINATE JFK IN TAMPA

The JFK motorcade planned for Tampa on November 18, 1963, was one of the longest amounts of time in the open for JFK of his presidency; the only longer exposed time was in Berlin. The motorcade in Tampa was scheduled to go from MacDill Air Force Base to Al Lopez Field to downtown Tampa and the National Guard Armory, then to the International Inn, ending back at MacDill.[404] In a 1996 interview with Waldron and Hartmann, Former Tampa Police Chief J. P. Mullins confirmed the existence of the assassination plot in Tampa. He also disclosed that while the Secret Service had warned the Tampa Police Department of the threat, no information had been shared about the assassination plot in Chicago earlier that month. Waldron and Hartmann also report that JFK had been briefed of the danger in Tampa; however, he did not feel a second motorcade could be canceled after Chicago without raising suspicion.[405] The Tampa assassination plot was never revealed to the Warren Commission or any of the government committees that investigated the JFK assassination. It was not brought to light until Waldron and Hartmann brought the plot to the attention of the JFK Assassination Review Board in 1995.[406]

Of particular concern in the forty-minute motorcade was the Floridian Hotel, the tallest building in Tampa at the time. JFK's motorcade had to make a hard left turn in front of the "tall, red-brick building with dozens of unguarded windows, in the days when hotel windows weren't sealed shut."[407] Tampa police expected the hotel to be packed with visitors who were planning to take advantage of the great view overlooking the JFK motorcade route. Tampa law enforcement went all out that day to protect JFK. Deputies from the sheriff's office controlled the roofs of the major buildings in the downtown and suburban areas; every overpass was lined with police officers on alert.

JFK rode in the back of the same SS-100-X Lincoln limousine he used in Dallas. Jackie Kennedy was not with her husband that day. The "bubbletop" typically used on the limo in bad weather was not deployed on that beautiful Tampa day, and given that the bubbletop was not bulletproof, JFK felt placing it on the car in good weather gave the wrong message. JFK stood in the limo for much of the motorcade, making him an easily visible target. In contrast to Dallas, two Secret Service agents rode on the running boards on the back of the JFK limo for much of the motorcade and the motorcycle escort was properly deployed, surrounding the limo in motorcycle escort coverage. "In spite of the pressure he must have been under, both from the threat and his packed schedule, JFK remained gracious, with the charm that had captured much of the nation," commented Waldron and Hartmann on the Tampa motorcade.[408]

THE TAMPA PATSY AND THE DALLAS PATSY: LOOK-ALIKES

The patsy in the Tampa assassination plot was Gilberto Policarpo Lopez, a young Cuban exile who had moved from the Florida Keys to Tampa in the fall of 1963 and was under surveillance by the FBI as a possible assassination threat. Waldron and Hartmann produced the following eighteen remarkable parallels between Lee Harvey Oswald and Gilberto Policarpo Lopez, as developed from government documents and sources:

- Both were white males, twenty-three years old during most of 1963.

- Both had returned to America in the summer of 1962 from a Communist country.

- Both spent part of 1963 in a Southern city that was headquarters for one of the two mob bosses that the House Select Committee on Assassinations says were most likely behind the Kennedy assassination.

- During 1963, each was frustrated by a lack of a government document, which could hamper his employment and the prospects for his future. This need to get a favorable determination on his status could make him amenable to taking risks for a U.S. agency or make him subject to manipulation by someone saying they could help with his document problems.

- Both are said by various sources to have been assets or informants for some U.S. agency, and both were of interest to Naval Intelligence, who kept files on them.

- In mid-1963, both men and their wives moved to another city and then became involved with the Fair Play for Cuba Committee.

- In the summer of 1963, some of their associates saw them as being pro-Castro, while others saw them as being anti-Castro. Both were living in a city where there was much anti-Castro activity.

- In the summer of 1963, both were involved in fistfights over "pro-Castro" statements they made.

- Though both appeared at times to be "pro-Castro," neither joined the Communist Party and neither regularly associated with local Communist party members.

- In the summer of 1963, their backgrounds would have made both of them a good, deniable, low-level intelligence asset inside Cuba. In addition to sometimes appearing to be a Castro supporter, each had a Russian connection in their background, meaning the CIA could blame any problem on the Russians if they were caught. These same attributes would also make both good Mafia patsies for the JFK assassination.

- By September 1963, both men were living apart from their wives as the result of marital difficulties.

- In the fall of 1963, both crossed the border at Nuevo Laredo and made a mysterious trip to Mexico City, where they were under photographic surveillance by the CIA. Both were trying to get to Cuba.

- Both went by car on one leg of their Mexico City trip. Neither was a very good driver and neither man owned a car.

- In the fall of 1963, each had a job in the vicinity of JFK's route for one of his November motorcades.

- A trusted FBI informant and a Tampa police informant placed both men in Tampa in the fall of 1963, in conjunction with the Fair Play for Cuba Committee.

- The week of 11/22/63, both men were in a Texas city where assassination was in the works for JFK.

- Following the events in Dallas, both men were investigated for involvement in JFK's assassination.

- Declassified documents indicate that both men were the subject of unusual U.S. intelligence activity.[409]

Waldron and Hartmann conclude the parallels strongly suggest that in the months preceding the JFK assassination, the same people were manipulating both men, for the same reasons. "The evidence shows that Oswald—like Lopez—was on a 'mission' for U.S. intelligence when they undertook their actions in November 1963, and that instead of intending to kill JFK on November 22, 1963, Oswald planned to go to Cuba as part of a U.S. intelligence operation," Waldron and Hartmann concluded. "In fact, after the Tampa assassination attempt, Lopez went to Texas, then actually made it into Cuba shortly after JFK's death, according to surveillance by the CIA."[410] Waldron and Hartmann reported that in Tampa, Lopez worked for a construction firm that had long-established organized crime connections with Key West; Lopez also had a brother living in the Soviet Union in 1963.[411]

The documents in Oswald's declassified CIA 201 file, otherwise known as a "personality file," clearly demonstrate the CIA had both Lee Harvey Oswald and Gilberto Policarpo Lopez under surveillance in 1963, as were the activities in Mexico of KGB foreign assassination head Valery Kostikov.[412] There is no indication Lopez met with Kostikov in Mexico City, as Oswald most likely did. But that Lopez was allowed to travel to

Cuba, while Oswald was denied a visa, may indicate that Lopez's KGB mission in Tampa was finished as soon as the assassination attempt was canceled due to increased security.

The CIA surveillance cables in Oswald's 201 file indicate that Lopez entered Mexico via Nuevo Laredo, Texas, en route to Havana, Cuba, on November 25, 1963, the Monday when JFK was buried at Arlington Cemetery.[413] On November 27, 1963, CIA surveillance photographed Lopez at the Mexico City airport, boarding Cuban flight number 465, as the only passenger.[414] No new information appears to have been developed on Lopez after he returned to Cuba five days after the JFK assassination; it is not known if he ever returned to the United States.

WILD CARDS IN DALLAS

Another strange case involves Miguel Casas Saez, who CIA surveillance documents identify under the nickname "Miguelito." On November 22, 1963, a Cubana Airlines flight from Mexico City to Havana, Cuba, was delayed for five hours awaiting a passenger. That afternoon, just hours after the JFK assassination, the airfield in Mexico City was particularly clogged with diplomatic personnel. Finally, around 10:30 p.m. local time, the passenger arrived aboard a private twin engine airplane. Reportedly, the passenger got out of the private airplane and boarded the Cubana flight directly, without going through customs. Once aboard, the passenger entered the cockpit of the airplane, where he remained for the duration of the flight. None of the passengers recognized him well enough to make a positive identification. Examination of various CIA declassified documents has identified the passenger as Miguel Casas Saez, also known as Angel Dominquez Martinez, the name under which he entered the United States in early November 1963.[415]

A CIA cable stamped January 25, 1964, identifies Miguel Casas as "an ardent revolutionary follower of Raul Castro, militiaman, and G-2."[416] The cable cites a report that Casas was in Dallas the day of the JFK assassination and that he managed to leave the United States through Laredo, Texas. He left Mexico on an airplane headed for Cuba. The CIA cable specifies that Casas "had firing practice in militias" and that he was "capable of doing anything." A source informed the CIA that Casas left Cuba on September 26, 1963, by small boat; after being caught in a hurricane off the coast of Florida, he landed in Puerto Rico and entered Miami from Puerto Rico, using the alias Angel Dominguez Martinez. Sources told the CIA that Casas spoke Russian well and that he was an infiltrator who entered the United States on an espionage mission. The CIA document described Casas as "age 22–23, 5'10", dark, strong build, dark brown hair, brown eyes."

A CIA report filed November 2, 1964, also gives a strange account of airplane activity the CIA investigators felt was possibly connected with the JFK assassination. A source identified only as "a well-known Cuban scientist" reported that by chance he was at the Havana airport on the afternoon of November 22, 1963, when at 5:00 p.m. local time an airplane with Mexican markings landed and parked at the far side of the field. "Two men, whom he recognized as Cuban 'gangsters,' alighted, entered the rear entrance of the administration building and disappeared without going through the normal customs procedures." The scientist determined the aircraft had just arrived from Dallas, Texas, via Tijuana and Mexico City. Engine trouble had forced the airplane to land in Tijuana. "By combining the date, the origin of the flight, and the known reputation of the two men, he theorized that the two men must have been involved in the assassination of President Kennedy," the CIA report continued. "He speculated that Lee Harvey Oswald had acted in the pay of Castro, and that the two Cubans had been in Dallas to organize or oversee the operation. He told the source that he had been greatly distressed by what he had seen and heard and had to tell someone about it."[417]

Again, there is no indication the CIA did anything to further investigate or to verify this report.

KGB DISINFORMATION

Former Romanian intelligence officer Ion Mihai Pacepa has repeatedly insisted that the various conspiracy theories regarding who killed JFK originated in Moscow as disinformation the KGB planned to disseminate through US journalists, researchers, and other authors of various kinds in order to cover the role of the Russian government under Khrushchev and the KGB's culpability in sending Oswald to the United States to assassinate JFK.

Pacepa recounts how on the evening of November 26, 1963, four days after the assassination of JFK, he was paid a surprise visit in Bucharest by General Sakharovsky, the chief Soviet intelligence advisor for Romania. "It turned out that Bucharest was Sakarovsky's first stop on a blitz tour of the main sister services," Pacepa wrote. "His task was to instruct the management of these services to unleash a diversionary intelligence effort aimed at directing world attention away from the Soviet Union and focusing suspicion for the killing of President Kennedy on the United States itself."[418] As Sakharovsky detailed Oswald's background, Pacepa became convinced the PGU had a hand in Oswald's getting a Soviet wife while he was in the Soviet Union. He was told Oswald's closest friend in the United States had been arranged to be a Russian émigré by the name of George DeMohrenschildt. This was enough to convince Pacepa that Oswald had been recruited to be a Soviet agent.

The next day, Pacepa and his intelligence colleagues in Romania began working on the ultra-secret directive Sakharovsky had brought with him. "Its bottom line was that we should immediately begin spreading the rumor in the West that President Kennedy had been killed by the CIA," Pacepa summarized. "Operational guidelines were included in the PGU center's directive, according to which the CIA hated Kennedy because, by toning down its plans to invade Cuba in 1962, he had compromised the CIA's presence around the world." That Kennedy wanted to end the Cold War was seen as a threat to the CIA's power. "Hence, the PGU line went, the old CIA cold warriors had decided to get rid of Kennedy and to do it in such a manner as simultaneously to increase the 'imperialist hysteria' against the Soviet Union."[419] Pacepa related that the cover story was to focus on Lee Harvey Oswald, an enlisted marine the CIA had chosen for carrying out the operation. Moscow instructed Romanian intelligence to represent Oswald as a CIA agent who had been dispatched to the Soviet Union under cover as a defector, who was repatriated to the United States almost three years later, after completing his CIA-assigned espionage mission in Russia. The directive instructed Romanian intelligence to construct the story so as to make the world believe the assassination had been perpetrated by the United States government.

Pacepa noted that Sakharovsky's directive had been transformed into a disinformation operational plan under the code name Operation Dragon. Soon, Pacepa found himself drafting an attachment to Operation Dragon containing guidelines for another rumor that was to be circulated, that Lyndon Johnson had orchestrated the JFK assassination because the vice president feared JFK would replace him with a member of the Kennedy clan for the 1964 elections. "The bottom line of this interpretation was that Johnson had seen though the clan's plot and had lured Kennedy to Texas, where Johnson could play on his home turf," Pacepa recalled. As proof, Russian intelligence sent Pacepa and his Romanian disinformation team an article that appeared in the Dallas newspapers the morning JFK was assassinated, reporting that former vice president Nixon, in a visit to Dallas the preceding day, had predicted JFK might drop LBJ from the 1964 Democratic Party presidential ballot.[420] In December 1963, Moscow added to Operation Dragon the theme that JFK was killed by the "military industrial complex" in the United States because he had become discouraged with waging a war in Southeast Asia and was making it known he wanted to begin withdrawing US advisors from Vietnam. Pacepa was bombarded with nearly frantic cables from the KGB demanding that Operation Dragon be put into high gear.[421]

Pacepa's assertion that a Soviet disinformation campaign was the origin of the various "conspiracy theories" that have sought to explain the JFK assassination in the last fifty years got strong support in 1992 when the British Secret Intelligence Service extracted retired KGB officer Vasili Mitrokhin, along with some twenty-five thousand pages of notes Mitrokhin had made in the course of twelve years, describing top-secret KGB files. "Among the most important revelations provided by the *Mitrokhin Archive* are the highly classified KGB documents proving that the so-called Kennedy assassination conspiracy, which so far generated thousands of books all around the world, was born in the KGB, and that some of it was financed by the KGB," Pacepa noted. "Equally significant are the documents in the *Mitrokhin Archive* showing that the KGB had constructed this conspiracy using some of the same paid KGB agents who were called upon to promote the disinformation operation designed to frame Pope Pius XII as having been pro-Nazi."[422]

In their 1999 book, *The Sword and the Shield: The Mitrokhin Archive and the Secret History of the KGB*, history professor Christopher Andrew and Vasili Mitrokhin listed a number of prominent books financed by the KGB to promote JFK assassination conspiracy theories.[423] Included on the list are books published in the 1960s that are referenced in earlier chapters: *Oswald: Assassin or Fall-Guy?* by Joachim Joesten and *Rush to Judgment* by Mark Lane. Joesten was a former member of the German Communist Party, whose book was published in the United States by KGB agent Carlo Aldo Marzini, who, according to documents in the *Mitrokhin Archive*, had received subsidies from Moscow totaling $672,000. The KGB identified New York lawyer Mark Lane as the most talented of the first wave of JFK assassination conspiracy theorists, citing his ties with the Democratic Party in the United States and his liberal views on a number of then-current American political problems. Together with student assistants and other volunteers, Lane founded what he called the "Citizens' Committee of Inquiry" in a small office in Manhattan and rented a small theater at which he gave nightly renditions of what became known as "The Speech," a rendition of Lane's conspiracy theories that Lane updated nightly, as his research progressed. Through a trusted intermediary, the KGB sent Lane fifteen hundred dollars to help finance his research. The same intermediary also provided five hundred dollars to pay for Lane to travel to Europe to continue his research.

WARREN COMMISSION DISINFORMATION

Remarkably, neither Khrushchev nor LBJ wanted a thorough and honest investigation. Conveniently, Lee Harvey Oswald was dead. Better to declare Lee Harvey Oswald the guilty party and move on, free of the risk that a trial could embarrass either Russia or the United States. So remarkably the Warren Commission's result—that neither the CIA, the FBI, nor the KGB knew anything about Oswald—was exactly the result the United States government wanted. The Soviets preferred a result that put the blame on the CIA, but in the final analysis, the Soviets were satisfied as long as the Warren Commission did not blame the Russian government or the KGB for having ordered and arranged that JFK be murdered. Neither Khrushchev nor LBJ wanted to go to war over JFK's assassination.

That Lee Harvey Oswald shot JFK and acted alone was a good story, and both Khrushchev and LBJ were sticking to it. According to Pacepa, Soviet disinformation was aimed at putting the blame back on the USA, as a defensive policy, just so no one would take too seriously Oswald's KGB ties. As demonstrated by the memo that Deputy Attorney General Nicholas deB. Katzenbach wrote LBJ presidential assistant Moyers, dated November 25, 1963, and referenced at the start of this chapter, the Warren Commission disinformation was aimed at making sure the American public did not blame either the CIA or the KGB.

As far as Pacepa is concerned, the success of the argument that the CIA was behind the JFK assassination is evidence not in the facts of the CIA's involvement but in how well designed and effective the Soviet disinformation campaign to blame the CIA turned out to be. "As Andropov once told me, after you start a disinformation story, it can gather momentum and then take on a life of its own. That's how so many innocent and imaginative dupes later picked up the multiple bullet/gunmen line and then promulgated it for their own purposes," Pacepa suggested in an e-mail he wrote me on January 13, 2012.[424] In the same e-mail, Pacepa explained that he and his wife, an American intelligence analyst, have spent ten years sifting through the several thousand books written on the JFK assassination, and they have concluded that there are only three substantive *sources* of *factual* information on JFK's assassination: the Warren Commission documents, the House committee documents, and Epstein's book *Legend, The Secret World of Lee Harvey Oswald.*

Pacepa's assessment was that Epstein unfortunately bought into some of the conspiracy theories later in his career. As noted earlier, Pacepa also felt "Epstein lacked the inside background knowledge that would have helped him to fit his bits and pieces together into one whole and reach a firm conclusion." As a consequence, Pacepa felt Epstein's "very well documented story is left hanging in mid-air," a defect Pacepa felt he could correct in a future manuscript, simply by providing insights gained from his years of experience with the techniques, codes, and ciphers common to agents communicating within the KGB sphere of intelligence operations.

In the end, the Warren Commission's disinformation campaign failed because the disinformation effort demanded manipulating the available evidence and sworn testimony to fit the investigation's pre-determined conclusion that Lee Harvey Oswald was alone guilty for killing JFK. That conspiracy theorists like Joesten or Lane knowingly or not knowingly accepted funding from Soviet intelligence sources does not disqualify the value of the questions asked. A particular argument or theory is not wrong simply because it can be traced to a KGB disinformation directive. Had the Warren Commission case against Oswald been ironclad, conspiracy theorists, no matter how creative, would not have been interesting enough to command an audience. The truth is, LBJ and the US Justice Department assigned the Warren Commission a fool's errand when assigning it the mission of finding Oswald guilty as the lone-nut gunman. LBJ wanted the Warren Commission to reach that conclusion as soon as possible, so a final report could be published before the 1964 presidential election. LBJ clearly wanted to run for president in 1964 as the successor to JFK determined to carry forth the JFK legislative agenda, not as a suspect under examination by a US public about to realize in a *Life* magazine exposé about to be published that revealed JFK planned on dumping LBJ from the 1964 Democratic Party ticket.

In the final analysis, the Warren Commission failed in its disinformation efforts to pin all the guilt on Oswald because the case against Oswald is not ironclad, while the Soviets succeeded in their disinformation campaign because the evidence supporting the conclusion the CIA was involved in the JFK assassination is more convincing than the official Warren Commission cover story.

A PAYOFF TO MARINA OSWALD

In the aftermath of the JFK assassination, the CIA brokered a substantial financial pay-off to Marina Oswald. The broker in the deal was C. D. Jackson who worked as the publisher of *Life* magazine. The anti-communist journalist and author Isaac Don Levine befriended Marina Oswald shortly after the JFK assassination. In response to a request from former CIA director Allen Dulles, Jackson helped broker a twenty-five-thousand-dollar book deal with New York publisher Meredith Press to publish Marina's life story, with Levine agreeing to be the ghost-writer. The book was never written, and Marina Oswald reportedly ended up receiving over $200,000 in what has been described as a "payoff" that Levine arranged.[425]

Both Jackson and Levine had extensive CIA ties. Frank Wisner, who had worked during World War II with Jackson in the Office of Strategic Services (OSS), the predecessor to the CIA, had transitioned to become the director of counter-intelligence for the CIA. In 1948 Wisner recruited Jackson to participate in Operation Mockingbird, a CIA project in which respected journalists were secretly paid by the CIA to publish stories favorable to the CIA. In 1948 Jackson had become managing director of Time-Life International. Jackson subsequently became the publisher of *Fortune* magazine, another Henry Luce creation. In February 1953 Jackson was appointed as a special assistant to President Eisenhower in a role that included coordinating with the CIA and advising Eisenhower on cold war planning and the tactics of psychological warfare.[426] As publisher of *Life* magazine, Jackson purchased the Zapruder film of the JFK assassination, from which he published only selected frames shown as still photographs. Jackson suppressed making the Zapruder film available for the public to view, arguing the film was too graphically violent for widespread distribution. None less than Carl Bernstein, the former *Washington Post* reporter of Watergate fame, dubbed C. D. Jackson as "Henry Luce's personal emissary to the CIA."[427]

Levine was born in Russia and spoke Russian fluently. He spent an intensive week coaching Marina Oswald just prior to her first session before the Warren Commission on February 3, 1964.[428] Since the end of World War II, Levine had become involved with what was then known as the China Lobby, a group of supporters for Nationalist China opposing Mao and the spread of Communism into China. Editing a magazine on behalf of the China Lobby called *Plain Talk*, Levine published a stream of articles analyzing the dangers to the United States from China after its fall to the Communist Chinese following Mao's revolution, which began in 1949. Levine's history as an anti-Communist also included credits for encouraging Whittaker Chambers to speak out against Alger Hiss. James Herbert Martin, who was then acting as Marina Oswald's literary agent and manager, believed that Levine's motivation at the time was to tie Oswald in with the Communist Party by coaching Marina on what to say when she testified to the Warren Commission.[429] The second possible interpretation of Levine's role was that he was "on the scene primarily for the purpose of gaining intelligence."[430] This was the impression of some of the FBI agents who questioned Levine about his relationship with Marina Oswald, including FBI counter-intelligence head William Sullivan. The conclusion assassination researcher Jerry Rose reached was that Levine was "to spread disinformation about Oswald, especially his 'Chinese communist' connections."[431]

OSWALD A HERO?

It did not matter whether Oswald was a committed Soviet KGB agent planning to assassinate JFK on his own, or a double agent playing out complex theatrics scripted by the CIA. In either event, Oswald perfectly fit the type of person sought out by serious assassination planners who needed a dupe to play the role they had written for the patsy. He could not have been more perfect, especially since he probably did not fully appreciate the extent to which he had been set up and abandoned, not until he saw Jack Ruby jump out at him with a gun in his hand in the basement of the Dallas Police Department.

Oswald often acted as if he expected to be misunderstood, or at least as if he were indifferent as to whether or not those in positions of authority understood him. He was vulnerable not because he wanted to be understood, but because he dreaded being seen as unimportant.

His mother seemed to share this fear.

"Lee Harvey Oswald, my son, even after his death, has done more for his country than any other living human being," Marguerite Oswald insisted, speaking to reporters at the gravesite of her son at Rose Hill Cemetery in Fort Worth, Texas, in late 1963.

Testifying to the Warren Commission, Marguerite told them she asked her son why he came back to the United States. She knew he had a good job in Russia because he sent her expensive gifts, and he was married to a Russian girl. "He said, 'Mother, not even Marina knows why I have returned to the United States.' And that is all the information I ever got out of my son."[432]

Until the day she died, Marguerite insisted her son, Lee Harvey Oswald, was innocent. She believed her son died in the service of his country—the United States of America—and that he laid down his life playing out his assigned counter-intelligence role as a loyal secret agent, whatever precisely that role may have been.

But Marguerite Oswald did not understand and certainly could not explain anything Lee Harvey Oswald had done, probably since he was a child, including why he went to Russia, or why he chose to come home.

And that, it appears, is exactly the way Oswald wanted it.

FIVE

ROOTS OF THE JFK ASSASSINATION—A BANANA REPUBLIC, THE CIA, AND THE MOB

"Anyone perched above the crowd with a rifle could do it."[433]

—President John F. Kennedy, in Fort Worth, Texas, the morning of November 22, 1963

"In Guatemala the political transition was unexpectedly smooth, and Castillo Armas became a popular elected president until his untimely assassination by a member of his personal bodyguard. Among the bodyguard's possessions were documents showing he had been a constant listener to Radio Moscow's Spanish-language broadcasts."[434]

—E. Howard Hunt, *Under-Cover: Memoirs of an American Secret Agent*, 1974

THE MORNING HE DIED, John F. Kennedy had talked about being assassinated.

Kenneth O'Donnell, the special assistant to JFK, in his testimony to the Warren Commission, described the conversation that November morning in Suite 850 of Hotel Texas in Fort Worth, before the presidential party set out for Dallas. O'Donnell was questioned by committee counsel Arlen Specter.

Mr. Specter: When did the conversation occur?

Mr. O'Donnell: The conversation took place in his room, with Mrs. Kennedy and myself, perhaps a half hour before he left the Hotel. It was to depart for Carswell Air Force Base.

Mr. Specter: That was in Fort Worth?

Mr. O'Donnell: That was in Fort Worth.

Mr. Specter: And tell us, as nearly as you can recollect, exactly what he said at that time, please.

Mr. O'Donnell: Well, as near as I can recollect he was commenting to his wife on the function of the Secret Service, and his interpretation of their role once the trip had commenced, in that their main function was to protect him from crowds, and to see that an unruly or sometimes an overexcited crowd did not generate into a riot, at which the President of the United States could be injured. But he said that if anybody really wanted to shoot the President of the United States, it was not a very difficult job — all one had to do was get a high building some day with a telescopic rifle, and there was nothing anybody could do to defend against such an attempt on the President's life.[435]

JFK had discussed being shot by a high-powered rifle from a tall building so frequently he appeared to have been obsessed with that assassination method. The reason he was obsessed with being assassinated by a sniper was because he had been warned that is precisely how he would be killed.

THE DAY JFK WAS SHOT

Jim Bishop, the author of *The Day Kennedy Was Shot*, recounts that the last time he saw JFK was on October 24, 1963, approximately one month before the assassination. JFK visited with Bishop and his wife in the Oval Office. Bishop was researching an article for *Good Housekeeping* magazine to be called "A Day in the Life of President Kennedy." Bishop recalled JFK selected assassination as the subject for their last chat, commenting how much he had enjoyed reading Bishop's earlier book, *The Day Lincoln Was Shot*. "My feelings about assassination are identical with

Mr. Lincoln's," JFK explained. "Anyone who wants to exchange his life for mine can take it." Bishop commented that JFK said this with bland good humor. "They just can't protect that much," JFK mused.[436] The comment suggested JFK was resigned to his fate, anticipating it meant not living out his term in office.

Every modern-day president is aware, at least intellectually, that the possibility of assassination is very real. Yet, with JFK there was a difference. The roots of his premonition were not psychic in nature; he was aware of the threat because he had been warned a plot to assassinate him was in the works. Before Dallas, JFK had been given ample warnings of specific and credible threats to his life. On the morning of November 22, 1963, the rain had stopped, probably a reason for the assassination to take place. The bubbletop would have been placed on the car if the rain had continued, and although it wasn't bulletproof, it might have caused refractions in the bullets' trajectories, which could have been sufficient to call off the mission. When JFK visited Ireland in June, five months before he was assassinated, the Irish police took extra security precautions after receiving three death threats, including a warning a sniper with a rifle would take up a position on a rooftop overlooking the president's motorcade route from the Dublin airport to the president's family residence.[437] Yet, November 1963 was different. There had been multiple recurring credible threats of assassination surfacing that indicated specific plans were in the works to assassinate JFK soon. Even more seriously worrisome, the plans all had a common element—a sniper with a high-powered rifle equipped with a scope, shooting from a tall building.

Digging deeper, we find the assassination plan had been tried before, crafted by public relations guru Edward Bernays and implemented by CIA operative E. Howard—all with the blessing of President Dwight D. Eisenhower. As we shall see in this chapter, disturbing parallels between the CIA-engineered assassination of Carlos Castillo Armas in Guatamala on July 26, 1957, and the assassination of JFK on November 22, 1963, suggest what the CIA had learned in Central America might have been duplicated in Dallas. If the JFK assassination was a rerun of Carlos Castillo Armas in Guatemala, professional politicians, such as Richard Nixon and Lyndon Johnson, could look the other way and deny complicity.

A STEPPED-UP THREAT LEVEL

On November 9, 1963, union organizer William Somersett, a former member of the Ku Klux Klan who had become a paid informant for the intelligence division of the Miami Police Department in 1962, allowed the Miami police to record surreptitiously a telephone conversation Somersett had with his old friend, the right-wing extremist Joseph Milteer. In the conversation, Milteer bragged that he had knowledge a plot was underway to assassinate JFK. "Well, how in the hell do you figure would be the best way to get him?" Somersett asked. "From an office with a high-powered rifle," Milteer bragged in response. Milteer insisted the plan was "in the works" and that a patsy would be blamed for the crime. "They won't leave any stone unturned there, no way," Milteer asserted. "They will pick up somebody within hours afterwards, if anything like that would happen, just to throw the public off." Somersett replied that somebody would have to go to jail if JFK got killed. Milteer responded by saying it would be just like Bruno Hauptman in the Lindberg kidnapping case, implying Hauptman had taken the punishment for a crime he did not commit.[438]

Miami police turned the transcript of the conversation over to the Secret Service on November 12, 1963, and the Secret Service, in turn, furnished the information to the agents planning JFK's trip to Tampa and Miami on November 18, 1963. Former prosecutor Vincent Bugliosi, convinced Lee Harvey Oswald acted alone, reported that Miami-based Secret Service Special Agent Robert Jamison took the threat seriously enough to have Somersett call Milteer on November 18 to verify that Milteer was in Valdosta, Georgia, that day and not in Miami, Florida.[439] When Somersett confirmed that no violence-prone associates of Milteer were in Miami that day, the Protective Research Section of the Secret Service closed the case. And they failed to notify the Washington, D.C., Secret Service detail in charge of the upcoming Dallas trip or the Secret Service in Dallas about Milteer's remarks. While Bugliosi chooses to interpret Milteer's recorded comments as nothing more than idle speculation in response to Somersett's leading questions, the conversation is one more indication that a wide conspiracy was in the works.

Secret Service Special Agent Forrest V. Sorrels, who was in charge of the Dallas District, described to the Warren Commission the advance work done to plan the JFK motorcade on November 22. In response to a question whether the buildings along the motorcade route presented any particular problems, Sorrels gave an extensive answer:

> All buildings are a problem, as far as we are concerned. That insofar as I have been concerned—and I am sure that every member of the Service, especially the Detail—that is always of concern to us. We always consider it a hazard. During the time that we were making this survey with the police, I made the remark that if someone wanted to get the President of the United States, he could do it with a high-powered rifle and a telescopic sight from some building or some hillside, because that has always been a concern to us, about the buildings.[440]

In an era of open-car motorcades and tall office buildings where the windows opened, the risk of assassination from a high-powered rifle with a scope was great. For a popular president in the JFK-era, the danger was unavoidable since riding in a motorcade in a closed limousine or under the cover of a bubble top would have conveyed a level of cowardice that itself would have been fatal to JFK's political future.

What remains intriguing about Milteer is that his information dovetails with what we now know about the plot to assassinate JFK in Tampa. Milteer told Somersett that JFK could have been killed in Miami, "but somebody called the FBI and gave the thing away, and of course, he was well guarded and everything went 'pluey,' and everybody kept quiet, and waited for Texas."[441] The motorcades in both Tampa and Miami were not canceled, but security was increased in both cities.

The House Select Committee on Assassinations concluded the Secret Service "failed to follow up" on Somersett's information about Milteer's threat, concluding a telephone call to Milteer to find out where he was on November 18 was not a sufficient precaution.[442] Similarly, the House Select Committee charged that the Secret Service failed to make appropriate use of the information supplied to it by the Chicago Police Department regarding the threat to assassinate JFK during his trip to Chicago.[443] The House Select Committee's conclusion was clear: "The fact was, however, that two threats to assassinate President Kennedy with high-powered rifles, both of which occurred in early November 1963, were not relayed to the Dallas region."[444] The Committee concluded that the Secret Service's failure to communicate the previous threats prevented Dallas officials from taking adequate precautions:

During the Secret Service check of the Dallas motorcade route, Special Agent in Charge Sorrels commented that if someone wanted to assassinate the President, it could be done with a rifle from a high building. President Kennedy himself had remarked he could be shot from a high building and little could be done to stop it. But such comments were just speculation. Unless the Secret Service had a specific reason to suspect the occupants or activities of a certain building, it would not inspect it. The committee found that at the time of the Dallas trip, there was not sufficient concern about the possibility of an attack from a high building to cause the agents responsible for the trip planning to develop security precautions to minimize the risk.[445]

Had the Secret Service office in Dallas been made aware of the threats in Chicago and Tampa earlier in the month, they likely would have taken extra precautions. A building survey conducted under a high "level of risk" criterion might well have included the Texas School Book Depository. Both the Secret Service and the Dallas police were unusually lax about allowing windows in tall buildings along the motorcade route to remain open.

The testimony of Secret Service agent Forrest Sorrels to the Warren Commission was important on these points. Sorrels rode in the lead car along with Dallas Police Chief Jessie Curry, immediately in front of JFK's limousine. Sorrels testified that his function in the lead car was "to observe the people and buildings as we drove along in the motorcade."[446] As the motorcade turned onto Houston Street, Sorrels observed the Texas School Book Depository. He continued watching the building as the motorcade turned left onto Elm Street. Sorrels testified that he saw two African-Americans watching the motorcade from a window a couple of floors from the top of the book depository, but he did not recall seeing any activity in the windows of the building that caused him particular concern. "I did not see any activity—no one moving around or anything like that," he testified, repeating the statement several times.[447] This statement confirms two key points: (1) Dallas police and the Secret Service took no special precautions to secure the Texas School Book Depository; and (2) any trained sniper positioned on the sixth floor of the building was sufficiently professional to avoid detection before the shooting started. And as noted earlier, there is nothing in the record to suggest Lee Harvey Oswald ever received specific training to be a sniper.

FBI AGENT DON ADAMS

In November 1963, FBI agent Don Adams was assigned to investigate Joseph Milteer's threats against JFK. In his 2012 book, *From an Office Building with a High-Powered Rifle: A Report to the Public from an FBI Agent Involved in the Official JFK Assassination Investigation*, Adams disputes the official Secret Service account that places Milteer in Georgia on November 22, 1963. "I spent five days, from November 22 to November 27, trying to locate Milteer and had no idea that there were lies being told about Milteer's whereabouts, effectively taking any pressure off any search or large-scale investigation into Milteer as a suspect," Adams wrote. "I can state with certainty that Milteer was not in Georgia on November 22; I was actively looking for him and he was nowhere to be found until five days later."[448]

Additionally, Adams recounted that at 10:30 a.m., on the morning of November 22, 1963, Milteer placed a telephone call to informant William Somersett in Miami. He reportedly told Somersett that he was in Dallas that day, commenting, "I don't think you'll ever see your boy again in Miami," referring to JFK.[449] Associated Press photographer James Altgens and amateur moviemaker Mark Bell took photographs in Dealey Plaza the day of the assassination. Their images of the JFK limousine proceeding down Houston Street show a man in the crowd who looks very much like Milteer. The House Select Committee on Assassinations, after an extensive photographic examination conducted by experts, concluded the man in the photo was "substantially taller," by more than six inches, than Milteer, who was estimated to be five feet four inches tall.[450] Adams disagreed: "I met, detained and stood toe-to-toe with Milteer. Granted, he was shorter than I was [6'7"]. However, I know he was taller than 5'4"; in fact, in my description of Milteer, I wrote that he was 5'8" tall."[451]

In a footnote, the House Select Committee noted that no evidence could be found that Milteer was in Dallas on the day of the assassination.[452] Again, Adams disagrees. Adams first saw the photograph of Milteer in the

Dallas crowd in 1993, when he picked up a copy of Robert Groden and Harrison Edward Livingstone's 1989 book, *High Treason*.[453] "I was flabbergasted," Adams wrote, describing his reaction the first time he saw the photograph. "I couldn't believe it. Here was someone who had threatened to kill the President of the United States, standing alongside the motorcade route that fateful day in Dallas. What was going on? I had been sent to find Milteer in Georgia the afternoon of the assassination, but didn't locate him until Wednesday the 27th. Was Milteer in Dallas? I'd say yes!"[454]

What Don Adams was suggesting is the strong likelihood the perpetrators of the JFK assassination were in Dallas that day, ready to watch. Milteer was not the only one.

E. HOWARD HUNT AND THE UNITED FRUIT COMPANY

In the 1950s, the United Fruit Company, then the world's largest importers of bananas to the United States, had some powerful friends in Washington, D.C. Allen Dulles, appointed by President Eisenhower to head the CIA in 1953, had ties with the United Fruit Company dating back to 1933 when the United Fruit Company hired Sullivan & Cromwell, the prestigious Wall Street firm in New York where Dulles was a lawyer at the time. After being retained as legal counsel, Dulles bought a large block of United Fruit stock.[455] On retainer for the United Fruit Company was Thomas G. Corcoran, the prominent New Deal attorney known as "Tommy the Cork" Corcoran. He was Harvard trained, a clerk for Supreme Court Justice Oliver Wendell Holmes, and a confidante of President Franklin D. Roosevelt. Since the 1940s, the company had also retained Edward L. Bernays, the genius consultant credited for inventing public relations as a profession, whose 1928 book, *Propaganda,* was openly admired by Nazi Minister of Propaganda Joseph Goebbels.[456]

The problem began in March 1951 when Jacobo Arbenz, a professional army officer who was the son of a Swiss pharmacist who migrated to Guatemala, took over the leadership of that country after a successful military coup. CIA operative E. Howard Hunt described Arbenz as "a man of modest intellect" who "had married the daughter of a prominent San Salvador family, and she, a doctrinaire Communist, had guided his career from army ranks to the presidency of Guatemala."[457] Arbenz's great sin was to initiate land reform, expropriating 225,000 acres of property from the United Fruit Company, then Guatemala's largest employer. The company's workers formed a union and demanded $2.50 a day for each worker, up from $1.36, cutting into the firm's profits. As was typical in Central America at that time, some 3 percent of the landholders held some 70 percent of the land in Guatemala. By 1954, the CIA in Washington became concerned Communists in Guatemala were organizing behind Arbenz, a concern that intensified when intelligence reports suggested the U.S.S.R. had begun covertly supplying the Arbenz regime with arms. Arbenz permitted the existence of a small Communist party in Guatemala, though he had no avid Communists at any top positions in his government. Ultimately, Arbenz nationalized over 1.5 million acres, including some of his family land, to turn over to the nation's peasants. Much of that land belonged to the United Fruit Company.

Finally, President Eisenhower and Vice President Richard Nixon ordered the National Security Council to overthrow the Arbenz regime in Guatemala. The CIA offered the assignment to E. Howard Hunt. "I was told that this was currently the most important clandestine project in the world," Hunt wrote "And that if I accepted the position, I would be the head of the project's propaganda and political action staff." After Hunt accepted the assignment, President Eisenhower called a meeting in the Oval Office to introduce Hunt to Edward Bernays, the public relations consultant retained by United Fruit to promote the company.

To advance the interests of United Fruit in the United States, Bernays had already recruited a group of well-known journalists and editors from prominent US publications to spend two weeks in Guatemala, in January 1952, as guests of the company so "they could report to the American people what they saw."[458] Bernays was jubilant when stories began appearing in Scripps-Howard newspapers reporting of efforts in Guatemala "to engender hatred of Yankee monopoly capitalism and imperialism."[459] Between early 1952 and the spring of 1954, Bernays had organized at least five two-week "fact-finding" junkets to Guatemala, with as many as ten news reporters on each trip. The trips took months to plan and were carefully timed and executed. The United Fruit Company spared no expense, claimed Thomas McCann, the former company official who worked with Bernays to organize the trips. Speaking candidly, McCann concluded the trips represented "a serious attempt to compromise objectivity" of the press.[460]

In discussing his plans for Guatemala, Hunt was particularly open that he was authorized to use covert methods to combat the spread of Communist influence in the Western Hemisphere. Hunt acknowledged that the United Fruit Company was known by locals as "El Pulpo," or "The Octopus," because the company "owned hundreds of miles of Guatemalan territory, while its tentacles bought up controlling interests in the railroad, electric power, communications, passenger and freight lines, and the administration of the nation's only port." Hunt openly stated that the company, the largest employer in Guatemala with some forty thousand employees, had gained its power "through the support of the corrupt former president, Jorge Ubico, who had given United Fruit most of the land, allowing them to pay almost no taxes on it."[461]

To provide the Eisenhower administration the required "plausible deniability," Hunt determined that within the CIA the Guatemalan operation would be conducted on a need-to-know basis. A cover program was set up under the code name PB/Success. Hunt's unit had its own funds, communications center, and chain of command within the CIA's Western Hemisphere Division. Hunt was issued forged documentation from the CIA's Central Cover Division, and he set up field headquarters in a two-story barracks at a former US Navy training camp at the Opa-Loca Airport in a suburb of Miami. "PB/Success did have a precedent that we planned to duplicate," Hunt wrote, describing the mission. "In August 1953, Operation Ajex had successfully deposed the Iranian premier Mohammed Mossadeqa in a bloodless coup after carefully preparing the minds of the target government and the population for such an event."[462] Hunt's job was to pull off the tactical, covert military part of the coup d'état the Eisenhower administration was planning to accomplish in Guatemala; Bernays was to handle the mind orientation. After all, the core idea of public relations as defined by Bernays rested with the techniques needed to help make up the public's mind—or, in today's terminology, to set and control the event's "narrative."

THE CIA-ENGINEERED GUATEMALAN COUP D'ÉTAT

In Honduras, Hunt and the CIA trained a small band of mercenaries under Colonel Carlos Castillo Armas, a Guatemalan military officer who had escaped from prison after an unsuccessful coup against Arbenz in November 1950, as Arbenz was assuming power. On June 17, 1954, Armas and his band of mercenaries crossed the Honduran border into Guatemala. For several days, Hunt and the CIA organized American jets and American pilots to strafe and bombard Guatemala City, the capital of Guatemala. The point of air attack was psychological. Hunt, in a videotaped recollection of the Guatemalan operation said, "Propaganda takes the place of armed combat—blood-letting—you just don't have to do it." The CIA-financed "rebel army" mercenaries numbered fewer than two hundred armed men, a "shadow army" at best. Yet, the CIA propaganda campaign was designed to make the Guatemalan people and government believe supporting Arbenz was hopeless. A CIA-funded and operated clandestine radio program recorded by the CIA in Miami and broadcast in neighboring countries pretended to be the "Voice of Liberation," broadcasting from within Guatemala, spreading false reports about legions of rebel soldiers who never existed defeating government troops in fierce battles that never happened.[463]

The truth is that Carlos Castillo Armas did not lead a popular uprising against a Communist regime, he lead a mercenary army financed and trained by the CIA in a CIA-engineered coup d'état. Behind the scenes were John Foster Dulles, secretary of state under President Eisenhower, and his brother Allen Dulles, who headed the CIA. The propaganda campaign designed by Hunt and Bernays was designed to make Arbenz and his government appear to be an "instrument of Moscow" and "a pawn in the Communist propaganda campaign" and a "spearhead of the Soviet Union," as the Arbenz government complained to the United Nations. In an emergency session of the Security Council held at the request of Guatemala, only the Soviet Union supported Guatemala. Henry Cabot Lodge, the US ambassador to the United Nations, in a very publicized statement warned that "the Soviet Union has got designs on the American Hemisphere." Lodge lectured the Soviet Union's ambassador in the Security Council to "stay out of this hemisphere and don't try to start your plans and your conspiracies over here." The Lodge family, including Henry Cabot Lodge, had investments in the United Fruit Company.

On June 25, 1954, Arbenz resigned and went into exile in the Mexican embassy. On July 3, 1954, Carlos Castillo Armas returned to Guatemala City aboard a US embassy airplane. He received a hero's welcome, all orchestrated by the CIA. One hundred thousand cheering Guatemalans gathered at the palace balcony to usher him into power. On July 8, 1954, a Guatemalan military junta elected Carlos Castillo Armas to power; in August 1954, Armas suspended all civil liberties. Within a week of taking power, the Armas government arrested four thousand people accused of participating in communist activity; within four months, some seventy-two thousand Guatemalans were registered as Communists.[464] Armas proceeded to reverse the reforms put into place by Arbenz. Land appropriated in nationalization efforts was taken away from the peasants and returned to the United Fruit Company. Former CIA director General Walter Bedell Smith, who had served in World War II as Eisenhower's chief of staff in the Tunisia Campaign and during the invasion of Italy, became a director of the United Fruit Company. Predictably, Hunt was proud of his achievement.[465] "For the first time since the Spanish Civil War a Communist government had been overthrown—and in 'Good Neighbor' Central America, at that," Hunt wrote.[466]

GUATEMALA 1957: THE ASSASSINATION AND THE PATSY

Within three years, the United States soured on Armas. On July 26, 1957, President Armas was assassinated at around 9:00 p.m., as he and his wife prepared to enter the dining room of the Presidential Palace. Two bullets were fired, one of which severed his aorta and killed him instantly. The assassin, identified as twenty-year-old Romeo Vasquez Sanchez, was said to have committed suicide immediately, using the same rifle he had used to kill Armas. The Guatemalan government identified Romeo Vasquez Sanchez as a disgruntled soldier dismissed from the military in June 1955 because of his "Communist ideology." Yet, somehow, Romeo Vasquez Sanchez managed to rehabilitate himself sufficiently to have been a member of the Presidential Palace Guard when he committed the assassination.

The Guatemalan Army claimed to have a forty-page handwritten diary in which the assassin referred to "a diabolical plan to put an end to the existence of the man who holds power." The diary reportedly read: "I have had the opportunity to study Russian Communism. The great nation that is Russia is fulfilling a most important mission in history . . . the Soviet Union is the first world power in progress and scientific research."[467] The Guatemalan government claimed to have evidence that linked Romeo Vasquez Sanchez to Moscow. The evidence produced was a card from the Latin American service of Radio Moscow that read: "It is our pleasure, dear listener, to engage in correspondence with you. We are very thankful for your regular listening to our programs."[468] No evidence was ever produced to prove Romeo Vasquez Sanchez was ever a member of the Guatemalan Communist Party.

The parallels between Romeo Vasquez Sanchez and Lee Harvey Oswald are obvious. Both were ex-military who left the service expressing distinct sympathies for Communist Russia. Waldron and Hartmann point out that Oswald was "a seemingly Communist ex-Marine who was able to get a job at a sensitive firm—a Dallas company that helped prepare maps from U-2 spy plane photos—even after he returned from his 'defection' to the Soviet Union." Waldron and Hartman note that in comparison, the Guatemala patsy was described by the Guatemalan government as a Communist fanatic who was expelled from the Guatemalan army only six months before he assassinated Armas, yet somehow Romeo Vasquez Sanchez had still been allowed to join the Presidential Palace Guard. How was that possible? Surely the Presidential Palace Guard would have been a sufficiently elite military unit to require a background check before they were hired. Waldron and Hartman further note that both men were ex-military who killed a president with a rifle. There were both described as Communist nuts who conveniently left behind diaries rambling in Communist propaganda.

There is no photographic evidence proving either Romeo Vasquez Sanchez or Lee Harvey Oswald were the assassins who pulled the trigger. There were no eyewitnesses in either case and both men have gaps and questions in their alibi timelines. For Oswald, what exactly was the route and travel time he used to go between the Texas School Book Depository where he was observed after the shooting and the Texas movie theater where he was apprehended? For Romeo Vasquez Sanchez, exactly how long did he wait after shooting the president before he killed himself? Why wait? What happened in the time between the assassination and the suicide? Neither made any confession of their crimes. Both died before there could be a criminal investigation or trial.[469]

Both the Armas assassination and the JFK assassination were considered open and shut cases, where responsible government and law enforcement authorities declared the guilt of Romeo Vasquez Sanchez and Lee Harvey Oswald was obvious, such that doubters could be dismissed as "conspiracy theorists." Both assassins were dead and buried a short time after the assassinations, avoiding a prolonged time for grief or for unanswered questions to surface. In neither case has any written record been released of any government interrogation—not in Oswald's case of the interrogation by Dallas Police, FBI, and/or Secret Service after his arrest—nor in Romeo Vasquez Sanchez's case of interrogation records prior to his being released from the military because of suspicions he was a Communist. In both cases, Romeo Vasquez Sanchez and Lee Harvey Oswald made perfect patsies because authorities openly proclaimed their guilt before trial and their deaths made sure neither would have the opportunity of a trial to counter the accusations leveled against them.

The fact that Armas was assassinated just four days after trying to close a casino owned by an associate of US mob figure Johnny Roselli, at a time when Roselli and Carlos Marcello, the "godfather" from New Orleans, were expanding their presence in Guatemala, received little coverage by the international press. With a view toward the mob's role in the JFK assassination, Lamar Waldron and Thom Hartman commented that both Marcello and Roselli would remember from the 1957 assassination of a president in Guatemala the importance of having a patsy to quickly take the blame and divert investigators.[470]

CARLOS MARCELLO: THE GODFATHER TALKS

In 1984, when serving a prison sentence at the maximum-security federal prison in Texarkana, Texas, mob boss Carlos Marcello from New Orleans was the subject of an undercover FBI sting operation code-named CAMTEX, for "Carlos Marcello, Texas." The sting involved a then-fifty-six-year-old prisoner named Jack Van Laningham. He was from Tampa and was serving an eight-year sentence in Texarkana for bank robbery. In March 1985, Van Laningham managed to befriend Marcello, and after being moved to share a cell with Marcello, Van Laningham agreed to work cooperatively in an FBI undercover operation directed by FBI agent Thomas Kimmel with the goal of recording Marcello to find out how he controlled his criminal organization from prison. CAMTEX evolved beyond taping the Texarkana phones to placing a bug in a transistor radio for Van Laningham to place in the private prison cell he shared with Marcello. In the course of their conversations, Marcello confessed to Van Laningham the role he played in the JFK assassination.[471]

Marcello explained to Van Laningham that his hatred of the Kennedy family traced back to the early 1960s, when then-Attorney General Robert Kennedy had Marcello deported to Guatemala where Marcello was dropped and left to his own devices to survive. Marcello, born in Tunisia, North Africa, had obtained false documentation claiming he had been born in Guatemala. In an arduous journey, aided by pilot David Ferrie, Marcello managed to make his way back to the United States through Florida. Ferrie, a shady character in his own right, traced back to Oswald because the two were photographed together at the New Orleans Civil Air Patrol in 1955, where Ferrie was a leader and Oswald a teenager. One of the first revelations Marcello made to Van Laningham was that David Ferrie had introduced him to Lee Harvey Oswald in New Orleans. Oswald and Marcello met at various locations in several subsequent meetings before Oswald left New Orleans for Dallas. Marcello also claimed to have set Jack Ruby up in the bar business in Dallas. Van Laningham told the FBI that Marcello knew Jack Ruby was a homosexual and understood Ruby was paying off the corrupt police in Dallas. Marcello claimed Ruby came to visit him in New Orleans regularly in order to report on what was happening in Dallas.[472]

In the course of their discussions, Marcello confessed to his involvement in the JFK assassination: "Yeah, I had the little son of a bitch killed, and I would do it again," Marcello said, referring to JFK. "He was a thorn in my side. I wish I could have done it myself."[473] Waldron and Hartmann noted that two former FBI agents who worked on the CAMTEX operation, including the supervisor of the operation, Thomas A. Kimmel, confirmed Van Laningham's credibility to them. A federal judge found

Van Laningham's reliability sufficiently credible to authorize extraordinary surveillance of Marcello while he was in prison, including putting an FBI bug in a transistor radio Van Laningham bought in prison to share with Marcello.[474] Regarding Marcello's comment that Jack Ruby was gay, Waldron and Hartmann note that information saying Ruby was homosexual or bisexual appears more than forty times in Warren Commission documents and Ruby's roommate at the time of the JFK assassination described Ruby as "my boyfriend."[475]

John H. Davis documented ties Ruby and Oswald both had to Marcello prior to the JFK assassination, in his 1989 book, *Mafia Kingfish: Carlos Marcello and the Assassination of John F. Kennedy.* In the summer of 1963, Oswald worked in Marcello's downtown bookmaking network as a runner, while his cousin Dutz Murret worked as a longtime bookie, working out of the Felix Oyster House, a mob-owned restaurant in the French Quarter of New Orleans.[476] Davis also reported that the New Orleans attorney who performed occasional legal services for both Marcello and Oswald in New Orleans during the summer of 1963 was certain Marcello was paying Oswald to hand out pro-Castro literature for the Fair Play for Cuba Committee on the streets of New Orleans. Davis questioned whether three months before the JFK assassination if Oswald was being unwittingly manipulated by the Marcello organization to play the role of the patsy in the plot to assassinate the president.[477]

Davis tied Jack Ruby to Joe Civello, one of the fifty-nine Mafia leaders arrested at the famous Appalachian meeting where he was representing Marcello. Davis reported Ruby was a frequent visitor of Civello and his partner Frank LaMonte at their Italian import business in Dallas—a business whose real purpose Davis suspected was importing narcotics.[478] These ties were confirmed in the final report of the House Select Committee on Assassinations. "The committee also established associations between Jack Ruby and several individuals affiliated with the underworld activities of Carlos Marcello," the House Select Committee concluded. "Ruby was a personal acquaintance of Joseph Civello, the Marcello associate who allegedly headed organized crime activities in Dallas."[479] Davis further reported the FBI deliberately suppressed evidence of the relationship between Ruby and Civello from the Warren Commission.[480]

SAM GIANCANA TALKS

In the 1992 book, *Double Cross: The Story of the Man Who Controlled America*, Chicago gangster Sam "Mooney" Giancana confessed to his younger brother, Chuck Giancana, the deepest secrets of how he had gained mob power.[481] As part of the confession, Sam Giancana revealed his role in the JFK assassination. "The hit in Dallas was just like any other operation we'd worked on in the past," Sam Giancana explained to his younger brother, "we'd overthrown other governments in other countries plenty of times before. This time, we just did it in our own background." Giancana went on to make sure the parallel between Guatemala and Dallas was clear. "On November 22, 1963, the United States had a coup. The government of this country was overthrown by a handful of guys who did their job so damned well . . . not one American even knew it happened."[482]

Giancana claimed Jack Ruby was a mobster with roots back to Chicago where Ruby was born Jack Rubenstein. He further claimed Ruby had demonstrated extreme loyalty and his ability to work with the CIA during the planning for the Bay of Pigs invasion. Giancana also insisted Lee Harvey Oswald was associated with the Marcello mob in New Orleans from the time he was born, given that Oswald's uncle was a Marcello lieutenant who worked as a bookie and "exerted a powerful influence over the fatherless boy."[483] Giancana claimed Oswald's alliance with the US intelligence community began when he was "an impressionable young man during a stint in the Civil Air Patrol with homosexual CIA operative and Outfit (i.e., mob) smuggling pilot David Ferrie—a bizarre, hairless eccentric"[484] who Marcello used to fly guns and drugs in and out of Central America. Giancana asserted Oswald had been a spy for the US government in the Soviet Union, and that he had been trained to speak fluent Russian. Giancana scoffed at the idea that Oswald was a Communist sympathizer, characterizing as misinformation the Warren Commission's argument Lee Harvey Oswald was a Fidel Castro supporter. "Lee Harvey Oswald was a right-wing supporter of the 'Kill Castro, Bay of Pigs Camp' . . . CIA all the way," Giancana said without hesitation.

He explained the mob ordered Ruby to silence Oswald. Ruby did the job, knowing it was better to be executed in the electric chair for having committed murder than suffering a death being tortured by the mob for failing to carry out an order. Giancana explained that when his superiors had ordered Oswald to Dallas, Oswald linked up with Giancana's representative in Dallas, Jack Ruby, at Ruby's Carousel Club, where Oswald also reestablished contact with David Ferrie. Giancana claimed that Russian exile George de Mohrenschildt was a CIA operative who helped him make a lot of money by introducing him to Texas oilmen, including Syd Richardson, H. L. Hunt, Clint Murchison, and Mike Davis. He claimed money raised for the JFK assassination came "from wealthy right-wing Texas oilmen."[485] He also claimed he sent his mob associate Johnny Roselli to New Orleans to check out Lee Harvey Oswald as a prospect to play the patsy in the JFK murder.

In New Orleans, Roselli met with Guy Bannister, a former Chicago FBI agent with intelligence community ties, at 544 Camp Street—the address of Bannister's office that was also found stamped on pro-Castro leaflets Oswald handed out on the streets of Dallas. Roselli also traveled to Dallas on Giancana's orders, coordinating with Ruby in preparation for the assassination. Giancana claimed it was early spring 1963 when he and his CIA associates made the decision to finalize plans for the elimination of the president. Oswald was the natural choice to play the role of fall guy, Giancana claimed: "They'd already laid the groundwork to make him look like a Commie nut, by goin' to Russia and with all that pro-Castro shit. He was perfect . . . he acted like a Commie . . . he smelled like a Commie . . . so they figured it would be no problem to convince people he was a Commie."[486]

Giancana claimed that the original plan to eliminate Oswald involved having Officer Tippit and Roscoe White kill Oswald in what would have been portrayed as an attempt to apprehend the escaping assassin. At that time, Tippit was a veteran on the Dallas Police Department, while Roscoe White was listed in Dallas Police Department records as being a police recruit in November 1963.[487] Under the guise of self-defense and in the line of duty, Tippit and White were expected to murder the "lone gunman." According to Giancana the plan went awry when Tippet lost his nerve. Then it fell to Roscoe White to kill Tippit, not just because Tippit failed to carry out his part in the plan, but also because Tippit knew too much about the conspiracy. When the plan to kill Oswald failed, the assignment went to Jack Ruby. Giancana claimed Tippit not killing

Oswald was "the only screwup" in the entire plan to assassinate JFK.[488]

Interestingly, Lee Harvey Oswald and Roscoe White had crossed paths before. They were both stationed at the Marine Corps Air Station in El Toro, California, in 1957.[489] That same year, they both sailed to Japan on the USS *Bexar*, and they served in Japan at the same time.[490] Oswald was sent to the Atsugi Naval Air Station, while White was sent to Tachikowa Air Base and then was flown to Okinawa. Even though Lee Harvey Oswald and Roscoe White crossed paths in the marines, there is no evidence they knew each other at the time.

Roselli, like Giancana, came up in the mob as a hit man for Al Capone in Chicago. When Giancana advanced to head the Capone mob, Roselli became his "eyes and ears" in Las Vegas and Los Angeles. Going back to the Eisenhower administration, Roselli had been the primary mob contact in the CIA plot to assassinate Fidel Castro, a plot that continued through the Kennedy administration. As part of this plot, Roselli had involved both Giancana in Chicago and Santo Trafficante in Tampa Bay. The plot to assassinate Castro was directed within the CIA by James Jesus Angleton's Executive Action program that was headed by William Harvey, and implemented through the Italian Mafia under Chicago mob boss Sam "Mooney" Giancana. Robert Maheu, the second-in-command under Howard Hughes, introduced Roselli to Harvey. Maheu had been second-in-command to Guy Bannister when Bannister was an FBI agent in Chicago.[491]

Roselli was born Fillippo Sacco in Esperia, Italy, on July 4, 1905. When he immigrated to the United States with his mother in 1911, they settled in Somerville, Massachusetts. When he fled to Chicago in 1922, after committing his first mob murder, he changed his last name to Roselli, in honor of the Italian Renaissance sculptor Cosimo Roselli, and to avoid any possible association with the anarchist Ferdinando Sacco who became infamous in the Sacco and Vanzetti robbery and murder case in South Braintree, Massachusetts, that was dominating news headlines in the 1920s. Known as "Handsome Johnny," Roselli joined the Capone mob, only to be ordered to relocate in Los Angeles in 1925, after skipping bail in a federal narcotics case. Once established in Los Angeles, Roselli spearheaded the mob entrance into the movie industry, welcoming Joseph P. Kennedy, the patriarch of the Kennedy clan, to Hollywood in 1926. In the early 1950s, Roselli helped the eastern mob to establish a foothold in the emerging gambling industry in Las Vegas. In the 1960s, after Castro closed the casinos in Havana run by mobster Meyer Lansky, Robert Maheu, a CIA operative who had served as a top aide and CEO of the Nevada operations for billionaire Howard Hughes, recruited Roselli to find mob assassins to participate in a planned CIA assassination of Fidel Castro. In carrying out this assignment Roselli was responsible for introducing Maheu to Sam Giancana in Chicago and to Santo Trafficante in Tampa.

Roselli went so far back with the Kennedy family that he had intervened at the request of Joseph P. Kennedy to cover-up a marriage that a youthful John F. Kennedy had entered into unwisely. At the request of JFK's father and the instructions of Sam Giancana, Roselli had completely wiped all legal documents from the public record that attested to the matrimony. The clean slate placed JFK back on his father's political agenda, planning for JFK to be elected president.[492] This was not the only time JFK was compromised over a sexual matter. In 1975 the Senate Select Committee to Study Government Operations with Respect to Intelligence Activities, better known as the Church Committee, named after chair Sen. Frank Church, a Democrat from Idaho, uncovered the fact that JFK, Sam Giancana, and Johnny Roselli all shared an extra-marital affair with the same woman: Judith Campbell, who Frank Sinatra introduced to JFK in Las Vegas on February 7, 1960, at the Sands Hotel. The FBI and Secret Service both tracked and documented JFK's affair.

On March 22, 1962, in a private lunch at the White House, J. Edgar Hoover made clear to the President that the FBI was aware of the affair he was having with Campbell, stressing the FBI had also documented Kennedy was sharing his mistress with Sam Giancana. Journalist David Talbot, in his 2007 book, *Brothers: The Hidden History of the Kennedy Years*, revealed that Robert Kennedy was also aware of the affair after one of his investigators tracking racketeers' phone calls came across the relationship. Talbot speculated that sending Hoover over to the White House may have been Robert Kennedy's way "of drilling into his sexually daring brother the urgency of stopping his liaison before it became a presidency-threatening scandal."[493] In a less generous manner, investigative reporter Seymour M. Hersh in his 1997 book, *The Dark Side of Camelot*, noted JFK's relationship with Judith Campbell "exposed the president to blackmail by the mob and friends of the mob."[494]

On June 19, 1975, five days before he was scheduled to testify to the Church Committee, Sam Giancana was murdered in his home in Oak Park, Illinois, just outside Chicago. Around midnight, he was shot once in the back of his head, once in the mouth, and five times under his chin, in a mob-style killing that suggested he was about to break the mob code of *omertá*, requiring silence on all mob related matters.

Since Roselli let Joseph P. Kennedy into the club by ushering Kennedy into Hollywood in the 1920s, it was Roselli who would have to take care of the problem, once the mob decided JFK had to go. When Joseph P. Kennedy experienced a disabling stroke on December 19, 1961, at the age of seventy-three, John F. Kennedy and his brother, Robert lost a major protector. After years of professing his innocence, Roselli finally confessed to his lawyer his involvement in the JFK assassination. Roselli claimed he knew a gunman shooting from the grassy knoll fired the first shot that hit JFK. This first shot supposedly went through the windshield of JFK's limousine and hit him in the throat. Roselli claimed the second and third shots came from gunman Charles Nicoletti, a Giancana hit man, who was shooting from the third floor of the Dal-Tex building behind JFK. Roselli claimed the second shot hit JFK in the back and the third shot hit Connally. Finally, according to Roselli, the fourth shot fired and the second shot from the grassy knoll was the fatal headshot that killed JFK.

On July 9, 1976, Johnny Roselli's legless body was found stuffed in a fifty-five-gallon oil drum, floating in Dumfoundling Bay near Miami, Florida. Roselli had completed two rounds of testimony before the House Select Committee on Assassinations. His murder prevented him from being called a third time to testify about the JFK assassination.

On March 29, 1977, Charles Nicoletti was murdered gangland style, with three .38 slugs pumped into the back of his head while he was sitting in his Oldsmobile in the parking lot of the Golden Horns Restaurant in Northlake, Illinois, another suburb of Chicago.

On the same day Nicoletti was murdered, George de Mohrenschildt supposedly committed suicide. At the time of their deaths, de Mohrenschildt, Roselli, and Nicoletti were all scheduled to testify before the House Select Committee on Assassinations, while Giancana was scheduled to testify before the Church Committee when he was killed. The murders of Sam Giancana, Johnny Roselli, and Charles Nicoletti remain even today unsolved open cases.

TRAFFICANTE AND HOFFA IMPLICATED

Mob lawyer Frank Ragano, years after the deaths of two of his clients—Jimmy Hoffa and Santo Trafficante—wrote a book, *Mob Lawyer*, in which he disclosed some remarkable information about the JFK assassination. At a lunch on July 23, 1963, Hoffa told Ragano, "something has to be done. . . . The time has come to kill John F. Kennedy." Hoffa knew Ragano was flying that day to New Orleans to meet Carlos Marcello and Santo Trafficante, and he wanted Ragano to deliver the message. At breakfast the next morning, Ragano explained to Marcello and Trafficante that Hoffa had a favor he wanted the two mob bosses to do. "You won't believe this, but [Hoffa] wants you to kill John Kennedy." Ragano reported their initial reaction was so icy he felt he had intruded into a minefield he had no right to enter.[495] On the Monday following the assassination, Ragano was in Jimmy Hoffa's office in Washington, D.C. As the meeting broke up, Hoffa pulled Ragano to one side. "I told you they would do it," he said, referring to Marcello and Trafficante killing JFK. "I'll never forget what Carlos and Santo did for me."[496]

In 1987 when Trafficante, then seventy-three years old, was on his death bed, he decided to confess to Ragano that he and Marcello had been involved in the JFK assassination. "We shouldn't have killed Giovanni [i.e. John Kennedy]," Trafficante explained. "We should have killed Bobby."[497] Ragano wrote that with this confession, the facts that had been suppressed for more than two decades could no longer be ignored. "Carlos [Marcello], Santo [Trafficante], and Jimmy [Hoffa] undoubtedly had roles in Kennedy's death," Ragano concluded. "They had planned to murder him and they used me as an unwitting accomplice in their scheme."[498] Ragano reasoned that Trafficante confessed to him because of "his perverse pride." Trafficante wanted the world to know "that he and his mob partners had eliminated a president, outwitted the government's top law-enforcement agencies, and escaped punishment."[499] Ragano concluded Marcello and Trafficante were uniquely capable of arranging the murder of a president. "Their minds performed unscrupulous and daring gymnastics that could befuddle and outmaneuver the best police and intelligence agents in the country," he wrote.[500]

The House Select Committee on Assassinations was critical of the Warren Commission for not investigating more thoroughly the role of organized crime in the JFK assassination. While the House Select Committee did not find evidence of a broad-based conspiracy, it did find "that the quality and scope of the investigation into the possibility of an organized crime conspiracy in the President's assassination by the Warren Commission and the FBI was not sufficient to uncover one had it existed." The committee's extensive investigation led it to conclude that "based on an analysis of motive, means and opportunity, that an individual organized crime leader, or a small combination of leaders, might have participated in a conspiracy to assassinate President Kennedy." Specifically, the committee found "the most likely family bosses of organized crime to have participated in such a unilateral assassination plan were Carlos Marcelo and Santo Trafficante."[501] They had the motive, means, and opportunity to have JFK assassinated, though it was impossible to develop conclusive evidence that would prove their guilt. The House Select Committee also discussed various threats that Hoffa had made regarding both John and Robert Kennedy and that JFK had been made aware of the threats. In direct contrast with the Warren Commission, the House Select Committee concluded Lee Harvey Oswald, much like Jack Ruby, had contact with organized crime, specifically with Marcello and Trafficante.

G. Robert Blakey, the Notre Dame law professor who served as the chief counsel and staff director for the House Select Committee on Assassinations concluded "that organized crime had a hand in the assassination of President Kennedy," Blakey wrote in his 1981 book, *The Plot to Kill the President: Organized Crime Assassinated J.F.K.—The Definitive Story*.[502] With this conclusion, the House Select Committee repudiated the Warren Commission's conclusion that Lee Harvey Oswald, a lone assassin, had killed the president.

THE MCCLELLAN COMMITTEE AND THE WESTERN MOB

The bad blood between the mob and the Kennedy family that led to the JFK assassination traces back to the 1957 McClellan Committee hearings, named after the chairman, Arkansas Democratic Sen. John L. McClellan. The committee was officially constituted as the Select Committee on Improper Activities in the Labor or Management Field. The initial focus of the committee was to investigate organized crime's penetration into the labor union movement, specifically the mob penetration of the Teamsters Union. While the target of the hearings at the start involved corrupt Teamster boss Dave Beck who lived and worked out of Seattle, the hearings are best known for the conflict that developed between Jimmy Hoffa, the infamous Teamster Boss from Detroit who took over the Teamsters after Beck resigned in disgrace, and the committee's chief counsel Robert Kennedy. On the committee was the freshman senator from Massachusetts John F. Kennedy.

Almost totally neglected by historians, the primary moving force behind the McClellan hearings was the committee's first star witness, crime boss James Butler Elkins from Portland, Oregon, better known as J. B. Elkins, or simply, "Big Jim." In 1957 two reporters for the Portland paper the *Oregonian*—William Lambert and Wallace Turner—won a Pulitzer Prize for a series of articles exposing the infiltration of organized crime into the Teamster Union operating in Washington State and Oregon. The source of the Lambert-Turner articles involved hundreds of hours of wiretaps the Elkins family had taken of various gangsters and public officials in Portland and Seattle as they bribed and extorted their way into control of the Teamster's Union in the northwest. The rub came after organized crime gained control of the Teamster's Union in Portland and the gangsters involved moved to take over the Elkins family's lucrative crime empire involving bootlegged liquor and gambling. The Elkins family, rather than concede a portion of their profits and control of the crime syndicate to the eastern mobsters, had decided to fight back, even if fighting back meant exposing themselves to criminal prosecution and the likely loss of their syndicate operations.

In 1956 then-Senator Jack Kennedy lost a bid to be the vice presidential candidate on the second run Adlai E. Stevenson was taking to be the Democratic Party's presidential candidate. In a hotly contested fight in which Stevenson preferred Kennedy to be his vice presidential running mate, the convention chose Senator Estes Kefauver who had come to national prominence as chairman of the Senate Special Committee to

Investigate Crime in Interstate Commerce, better known as the Kefauver Committee, which held a series of nationally televised hearings investigating organized crime. After being forced to concede to Kefauver in 1956, the Kennedy family realized the importance of the media, especially television, in gaining national political prominence. Wanting to duplicate what Kefauver had accomplished, the Kennedy family seized upon the Lambert-Turner articles as evidence new labor racketeering hearings could be held to investigate the Teamsters.

The Kennedy family quickly realized the importance of the exhaustive wiretapping done by the Elkins family. If these tapes had not existed, the Kennedy family might never have gone forward with the McClellan Committee hearings. Democrats depended on union votes to win elections. The Kennedy family could never afford the wrath of organized labor if the evidence of organized crime penetration of the Teamsters was not certain. After a series of discussions with organized labor figures, including those in the then-five railroad operating unions, the conclusion was reached that the union movement would not oppose the public hearings, provided the Kennedy family limited the investigation to the organized criminals who had taken over the Teamsters Union, being careful to distinguish that the target of the investigation was not the union itself. The consent of the railroad unions at the time was critical, given the extent to which the railroad unions cooperated at the time with the Teamsters. Before the interstate highways truck trailers "piggy backed" on railroad train flat cars for transit across the nation, and then they were picked-up by Teamster Union truck cabs for local delivery.

A TALE OF TWO FAMILIES

In the months leading up to the hearings, the Kennedy family realized the mob takeover of the Teamster Union involved a move by the eastern mobs to muscle into the territory of the western mobs. In the 1950s the eastern mobs were largely Catholic and Jewish, controlled back to the 1930s by Al Capone in Chicago, Lucky Luciano in New York, and Meyer Lansky in Florida and Cuba. The western mobs were largely Protestant, as evidenced by the Elkins family. At stake was not only the Elkins family crime empire in the Pacific Northwest, but the future development of what was expected to be a highly lucrative gambling industry, originally developed in Reno and Las Vegas by the Elkins mob. Joseph Kennedy, a mobster who had controlled the importation of Scotch liquor into the United States going back to the days before Prohibition, had never comfortably been accepted by the eastern mobs even though he was Catholic. Rejected largely because he was of Irish descent, not Italian, Joseph Kennedy encouraged his sons to develop a partnership with the Elkins family to launch the McClellan hearings as a springboard to advance JFK's presidential ambitions.

The strategy worked. J. B. Elkins began his testimony to the McClellan Committee on the opening day of the hearings, February 26, 1957. The issue of *Life* magazine dated March 11, 1957, carried a full-page color photograph of JFK on the cover with the headline, "Where Democrats Should Go From Here." The same issue featured a news article on the McClellan hearings entitled "Senators Hear Tales of Scandal." The article featured a full-page black-and-white photograph of J. B. Elkins. "James Elkins, 56, had been a racketeer in Portland, operating mainly gambling and bootlegging joints," the article read. "At first he had welcomed the help offered by the Teamsters' agents when they appeared on his home grounds. Then, outraged by their self-aggrandizing tactics and prodded by the *Oregonian*, he squealed. Before the Senate committee he was by far the most articulate member of the cast of witnesses."[503]

In Robert Kennedy's 1960 bestselling book on the McClellan Committee, *The Enemy Within*, he described racketeer J. B. Elkins as "a slim, rugged-looking man with a rather kindly face and a very attractive and devoted wife."[504] Kennedy said Elkins was "one of the most interesting and controversial witnesses that appeared before the McClellan Committee, noting that Elkins was very guarded in what he said and to whom he said it. Kennedy admitted Elkins was reluctant to talk the first time they met, but in subsequent meetings, Elkins talked freely. "Once he made up his mind that he was going to co-operate, he went the whole way," Kennedy wrote. What Robert Kennedy did not detail in the book was that getting J. B. Elkins required a series of meetings held near Phoenix, Arizona, between Robert, JFK, J. B. Elkins, and one other trusted member of the Elkins family. In those discussions, J. B. Elkins warned the Kennedys that going after the Teamsters might cost them their lives. Despite the risk, all four committed to working together to expose the organized criminals who had penetrated the Teamsters Union. Once the agreement had been reached, the Elkins family turned over to the Kennedy family the entire collection of wiretap recordings that incriminated the mobsters posing as Teamsters.

Elkins assisted Robert Kennedy in running a complete background check, disclosing to the Kennedy family details that had not before been shared with anyone outside the family. "I learned that [Elkins] had manufactured illicit whiskey during prohibition, been given a twenty-to-thirty-year sentence for assault with intent to kill, a one-year sentence for possession of narcotics, and had been arrested several times on gambling charges," Robert Kennedy wrote. To get out of prison, the Elkins family paid a substantial fifty-thousand-dollar bribe to Arizona's first governor, George W. P. Hunt. Robert Kennedy also documented that Elkins had worked with military intelligence during World War II, although the nature of that work was never fully disclosed. In *The Enemy Within*, Robert Kennedy gave Elkins one of the most positive endorsements he ever gave regarding testimony before the McClellan Committee:

> Nevertheless, Jim Elkins was one of the three or four best witnesses the Committee ever had. Because his background was so unsavory, we checked his story up and down, backward and forward, inside out. We found he didn't lie, and that he didn't exaggerate.
>
> Occasionally, at the beginning, he would not answer a question. He would ask me to go on to something else. Later, as we came to know each other better, he would answer the question but tell me not to use the information. And sometimes when I pressed him for an answer, he would say, "You don't want to know the answer to that."
>
> He was bright. He had a native intelligence. He was highly suspicious—and a fund of information. He never once misled me. He never once tried.[505]

Robert Kennedy further disclosed that he spent more time with J. B. Elkins than he did with any other witness, both because of the tremendous amount of information he had and because of the difficulty he feared the Committee would have in understanding him. Kennedy wrote that he "needed to know the story almost as well as [Elkins] did, so that I could clarify some of his complicated answers.[506]

What Robert Kennedy did not disclose was that the relationship had been so close that Elkins and the family associate that accompanied him to Washington stayed in Robert Kennedy's home in McLean, Virginia. This was confirmed by a note found in 1986 in the correspondence collection of the JFK Library at Columbia Point in Boston. On December 17, 1957, Elkins posted a Christmas card to Robert Kennedy and his family, addressed to the Kennedy offices in the Senate Office Building. A personal handwritten note written by Colleen Elkins, J. B.'s wife, addressed to Robert and Ethel Kennedy and family, commented that Colleen and J. B. had watched the Edward R. Morrow television show *Person to Person*. "We watched Edward R. Murrow's program the night he was at your home," Coleen wrote. "We certainly enjoyed it. Jim said it reminded him of 'Old Home Week.' The children were just as cute as could be and the baby had grown so we hardly knew her."[507]

The importance of Elkins to the McClellan Committee cannot be overemphasized. "It was Elkins' passion for detail that made him the star witness before Sen. John L. McClellan's Select Committee investigating labor racketeering," *Newsweek* commented, crediting Elkins with a phenomenal memory. "The mother lode of evidence Elkins turned up made it possible for committee counsel Bobby Kennedy to crack the Teamster case wide open. Without Elkins, there might have been no indictment of Teamster vice president Jimmy Hoffa. Without Elkins, the Teamsters' powerful president Dave Beck would not be defending himself on the witness stand this week."[508]

Communication between the Elkins family and the Kennedy family continued as long as John and Bobby were alive. The Elkins family continued to advise Attorney General Robert Kennedy in his war on organized crime, a war the Elkins family interpreted as having been ordered by the Kennedy family patriarch, Joseph Kennedy, to even the score and get revenge for perceived slights the Kennedy family had suffered at the hands of the eastern mob going back decades. The Kennedy war on organized crime particularly rankled the eastern mob, given the effort the Giancana family and Chicago mayor Richard Daley went to in order to deliver, both legally and illegally, the critical votes in Cook County that JFK needed to win the 1960 presidential campaign. The eastern mob felt betrayed that the Kennedy family did not have more respect and appreciation for the mob efforts taken to make sure JFK became president. The Elkins family joined the Kennedy family in the grudge match between Robert Kennedy and Jimmy Hoffa. Truthfully, Robert Kennedy and Jimmy Hoffa hated each other in part because they were both so very much alike—small men with an irrepressible determination to prove how tough they were. Pulitzer Prize–winning journalist Clark Mollenhoff reported that at the arraignment of Jimmy Hoffa for having McClellan Committee papers in his possession, Robert Kennedy and Jimmy Hoffa got into a friendly debate, arguing with each other who could do the most push-ups, although neither actually did any.[509]

In 1963 the Elkins family warned the Kennedy brothers that a mob hit had been called on JFK. Elkins explained to JFK the details of the hit, that it was planned to be done from a tall building by a shooter armed with a high-powered rifle with a scope with the intent to shoot JFK in a motorcade. The top Elkins family consigliere flew to Portland, Oregon, in 1968 to warn Robert Kennedy an assassination attempt had been planned on him in Los Angeles during the California presidential primary. RFK was warned that when the shooting started a small-caliber handgun discharged from the rear would be used to kill him. RFK was advised the assassin being a person who was supposedly there to protect Robert Kennedy. The Elkins family consigliere urged Robert Kennedy to postpone his planned return to Los Angeles, under the assumption that even a few hours change in schedule might derail the plan. If Robert Kennedy resolved to go ahead as planned and return to Los Angeles to be there for the primary results, the Elkins family warned him to fire his bodyguards and hire new ones.

On Friday, October 17, 1968, J. B. Elkins died under suspicious circumstances. The car he was driving was pushed off the road by another driver who was never apprehended or identified. He veered off the road and crashed into a utility pole. Elkins reportedly died of massive chest injuries suffered when he collided with the steering wheel of his car. Representatives of the Portland Police Department were sent to Arizona to view Elkins' body to validate the Portland crime czar was actually deceased. At the time of his death, Elkins was free on a twenty-thousand-dollar bond. He was facing indictments in Portland, Oregon, for possession of a firearm, conspiracy to commit a felony, possession of dangerous drugs, and several counts of receiving and concealing stolen property.[510]

SIX

CUBA, NIXON, AND WATERGATE

"[E. Howard] Hunt and [CIA psychological specialist] David Phillips were both veterans of the CIA's 1954 Guatemala campaign. The Cuba Project [Bay of Pigs invasion] was to be a carbon copy. In Guatemala the CIA trained a 'patriotic' opposition army, gave it logistical support and orchestrated an 'invasion'."[511]

—Warren Hinckle and William Turner, *The Fish Is Red: The Secret War Against Castro*, 1981

THE CIA-ENGINEERED COUP D'ÉTAT in Guatemala going back to 1954, set the stage both for the Bay of Pigs and for the JFK assassination. Although the Bay of Pigs typically is considered a Kennedy administration initiative, the historical record demonstrates the CIA undertook the planning for the Bay of Pigs invasion during the last year of the Eisenhower administration. The original plan was to provide Vice President Richard Nixon with an "October Surprise" that Nixon could use to defeat John F. Kennedy in the 1960 presidential election.

The idea was that the American public would rally around Vice

President Nixon taking the lead in an Eisenhower administration effort to support a popular uprising of Cuban patriots invading Cuba from the United States in order to rescue their homeland from Castro and Communism. The plan was to allow the American public to see Richard Nixon directing the American military in support of the Bay of Pigs invasion from within the White House. Nixon would score a knockout blow over Kennedy as the American public saw Nixon using his superior foreign policy expertise to depose Castro via a popular uprising in Cuba stirred by the invasion.

Nixon's plan to win the 1960 election was disrupted when insider sources tipped-off the Kennedy campaign that the Bay of Pigs invasion was planned for the last weeks of the 1960 presidential campaign.

THE EISENHOWER PLAN TO INVADE CUBA

In March 1960 President Eisenhower approved a plan to train a group of Cuban exiles to invade their homeland, with the anticipation that the Cuban people and various elements of the Cuban military would support the invasion. The goal was to overthrow Castro and to establish a non-Communist government favorable to the United States. Richard Bissell, the CIA deputy director for plans who had successfully developed the Lockheed U-2 spy plane program, spearheaded the plan within the CIA to invade Cuba that ultimately became the Bay of Pigs fiasco.[512] Bissell, a graduate of Yale University and the London School of Economics, had never spent a day in the US military, though he was ensconced in a group of journalists and government officials that became known as the "Georgetown Set," a group that included CIA officials James Jesus Angleton, Allen Dulles, and Cord Meyer—three figures that played roles in the JFK assassination.

Once Eisenhower approved Bissell's plan to invade Cuba, the CIA set up training camps in Guatemala where a small army was prepared for an amphibious assault landing and guerrilla warfare. E. Howard Hunt was selected to train the Cuban invasion army in Guatemala. Hunt leaves no doubt that the plan to invade Cuba was a direct copycat of his plan to overthrow Arbenz in1954. "As principal assistant to Bissell, Tracy Barnes told me, I was needed for a new project, much like the one on which I had worked for him in overthrowing Jacobo Arbenz," Hunt wrote in his 1974 book, *Under-Cover: Memoirs of an American Secret Agent.* "My job, Tracy told me, would be essentially the same as my earlier one—chief of political action for a project recommended by the National Security Council and just approved by President Eisenhower: to assist Cuban exiles in overthrowing Castro."[513] Hunt also affirmed that Nixon was in charge of executing the plan. "Nixon, however, had little to say on the subject in public," Hunt explained. "Secretly, however, he was the White House action officer for our covert project, and some months before, his senior military aide, Marine General Robert Cushman, had urged me to inform him of any project difficulties the Vice President might be able to resolve. For Nixon was, Cushman told me, determined that the effort should not fail."[514]

Operating under the code name "Eduardo," E. Howard Hunt began organizing a government-in-exile that would form a provisional government in Cuba once Castro was deposed. Hunt's principal assistant was a Cuban-American named Bernard "Macho" Barker who had worked for years for the CIA station in Havana. Baker and Hunt chose then-twenty-seven year old Manuel F. Artime to head the provisional government. Artime, a Jesuit-trained psychiatrist, had joined Castro's forces in the Sierra Maestra and served as a regional agricultural official after Castro ousted Cuba's ruling dictator Fulgencio Batista. Artime fled to Miami after becoming disillusioned with the number of anti-Communist friends who were being executed by Castro even though they had supported the revolution. Bernard Barker later turned up as one of the burglars apprehended in the break-in of Larry O'Donnell's Democratic National Committee offices in the Watergate complex. Artime later figured into the many plots to assassinate Castro that Robert Kennedy advanced in the Kennedy administration, right up to the time of the JFK assassination. The Kennedy plan was to replace Castro with the commander of the Cuban army, Juan Almeida, another Castro supporter who reportedly had turned against the revolution after Castro took power.[515]

According to Hunt, the plan developed by Bissell and the CIA in the Eisenhower administration called for "a total wipeout of Castro's air power by a series of strikes just prior to the invasion landing."[516] Once the invasion of Cuban exiles cleared the perimeter around the airstrip at the Bay of Pigs, Hunt planned to fly to Cuba with the provisional government. From Cuba, the provisional government would broadcast to the world a declaration that it was a government-in-arms, making an appeal for aid in overthrowing Castro. Following this declaration, a sizable contingent of US Marines waiting offshore in the US aircraft carrier *Boxer* was ready to land on the island once the provisional government was establish and had a chance to appeal to the United States for assistance. Because what the Eisenhower administration was planning was illegal under international law, the entire Cuban project was run under the principle of "plausible deniability." To hide the secret war planning, the CIA trained the Cuban exiles in Guatemala and utilized agency covers in the United States that included businesses and individuals who shared rentals with organized crime and radical right-wing paramilitary organizations. "In time it became impossible to separate the wheat of intelligence from the chaff of the underworld," commented journalist Warren Hinckle and his coauthor William Turner, a former FBI agent, in their 1981 book, *The Fish Is Red: The Secret War Against Castro.*[517]

CANDIDATE KENNEDY'S GAMBIT ON CUBA

On July 23, 1960, CIA director Allen Dulles visited JFK at the family compound at Hyannis Port on Cape Cod to brief the candidate on the Eisenhower administration's anti-Castro efforts. This put the Kennedy campaign on notice that the invasion of Cuba was possibly an October Surprise, an event to effect the election. Increasingly, the Kennedy camp became paranoid as rumors out of Miami talked about the creation of a CIA-sponsored invasion force consisting of Cuban exiles.[518] After confirming an invasion of Cuba was being planned, the Kennedy campaign decided to step up the candidate's rhetoric. On October 6, 1960, at a Democratic Party dinner in Cincinnati, Ohio, JFK insisted the country "must firmly resist further Communist encroachment in this hemisphere—working through a strengthened organization of the American States—and encouraging those liberty-loving Cubans who are leading the resistance to Castro."[519] This sounded close to an endorsement of a US policy of assisting Cuban exiles in an effort to oust Castro. On October 20, 1960, on the eve of the fourth and final presidential debate, JFK put out a statement that said the United States "must attempt to strengthen the non-Batista democratic anti-Castro forces in exile, and in Cuba itself, who offer eventual hope of overthrowing Castro. Thus far these fighters for freedom have had virtually no support from our Government."[520] Again, while the statement stopped short of endorsing a US government–sponsored invasion of Cuba, JFK was trying to pre-empt the aggressive rhetoric on Cuba, positioning himself to claim credit for the idea, if Nixon and the Eisenhower administration were to go forward with the Cuban exile plan prior to election day.

Then, during the fourth debate, on October 21, 1960, in New York City, in his opening statement, JFK again returned to the theme of Cuba. "I look at Cuba, ninety miles off the coast of the United States," Kennedy began. "In 1957, I was in Havana. I talked with the American ambassador there. He said he was the second most powerful man in Cuba. And yet even though Ambassador Smith and Ambassador Gardner, both Republican ambassadors, both warned of Castro, the Marxist influences around Castro, the Communist influences around Castro, both of them have testified in the last six weeks, that in spite of their warnings to the American government, nothing was done." The Kennedy campaign had correctly calculated that Nixon's training as a debater would induce him to take the opposite approach, urging a policy of restraint while charging that Kennedy was being irresponsible in suggesting a US military invasion of Cuba. This is exactly what Nixon did in the fourth debate, calling JFK's Cuba policy the "most dangerously irresponsible recommendations he's made during the course of this campaign."[521] Kennedy's calculated move effectively checkmated Nixon on Cuba. Nixon was furious.

In his 1962 book, *Six Crises*, Nixon describes how as he was preparing the day before the fourth debate, he saw huge black headlines in the afternoon papers that read: "Kennedy Advocates U.S. Intervention in Cuba, Calls for Aid to Rebel Forces in Cuba."[522] Nixon recalled that as early as September 23, 1960, Kennedy had given an exclusive statement to the Scripps-Howard newspapers in which he said, "The forces fighting for freedom in exile and in the mountains of Cuba should be sustained and assisted." In briefing Kennedy, Dulles was doing nothing wrong. Nixon acknowledged in *Six Crises* that he knew President Eisenhower had arranged for Kennedy to receive regular briefings by Allen Dulles on

CIA covert activities around the world. But, when Nixon read the headlines in the newspapers, he could hardly believe his eyes. Nixon asked his aides to call the White House and find out if Allen Dulles had briefed Kennedy specifically on Cuba, on the fact that for months the CIA had been training Cuban exiles in Guatemala for the purposes of an invasion.

Within a half hour, Nixon discovered Dulles had briefed Kennedy on the impending Cuban invasion. Nixon's reaction was rage, not at Dulles for informing Kennedy, but at Kennedy for exploiting this highly sensitive information for political advantage. "For the first and only time in the campaign, I got mad at Kennedy—personally," Nixon wrote. "I understand and expect hard-hitting attacks in a campaign. But in this instance I thought that Kennedy, with full knowledge of the facts was jeopardizing the security of a United States foreign policy operation. And my rage was greater because I could do nothing about it."[523] Nixon was particularly enraged that, although the idea of providing the Cuban exiles cover training was actually his idea, Kennedy, by exploiting the classified information Dulles had shared with him about US training activities, managed to pull off the illusion he had thought of it first.[524] Kennedy had robbed Nixon of his October Surprise that he was sure would catapult him into office. If Eisenhower and Nixon were successful with the Cuban invasion, Kennedy could claim they were simply implementing a plan Kennedy himself was the first to advocate publicly.

Nixon felt cornered. He had been planning the operation—the arms, ammunition, and training for the Cuban exiles—for six months before the 1960 campaign had gotten under way. It was Nixon's program, but now he could not say a single word about it. "The operation was covert," Nixon wrote. "Under no circumstances could it be disclosed or even alluded to. Consequently, under Kennedy's attacks and his new demands for 'militant' policies, I was in the position of a fighter with one hand tied behind his back. I knew we had a program under way to deal with Castro, but I could not even hint at its existence, much less spell it out."[525] Nixon wrote that because Kennedy had him at such a tremendous disadvantage, he was faced with one of the most difficult decisions of the campaign. "Kennedy was now publicly advocating what was already the policy of the American Government—covertly—and Kennedy had been so informed," Nixon groused. "But by stating such a position publicly, he obviously stood to gain the support of all those who wanted a stronger policy against Castro, but who, of course, did not know of our covert programs already under way."[526] Nixon decided that, as the Kennedy camp predicted he would do, he had to protect the covert operation at all costs. He had to go to the other extreme. He had to "attack the Kennedy proposal to provide such aid as wrong and irresponsible because it would violate our treaty obligations," Nixon explained.[527]

The Kennedy ploy had worked. By taking the aggressive position on Cuba, JFK effectively blocked the October Surprise by exposing it. But that was hardly the end of the story. While Kennedy's stratagem may well have been critical to preserving JFK's chance to beat Nixon in 1960, the strategy ultimately backfired. Once JFK was elected president, he suddenly became vulnerable to Bissell and the CIA, who blackmailed him over Cuba. If JFK as president did not keep good on his campaign promise to support the Cuban exiles in their effort to regain their country, Bissell and the CIA would leak to the public the reality that JFK's hard-line stand against Cuba during the campaign was nothing more than a stratagem to get elected. Once JFK blocked Nixon from executing the CIA covert plan to invade Cuba, he committed himself to following through with the plan shortly after taking office, with no assurance the plan would work.

THE RELUCTANT WARRIOR

JFK approved the Bay of Pigs operation despite serious reservations the plan had any chance of success. Presidential historian Robert Dallek reported that two days after JFK became president, the CIA began pushing him to move against Cuba. At a January 22, 1961, meeting of Secretary of State Dean Rusk, Secretary of Defense Robert MacNamara, Attorney General Robert Kennedy, Army General Lyman Lemnitzer, the Chairman of the Joint Chiefs, and various national security and foreign policy experts, CIA director Allen Dulles stressed the United States had only two months "before something had to be done about" the Cubans being trained in Guatemala.[528] The CIA knew they had Kennedy over a barrel. To abandon the invasion would make Kennedy look like an appeaser of Castro, appearing as if Eisenhower had approved the plan and JFK dropped it. A JFK confidante and political advisor warned him that canceling the Bay of Pigs operation would present JFK with "a major political blowup."[529] Besides, if the invasion plans were scrapped, what was JFK supposed to do with the Cuban exiles who had been trained by the CIA in Guatemala?

Kennedy's own military instincts told him the plan was harebrained. Even his adviser Arthur Schlesinger and the chairman of the Senate Foreign Relations Committee Senator William Fulbright agreed. There was no assurance the invasion would trigger a popular uprising, and there was little likelihood the invasion would succeed even with direct US military support. Still, Allen Dulles was insistent. "Mr. President, I know you're doubtful about this," Dulles told JFK in the Oval Office. "But I stood at this very desk and said to President Eisenhower about a similar operation in Guatemala, 'I believe it will work.' And I say to you now, Mr. President, that the prospects for this plan are even better than our prospects were in Guatemala."[530] The covert invasion began on Saturday, April 15, 1961, when eight B-26s marked deceptively as Cuban air force planes, flew from Puerto Cabezas, Nicaragua, to bomb three Cuban airfields near Havana. The mission turned into an unmitigated disaster, much as JFK feared, when two days later, on April 17, 1961, the invasion of the Cuban exile forces trained by the CIA began parachuting into strategic locations in Cuba.[531]

JFK blamed the CIA. Presidential historian Robert Dallek summarized the problem with the invasion as follows: "the willingness of the Cubans, the CIA, and the US military to proceed partly rested on their assumption that once the invasion began, Kennedy would have to use American forces if the attack seemed about to fail." That was the crux of why JFK ultimately felt the CIA had betrayed him. The CIA, knowing JFK would never go along with direct US military involvement, calculated the only plan with any chance of success was to promote an invasion plan the CIA knew would fail, in order to force JFK's hand to approve the B-26 air attacks and approve US jets from the aircraft carrier USS *Essex* thirty miles offshore to provide support. Bissell and Dulles had calculated incorrectly. On Sunday night, April 16, 1961, the last thing JFK did before he went to bed was to call Dean Rusk and tell him to order the cancellation of a dawn aerial attack by the entire exile force of sixteen B-26s, leaving Castro with airplanes to use in strafing the invading exiles on the ground, in what was called Brigade 2506, that were planning to hit the beach in the Bay of Pigs at dawn. On Monday morning, April 17, 1961, JFK refused to allow the US jets from USS *Essex* to provide air cover.[532] That decision marked the moment the invasion was certain to fail. On April 19, destroyers USS *Eaton* and USS *Murray* moved into the Bay of Pigs, in the face of fire from Cuban tanks on shore, to evacuate from the beaches the retreating soldiers of what had been the invading Brigade 2506 of paramilitary Cuban exiles.

The Bay of Pigs scarred JFK badly. Within days of becoming president, he realized how little power he truly had. The CIA had played him, disregarding his expressed concern that the United States not be involved militarily and only *support* an invasion by Cuban exile patriots trying to take back their country for democracy. JFK fired Bissell and Dulles in a threat to break the CIA up into a thousand pieces. Unfortunately, that impulse—to destroy the CIA—was one JFK never followed to completion, a mistake that contributed to him losing not only his presidency, but also his life.

"THE WHOLE BAY OF PIGS THING . . . "

Three members of Nixon's Watergate burglary team—E. Howard Hunt, Bernard Barker, and Frank Sturgis—were also involved in the planning of the invasion of Cuba. Why were so many men who were involved with the Bay of Pigs fiasco part of the Watergate break-in? Because dating back to the Eisenhower administration, Nixon became closely involved with the CIA and Mafia when he helped plan the Guatemala coup. He continued those relationships when he called on the CIA and Mafia to kill Castro. JFK assassination researcher Lamar Waldron has documented that Nixon received a $1 million Mafia bribe from Carlos Marcello and Santo Trafficante just prior to the start of the 1972 presidential campaign as part of a deal to release Jimmy Hoffa from prison, which occurred less than four months before the first Watergate break-in.[533] These men were veterans of the Eisenhower administration plots and had worked Nixon in the past.

G. Gordon Liddy has long maintained that the Watergate burglary was motivated by the desire to wiretap a telephone in the Democratic National Committee (DNC) headquarters that top Democratic officials and their political friends were using as part of a call girl ring.[534] But that does not explain the thousands of pages of documents the Watergate burglars copied or the many different locations that were burglarized over a period of several months, continuing by other secret White House operatives even after the Watergate burglars were apprehended.

The "smoking-gun" discussion in the White House during Watergate involved a meeting between then-White House chief-of-staff H. R. Haldeman and President Richard Nixon in the Oval Office on June 23, 1972, from 10:04 a.m. to 11:39 a.m. Haldeman was concerned about the FBI's investigation into Watergate. He was looking for a way to justify telling then-FBI acting director Patrick Gray to back off. Nixon was concerned the FBI was going to look into the background of E. Howard Hunt:

> **Nixon:** Of course, this is a—[E. Howard] Hunt will—that will uncover a lot [unclear] when you open that scab there's a hell of a lot of things and then we just feel it would be very detrimental to have this thing go any further, that this involves these Cubans, and Hunt, and a lot of hanky-panky that we have nothing to do with ourselves.

Nixon recommended having the CIA instruct the FBI to stop investigating Watergate on national security concerns. Specifically, Nixon instructed Haldeman to have Gen. Vernon A. Walters, deputy director of the CIA, call L. Patrick Gray. Nixon's chief-of-staff H. R. Haldeman, in his 1978 book, *The Ends of Power*, argued that Nixon's references in the Watergate tapes to "the whole Bay of Pigs thing" suggested the Watergate burglars were also involved with the JFK assassination. "It seems that in all of those Nixon references to the Bay of Pigs, [Nixon] was actually referring to the Kennedy assassination," Haldeman wrote.[535]

> **Nixon:** When you get in these people when you . . . get these people in, say: "Look, the problem is that this will open the whole, the whole Bay of Pigs thing, and the President just feels that" ah, without going into the details . . . don't, don't lie to them to the extent to say there is no involvement, but just say this is sort of a comedy of errors, bizarre, without getting into it, "the President believes that it is going to open the whole Bay of Pigs thing up again. And, ah because these people are plugging for, for keeps and that they should call the FBI in and say that we wish for the country, don't go any further into this case," period![536]

In a separate conversation with Haldeman in the Oval Office on June 23, 1972, from 1:04 p.m. to 1:13 p.m., Nixon returned to the Howard Hunt theme.

> **Nixon**: And I would just tell them that it'd be very bad to have this fellow [E. Howard] Hunt, you know, it's—"he knows too damn much, and he was involved, we happen to know that. And if it gets out that the whole. . ." this is all involved in the Cuban thing, that it's a fiasco, it's going to make the FBI—the CIA—look bad, it's going to make Hunt look bad, and it's likely to blow the whole Bay of Pigs thing, which we think would be very unfortunate for [the] CIA and for the country at this time, and for American foreign policy. And he's just got to tell [L. Patrick Gray and the FBI] to lay off. Is that what you—

> **Haldeman**: Yeah, that's the basis we're going to do it on and just leave it at that.[537]

In the later years of Haldeman's life, he repudiated the "Bay of Pigs meaning the JFK assassination" statement, attributing it to the invention of his ghostwriter, Joseph DiMona.[538] From the time Nixon fired Haldeman in 1973 until 1978, when he was released from prison, Haldeman and Nixon were not on speaking terms. By 1990 Haldeman was repudiating much of what he wrote in *The Ends of Power*, the book he published as he was preparing to be released from prison on parole.[539]

Nixon's seemingly out-of-context comment forced Watergate inquiries to circle back to the invasion plans against Cuba that began under Richard Bissell at the CIA when Nixon was vice president under Eisenhower. Hunt was beginning to demand as much as one million dollars in hush money and Nixon was concerned at how many dark secrets would be exposed if Hunt began to talk. The FBI had begun to suspect the Nixon White House had begun to solicit one million dollars from the Teamsters to keep the imprisoned Watergate burglars quiet.[540] In early 1973, in the final stages of the Watergate cover-up, White House counsel John Dean seemed to confirm this when he told Richard Nixon face-to-face that one million dollars might be needed to keep the Watergate burglars quiet. "We could get that—you could get a million dollars," was Nixon's response. "You could get it in cash. I know where it could be gotten."

Nixon's extreme tactics suggest there was a deeper secret behind the Watergate break-in, that the Bay of Pigs plotters, including Howard Hunt, were also Watergate burglars and very possibly participants in the JFK assassination. Many have speculated that the Watergate burglary was about making sure Larry O'Brien and the Democratic Party did not have highly sensitive information that would have shown Nixon knew the truth about the JFK assassination and did nothing about it, or possibly even incriminating evidence that might have tied Nixon to the JFK assassination. "Could [Haldeman and Nixon] have been circuitously referring to the interlocking connections between CIA agents, anti-Castro Cubans, and mobsters that likely resulted in the Kennedy assassination?" conspiracy researcher Jim Marrs asked. "Did they themselves have some sort of insider knowledge of this event?"[541]

"What did the president know, and when did he know it?" Sen. Howard Baker, the vice-chairman of the Senate Watergate hearings, famously asked about Watergate. Perhaps this question should have been asked of Richard Nixon about not only the Watergate break-in, but also about the JFK assassination. What did Richard Nixon know about the JFK assassination, and when did he know about it?

Nixon knew that E. Howard Hunt not only was a culprit in Watergate, but was also involved in the coup d'état in Guatemala in 1954 and the staged political assassination that followed in 1957. Then, too, Nixon may have been keenly aware of the evidence that suggested E. Howard Hunt was involved not only in the Bay of Pigs and the various plots to assassinate Castro, but very possibly in the JFK assassination as well.

THE DEATH OF DOROTHY HUNT

On Friday, December 8, 1972, Dorothy Hunt, E. Howard Hunt's wife, was killed when United Flight 553 from Washington National Airport to Midway Airport in Chicago crashed under suspicious circumstances at approximately 2:29 p.m. local time. Captain Wendell L. Whitehouse, a seasoned veteran with eighteen thousand flying hours, piloted the airplane, a Boeing 737 with sixty-one passengers and six crewmembers on board. E. Howard Hunt had just been indicted some months before for his role in the Watergate affair and he was prohibited from traveling. Assassination researcher Harrison Edward Livingstone, believes Dorothy Hunt was carrying White House hush money to pay off the Cuban exiles whose involvement with Hunt stretched from the Bay of Pigs through the JFK assassination to Watergate.[542] At the crash site, Dorothy Hunt was found to be carrying ten thousand dollars in cash in her purse. She was traveling with Michelle Clark, a CBS reporter, who had learned from her sources that the Hunts were getting ready to "blow the White House out of the water," such that before Howard Hunt was hung out to dry, he would "bring down every tree in the forest."[543] Forty-five people died in the crash, including Dorothy Hunt and Michelle Clark.

Witnesses to the crash charged that immediately after the crash, some two hundred FBI and Defense Intelligence Agency officials came in and took over the crash scene. The FBI admitted fifty FBI agents were on the crash scene. Finally, William Ruckelshaus, the acting director of the FBI, explained to the *Washington Post* on June 14, 1973, that the FBI had primary jurisdiction in possible cases of sabotage, including airline crashes.[544] The day after the crash, Egil Krogh Jr., the former head of Nixon's "plumber's unit" that employed E. Howard Hunt, was named undersecretary of the Department of Transportation. This appointment put Krogh in a position to supervise the National Transportation Safety Board and the Federal Aviation Agency in their investigation of the United Flight 553 crash. Krogh ultimately went to prison for his role in burglarizing the offices of the psychiatrist for Daniel Ellsberg who had achieved fame for the release of the *Pentagon Papers*. On December 19, 1972, Nixon moved former CIA agent Alexander Butterfield to serve as the head of the Federal Aviation Agency. Butterfield had been secretary to the Cabinet and he achieved fame for revealing to the Senate Watergate Committee that he had been responsible for maintaining for Nixon a secret audiotaping system in the White House. Finally, in January 1973, Dwight Chapin, Nixon's appointments secretary and dirty tricks supervisor was made an executive in the Chicago headquarters office of United Airlines.[545]

The death of Dorothy Hunt was the first evidence available publicly indicating the Nixon administration was in the business of paying hush money to the Watergate burglars. To go to such lengths as to bring down a jet liner and cover it up with high-level appointments suggest the deep politics behind the Watergate burglary involved more than an effort to embarrass the Democrats with information about a prostitution ring being run out of the DNC. Nixon's obsession with the JFK assassination appears out of place in his discussions over Watergate, suggesting Nixon was trying to hide a secret about JFK's assassination that had to remain secret at all costs — a secret that suggests Nixon may have had reason to have a guilty conscience stemming from his personal involvement in "the whole Bay of Pigs thing."

THE STRANGE CASE OF MARITA LORENZ

A self-proclaimed mistress and long-time lover of Fidel Castro, Marita Lorenz set off a firestorm of speculation with a story that involved soldier-of-fortune Frank Fiorini, also known as Frank Sturgis, as well as E. Howard Hunt and the various CIA-mob plans to assassinate Castro. On May 31, 1978, in sworn testimony before a closed session of the House Select Committee on Assassinations, Lorenz testified to having been involved with E. Howard Hunt and Frank Sturgis in the CIA training provided to Cuban exiles in the Everglades in Florida after the Bay of Pigs attack.[546] She also claimed to have met Lee Harvey Oswald in early 1961, at a CIA safe house in Miami. It was a meeting of several key players—Frank Sturgis, Pedro Diaz Lanz, Alexander Rorke (a rabid anti-Communist and former-FBI agent who was the wealthy son-in-law of Sherman Billingsley), Orlando Bosch, Guillermo and Ignacio Novo (brothers and Cuban exile leaders), and Jerry Patrick Hemming—in the CIA assassination unit known at the time as Operation 40.[547]

Lorenz claimed the participants in Operation 40, including herself, were receiving military training in guerrilla warfare, plastic explosives, M-1 rifles, automatic weapons, attack techniques, and self-defense. Lorenz testified she called Oswald by the nickname "Ozzie." She also testified that E. Howard Hunt was known as "Eduardo," and that his role in the group appeared to involve periodically bringing Frank Sturgis large quantities of cash delivered in an envelope.

Lorenz testified that in a private meeting with several of the Operation 40 players in September 1963, Frank Sturgis led the group as they studied street maps of Dallas that Sturgis laid out on a coffee table. Lorenz placed Oswald at the meeting, saying that at the conclusion of the discussion, Sturgis folded up the maps and put them in his pocket. "Okay, that's it," Sturgis reportedly said. "We are ready." Then, about a week before November 22, 1963, Frank Sturgis, Lorenz, and the Novo brothers left Orlando, Florida, in a two-car caravan with the second car containing Lee Harvey Oswald; Petro Diaz Lanz, the former chief of the Cuban Air Force; Orlando Bosch, a Cuban exile leader and CIA operative; and Jerry Patrick Hemming, a former US Marine who became a mercenary and a CIA operative. She testified that on the trip they rotated drivers and stopped to eat only at drive-in roadside restaurants. They drove nonstop over two days from Orlando to Dallas, Texas, where the group checked into adjoining hotel rooms in a hotel outside Dallas.

She further testified that once the group had settled into the two adjoining hotel rooms, Frank Sturgis took rifles and scopes that had been wrapped in green waterproof paper, with blankets thrown on top, from the trunk of his car. Sturgis placed the rifles and scopes between the two twin beds in his hotel room. Lorenz said she recognized three or four automatic rifles, but she did not know the specific makes, and she did not pay attention to the rifles or scopes, except to notice the rifles were equipped with slings. She testified that Jack Ruby showed up at the hotel to have a private discussion with Frank Sturgis, and that Ruby ignored Oswald during this visit. She also claimed E. Howard Hunt showed up with more money.

Lorenz claimed not to know the purpose of the trip. She assumed the goal was to attack an armory and steal weapons. She claimed she had acted as a decoy in several such missions previously staged in Florida and adjoining states. Why a CIA-supplied operation needed to steal weapons from an armory, Lorenz did not explain. After a few days in the hotel, Lorenz began to feel homesick for her daughter and wanted to go home. She testified that Frank Sturgis took her to the airport in Dallas and she flew home to Miami on November 19 or 20, 1963. She claimed she was on an airplane with her daughter on November 22, 1963, going from Miami to New York, when JFK was shot. The flight was diverted to land at Newark, she testified, after the copilot came on the intercom and announced, "Ladies and gentlemen, the president was shot."

In her 1993 autobiographical book, *Marita: One Woman's Extraordinary Tale of Love and Espionage in the CIA*, Lorenz details her experiences in Cuba, disclosing her belief that Joseph Kennedy, the patriarch of the Kennedy clan, had financed Castro with the expectation that if Castro managed to depose Cuban president Batista, then Kennedy would be able to take control of the Havana nightlife and destroy mobster Meyer Lansky's influence. Confirming the tension between Joseph Kennedy and the eastern mob (controlled at that time by the Italians under Lucky Luciano and the Jews under Meyer Lansky) Lorenz noted Joseph Kennedy "had hated Lansky since bootlegging days of prohibition when they were rivals."[548] Lorenz claimed that when she was growing up she had only been vaguely aware of the dark side of Cuba—the prostitution, the gambling, the gangsters, and the political graft. "I didn't know then about organized crime figure Meyer Lansky and his friends Charles 'Lucky' Luciano and Benjamin 'Bugsy' Siegel, who dominated the Havana casinos, or his brother Jake, who handled the day-to-day management, or about syndicate members such as Carlos Marcello of New Orleans and Santo Trafficante, Jr., who let underlings including a nightclub owner named Jack Ruby, run guns to whomever wanted them," she wrote.[549] She also claimed Teamster Union boss Jimmy Hoffa and Bill Bresser, a labor union boss in Cleveland, Ohio, made money selling guns "to both sides"—namely Batista and Castro—and that Santo Trafficante, Jack Ruby, and Frank Fiorini/Sturgis were among the gun runners providing weapons to Castro in his fight against Batista. Finally, she wrote "that all these men, like Sam Giancana of Chicago, just wanted the Havana nightclub scene to be business as usual after the revolution."[550]

WHERE WAS E. HOWARD HUNT ON THE DAY JFK WAS SHOT?

Gaeton Fonzi, a lead investigator for the House Select Committee on Assassinations, ultimately concluded that Lorenz's story was unreliable; he successfully urged the House Select Committee to ignore the account when it could not be independently corroborated. Marita Lorenz would have become just another weird footnote to the JFK assassination investigation except that she figured into an important libel case as a key witness where Lane set out to prove E. Howard Hunt had been in Dallas on November 22, 1963.

The case developed when *The Spotlight*, a newspaper published by Liberty Lobby, Inc., ran an article in 1978 authored by former-CIA officer Victor Marchetti in which Marchetti accused E. Howard Hunt of having been in Dallas on November 22, 1963, and of having played a role in the

JFK assassination. Marchetti had achieved notoriety in 1974 by publishing a heavily redacted book entitled *The CIA and the Cult of Intelligence*.[551] Hunt won a libel judgment of $625,000. Mark Lane, even though he disagreed with the Liberty Lobby, took the case on appeal because the case offered him a chance to apply the knowledge he gathered in two decades he had then spent studying the JFK assassination.

A critical point in the retrial was reached when Hunt, under cross-examination by Lane, was forced to admit his children were never fully convinced Hunt was in Washington, D.C., on November 22, 1963, as he had always claimed. Lane asked Hunt about his testimony in the first trial of the Liberty Lobby case, on December 16, 1981. In his book on the Liberty Lobby retrial, Lane recreates the cross-examination sequence from the second trial:

> **Lane Question**: Do you recall testifying back on Dec. 16, 1981, that when the allegation was made that you were in Dallas, Texas, on Nov. 22, 1963, your children were really upset? Do you recall testifying to that?
>
> **Hunt Answer**: Yes.
>
> **Lane Question**: Do you recall testifying that you had to reassure them that you were not in Texas that day?
>
> **Hunt Answer**: Yes.
>
> **Lane Question**: That you had nothing to do with the Kennedy assassination?
>
> **Hunt Answer**: That's right.
>
> **Lane Question**: And that you were being persecuted for reasons that were unknown to you.
>
> **Hunt Answer**: Yes.
>
> **Lane Question**: Did you say that the allegation that you were in Dallas, Texas, on November 22, 1963, was the focus of a great deal of interfamily friction and tended to exacerbate difficulties in the family?
>
> **Answer**: I did.[552]

Through the years, Hunt had produced several explanations of the day JFK was assassinated, including a claim he had stopped to get Chinese food on his way home from the office. Records, however, showed Hunt had not been at CIA headquarters in Langley, Virginia, on November 22, 1963. Hunt's coworker at the CIA said he could not recall seeing Hunt at work between November 18, 1963, and sometime in December 1963.[553] On August 20, 1978, Joseph Trento and Jacquie Powers, reporters for the *Wilmington Sunday News Journal*, wrote an article very similar to the Marchetti article, claiming a secret 1966 CIA memo placed Hunt in Dallas on November 22, 1963.[554]

At the 1985 retrial, Lane pressed Hunt, asking him how his children could ever have wondered how one of the three tramp photos, photos of three transients taken by several Dallas-area newspapers, that purported to show him in Dealey Plaza on November 22, 1963, could be authentic, when his children knew he was in Washington that day. Hunt claimed his children were not fully aware he worked for the CIA. He claimed when the tramp pictures were made public, he had to "remind" his children he was never in Dallas that day. Finally, Lane got Hunt to admit that each time a new allegation asserting Hunt had been in Dallas on the day JFK was assassinated was made, his children, even as adults, demanded to know if it was true. "Rarely does a witness testify that he had to remind his alibi witnesses where they were at the crucial moment in the case," Lane wrote.[555]

Lane's sole witness was Marita Lorenz, who appeared at the trial via a deposition read to the jury. In a unanimous decision, the jury agreed with the Liberty Lobby and decided against the plaintiff E. Howard Hunt. The jury foreman, Leslie Armstrong, told reporters "the evidence was clear The CIA had killed President Kennedy. Hunt had been part of it, and that evidence, so painstakingly presented, should now be examined by the relevant institutions of the United States government so that those responsible for the assassination might be brought to justice."[556] Despite continuing concerns that the testimony of Marita Lorenz was unreliable, Lane demonstrated two key points with the 1985 retrial: (1) the jury refused to believe E. Howard Hunt's insistence he was in Washington on the day Kennedy was killed, and (2) the jury believed the CIA played a role in the assassination.

THE SILVIA ODIO INCIDENT

House Select Committee on Assassinations investigator Gaeton Fonzi wrote that meeting Cuban exile Silvia Odio played an important role in his conviction that a conspiracy was involved in the JFK assassination. "My investigation with the House Select Committee on Assassinations revealed that there was evidence that proved Odio was telling the truth about three men visiting her almost two months before the assassination," Fonzi wrote.[557]

On July 22, 1964, a then-twenty-seven-year-old Silvio Odio testified to the Warren Commission that she had a meeting with a man she later identified as Lee Harvey Oswald. In 1963 Odio was a member of the Cuban Revolutionary Junta, known as JURE, and both her parents were then political prisoners of the Castro regime. She testified that in late September 1963, three men came to her apartment in Dallas and asked her to help them prepare a letter soliciting funds for JURE. She said two of the men appeared to be Cubans, although she also thought they had characteristics associated with Mexicans. She said the two men did not state their full names, but identified themselves only by their underground "war names." She remembered one of the two Cubans as "Leopoldo." The third man, an American, was introduced to her as "Leon Oswald," and she was told he was interested in the Cuban cause.

She further told the Warren Commission that the next day, after the meeting in her apartment, Leopoldo called her and asked her what she thought of the American. When Odio replied, "I didn't think anything," Leopoldo went on to describe the American in more detail. This is what Odio told the Warren Commission: "[Leopoldo] said, 'You know our idea is to introduce [Leon Oswald] to the underground in Cuba because he is great, he is kind of nuts.' That was more or less—I can't repeat the exact words, because he was kind of nuts. He told us we don't have any guts, you Cubans, because President Kennedy should have been assassinated after the Bay of Pigs, and some Cubans should have done that, because he was the one that was holding the freedom of Cuba actually." Leopoldo also told Odio that this Leon had been a marine and he was interested in helping the Cubans.[558] On November 22, 1963, seeing photographs of Lee Harvey Oswald on television, Sylvia Odio recognized him as Leon

Oswald, the man who came to her house.

The Warren Commission rejected Odio's testimony largely because the dates deemed most likely for the suspect visit to Odio's apartment, September 26 and 27, 1963, were the same dates the Commission placed Oswald in Dallas. In so concluding, the Warren Commission discounted the possibility that someone was using the Oswald identity to create the impression Oswald had visited Mexico in the time period of late-September 1963. As noted in chapter 4, no US government agency has released a photograph that confirms Oswald had visited the Cuban and Russian embassies in Mexico City in late-September 1963, despite extensive US intelligence surveillance of both embassies at that time. "In spite of the fact that it appeared almost certain that Oswald could not have been in Dallas at the time Mrs. Odio thought he was, the Commission requested the FBI to conduct further investigation to determine the validity of Mrs. Odio's testimony," the Warren Commission final report noted.[559]

Fonzi, after locating Sylvia Odio and conducting extensive research on the incident, wrote a special report for the House Select Committee on Assassinations. "It appears that Sylvia Odio's testimony is essentially credible," Fonzi concluded in the special report, noting that Sylvia's sister Annie also witnessed the visit in question. "From the evidence provided in sworn testimony of the corroborating witnesses, there is no doubt that three men came to her apartment in Dallas prior to the Kennedy assassination and identified themselves as members of an anti-Castro Cuban organization. From a judgment of the credibility of both Silvia and Annie Odio, it must be concluded that there is a strong probability that one of the men was or appeared to be Lee Harvey Oswald."[560] The problem was that Oswald had clearly been identified as a pro-Castro activist on the left, for instance, when he was arrested in an altercation that occurred as he distributed "Fair Play for Cuba" literature on the streets of New Orleans, an incident discussed in chapter 4. Was Oswald pro-Castro or anti-Castro? Was there an attempt by a look-alike to use the Oswald identity in situations where Oswald himself could not have been physically present? The House Select Committee was unable to reach a conclusion regarding Oswald's motives, assuming the visit had come from Oswald himself. The House Select Committee also could come to no definite conclusion regarding the precise date of the visit, or whether Oswald might have been in Dallas on those dates.

As far as Fonzi was concerned, the important conclusion was that Sylvia Odio was telling the truth. What the incident proved, Fonzi concluded, was not that Oswald himself had visited Odio's apartment, but that a conspiracy was involved to assassinate JFK. "Validating Silvia Odio's report that Oswald, or someone who closely resembled him (it matters not), appeared at her door in Dallas with two associates, one of whom would link Oswald to the assassination before the assassination, confirms—no, cries out without a shadow of a doubt—that there was a conspiracy to assassinate President John F. Kennedy," Fonzi concluded.[561]

E. HOWARD HUNT'S DEATHBED CONFESSION

In 2007 St. John Hunt, the son of E. Howard Hunt, began making public the deathbed confessions of his father. He released a 2004 audio file of revelations Hunt taped before his death that was broadcast nationally on George Noory's nationally syndicated nightly *Coast-to-Coast AM* radio show. St. John Hunt then was interviewed for an article in *Rolling Stone* magazine, started a website, and self-published a book called *Bond of Secrecy: My Life with CIA Spy and Watergate Conspirator E. Howard Hunt.*

Hunt's deathbed confession must be evaluated cautiously. If the deathbed confession is truthful, then Hunt had been lying since 1963 and was not in Washington D.C. on November 22, 1963, and did have something to do with JFK's murder. Conceivably, the deathbed confession represents Hunt's last effort to come to grips with the truth, or perhaps his first effort to gain notoriety by confessing his guilt when it was too late to bring him to justice. The problem is that Hunt could have still been lying, trying as his last public act to bring calumny and doubt on enemies he had battled for years within the CIA. What Hunt's deathbed confession manages to accomplish then is not to solve the case, but to confirm the CIA's involvement from the beginning, and highlight the failure of the Warren Commission and the House Select Committee on Assassinations to investigate thoroughly the CIA's role in the JFK conspiracy.

E. Howard Hunt claimed he was a "benchwarmer" on the CIA operation to assassinate JFK, a mission Hunt called "the big event." By so characterizing his role, Hunt implies he played a role in the JFK assassination, but that he was not the first team on the field, and/or that he may have had organizational responsibilities but more qualified players had been assigned the operational roles.

Hunt claimed Vice President Lyndon Johnson enlisted the help of Cord Meyer in the CIA to prepare the operational plan and organize the team of co-conspirators. This was not the first time that Hunt had fingered LBJ as the prime mover in the JFK assassination. "Conspiracy nuts say that the person who had the most to gain from Kennedy's assassination was LBJ," E. Howard Hunt wrote in his 2007 book, *American Spy: My Secret History in the CIA, Watergate & Beyond.* "There was nobody with the leverage that LBJ had, no competitor at all. He was the vice president, and if he wanted to get rid of the president, he had the ability to do so by corrupting different people in the CIA."[562] Hunt knew that LBJ would never be satisfied being dumped from the 1964 ticket and that LBJ was sufficiently ruthless to do whatever it took to become president. With LBJ in the White House, *Life* magazine would have little to gain pressing ahead with the Bobby Baker scandal. LBJ could have reasonably calculated a grieving nation would rally behind him as JFK's successor. On this point, Hunt was right. LBJ had ample motives to remove the sitting president, motives LBJ shared with many other powerful people, including Allen Dulles, who equally had come to want to see JFK's presidency come to an end.

THE MARY PINCHOT MEYER SAGA

E. Howard Hunt explained Meyer was another person with motive since John F. Kennedy had been having an affair with his wife, Mary Pinchot. JFK first met Mary Pinchot in 1936. A then-young JFK spotted Pinchot on the dance floor at Choate Rosemary Hall, in Wallingford, Connecticut, where JFK had attended prep school. That weekend, JFK returned to Choate to attend the Winter Festivals Saturday Night Dance. JFK tapped her date, William Attwood, on the right shoulder to cut in so he could dance with Mary. The incident occurred when JFK was spending his brief time as an undergraduate at Princeton, before his father had him transfer to Harvard. JFK's relationship with Meyer, however, did not become intimate until many years later, after Jack was in the White House.

Mary Pinchot met Cord Meyer, a Yale graduate, in 1944, when he was a Marine Corps lieutenant. During World War II, Meyer distinguished himself in combat, losing an eye from shrapnel wounds suffered in the Pacific when a hand grenade rolled into his foxhole on Guam and exploded in his face. His twin brother died fighting on Okinawa. Cord emerged from World War II determined that those who died in combat, including his twin brother, would not have died in vain. Meyer joined the CIA in 1951 and became "part of a wave of idealistic, anti-Communist liberals who enlisted in the CIA after the war."[563]

As Cord Meyer's anti-Communist fervor intensified, he and the more free-spirited Mary Pinchot Meyer drifted apart. The couple split apart in 1958, two years after their middle son, nine-year-old Michael, was killed in an auto accident outside their home in McLean, Virginia. "Mary threw herself into the Washington art scene, starting an affair with a younger artist—the rising abstract painter Kenneth Noland—and embracing a pre-hippie lifestyle that included a wardrobe of peasant blouses and blue tights and a round of Reichian therapy, which promised enlightenment through orgasmic release," explained David Talbot in his 2007 book, *Brothers: The Hidden History of the Kennedy Years.*[564] When Mary Pinchot Meyer and JFK got back together again in late 1961, with Jack now in the White House, it was easy to see why they got together. She was "the same blond beauty with sparkling green-blue eyes" that JFK met when they were both teenagers; but now, "her mischievous and witty personality promised something deeper, an earthy and wry wisdom that must have matched his own acute sense of life's tragedy."[565]

In 1962 Mary Meyer became involved with Harvard University psychology lecturer Timothy Leary, noted for his experimentation with psychedelic drugs and for leading a cultural revolution in the 1960s distinguished by phrases such as, "Turn on, Drop out." In 1962 and 1963 Pinchot reportedly brought marijuana and LSD into the White House to enhance her sexual escapades with JFK. CIA spymaster James Angleton leaked to reporters that Mary Meyer and JFK experimented with drugs, smoking marijuana and dabbling with LSD. Reporter David Talbot picked up on Angleton's story, writing: "According to the spy, Meyer and Kennedy took one low dose of the hallucinogen, after which, he noted with a cringe-inducing delicacy, 'they made love.'"[566] Angleton knew his information was reliable because he had been bugging the telephones and various rooms of Meyer's Georgetown home. David Talbot reported that Mary Meyer consulted Timothy Leary about JFK. "[Mary Meyer] wanted Leary's advice about how to guide him on a psychedelic journey," Talbot wrote. "Though Mary didn't name her powerful friend she left little doubt who he was. 'I've heard Allen Ginsberg on radio and TV shows saying that if Khrushchev and Kennedy would take LSD together they'd end world conflict,' she told Leary. 'Isn't that the idea—to get powerful men to turn on?'"[567]

Certainly JFK found Mary Pinchot Meyer intriguing; what he thought of marijuana and LSD, if he actually did experiment with the drugs, is unrecorded.

Mary Pinchot's sister, Antoinette, better known as "Tony," married Ben Bradlee, the managing editor of the *Washington Post*. He is best known for publishing the Watergate stories investigated and published by Carl Bernstein and Bob Woodward. When JFK was a US Senator from Massachusetts, the Kennedys' and Bradlees' homes were literally across the street from one another in Georgetown. In those years, the Kennedys and Bradlees were close friends, prominent Georgetown socialites, and frequent dinner companions. Mary Pinchot reconnected with Georgetown after she divorced Cord Meyer and moved into a studio behind the Bradlees' home on N Street in Georgetown, determined to focus her energies on her emerging career as an artist.

Hunt had discussed Cord Meyer's role in the assassination not only in his deathbed confession, but also in his 2007 book, *American Spy*. "[Cord Meyer] was a high-level CIA operative whose wife, journalist Mary Pinchot, was having an affair with John F. Kennedy," Hunt wrote. "Meyer was the Yale-educated, blue-blooded son of a wealthy diplomat, who had once been elected the president of the United World Federalists—an organization supported by many intellectuals, such as Albert Einstein—which worked with the United Nations to build a 'just world order,' hoping to prevent another world war." Hunt noted Allen Dulles recruited Meyers to the CIA in 1951, placing him under Frank Wisner in what was then known as Operation Mockingbird, a CIA operation in which journalists were secretly paid by the CIA to report on world affairs with a CIA perspective, all unbeknownst to the American public. "The theorists suggest Cord would have had a motive to kill Kennedy because his wife was having an affair with the president," Hunt continued. "In 1954, the Kennedys bought an estate outside Washington, D.C., where they became neighbors of the Meyers. Cord's wife and Jackie apparently became rather friendly and went on walks together."

The rivalry with JFK was not only that both shared a love interest in Mary Meyers, but also that each had contrasting views about foreign policy. Meyer believed that JFK's view of foreign policy was dangerously set on pre-World War II ideas of US national interests. JFK was suspicious of the CIA based on his experience in Cuba and, as we will see in the next chapter, with his experiences with the CIA in Laos and Vietnam. Meyer aligned with Dulles and believed in an internationalist "one-world government" view that transcended nationalism. Because of their rivalry Cord Meyer would have been ripe for LBJ to recruit into organizing a JFK assassination plot.[568]

On October 12, 1964, less than a year after JFK was killed, Mary Meyer was attacked as she left her painting studio to take a walk along the Chesapeake and Ohio Canal towpath in Georgetown. In what police judged to be an apparent rape attempt, Meyer fought for her life, only to be killed by two bullet shots, one to the head and the other to the heart, both fired at close range. Within minutes of the assault, Raymond Crump, an African-American, was arrested near the murder scene. Failing to find any gun or forensic evidence, such as hair, clothing fibers, blood, semen, skin, urine, or saliva, that linked Raymond Crump to either the murder scene or the body and clothing of Mary Meyer, the jury voted to acquit Crump.[569] The case has never been solved. Longtime Pinchot family friend Peter Janney accused the CIA of murdering Pinchot and of setting Crump up to be the patsy.[570]

On the morning after Mary Meyer's death, Ben Bradlee and his wife, Tony, Mary's sister, talked to one of Mary's closest friends, Anne Truitt, who was in Tokyo at the time of Mary's death. She encouraged the Bradlees to go to Mary Meyer's home to recover her diary. When Ben and Tony Bradlee got there, they found high-ranking CIA official James Jesus Angleton inside. After a search, the three of them failed to find the diary. After Ben Bradlee realized they had not searched Mary's studio, he and his wife returned to the house, only to run into Jim Angleton again.

This time Angleton was in the process of picking the padlock. According to Ben Bradlee, after Angleton left, he and his wife found the diary and took it home with them. They claimed they found a few phrases that confirmed the relationship between Mary Meyer and JFK, and that they were stunned. "Tony, especially, felt betrayed, both by Kennedy and by Mary," wrote Ben Bradlee in his 1991 book, *A Good Life*.[571] Other than establishing the fact of Mary's affair with JFK, Bradlee maintained the diary included little of interest to assassination researchers, with most of the diary discussing Mary's artwork.

Still, there is a second, more sinister version of what happened to Mary's diary. Author Peter Janney argued that Ben and Tony Bradlee could not have recovered the diary because Angleton recovered Mary's diary on the night of her murder. Janney wrote that the night of Mary's murder, the Bradlees were unable to find the diary, and that Anne Truitt called Angleton to tell him where in the house to find the diary. According to Janney's reconstruction of events, after getting the phone call from Anne Truitt, Angelton returned to Mary's home a second time on the night of her murder and found the diary. Angleton destroyed the diary, Janney argued, because it contained information "highly incriminating of Angleton himself and the CIA's role in orchestrating what had happened in Dallas." Angleton was back in the house the morning after Mary's murder, Janey argued, to "take into his possession and eliminate any *other* documents, papers, letters, or personal effects that might further jeopardize the Warren Report and the public's acceptance of Lee Harvey Oswald's guilt." Janney concluded that Angleton returned to Mary's home a third time and that is when Ben and Tony Bradlee walked in on him searching through Mary's belongings, because Angleton "wanted to be seen searching for the diary so that no one would suspect that it was already in his possession."[572] The only ones who really knew what had happened in Mary's death, Janney insisted, were "the mastermind," Jim Angleton, and "his colleague," Cord Meyer, and to a lesser extent Ben Bradlee.

Remember, within the CIA the Executive Action program involved the mob, and specifically Sam Giancana in Chicago through the urging of Johnny Roselli, to provide assets to work with the CIA in assassinating JFK.[573] William Harvey headed the Executive Action program and E. Howard Hunt in his deathbed confession named William Harvey as an operative recruited to participate in the JFK assassination. It strains credibility to believe that a mature woman such as Mary Pinchot, with her access to the smug Georgetown elite of the early 1960s, would have confided intimate details of her relationship to JFK to a diary. Angleton was not interested in Mary because of Mary's affair with JFK or because of what Mary might have written in her diary about that love interest. Angleton was interested in Mary and her diary because of what Mary knew and might have written about Angleton himself.

In the end, E. Howard Hunt argued Mary's death was a contract job. "I think [Mary Pinchot Meyer's murder] was a professional hit by someone trying to protect the Kennedy legacy," Hunt wrote in *American Spy*. "I don't think that Cord Meyer killed his ex-wife, and I don't think it was Angleton either, although [Angleton] did apparently know that Mary and Kennedy had carried on the affair."[574] When he was in a nursing home at the end of his life, Cord Meyer is supposed to have speculated that Mary Pinchot's death was tied somehow to the JFK assassination. The story is that author C. David Heymann, author of *The Georgetown Ladies' Social Club*, asked Meyer some six weeks before his death if he thought he knew who killed Mary.[575] "The same sons of bitches that killed John F. Kennedy," the mortally-ill CIA man is said to have alleged.[576] Author David Talbot doubted the veracity of this story, yet Talbot had no doubt about the CIA's interest in Mary Pinchot Meyer. "What is clear is that Mary Meyer's personal life was of immense interest to the CIA, before and after her death," Talbot wrote. "Angleton was fully aware of the ecstatic sway she had over the president. And he believed that she actually influenced administration policy, nudging it in a more dovish direction."[577] That may have been a concern Mary had. But from the beginning of her marriage to Cord Meyer, Mary knew her husband and Angleton were close, as both men in their earlier years shared literary ambitions. What Angleton suspected Mary might have connected together was the degree to which Cord Meyer and Angleton's close relationship continued, right up until the day both men participated in the plot to kill JFK. Angleton, as we shall see in the next section, also had reason to know Lee Harvey Oswald, for nearly a year before Oswald's name surfaced as the likely suspect in the JFK murder case.

ANGLETON AND OSWALD'S INTELLIGENCE FILE

James Angleton, a well-educated and highly literate individual, directed ░░░░░░ ░░░░lligence for the CIA from 1954–1975. Most intelligence pro░░░░░░░░ ░░░░ ░░░░ ░░░░ ░░░░ ░░░░ ░░░ ░░░░lligence before joining the CIA he edited a literary journal that published the works of c. c. cummings and Ezra Pound—and his fierce loyalty to the agency. Angleton appears to have become involved in the JFK assassination primarily to cover-up the agency's involvement. Angleton is typically not named as a coconspirator in planning the JFK assassination but clearly appears in the narrative when he was assigned after JFK's death to be the CIA liaison to the Warren Commission. According to the House Select Committee on Assassinations, Angleton, in his role of directing counter-intelligence at the CIA, opened a 201 personality file on Oswald as far back as December 9, 1960, after Oswald's defection to the USSR.[578]

But the clincher is that among Angleton's responsibilities for counter intelligence at the CIA, Angleton ran the false defector program.[579] False defectors were double agents that "defected" to the Soviet Union with the intention of acting as undercover assets or spies. In the CIA, an important part of Angleton's job involved recruiting soldiers among the US military who were intelligent enough to learn Russian and clever enough to convince the Russians they were disgruntled idealists disillusioned with the United States and eager to adopt a political system that embraced real social justice, such as Soviet Communism. Even if Angleton had not recruited Oswald to defect, Angleton most likely managed Oswald through the process of defection and engineered Oswald's return to the United States the moment his return met the needs of the Agency.

As early as October 1960, the Department of State undertook a project to identify and research all Americans who had defected to the Soviet Union, to Soviet bloc nations, or to Communist China. At the Department of State's Office of Intelligence/Resources and Coordination, Robert B. Elwood wrote to Richard Bissell, the CIA's then-deputy director of plans—the position from which Bissell began planning the Bay of Pigs invasion of Cuba under the Eisenhower administration. Elwood wanted to identify all CIA assets that as former US military had participated in the "false defector" program. The assignment to follow through at the

State Department fell to Otto F. Otepka, deputy director of the State Department Office of Security. Bissell shipped the "false defector" file to James Angleton at CIA Counter Intelligence and to Robert L. Bannerman, Deputy Chief of Security at the CIA.[580] According to former military intelligence officer John Newman in his 1995 book, *Oswald and the CIA*, Bannerman told him that the opening of Oswald's 201 file regarding his defection to the Soviet Union "would have all gone through Angleton." The 201 opening was something on which "we worked very closely with Angleton and his staff," Bannerman recalled.[581] Given the documents on the JFK assassination released by the federal government in the past few years, we know Oswald's CIA file was numbered #39-61981, with the "39" denoting an intelligence file. From sometime shortly after he joined the Marines in 1957, Oswald was likely targeted and recruited by the CIA to be a top player in the CIA "false defector" program.

At the State Department, Otepka continued to add to Oswald's 201 file, noting key "red flags," for instance when Oswald applied for and received a US passport on one day's notice to return to the United States, as well as Oswald receiving an extra visa a month and a half before he actually left Russia, evidently so his Russian wife could accompany him home. Otepka also added to Oswald's file when he learned Oswald had received a State Department loan that made his return to the United States financially possible. There are indications in the file that the attorney general Bobby Kennedy was aware of Oswald and his 201 file a year and a half before the JFK assassination.

When the supposed assassination attempt was made on Gen. Walker, the Justice Department evidently also got involved in the Oswald file. The Justice Department evidently intervened, asking the Dallas Police not to pursue, investigate, or arrest Lee Harvey Oswald in the matter of Oswald supposedly having fired a shot at Gen. Edwin Walker in Dallas. Walker urged the House Select Committee on Investigations to look into this extraordinary intervention that he believed had to trace back to Robert Kennedy.[582] From the pieces of the CIA records on the JFK assassination we have available, we can assume that when his brother was assassinated in Dallas it was not the first time Robert Kennedy heard the name "Lee Harvey Oswald." Conceivably, as we saw in chapter 4, a trained Soviet bloc intelligence officer like Pacepa had good reason for perceiving everything

Oswald did resulted from Oswald being a KGB asset, and the CIA may have assumed Oswald was a KGB asset. When we ask the question, "Who did Oswald work for?" the answer may end up being that Oswald worked for both the CIA and the KGB. The likelihood is that prior to the JFK assassination, the FBI's file on Oswald was fairly extensive. As remarkable as it seems, the evidence suggests Lee Harvey Oswald prior to the assassination was on the payroll of the FBI. J. Lee Rankin, the general counsel of the Warren Commission, wrote a memo to the file in January 1964 documenting that a reliable source informed him of journalists in Texas who commonly knew Oswald was receiving a monthly check of $200 from the FBI.[583] Knowing this it is remarkable to think the Warren Commission insisted Lee Harvey Oswald was operating alone. The alternative reality may have been that Lee Harvey Oswald was a patriotic US citizen who earned his employment as a well-trained intelligence operative with his primary allegiance to the CIA. This could be a key part of the deep secret the CIA could not afford the US public to know in the aftermath of the JFK assassination when the Warren Report was issued in 1964.

THE CONSPIRACY EXPANDS

In his deathbed confession, E. Howard Hunt identified a small group of people from within the CIA that Cord Meyer recruited into the assassination plot. In an organizational chart designed to describe the plot, Hunt placed David Morales below Cord Meyer but with a direct line to the contract killers on the grassy knoll. On the same level as Morales, but off to the side, Hunt placed CIA agent William Harvey.

David Morales had a dark Latin, possibly even Mexican or Indian appearance. He first showed up as El Indio ("The Indian") in the CIA training of guerillas for the staged "invasion" of Guatemala engineered by E. Howard Hunt in 1954. House Select Committee investigator Gaeton Fonzi describes Morales simply: "David Sanchez Morales was a hit man for the CIA." Fonzi notes Morales bragged of killing people for the CIA in Vietnam, in Venezuela, and in Uruguay, among other places. "These were not murders in the heat of military combat—although they were done in what he considered the performance of his duty for his country," Fonzi wrote. "(T)hese were assassinations of individuals or groups selected for annihilation."[584] In the 1960s, Morales was chief of operations at the CIA's large JMWAVE facility in Miami, an operation that began providing covert training for the Bay of Pigs invasion and evolved into an operations center for Operation Mongoose, a CIA effort to assassinate or otherwise overthrow Fidel Castro. JMWAVE operated under the guise of Zenith Technical Enterprises, Inc, a front company created as a cover for the covert operations JMWAVE staged against Cuba. Fonzi described an all-night drinking session during which Morales flew off the handle at the mention of JFK's name. Morales started yelling about what a wimp JFK was and talking about how JFK was responsible for the men who died in the Bay of Pigs operation. Finally, Morales stopped, sat down on the bed and remained silent for a moment. "Then, as if saying it only to himself, he added, 'Well, we sure took care of that son of a bitch, didn't we,'" Fonzi related in his book *The Last Investigation*.[585]

As noted above, while working for the CIA, William Harvey came to direct a policy that became known as Executive Action, a determination to remove a foreign head of state from power by any means required, including staging a coup d'état and/or assassination. Harvey, like Morales, was involved in the CIA staged coup d'état in 1954 that overthrew the government of Jacobo Arbenz in Guatemala. Harvey, head of ZR/RIFLE—the operation assigned to eliminate foreign political leaders—also directed Task Force W, a group appointed to oversee JMWAVE operations. As documented by Claudia Furiati in her 1994 book, *ZR Rifle: The Plot to Kill Kennedy and Castro*, Harvey drew up policies and oriented the execution of the Cuba project for all CIA foreign stations, as well as for CIA operatives who worked in embassies in countries where Cuba had strong diplomatic representation.[586] Ultimately, Harvey fell out of favor with JFK as evidenced by the fact that Harvey continued to send clandestine operations into Cuba during the Cuban Missile Crisis, ignoring Robert Kennedy's instructions to then-CIA director John McCone to halt all covert operations against Cuba. On October 30, 1962, Harvey was removed as commander of ZR/RIFLE.[587]

E. Howard Hunt wrote at length in *American Spy* that he doubted Lee Harvey Oswald had the accuracy of marksmanship required to hit JFK with a mail-order 1938 Italian-manufactured Mannlicher-Carcano rifle. "There has been suggestion in some circles that CIA agent Bill Harvey had something to do with the murder [of JFK] and had recruited several Corsicans, especially a crack shot named Lucien Sarti, to back up Oswald and make sure the hit was successful," Hunt wrote, "Supposedly, Sarti was dressed in a Dallas police uniform and fired the fatal bullet from the grassy knoll behind the picket fence."[588] Hunt considered another possibility. "Is it possible that Bill Harvey might have recruited a Mafia criminal to administer the magic bullet?" he speculated. "I think it's possible. I can't go beyond that. Harvey could definitely be a person of interest, as he was a strange character hiding a mass of hidden aggression. Allegations have been made that he transported weapons to Dallas. Certainly it is an area that could use further investigation." Hunt noted the association between Harvey and the Corsican assassins involved in the Marseilles drug connection known as the "French Connection," stemmed from a memo Harvey authored when running the Executive Action program, advocating a desire to hire Corsicans because of their expertise and proficiency as contract hit men.[589]

Hunt had little regard for Harvey, a man he described as "the perfect concentration camp guard"—a "brain-addled pistol-toting drunk . . . very much under the control of his wife." Hunt felt certain Harvey, out of resentment over losing his job as head of ZR/RIFLE, could easily have teamed with LBJ to form "some kind of a thieves' pact" to assassinate JFK.[590] In his deathbed confession, Hunt claims he personally bowed out of the JFK assassination plot when he learned Cord Meyer had recruited William Harvey, a man Hunt described as an "alcoholic psycho."[591]

DAVID PHILLIPS AND ANTONIO VECIANA

At the next level of the conspiracy, Hunt claimed Cord Meyer recruited David Phillips, the CIA operative who had played a major role in the propaganda campaign overthrowing the Arbenz government in Guatemala in 1954. Hunt slyly commented that Phillips, "a consummate CIA officer" was not above "a bit of disinformation."[592] Phillips, widely regarded as a propaganda specialist, ultimately rose to be chief of the CIA's Western Hemisphere. The House Select Committee on Assassinations concluded that Phillips, assuming the identity of the mysterious Maurice Bishop, worked with Antonio Veciana, the Cuban exile leader who established Alpha 66 to oppose Castro after the Communists assumed power in Cuba in 1959. Veciana claimed that it was Maurice Bishop who suggested to him that in 1963 Alpha 66 should attack Soviet ships docked in Cuba as a means to prevent an improvement in the relationship between the United States and the U.S.S.R. after the conclusion of the Cuban Missile Crisis. When Alpha 66 attacked a Soviet ship on March 23, 1963, a furious JFK ordered that Veciana and other leaders of Alpha 66 should be arrested and placed in confinement in Florida.[593]

Veciana claimed that in August 1963, he saw Lee Harvey Oswald in the company of Maurice Bishop. Veciana met Bishop in the lobby of a large downtown office building that House Select Committee investigator Gaeton Fonzi believed was the Southland Center, a forty-two-story office complex built in Dallas in the late 1950s. Veciana noticed a young man with Bishop that day. After seeing the news photographs and television coverage portraying Lee Harvey Oswald as the long-gun shooter of JFK, Veciana told Fonzi he was certain the man with Bishop that day had been Oswald. "Well, you know, Bishop himself taught me how to remember faces, how to remember characteristics," Veciana explained to Fonzi. "I am sure it was Oswald. If it wasn't Oswald, it was someone who looked exactly like him. *Exacto. Exacto.*"[594]

After investigating thoroughly, Fonzi was convinced Veciana's story was true. "Maurice Bishop was David Atlee Phillips," Fonzi wrote in his book, *The Last Investigation*. "I state that unequivocally."[595] Fonzi continued to state he was convinced David Atlee Phillips played a key role in the JFK assassination. "I don't embrace the assumption that Phillip's relationship to Oswald may have been extraneous to any conspiratorial role. If there was one most meaningful revelation that emerged from further digging into Phillips's background after the Assassinations Committee probe, it was the fact that David Phillips, the consummate actor, maintained a personal and even familial façade that was in direct contrast to the political realities of his professional life."[596]

Fonzi believed what motivated Philips was his deep ideological commitment to getting rid of Castro in Cuba. Fonzi also believed Philips rose to be CIA chief of the Western Hemisphere Division not by accident, but because key CIA field operatives shared his view that JFK's "deal" with Khrushchev that ended the Cuban Missile Crisis was treasonous because JFK promised that the U.S. would not invade Cuba if the Soviet Union withdrew nuclear weapons from the island. Fonzi was convinced anti-Castroism was the unifying theme within the CIA that served as the trigger to the CIA's decision to participate in the JFK assassination. He was skeptical that Oswald actually made his controversial trip to Mexico, believing instead that the CIA staged the entire sequence of events in Mexico by using a CIA operative who was instructed to assume the Oswald identity. Phillips was CIA station chief in Mexico City at the time of Oswald's visit. Commenting about his certainty David Atlee Phillips was the man who assumed the Maurice Bishop persona. Fonzi wrote, "It is no coincidence that the man who emerges as the Maurice Bishop who planned Alpha 66 attempts to sink Russian ships in Havana harbor with the aim of embarrassing Kennedy and sabotaging his negotiations with Khrushchev, was the same man responsible for staging the entire Mexico City scenario designed to link Lee Harvey Oswald to Fidel Castro."[597] Fonzi stressed that Phillips had a tight working association with some of the CIA's most lethal anti-Castro operatives, including E. Howard Hunt and William Harvey.

In September 1979 Veciana was ambushed on his way home from work in an apparent assassination attempt. Four shots were fired, one of which hit him in the left temple. Veciana survived, but after the attack he refused to discuss his work with Alpha 66. He was convinced a Castro agent made the attempt on his life.[598]

Reflecting on Veciana, Fonzi wrote there is "a preponderance of evidence that indicates Lee Harvey Oswald had an association with a U.S. Government agency, perhaps more than one, but undoubtedly with the Central Intelligence Agency."[599]

ROSCOE WHITE AND HONEST JOE

In chapter 5, we saw that Roscoe White was named by Sam Giancana as a suspect in the murder of Dallas Policeman J. D. Tippit, and was also suspected of having been a shooter in the JFK assassination. White's history is intertwined with that of Lee Harvey Oswald. White also served in the same marine platoon with Oswald in Japan and later in the Philippines. Both Roscoe White and Lee Harvey Oswald were candidates for having been recruited into the CIA when they were marines. As discussed in chapter 2, Former marine sniper Craig Roberts argued that Roscoe

White was recruited by William Harvey to participate in ZR/RIFLE under the codename Mandarin. In his 1994 book, *Kill Zone*, Roberts noted that Roscoe White had access to a Dallas police uniform and badge on November 22, 1963.[600]

Long-time assassination researcher Jones Harris linked Roscoe White with a strange incident involving an old Edsel automobile tied to Honest Joe's Pawn Shop, a well-known Dallas fixture at 2524 Elm Street owned by Rubin Goldstein, a Dallas resident since 1931. The address is approximately ten blocks to the east of Dealey Plaza on Elm Street. The distinctive Edsel automobile, customized as an advertising vehicle, featured on its hood an oversized mock fifty-caliber machine gun. There is ample testimony in the Warren Commission hearings, typically ignored by the Warren Commission in its final report, that the Honest Joe's Pawn Shop vehicle was parked behind the concrete monument on the Elm Street spur in front of the Texas School Book Depository on the day of the shooting. In an extreme blow-up of a frame from the film taken by Orville Nix on November 22, 1963, Harris identified Roscoe White as the shooter crouching on top of the Honest Joe's Pawn Shop vehicle, firing at JFK.[601] From the vantage point of having jumped on top of the car, White may have been the shooter who hit JFK's neck.

There is ample testimony in the Warren Commission hearings about the Honest Joe's Pawn Shop vehicle being driven in the motorcade route the day of the assassination. Jean Hill and Mary Moorman, two assassination witnesses who were on Elm Street directly across from the concrete monument when JFK was shot, both reported observing the Honest Joe's vehicle. In an interview with the FBI conducted on March 13, 1964, Jean Hill described how she and Mary Moorman walked around the parkway area near the Texas School Book Depository looking for the best vantage point from which to take photographs of the president. Hill recalled talking to a uniformed policeman of the Dallas Police Department on the sidewalk near the main entrance to the Depository building. "While conversing with the policeman, Mrs. Hill noticed an automobile circling the area," the FBI report of her interview noted. "The windows of the vehicle were covered with cardboard and the name 'Honest Joe's Pawn Shop' was painted on the side of the car. Mrs. Hill made a remark about the automobile and the policeman told her the driver had permission to drive in the area."[602] Hill jokingly said to Moorman, "Do you suppose there are murderers in the van?"[603]

Assassination witness A. J. Millican gave testimony to the Dallas County Sheriff's office that he was standing on the north side of Elm Street about halfway between Houston Street and the triple underpass. "About five or ten minutes before the President's car came by I observed a truck from Honest Joe's Pawn Shop parked by the Book Depository store," he stated in a signed statement. Millican contradicted Jean Hill in claiming the Honest Joe's vehicle drove off five or ten minutes before the JFK motorcade came by.[604]

Secret Service Agent Forest V. Sorrels questioned Jack Ruby about Honest Joe in the first minutes after Ruby shot Oswald. Sorrels interviewed Ruby on the fifth floor of the Dallas Police Department in the city jail for about five to seven minutes, while Ruby was standing there dressed only in his shorts with a Dallas Police officer on either side of him. "[Ruby] appeared to be considering whether or not he was going to answer my questions, and I told him that I had just come from the third floor and had been looking out the window, and that I had seen Honest Joe, who is a Jewish merchant there, who operates a second-hand pawn loan shop, so to speak, specializing in tools on Elm Street, and who is more or less known in the area because of the fact that he takes advantage of any opportunity to get free advertising," Sorrels testified to the Warren Commission. "He at that time had an Edsel car, which is somewhat a rarity now, all painted up with 'Honest Joe' on there. He wears jackets with 'Honest Joe' on the back. He gets write-ups in the paper, free advertising about different things he loans money on, like artificial limbs and things like that. And I had noticed Honest Joe across the street when I was looking out of Chief Batchelor's office."

Evidently, Sorrels thought mentioning Honest Joe to Ruby would break the ice because Ruby was also Jewish. It worked. "So I remarked to Jack Ruby, I said, 'I just saw Honest Joe across the street over there, and I know a number of Jewish merchants here that you know.'" Sorrels continued in his testimony. "And Ruby said, 'That's good enough for me. What is it that you want to know?' And I said these two words, 'Jack, why?'" This is where Ruby explained to Sorrels he had been emotionally upset by the JFK assassination, and he did not want Jackie Kennedy to have to go through the ordeal of Lee Harvey Oswald's trial.[605]

Sorrels repeated the story in a signed report he filed on February 3, 1964, with the Secret Service office in Washington.[606] Dallas Police Department Sergeant Patrick Trevore Dean, the officer who brought Sorrels to interview Ruby after he shot Oswald, in his testimony before the Warren Commission validated that Sorrels had talked to Ruby about Honest Joe.[607] An FBI report filed in the Warren Commission documents identified Honest Joe as Rubin Goldstein. The report indicated:

> GOLDSTEIN advised on the morning of November 22, 1963, he was driving an old Edsel sedan in the vicinity of the Texas School Book Depository. He stated the car was brightly painted and carried slogans advertising his pawnshop. GOLDSTEIN said the police permitted him to drive on the route used by President JOHN F. KENNEDY's Motorcade. He stated, however, that he was parked on Pacific Avenue, one block from the parade route, when President KENNEDY was shot.[608]

The FBI report further stated that while Rubin Goldstein claimed not to know Lee Harvey Oswald, Goldstein admitted that he knew Jack Ruby. Goldstein told the FBI that Ruby purchased some equipment from him several years prior to the JFK assassination. Goldstein insisted he was not a personal friend of Jack Ruby and that he had no other business dealings with Ruby since Ruby bought the equipment from him.

Almost immediately after the assassination, Sorrels had suspected Goldstein and his Honest Joe vehicle were involved. Assassination researcher Jones Harris had the relevant frame from the Nix film enlarged. It shows the Honest Joe's vehicle parked on Pacific Avenue, the spur running directly behind the Texas School Book Depository parallel to the Elm Street spur that runs in front of the Texas School Book Depository as a short extension of Elm Street west past Houston Street. Startlingly there appears to be a man standing on the running board of the Honest Joe vehicle, with a weapon in his hands, shooting at JFK as the limo passes on Elm Street. Harris interviewed Sorrels shortly after the assassination, and Sorrels admitted he had visited Honest Joe's store on the afternoon of November 22, 1963. Harris believes Sorrels was well along the way to solving almost single-handedly the JFK assassination. Harris is convinced Sorrels was in the process of implicating both Goldstein and Roscoe

White, the shooter Harris insists fired from the running-board of the Honest Joe vehicle visible in the early versions of the Nix film. Sorrels was largely taken off the case after the FBI began assuming jurisdiction over the investigation. By Sunday morning, when Jack Ruby shot Lee Harvey Oswald, there was no possible way Washington would allow Sorrels to continue his investigation in Dallas, even though Sorrels was the special agent in charge of the Dallas district of the US Secret Service. If Sorrels had been given enough time, he would have located James P. Hosty Jr., the FBI agent in charge of Oswald's case in Dallas, so as to begin probing Oswald's relationship to the FBI prior to the assassination.

Beverly Oliver was a performer in Jack Ruby's Carousel Club who also turned out to be the long-unidentified "Babushka Lady," and an eyewitness to the JFK assassination. Taking photographs of the JFK limo as it traveled along Elm Street in Dealey Plaza, she positively identified Roscoe White on the grassy knoll in the immediate aftermath of the shooting. Oliver is the witness that was cited in chapter 3 as having been introduced to Lee Harvey Oswald in the Carousel Club by Jack Ruby who described Oswald as a CIA agent. In her book, *Nightmare in Dallas*, Oliver describes running across Elm Street to join the people running up the grassy knoll as JFK's limousine sped under the triple underpass. As she ran up the steps heading to the concrete pergola monument, she felt scared. Her heart was pounding, her hands were perspiring, and her stomach was in knots. That's when she describes encountering the man she knew as "Geneva [White's] husband" walking across the steps in front of her.[609]

"He was wearing part of his policeman's uniform but not all of it. He was wearing his shirt, his badge, his trousers, but he was not wearing a hat, nor was he carrying a gun."[610] Oliver says she caught White's attention, and she was sure he recognized her even though she was wearing a wig because White had seen her in wigs before. Oliver reported that Jack Ruby had hired Geneva White to be a hostess at the Carousel Club and Geneva relied on her husband to pick her up after work.[611]

The officer seen in the Hughes film in the railroad yard behind the fence on the grassy knoll is wearing a Dallas Police Department uniform, but he is conspicuously seen not wearing a Dallas Police Department cap and not carrying a gun. Viewing the Hughes film, Oliver identified Roscoe White as the Dallas Police officer seen in the Hughes film standing in the railroad yard behind the picket fence on the grassy knoll in the moments following the assassination.[612] The officer in the railroad yard in the Hughes film bears a striking physical resemblance to Roscoe White.

After Roscoe White's death in 1971, his son, Ricky White, claimed to have found a military footlocker belonging to his father. In it, Ricky claimed, was a handwritten diary in which his father supposedly admitted to shooting JFK and some never-before-seen photos of the assassination and Lee Harvey Oswald. When Ricky later went to sell the footlocker, he discovered that the diary and photos were missing.

About a year later, Ricky White claimed to find a metal artillery powder canister in his grandmother's attic that contained Roscoe White's Marine Corps service papers and his dog tag, as well as three messages written in military style and addressed to an individual code-named Mandarin. Former Marine sniper Craig Roberts claims to have seen the messages and verified that the number in the top right-hand corner of each was identical to Roscoe White's Marine Corps serial number.[613] Roberts declared the "facts ring true: Roscoe White was in Lee Harvey Oswald's platoon in Japan and later in the Philippines; Roscoe White worked in the intelligence community; he had access to a Dallas police uniform complete with badge; his serial number matched that of the message addressee number; and finally, the messages were of standard military format down to the last detail."[614] Roberts noted the messages were sent in September 1963, while Roscoe White was waiting to start the Dallas Police Academy and was still associated with William Harvey's ZR/RIFLE project. The messages called for White to be prepared to eliminate a national security threat in Dallas, assumed to be a reference to JFK. Roberts insists he has personally inspected the three messages and believes them to be authentic, with the format, content, and composition of the messages exactly as he would expect, given his extensive military experience as a sniper.

NIXON IN DALLAS ON NOVEMBER 22, 1963

Richard Nixon did not want the American public knowing he was in Dallas, Texas, on November 23, 1963, when JFK was assassinated. Otherwise, why would he have invented several different versions of the story? L. Fletcher Prouty, the retired US Air Force colonel who was the real-life model for the "Mr. X" character played by actor Donald Sutherland in Oliver Stone's 1991 movie, *JFK*, notes Nixon told three different stories designed to cover up the truth that he was in Dallas at the very moment JFK was killed.[615]

In a *Reader's Digest* article that appeared in the November 1964 issue, Nixon claimed he boarded an airplane in Dallas on the morning of November 22, 1963, and that the airplane arrived on time, at 12:56 p.m. local time in New York. "I hailed a cab," Nixon said in the *Reader's Digest* article. "We were waiting for a light to change when a man ran over from the street corner and said that the President had just been shot in Dallas." So, in the first version, Nixon claims he was in the air when Kennedy was shot and a man told him the news.

In the November 1973 issue of *Esquire* magazine Nixon said he attended a Pepsi-Cola convention in Dallas, leaving on the morning of November 22, 1963, on a flight from Love Field back to New York. In this second version, Nixon claims he caught a cab and headed for New York City, when the cab missed a turn, throwing the taxi off the freeway. A woman came screaming out of a house, and when Nixon rolled down the window of the taxi, the woman told him JFK had been shot in Dallas.

In the third version that Nixon provided Jim Bishop for his book, *The Day Kennedy Was Shot*, reporters met Nixon's plane from Dallas and Nixon gave an interview before anyone knew JFK had been shot. " [Nixon] was barely out of the airport when one of the reporters got the message: 'The President has been shot in Dallas,'" Bishop wrote.[616]

Prouty later learned the truth was that at the exact time JFK was shot, Nixon was yet in Dallas, attending a Pepsi-Cola Company convention on behalf of his Wall Street law firm, Mudge, Rose, Guthrie, Alexander, & Mitchell. Nixon was there representing outside counsel to work with Harvey Russel, Pepsi-Cola's general counsel. Further documenting this was a news story the *Dallas Morning News* ran on November 22, 1963, entitled "Nixon Predicts JFK May Drop Johnson." The *Dallas Morning News* also printed a picture of Nixon staying in the Baker Hotel at 1400 Commerce in downtown Dallas, six blocks from the spot where JFK was assassinated. The newspaper reported Pepsi-Cola had rented the entire third floor of the hotel for their "convention" that included a suite for Pepsi heiress and movie star actress Joan Crawford, a suite for attorney Richard Nixon, and various rooms for Pepsi executives and unnamed dignitaries.

Further documenting Nixon in Dallas, on Friday morning, November 22, 1963, the *Dallas Herald Times* published a story noting that the previous evening Nixon was a guest at the Empire Room of the Statler Hilton, along with a group from Pepsi-Cola that included "the chic and glamorous as ever Joan Crawford." When Nixon entered the room, the Don Ragon Band was playing "April in Portugal," a song Nixon said was his wife's favorite. The newspaper further reported that Nixon and Crawford sat ringside in the Empire Room during the dinner show and drew tremendous applause when introduced.[617]

The Pepsi meeting in Dallas on November 22, 1963 was interrupted by the announcement JFK had been shot. With that deeply disturbing news, the convention session Nixon was attending broke up. Nixon returned to his hotel room and was driven later that afternoon to Love Field by a Pepsi-Cola official named DeLuca.[618]

Don Fulsom, a longtime White House reporter and former United Press International Washington bureau chief, has credited Nixon's ties to the JFK assassination as his greater cover-up, one that worked, compared to the cover-up Nixon attempted over Watergate—Nixon's final cover-up that unraveled as he resigned the presidency on August 4, 1974.[619] The morning after the JFK assassination, Nixon called a meeting in his New York apartment of top Republican leaders to assess how JFK's murder would change the possibilities of Nixon running for president.[620] Even when they were both US Senators, Nixon resented JFK for the attention he got from a loving press, attention that Nixon felt reflected the privileges including an Ivy League education that JFK enjoyed because his father, Joseph P. Kennedy, was wealthy. In 1960 Nixon was convinced Chicago mayor Richard Daley had stolen enough votes at the order of Kennedy family boss, Joseph P. Kennedy, and with the help of Chicago crime boss Sam Giancana to tip the narrow balance of the presidential election away from Nixon.

By the time of the JFK assassination, the mob's 1960 honeymoon with JFK was over, and Giancana had abandoned JFK, feeling betrayed by Bobby Kennedy's war against the Italian and Jewish mobs in the east. Giancana maintained the JFK assassination had taken months to mastermind and dozens of men were involved, planning the assassination hit for several different cities, including Chicago, Tampa/Miami, Los Angeles, and Dallas. Giancana claimed that ultimately JFK had to be lured to Dallas because Dallas afforded the best opportunity for a successful assassination. "Richard Nixon and Lyndon Johnson knew about the whole damn thing," Giancana wrote about the JFK assassination, disclosing both Richard Nixon and LBJ had met with him in Dallas several times prior to the JFK hit to discuss the assassination planning.[621]

Giancana insisted the JFK assassination was a joint mob-CIA action, done with the approval and complicity of both Lyndon Johnson and Richard Nixon. "The politicians and the CIA made it real simple," Giancana said. "We'd each provide men for the hit. . . . I'd oversee the Outfit [organized crime] side of things and throw in Jack Ruby and some extra backup and the CIA would put their own guys on to take care of the rest." Giancana further claimed Dallas mayor Earle Cabell, the brother of former CIA deputy director Charles Cabell, made sure security along the motorcade in Dallas was lax at best. Charles Cabell also had a grudge with JFK because he was one of the CIA officials JFK forced to resign in January 1962 after the Bay of Pigs invasion. Giancana specifically mentioned Roscoe White as one of the shooters, and he insisted both Lee Harvey Oswald and Dallas Police officer J. D. Tippit were part of the conspiracy, with Oswald unbeknownst to him having been marked to play the role of the patsy.[622]

According to Giancana the actual hit came down on November 22, 1963, from a CIA command center operated out of a hotel. They coordinated with field operatives via state-of-the-art walkie-talkie telecommunications equipment at that time available only to government spooks. Inconspicuously positioned along the motorcade route, spotters with unseen field communications gear reported the progress of the JFK limo to alert sniper teams positioned for action. The best shooters were reserved for final shots planned to occur as the limo approached the sweet spot of the kill zone, along Elm Street before the final curve of the street into the triple underpass.

"And the rest is history," Giancana bragged. "For once, we didn't even have to worry about J. Edgar Hoover. . . . He hated the Kennedys as much as anybody, and he wasn't about to help Bobby find his brother's killers. He buried his head in the sand, covered up anything and everything his 'Boy Scouts' found."

SEVEN

VIETNAM, DIEM, THE FRENCH CONNECTION, AND LBJ

"I remember [JFK] saying that the CIA frequently did things he didn't know about, and he was unhappy about it. He complained that the CIA was almost autonomous. He told me he believed the CIA had arranged to have Diem (South Vietnam) and Trujillo (Dominican Republic) bumped off. He was pretty well shocked about that. He thought it was a stupid thing to do, and he wanted to get control of what the CIA was doing.'"

—Senator George Smathers, quoted in *The Assassinations: Dallas and Beyond,* 1976[623]

In the final months, [JFK] spoke with friends about his own death with a freedom and frequency that shocked them. Some found it abnormal. Senator George Smathers said, "I don't know why it is, but death became kind of an obsession with Jack."

—Senator George Smathers, quoted in James W. Douglass, *JFK and the Unspeakable,* 2008[624]

J FK WAS DEEPLY MOVED by the poem "Rendezvous," a poem about death. Written by Alan Seeger, who graduated from Harvard in 1910 and volunteered for the French Foreign Legion before the United States entered World War I, the poem first seems to prefigure his own death. Seeger was killed on July 4, 1916, at Belloy-en-Senterre, attacking a French position. The poem ends:

> But I've a rendezvous with Death
> At midnight in some flaming town,

When Spring trips north again this year,
And I to my pledged word am true,
I shall not fail that rendezvous.

Writing about Seeger's poem and the profound meaning it had for JFK, James W. Douglass commented, "John Kennedy had been listening to the music of death for years."[625]

Kennedy lived much of his life in pain. He suffered from Addison's disease and had a degenerative back ailment that plagued him for life. Presidential historian Robert Dallek, after gaining access to a collection of JFK papers for the years 1955–1963 that contained various medical records, including X-rays and prescription records, revealed Kennedy "was taking an extraordinary variety of medications: steroids for his Addison's disease; painkillers for his back; anti-spasmodic for his colitis; antibiotics for urinary-tract infections; antihistamines for allergies; and, on at least one occasion, an anti-psychotic (though only for two days) for a severe mood change that Jackie Kennedy believed had been brought on by anti-histamines." Kennedy's charismatic appeal rested heavily on the image of youthful energy and good health he projected. Dallek concluded it was a myth. The real story was more heroic—the story of "iron-willed fortitude in mastering the difficulties of chronic illness."[626]

JFK became dependent on Max Jacobson, better known as "Dr. Feelgood"—a doctor who had emigrated from Germany to New York and who gave JFK injections of amphetamines and pain killers that made him less dependent on crutches. Among those he trusted, Jack (JFK) could be seen occasionally during the middle of a meeting calmly taking a syringe and injecting himself into his thigh, passing the needle straight through his pants—an act he performed without comment, not breaking a sentence as he kept stride with the conversation. Dallek commented that JFK's medical ailments in a strange way contributed to his demise. He wore a corset-like back brace every day, and after an initial shot hit him in the back, the corset held him upright, positioning him perfectly for the final fatal headshots.

Jack's preoccupation with death may have been due to the fact that he knew he would almost certainly become a cripple in old age, confined to a wheelchair. When JFK was told that an assassination plot was underway, that he would be shot by a high-powered rifle from a tall building, Jack took the information stoically. Rather than take extraordinary precautions to protect his safety, he commented matter-of-factly that sometimes a person has no choice but to do what they must do. Still, as his rendezvous with death approached and the calendar entered November 1963, news from South Vietnam did not permit Jack Kennedy to view the potential of an assassination attempt in a fateful or stoic manner. Suddenly, the prospect he might be assassinated, and soon, became all too real a prospect for JFK to dismiss. The emotional impact of the realization of his impending death finally hit JFK uncharacteristically hard.

THE CIA HIT ON DIEM

On Saturday, November 2, 1963, less than three weeks away from his own assassination, President John F. Kennedy was deeply disturbed to learn that South Vietnamese President Ngo Dinh Diem and his younger brother Ngo Dinh Nhu had been arrested and killed by the South Vietnamese army. They were victims of a CIA-engineered coup led by South Vietnamese Maj. Gen. Duong Van Minh. The moment JFK heard Diem had been killed, he knew the CIA had most likely signed his own death warrant.

At 7:00 a.m. Washington time, Ambassador Lodge sent a cable from Saigon to the White House describing the death of Diem and Nhu. National Security Council staff aide Michael V. Forrestal handed the message to JFK in the Cabinet Room of the White House as a crisis meeting of the National Security Council was about to begin. Reading the cable, Kennedy "leaped to his feet and rushed from the room with a look of shock on his face," as described by General Maxwell Taylor who was attending the meeting.[627] Even more embarrassing to the United States, Diem was murdered while his wife, Madame Nhu, was in the United States on a speaking tour promoting the interests of her husband's government.

Presidential historian Robert Dallek, in his 2003 book, *An Unfinished Life*, noted Taylor attributed Kennedy's reaction to his belief that any change of government in South Vietnam would be carried out without bloodshed. Even more precisely, JFK had specifically ordered the CIA not to assassinate Diem in a coup d'état.[628] JFK could not easily dismiss the problem of Diem's execution. If Diem could be assassinated despite his orders, JFK knew he, too, could be assassinated. He suspected the same people in the CIA who had disregarded his instructions to Ambassador Lodge were capable of plotting directly against him as well. Trusted JFK advisor Arthur Schlesinger saw JFK shortly after the Diem assassination and found the president to be "somber and shaken." Insightfully, Schlesinger commented he had not seen JFK so depressed since the Bay of Pigs crisis.[629] Instantly on hearing the news Diem and his brother had been killed, JFK realized the instrument of his death was the CIA. If a CIA coup d'état was underway to remove him from office by assassination, what could Jack Kennedy do to prevent it?

On Monday, November 4, 1963, JFK taped a message on the Diem assassination for future historians. "I was shocked by the death of Diem and Nhu," JFK recorded. "I'd met Diem with Justice Douglas many years ago. He was an extraordinary character. While [Diem] became increasingly difficult in the last months, nevertheless over a ten-year period, he'd held his country together, maintained its independence under very adverse conditions. The way he was killed made it particularly abhorrent."[630] Kennedy believed the $1 million in large denominations that Diem had with him in a briefcase at the time he was murdered was evidence Diem had planned to escape and live comfortably in exile. Kennedy refused to accept the official story Diem had committed suicide by poison, believing instead the military loyal to General Minh had assassinated Diem, at the orders of Minh and with the approval of the CIA. Diem and his brother placed themselves at risk by agreeing to surrender to forces loyal to General Minh. In exchange for the trust Diem and his brother placed in JFK, they were brutally killed. On orders from General Minh, Captain Nguyen Van Nhung assassinated Diem and Nhu with a pistol at point-blank range in an armored personnel carrier, finishing the job off with a bayonet, as Diem and Nhu were en route to a South Vietnam military base and then out of the country.

The Diem murder was especially ironic due to the fact that the CIA positioned Diem to head South Vietnam after the Geneva Agreements of 1954 partitioned Vietnam and after the defeat of the French at Dien Bien Phu.[631]

Ngo Dinh Diem established his nationalist credentials in the early 1930s when he resigned his position as Vietnam's Interior Minister.

Living in the United States in the 1950s, he won over key US legislators who began to see him as the best hope for anti-Communist leadership in Vietnam. The CIA had restored the Shah of Iran to his throne in 1953, and in March 1954, just before the French defeat at Dien Bien Phu, the CIA had engineered a successful military coup against the government of Guatemala, CIA operative Thomas L. Ahern Jr. noted in a secret CIA document, declassified in 2009, *CIA and the House of NGO: Covert Action in South Vietnam, 1954–63*. By mid-1954 there was ample precedent for the CIA to take a lead role in Vietnam.[632]

The CIA first crafted a case officer relationship with Diem's brother Ngo Dinh Nhu as early as 1952; the next year, Secretary of State John Foster Dulles and his brother, then-CIA Director Allen Dulles, came to the conclusion that Diem was best suited to be the first president of a non-Communist South Vietnam. On June 18, 1954, at the direct encouragement of the CIA, Vietnamese Emperor Bao Dai invited Diem to form a government to replace that of the Francophile courtier Prince Buo Loc.[633] "Ngo Dinh Diem's attractiveness to his first American patrons derived from three qualities: he was a certified anti-Communist nationalist, he was a Roman Catholic and he understood English," Ahern concluded.[634] That the CIA assassinated Diem after having created him was particularly shocking.

While the Diem murder soured JFK on South Vietnam, the removal of Diem had exactly the opposite effect on the CIA. It calculated that the overthrow of Diem committed Washington to Saigon more deeply. "Having had a hand in the coup, America had more responsibility for the South Vietnamese governments that followed Diem," wrote John Prados, a senior fellow of the National Security Archive at George Washington University.[635]

For JFK, hearing the news on November 2, 1963, was much more immediate of a problem than the impact of the Diem assassination on the progress of the Vietnam War. After the assassination of Diem, JFK found it impossible to dismiss the warning from the Elkins family. Kennedy knew being vice president had humiliated LBJ, but would LBJ go so far as to participate in an assassination plot?

DIEM AND THE CANCELED TRIP TO CHICAGO

November 2, 1963, was coincidentally the day Chicago police arrested a well-armed Thomas Arthur Vallee on suspicion of planning to assassinate the president.[636] After November 2, 1963, the two heavily armed men suspected of conspiring with Vallee had been apprehended, questioned, and released; the other two members of the suspected four-man sniper team vanished. "Higher orders ensured the necessary amnesia. A Treasury Department official ordered Chicago Police Lieutenant Berkeley Moyland to forget his encounter with Thomas Arthur Vallee. The Secret Service Agent in Charge, Maurice Martineau, ordered his Chicago agents to forget their investigation of the four-man sniper team. The Dallas assassination was allowed to happen, unimpeded by the intelligence community's knowledge of its forerunner," wrote James W. Douglass in his 2008 best-selling book, *JFK and the Unspeakable*.[637] The Secret Service investigation that disrupted the Chicago plot to assassinate JFK should have been used to disrupt the Dallas plot, Douglass argued. Yet, curiously, the intelligence about the Chicago assassination plot never surfaced beyond Chicago.

Kennedy, on being briefed about the danger in Chicago, decided the trip had to be canceled. That some of the potential assassins had escaped was devastating news. So at 10:15 a.m. on November 2, at the last possible moment, White House Press Secretary Pierre Salinger announced to the press that JFK had decided to cancel his scheduled visit to Chicago, implying concerns over Vietnam were the reason. The White House never specifically attributed the Diem assassination as the reason for canceling the Chicago trip, nor did the White House make public the intelligence information about the arrest of Thomas Arthur Vallee.

Author James Douglass noted the parallels between the Chicago assassination plot and the assassination in Dallas: "Just as Chicago was the model for Dallas, Saigon was the backdrop for Chicago."[638] Douglass suggested that "[i]f Kennedy had been murdered in Chicago on the day after Diem's and Nhu's murders in Saigon, the juxtaposition of the events would have created the perfect formula to be spoon-fed to the public: 'Kennedy murdered Diem, and got what he deserved.'" It didn't matter that Chicago failed, reasoned Douglass, because Dallas followed a similar pattern. "From the claims made by a series of CIA officers to the authors of widely disseminated books and articles, John Kennedy has been convicted in his grave of having tried to kill Fidel Castro, whose supposedly deranged surrogate, Lee Harvey Oswald then retaliated," Douglass continued. "As a successful Chicago plot would have done, the Dallas plot ended up blaming the victim: 'Kennedy tried to murder Castro, and got what he deserved.'"[639] Kennedy's problem, Douglass believed, was that he wanted to pursue peace, but that "in his critics' eyes, made him soft on Communism."[640] Kennedy's opponents within the US government were resolved that JFK had to be removed. "The absolute end of victory over the evil of Communism justified any means necessary, including the assassination of the president," Douglass concluded. "The failed plot in Chicago had to be followed by a successful one in Dallas."

THE HUNT DISPATCHES

In The *Ends of Power* H. R. Haldeman discusses State Department cables that E. Howard Hunt had in his safe at the White House. The cables apparently linked JFK to the Diem assassination. Haldeman admits there were many indicators along the way that the investigation of the Watergate burglary was only the tip of the iceberg. "In retrospect, I must admit that there were certainly many indications along the way that, had I heeded them, would have at the very least caused me to wonder exactly what was really going on," Haldeman wrote. "But at the time, I didn't want to know, and I made no effort to find out."[641]

In his testimony to the Senate Watergate Committee, Hunt admitted to forging CIA cables linking JFK to the Diem assassination under questioning from committee counsel Samuel Dash. Hunt established that his analysis of authentic State Department cables indicated "a gap" in the sequence leading up to the Diem assassination. In the segment of Hunt's testimony presented below, Charles Colson, who served in the White House as special counsel to President Nixon from 1969 to 1973, is exposed as playing a central role in the Watergate cover-up.

> **Mr. Hunt**: I told him [Charles Colson] that the construction I placed upon the absence of certain cables was that they had been abstracted from the files maintained by the Department of State in chronological fashion and that while there was every reason to believe, on the basis

of an accumulated evidence of the cable documentation, that the Kennedy administration was implicitly, if not explicitly, responsible for the assassination of Diem and his brother-in-law, that there was no hard evidence such as a cable emanating from the White House or a reply coming from Saigon, the Saigon embassy.

Mr. Dash: What was Mr. Colson's reaction to your statement and the showing of the cable to him? Did he agree that the cables were sufficient evidence to show any relationship between the Kennedy administration and the assassination of Diem?

Mr. Hunt: He did.

Mr. Dash: Did he ask you to do anything?

Mr. Hunt: He suggested that I might be able to improve upon the record. To create, to fabricate cables that could substitute for the missing chronological cables.

Mr. Dash: Did you in fact fabricate cables for the purpose of indicating the relationship of the Kennedy administration and the assassination of Diem?

Mr. Hunt: I did.

Mr. Dash: Did you show these fabricated cables to Mr. Colson?

Mr. Hunt: I did.

Mr. Dash: What was his response to the fabricated cables?

Mr. Hunt: He indicated to me that he would be probably getting in touch with a member of the media, of the press, to show the cables.[642]

In establishing the basis for this testimony, Dash had explained to the Senate Watergate Committee that he expected Hunt's testimony "will show an effort by Mr. Colson to try to discredit the Kennedy administration and therefore the Democratic Party during the election and relating it to the assassination of Premier Diem and for that purpose attempting to bring the Catholic vote away from the Democratic Party, and to show that a Democratic President had a role in the assassination of a Catholic premier."[643]

Hunt further testified that he had given a copy of the forged cables to William Lambert of *Life* magazine, the same Lambert who won a Pulitzer Prize with Wallace Turner when they published a series of articles, discussed in chapter 5, revealing the Teamster penetration into the western organized crime mob headed by J. B. Elkins. Lambert was suspicious of the authenticity of the cables, based in large part on the advice from the surviving members of the Elkins family that the document had been falsified and that JFK had nothing to do with ordering the Diem assassination. Lambert never published the cables.

On August 3, 1973, L. Patrick Gray, the former acting director of the FBI, testified to the Senate Watergate Committee that on the evening of June 28, 1972, in a meeting with White House counsel John Dean, H. R. Haldeman, and John Erlichman, counsel and Domestic Affairs assistant to President Nixon, Dean handed to Gray two legal-sized white manila folders that contained copies of classified papers that E. Howard Hunt had been working on while in the White House. Dean explained the files had "national security implications or overtones," but that they had nothing to do with the Watergate burglary or investigation. "The clear implication of the substance and tone of these remarks was that these two files were to be destroyed, and I interpreted this to be an order from [John Dean] issued in the presence of one of the two top assistants to the President of the United States."[644]

Gray further testified that he took these files to his home in Stonington, Connecticut, in late September or early October 1972, and he burned them along with the wrapping paper from Christmas. Before putting the files in the fire, he opened one and saw that it contained what appeared to be copies of "top secret" State Department cables. "I read the first cable," he testified. "I do not recall the exact language but the text of the cable implicated officials of the Kennedy administration in the assassination of President Diem of South Vietnam. I had no reason then to doubt the authenticity of the 'cable' and was shaken at what I had read." He continued to explain he thumbed through the other cables in the file and they appeared to be duplicates of the first cable.[645]

In 2005, Gray said, "the gravest mistake of my eighty-eight years was getting involved with Nixon," explaining he had "refused all contact" with the former president after Watergate, even though Nixon "sent me book after book after book" with personalized inscriptions. "If you could have known what was in my heart and mind then, you would have thought I was a vigilante," Gray said. "I was hurt and so angry at this man, who had not only junked his presidency, but junked the career of so many other people, many of whom had to go to jail."[616] Gray was forced to resign from the FBI on April 27, 1973, after it became known publicly that he had destroyed the two Hunt files given to him by John Dean.

Had there been proof JFK had ordered the Diem assassination, E. Howard Hunt would never have needed to forge State Department documents. Moreover, that Hunt broke the law to create falsified State Department documents underscores the explosive nature of the Diem assassination, even in 1972 and 1973, ten years after the JFK assassination.

One of the tantalizing aspects of the Watergate investigation involves the possibility that the "plumbers unit" in the White House fabricated and stole yet unseen documents that would tarnish the record or the character of JFK and his two brothers.

Why then exactly did Richard Nixon employ E. Howard Hunt in the White House?

Nixon's purpose very possibly was not just to change the historical record regarding the Diem assassination, but to make sure no evidence existed that could implicate him in the JFK assassination.

Why then did Richard Nixon pay E. Howard Hunt hush money after the burglars at the Watergate were caught?

Quite possibly Nixon feared that Hunt knew enough about the JFK assassination to implicate him. Even if in revealing the truth Hunt implicated himself, Nixon feared he might do it if he got a good deal for trading off the information.

What is certain is that if Hunt knew the full extent of the CIA's involvement in the JFK assassination, Nixon knew it too.

UNWISE TO FIGHT IN LAOS

In the first one hundred days after taking office, President Kennedy was faced with escalating Soviet military involvement supporting the Pathet Lao, a Communist nationalist group in Laos engaged in a civil war seeking to overthrow the Royal Laotian Government. On March 23, 1970, JFK held a press conference in the then-new State Department auditorium. He spoke against a background of three maps of Laos illustrating the advance of the Russian-supported Pathet Lao. In his opening statement, JFK made clear there could be no peaceful solution in Laos without "a cessation of the present armed attacks by externally supported Communists."[647]

On Thursday April 27, 1961, only ten days after the launch of the failed Bay of Pigs invasion, JFK held a meeting of the National Security Council in the White House—a meeting historian Arthur Schlesinger, Jr., described as a "long and confused session."[648] At the meeting, the Joint Chiefs, cautioned by the Bay of Pigs fiasco, refused to guarantee the success of a US military operation in Laos, even with the sixty thousand troops the Joint Chiefs had recommended only a month before being committed to Laos to block the Russians and stop the advance of the Pathet Laos. How could a US military incursion in Laos, some five thousand miles away, succeed when military intervention in Cuba had just failed, only ninety miles off the shore of Florida? Moreover, for JFK, the problem remained of justifying the intervention against Communism in Laos if we were resolved to reject intervention against Communism in Cuba.

Coincident with these discussions, General McArthur gave a speech in New York City where he once again expressed the views he espoused at the end of World War II that, as Arthur Schlesinger, Jr. characterized it, "anyone wanting to commit American ground forces to the mainland of Asia should have his head examined."[649] McArthur advised strongly that the United States should never again fight a land war in Asia, a part of the world where indigenous military forces could subsist for days on a pocketful of uncooked rice, while the US military required extensive bases and forward supplies just to sustain battle-ready troops. McArthur added that if we intervened in Southeast Asia, the United States must be prepared to use nuclear weapons, should China enter in force. The lesson of the Korean War was that fighting a limited warfare war fought with conventional troops and conventional weapons was a risky strategy. When the Korean War was being fought, China was still more than a decade away from developing its own nuclear war capability. Yet, China could enter the war at any moment with thousands of fresh troops at precisely the right moment, calculating to overwhelm US troops fighting at near exhaustion in the bitterest of winter conditions.

Combat in Southeast Asia promised to be even more difficult than combat in Korea. In Korea, China was still forced to rely on regular army troops to secure victory. In Laos or Vietnam, combatants fighting against the United States included a shadow army that could easily blend back unseen into the village and countryside. Even when regular North Vietnamese troops entered the war, the North Vietnamese were fighting in their own country, in terrain they knew and understood. In Laos and Vietnam, US troops were vulnerable to defeat in what was asymmetrical combat against an enemy that could be organized loosely as guerilla insurgents. War in Laos and Vietnam was as much about controlling the infrastructure of the local communities as gaining or losing territory in a conventional sense. In the peasant civil war typically fought in Southeast Asia, fighters lived where they fought, often with only a pocketful of uncooked rice to sustain them. Insurgent guerilla fighters entered and exited the field of battle as often as not unseen, if not necessarily unsuspected, typically without the niceties of uniforms or a formal command structure.

The Laos crisis ended when the Russians stepped down and Khrushchev decided to negotiate. But this did not occur before Kennedy had given the order, on April 20, 1961, for the corps of American military advisors in Laos to discard their civilian clothes and to put on their military uniforms, transforming into a Military and Advisory Group authorized to accompany Laotian troops into combat.[650] In Laos, JFK was not willing to commit US military forces, but he was willing to commit military advisors. With Laos, JFK had begun to develop a limited warfare theory for Southeast Asia that would rely upon military assistance and foreign aid, not combat troops. As Kennedy reflected on Laos, he resolved he would not make in Vietnam the mistake he had avoided in Laos. As he studied Vietnam, JFK came to the conclusion he would not make the mistake Truman had made in Korea. JFK had no intention whatsoever of committing to Vietnam regular US troops, as he had also refused to commit in Laos.

THE SPEECH JFK NEVER GAVE

On the day JFK was assassinated, he was on his way to the Dallas Trade Center to give a luncheon address. This, the "Unspoken Speech," contained a strong and clear statement of Kennedy's determination to support our allies and to fight back Communism worldwide through a military and economic assistance program, not through the direct intervention of US military forces. JFK's prepared remarks read:

> But American military might should not and need not stand alone against the ambitions of international Communism. Our security and strength, in the last analysis, directly depend on the security and strength of others, and that is why our military and economic assistance plays such a key role in enabling those who live on the periphery of the Communist world to maintain their independence of choice. . . . For our assistance makes possible the stationing of 3–5 million allied troops along the Communist frontier at one tenth the cost of maintaining a comparable number of American soldiers. . . . A successful Communist breakthrough in these areas, necessitating direct United States intervention, would cost us several times as much as our entire foreign aid program, and might cost us heavily in American lives as well.[651]

With this speech, JFK would have expressed a clear policy preference for providing military aid to nations such as Vietnam, rather than committing troops. Beginning in the first days of his administration over Laos to the last hours of his administration over Vietnam, JFK was constantly pressured by the military to ramp up the US military presence in Southeast Asia. White House historian Arthur Schlesinger Jr. observed that starting with Laos, "the military left a predominant impression that they did not want ground troops at all unless they could send at least 140,000 men equipped with tactical nuclear weapons."[652] The Pentagon was unrelenting in this position, calling for the possibility even of dropping a nuclear bomb on Hanoi and Beijing. Kennedy was moving in the opposite direction, even when Gen. Edward Lansdale presented to him the same proposal he had developed for Eisenhower.

General Lansdale was a product of the OSS formed in World War II as the predecessor of what became the CIA. He had a swashbuckling reputation and was often cited as the model for William J. Lederer and

Eugene Burdick's 1958 novel *The Ugly American.*[653] Until LBJ came along, General Lansdale's only supporter was E. Howard Hunt in the CIA who saw benefits to Lansdale's thinking in covert coups, such as what the CIA engineered in Guatemala in 1954 and 1957. Landsdale recommended to JFK a direct US military intervention in Vietnam, just as he had recommended the same to Eisenhower in 1954 when the French faced defeat at Diem Biem Phu, and were at the point of being pushed out of what was then known as Indochina.

THE PLAN TO WITHDRAW

JFK properly worried that no direct US military intervention in a region like Southeast Asia could succeed, regardless how many troops were sent or what type of arms they had, unless the indigenous population was ready to fight and die for their own freedom. JFK also worried about the corrupt regimes. How could a constitutional republic modeled on the United States possibly survive in a political environment where corrupt politicians oppressed the citizens in the name of liberal democracy?

By offering a wide range of financial assistance, military training, and sophisticated military equipment, JFK felt he could test the resolve and the ability of the citizens of a nation like Vietnam to help them win in a war against indigenous Communists supported by China and Russia. Listening to the Pentagon's enthusiasm for bombing, JFK harkened back to the Strategic Bombing Study that FDR ordered at the end of World War II. It proved that strategic bombing achieved no true military advantage unless there were strategic targets to bomb, especially fuel and chemical production sites. What was going to be achieved by carpet-bombing the jungle in Southeast Asia, Kennedy asked? Yes, the "rolling-thunder" effect of massive B-52 raids would be frightening. But in a theater of war where supply routes like the Ho Chi Minh trail were little more than footpaths through dense tropical undergrowth, what military advantage would massive strategic bombing raids achieve?

On the day JFK died, the United States had fifteen thousand American military advisors in South Vietnam; the same number JFK had decided to send there in 1961.[654] Presidential historian Robert Dallek has argued that JFK was moving in the direction of reducing the US military involvement in Southeast Asia. "But we do know that in November 1963 Kennedy was strongly leaning both toward reducing tensions with Castro and against expanding commitments in Vietnam." Dallek argued. "And most historians agree that Kennedy, like Johnson, would have faced Barry Goldwater in the 1964 election and defeated him by a wide margin, just as Johnson did. This would have given Kennedy, now free from concern about re-election, the mandate to make a bold foreign-policy change while staring down his military advisers."[655]

James W. Douglass in his 2008 book, *JFK and the Unspeakable*, describes a conversation JFK had in the White House with Senate Majority Leader Mike Mansfield in the spring of 1963, after Mansfield criticized Kennedy over Vietnam. JFK aide Kenneth O'Donnell who sat in on part of the meeting described the discussion as follows: "The President told Mansfield that he had been having second thoughts about Mansfield's arguments and that he now agreed with the Senator's thinking on the need for a complete military withdrawal from Vietnam." Kennedy told Mansfield that while he was in agreement, a pull out was not possible until 1965, if JFK were reelected. "President Kennedy explained and Mansfield agreed with him, that if he announced a withdrawal of American military personnel from Vietnam before the 1964 election, there would be a wild conservative outcry against returning him to office for a second term," O'Donnell continued. "After Mansfield left the office, the President said to me, 'In 1965, I'll become one of the most unpopular Presidents in history. I'll be damned everywhere as a Communist appeaser. But I don't care. If I tried to pull out completely now from Vietnam, we would have another Joe McCarthy red scare on our hands, but I can do it after I'm reelected. So we had better make damned sure I *am* reelected."[656]

That policy to withdraw the bulk of US military personnel from Vietnam by the end of 1965 became official government policy on October 11, 1963, when JFK signed National Security Action Memorandum Number 263. Nine days later, JFK signed National Security Action Memorandum Number 263, making into official government policy the recommendation of Secretary of Defense Robert McNamara and Gen. Maxwell Taylor for the withdrawal of one thousand US military personnel by the end of 1963 and by the end of 1965, the withdrawal of the bulk of US military personnel.

On Monday, September 2, 1963, Labor Day, at Hyannis Port, JFK had a relaxed interview outdoors with CBS television anchorman Walter Cronkite, who that sunny day was inaugurating a new CBS television news program. About midway into the interview, Cronkite asked about Vietnam: "Mr. President, the only hot war we've got running at the moment is of course the one in Viet-Nam, and we have our difficulties there, quite obviously." Kennedy answered directly, careful to set the stage for explaining why a military withdrawal from Vietnam was beginning to make sense to him. "I don't think that unless a greater effort is made by the Government [of South Vietnam] to win popular support that the war can be won out there," Kennedy explained. "In the final analysis, it is their war. They are the ones who have to win it or lose it. We can't help them, we can give them equipment, we can send our men out there as advisers, but they have to win it, the people of Vietnam, against the Communists."[657] In the interview, JFK distanced himself from saying the U.S. should withdraw from Vietnam, saying to withdraw would "be a great mistake." James W. Douglass argued when he spoke with Cronkite, that Kennedy "knew he was headed in that contentious direction, but he was not prepared to admit it in advance on national television."[658] Douglass commented that even when Kennedy had implemented a policy of withdrawal from Vietnam by signing National Security Action Memorandum 263— a document not declassified for some thirty years—he "still hesitated how to justify it politically during the final last weeks of his life."[659]

LBJ AND THE GENERALS

Only four days after JFK was shot, on November 26, 1962, LBJ signed National Security Action Memorandum Number 273. Contrary to moviemaker Oliver Stone's contention that by signing this document LBJ reversed JFK's withdrawal policy on Vietnam, the second point in National Security Action Memorandum 273 makes clear that, "the objectives of the United States with respect to the withdrawal of U.S. military personnel remain as stated in the White House statement of October 2, 1963." That document was a public White House statement of policy recommendations received from Defense Secretary Robert McNamara, Gen. Maxwell Taylor, and

Ambassador Henry Cabot Lodge Jr. The key paragraph of the White House statement of October 2, 1963, read as follows:

> Secretary McNamara and General Taylor reported their judgment that the major part of the U.S. military task can be completed by the end of 1965, although there may be a continuing requirement for a limited number of U.S. training personnel. They reported that by the end of this year, the U.S. program for training Vietnamese should have progressed to the point where 1,000 U.S. military personnel assigned to South Vietnam can be withdrawn.[660]

Even though Kennedy made public on October 2, 1963, the recommendations he received from McNamara and Taylor, Kennedy kept secret that he agreed with the recommendation.[661] He assured his decision would remain secret by designating Security Action Memorandum Number 263 as top secret, and specifying in a cover letter that no formal announcement of the presidential decision to withdraw one thousand US military personnel from Vietnam would be made before the end of 1963.[662]

The military obviously had the ear of LBJ, even though LBJ's escalation of the Vietnam War did not begin in earnest until after the 1964 election. LBJ made a few alterations in the draft of National Security Action Memorandum Number 273 that had been prepared for JFK's review. The draft prepared by JFK national security advisor McGeorge Bundy for JFK's review allowed for maritime operations against North Vietnam, but only by the government of South Vietnam. Johnson changed this, realizing South Vietnam really had no navy of any consequence. Johnson allowed American naval vessels to be involved in missions against North Vietnam. This resulted in what was called OPLAN 44, specifying attacks be undertaken by fast patrol boats manned by South Vietnamese sailors, with the support and preparations undertaken by Americans. Included in the mission specification were US destroyers offshore North Vietnam monitoring enemy actions through electronic surveillance. These patrols, code-named DESOTO, resulted in what became known as the Gulf of Tonkin Incident in which three North Vietnamese torpedo boats attacked the US Navy destroyer *Maddox* on August 2, 1964. Although the North Vietnamese launched a torpedo attack, the total damage done to the *Maddox* consisted of one bullet through the hull. LBJ leveraged the incident into the congressional resolution known as the Gulf of Tonkin resolution that was subsequently utilized as constitutional authority for allowing the president to wage the Vietnam War.[663]

LBJ's first Vietnam meeting as president was held in the White House at 3:00 p.m., on November 24, 1963, the Sunday that JFK's body lay in state for public viewing in the Rotunda of the Capitol. In attendance at the meeting in the White House were Secretary of State Dean Rusk, Secretary of State Robert McNamara, National Security Advisor McGeorge Bundy, Undersecretary of State George Ball, CIA Director John McCone, and Ambassador Lodge. John Newman in his 1992 book, *JFK and Vietnam,* reported that LBJ made several dramatic statements about the course of the Vietnam War. "I am not going to lose Vietnam," Johnson said. "I am not going to be the President who saw Southeast Asia go the way China went."[664] Newman believed that JFK "would never have placed American combat troops in Vietnam."[665] The problem, according to Newman, was that by the time JFK ruled out once and for all sending U.S. combat troops to Vietnam, "the size of the Viet Cong had grown to the point where there was little hope that the South Vietnamese Army could contain it."[666] Newman argued the most tragic consequence of JFK's assassination was the subsequent escalation of the Vietnam War.[667]

In a daring passage, Newman derided that conventional wisdom had placed off limits for serious political scientists and historians an examination of the conspiratorial possibility JFK had been assassinated precisely to reverse his decision to withdraw from Vietnam. "The implication seems to be that any study that dares examine the possibility of a recent conspiracy is somehow un-American," Newman wrote. "Yes, in fact, it is *that* idea that is un-American. That we the people not only have the right but the duty to examine such questions is a basic assumption of our most treasured institutions."[668] Kennedy concluded, unfortunately, that he could not win reelection in 1964 if he served up to his Republican challengers the argument the United States should withdraw from Vietnam. Former vice president Nixon was already calling for bombing North Vietnam as a strategy to win the war, and Arizona Senator Barry Goldwater, JFK's most likely presidential challenger in 1964, would gain perhaps decisive political advantage in painting JFK as ineffective in foreign policy, having been embarrassed at the Bay of Pigs, unable to stop Khrushchev from erecting the Berlin Wall, and now, having abandoned South Vietnam to Communism. But, as Newman pointed out, JFK also concluded correctly that a retreat from Vietnam could not happen unless he was reelected in 1964.

THE LBJ MISTRESS SAGA

One of the more controversial sagas concerning LBJ involves Madeleine Duncan Brown and her claim to have been a long-time mistress to LBJ who bore him a son out of wedlock. In her 1997 book, *Texas in the Morning*, Brown describes attending a party at the home of Texas oilman Clint Murchison on Thursday, November 21, 1963, the night before JFK was assassinated. "It was my understanding that the event was scheduled as a tribute honoring his longtime friend, J. Edgar Hoover, whom Murchison had first met decades earlier through President William Howard Taft, and Hoover's companion and assistant, Clyde Tolson," Brown wrote.[669] She claimed that other guests attending the party included former Vice President Richard Nixon who was in Dallas to attend a Pepsi-Cola convention, Texas oilman H. L. Hunt, lawyer and former World Bank president John J. McCloy, Houston construction company entrepreneur George R. Brown, and philanthropist and former Dallas mayor Robert L. Thornton.

She described how LBJ arrived unexpectedly just as the party was breaking up. "Tension filled the room upon his arrival," Brown wrote. "The group immediately went behind closed doors. A short time later Lyndon, anxious and red-faced, re-appeared. Squeezing my hand so hard it felt crushed from the pressure, he spoke with a grating whisper—a growl into my ear not a love message, but one I will always remember: '*After tomorrow those goddamn Kennedys will never embarrass me again—that's no threat—that's a promise.*'"[670] The clear implication was that LBJ was part of a cabal that was planning JFK's demise the following day. In a final meeting with the co-conspirators, including both Richard Nixon and J. Edgar Hoover, evidently confirmation of the attempt to be made the next day on JFK's life was given.

The problem with this spectacular revelation is that it is unlikely to be true. On the evening of Thursday, November 21, 1963, JFK and LBJ attended a testimonial dinner honoring Texas Congressman Albert

Thomas held in the Houston Coliseum. William Manchester in his 1967 book, *The Death of a President*, noted it was after 9:30 p.m. when JFK and the presidential party including LBJ left the head table to travel to Dallas.[671] Manchester noted it was 11.07 p.m. when Air Force One and the other two airplanes in the presidential party touched down at Carswell Air Force base in Fort Worth. When the presidential party arrived at the Hotel Texas in Fort Worth, JFK and Jackie went immediately to retire for the night in Suite 850, while LBJ entertained guests in the hotel's Will Rogers Suite. It is difficult to imagine how LBJ slipped away from Fort Worth, drove to Dallas, showed up while guests were still at the Murchison estate, and returned to Fort Worth, all the while unnoticed that he was gone. The same goes for Richard Nixon, especially when Dallas newspapers noted he was out late in the evening dining with actress Joan Crawford at a well-known Dallas dinner nightclub, with both of them very visible guests at the Pepsi-Cola convention.

Madeleine Brown may well have been an LBJ mistress, but her claim that LBJ was the father of her son was called into question when his lawsuit seeking rights as an LBJ heir was dismissed because son Stephen failed to appear in court. Madeleine also did permanent damage to her own reputation when she was convicted of fraud in 1988 for forging the will of a relative, only to have the conviction reversed on appeal in 1994 because of a procedural error.[672] Her claims of a late-night celebration in Texas among the co-conspirators in the JFK assassination, including LBJ and Richard Nixon, lack any supporting documentary evidence. Criminal conspirators obviously need to get together to plan their dirty deeds, but do they need to break away from the guests at a party, where everyone is looking, so they can go into a backroom, only to come out and announce what they have been plotting? Still, it is highly possible, as we will soon discuss, that LBJ had some advanced warning that a plot to assassinate JFK was in the works, just as it is possible some wealthy Texans on the radical right might have provided funds to make sure LBJ would be president sooner rather than later. Yet, the idea of a grand cabal meeting for a celebratory pre-assassination party at the home of a wealthy Texas oil family on the eve of the JFK assassination lacks solid documentary proof and strains credibility.

THE BOBBY BAKER SCANDAL

In November 1963, the scandal that most threatened LBJ's political future involved Bobby Baker, a Senate page who rose to the position of being secretary to Lyndon Johnson when Johnson was Senate Majority Leader. After LBJ became vice president, Baker continued as his personal secretary and close private advisor. The crux of the Bobby Baker scandal involved a vending machine company, Serve-U Corporation, from which Baker was deriving an annual gross income of $3.5 million at a time when his compensation from the Senate was under twenty thousand dollars a year. Serve-U Corporation had links to Texas oil millionaire Clint Murchison, as well as ties to mobsters Sam Giancana and Meyer Lansky. The company derived most of its earnings by placing vending machines in aerospace companies dependent upon the government for contract work.

What made the Bobby Baker scandal particularly titillating was a sex scandal involving what was known in Washington as the "Quorum Club," a hostess affair Bobby Baker helped create. The Quorum Club was run out of the Carroll Arms Hotel near the Senate Office buildings on Capitol Hill. Basically, the "Q Club" operated to provide call girls to prominent lobbyists and influential members of Congress, with Baker positioned centrally, ready to advance his career politically and financially by trading on sex and power.

The Bobby Baker scandal broke wide open with a *Life* magazine cover story published on November 8, 1963, only three weeks before JFK was killed. That issue of *Life* featured a front-page photograph of Bobby Baker in a costume with his mask lifted to show his laughing face at an unspecified Washington masquerade party. A yellow banner across the cover of the magazine proclaimed: "Capitol Buzzes over Stories of Misconduct in High Places."[673] The article explained that "a Senate committee was investigating Bobby Baker." The second page of the article featured a full-page photograph of a smiling LBJ with his arms around the shoulder of Bobby Baker. The caption under the photo noted that Bobby Baker was "an indispensable confident . . . a messenger, a pleader of causes, a fund-raiser and a source of intelligence."[674] A two-page spread featured a picture of scantily clad waitresses sitting on bar stools, waiting to greet guests during the opening of the Carousel motel for the 1962 summer season in Ocean City, Maryland.[675] The *Life* article cleverly placed next to the waitresses a photo of Bobby Baker greeting newly elected Senator Daniel Inouye, from Hawaii, and Ted Kennedy, who had just taken over his brother John's Senate seat. The photograph was taken in the office of Senate Majority Leader Mike Mansfield, with Mansfield shown in the part of the photograph that continued past the magazine fold to adjoin the photo of the leggy ladies sitting on the Carousel motel's barstools. The article pointed out that in addition to his interest in the vending-machine business, Baker was half owner of the Carousel motel and nightclub in Ocean City, Maryland, as well as having business interests in a law firm, a travel agency, an insurance agency, and a Howard Johnson motel. Commenting that Baker had just resigned from the Senate under fire, *Life* asked how his $19,612 annual salary had provided him sufficient resources to permit his family, consisting of wife, Dorothy, and five children ages ten to one, with the youngest named Lyndon Baines Johnson after the then-Senate majority leader, to move into the $124,500 Washington home a short walk from where LBJ and his family lived.

TARGETING LBJ

The *Life* exposé escalated in seriousness when *Life's* associate and Pulitzer Prize-winning journalist William Lambert sought out George P. Hunt, the magazine's managing editor, to explain that the nine-person investigative team assigned by *Life* to look into Bobby Baker had expanded the inquiry to look into how LBJ acquired his fortune.[676] Lambert explained to Hunt his concern that LBJ had used his public office to enhance his private wealth. Lambert asked for permission to expand the investigative team to pour over LBJ's entire financial picture. Lambert wanted to know how LBJ had managed to accumulate millions in personal net worth when he had been on the public payroll ever since he got out of college. Hunt authorized Lambert to put together a "task force."[677]

The *Life* magazine issue that hit the newsstands on November 18, 1963, the Monday of the week JFK left for Texas, contained the second bombshell on the Bobby Baker scandal. Entitled, "The Bobby Baker Scandal: It Grows and Grows as Washington Shudders," the article disclosed to readers that *Life* had assigned a nine-member team to investigate

Bobby Baker.[678] This second piece exposed in-depth Bobby Baker's corrupt business dealings and his sleazy use of sex, employing what amounted to nothing more than prostitutes employed as "hostesses" to escort lobbyists, legislators, and businessmen so Bobby Baker could rack up political favors and make lucrative business deals. "But in the peculiar Washington world here under review, wives were not the only women involved in social activity," the article read. "This may have been because simple congeniality often carried the burdens of business. The lines between having fun and furthering important actions were often hard to draw."[679] The article continued: "Girls, a former Baker business associate said, were often around as business adjuncts. As he put it, in describing one planning session, 'They had a bunch of girls who, they say, work in the government and during their lunch hour they make a little extra money.'"[680]

Life magazine made clear that everything about Bobby Baker led back to Lyndon Johnson. Noting the US Senate was "Baker's base of operations," *Life* pointed out that the Senate was controlled by a small group of southern senators and conservative Republicans called the "Establishment." At the center of the Establishment, *Life* found LBJ. "In a very real sense the present Establishment is the personal creation of Lyndon Baines Johnson who, from the day he took over as majority leader until he went to the Vice Presidency, ruled it like an absolute monarch," *Life* wrote.[681]

In his 2012 book, *The Passage of Power*, Robert A. Caro, the Pulitzer Prize–winning biographer of LBJ noted that following the publication of this second article, Wheeler and Lambert scheduled a meeting with Hunt.[682] The *Life* investigation that started with the Bobby Baker scandal had morphed to focus on LBJ. As Robert Caro explained, it was clear "that the Bobby Baker case was inevitably going to become the Lyndon Johnson case as well."[683] The meeting was scheduled for late Friday morning, November 22, 1963, in the managing editor's office, at which all the members of the team who were in New York were invited to attend.

With these two *Life* magazine articles appearing as JFK was preparing to leave for his trip to Texas, the Bobby Baker scandal and the political future of LBJ were very much at the center of attention. John Kennedy knew Lambert well enough from the McClellan hearings to appreciate that Lambert was like a bulldog, in that he was loathe to let go of a story once he sank his teeth into it. With the resources of *Life* magazine behind him,

Lambert was at the pinnacle of his career, able to leverage the magazine's immense popularity and prestige to provide his investigative journalism with a stage nearly unequalled in the world of publishing at the time. Now, with the increasing backing of the magazine's managing editor, Lambert was on track to use the same dogged investigative research methods he had used in Portland, Oregon, to put the organized crime penetration of the Teamsters Union onto front pages of newspapers across the nation. This time, he was on track to use the good graces of the ever-popular *Life* magazine to bring down not only the well-connected, powerful, and wealthy Bobby Baker, but also very possibly the vice president of the United States, Lyndon Baines Johnson.

So who put *Life* magazine on the Bobby Baker story in the first place? The first suspect would have to be the president's brother, Attorney General Robert Kennedy. From the Los Angeles Democratic National Convention in 1960 where Jack beat out Lyndon for the presidential nomination, to the end of his life, Bobby Kennedy's enmity for LBJ was impossible to overestimate.

All it took for J.B. Elkins to bring down Dave Beck and go after Jimmy Hoffa was a casual word or two in a coffee shop in Portland, Oregon. "What's the matter, J.B.?" Lambert or his partner Wallace Turner would ask. "Nothing," a downtrodden J.B. would respond. "Except maybe for those Teamsters." That led to hundreds of hours of wiretaps, a Pulitzer-Prize series Lambert and Turner wrote for the *Oregonian*, and Senate crime hearings that springboarded Jack to national status, positioning JFK for a 1960 run for the presidency.[684]

Now, with Lambert positioned as an associate editor at *Life* magazine, Robert Kennedy knew he could play the J.B. Elkins game on his own, dropping comments in casual with the goal of putting Lambert on the trail of Baker. After Lambert got started, RFK was ready to spoon feed leads to Lambert, acting as a "deep throat" source willing to hand over information from within the Justice Department and FBI, all the while calculating the story would necessarily lead to LBJ's downfall.

What worried Robert Kennedy was that Jack, left to his own devices, might have settled to keep LBJ on the ticket a second time, preferring if possible to avoid the political uproar a scorned LBJ would most certainly cause. What Robert Kennedy figured was that the LBJ lion's roar would be a lot tamer with the Bobby Baker thorn placed painfully in the lion's paw. But certainly after the first article was published, LBJ was aware *Life* magazine was gunning for him. Rather than sit idly by waiting for the disclosures to ruin his political career, LBJ's political instincts demanded he protect himself. While the Kennedy administration took pains to keep from the public the assassination plots that had been stymied in Chicago and Tampa, surely LBJ was aware the talk of assassinating Kennedy was in the air in November 1963. While the proof is not definitive, assassination researchers insist that in the Dallas motorcade on November 22, 1963, LBJ ducked down in his seat as the follow-up car he was riding in, trailing JFK's limo, moved into the kill zone by turning left from Houston Street onto Elm Street. In the famous photograph taken by Associated Press photographer Altgens, Lady Bird Johnson can be clearly seen in the open car following JFK's limo. Curiously, LBJ, a physically large man, is not apparently visible. Many observers have suspected LBJ knew the motorcade was entering the pre-determined kill zone, and he ducked down as his car turned the corner in order to stay out of the crossfire.

JFK DECIDES TO DUMP LBJ

Robert Caro reported in his 2012 book, *The Passage of Power,* that on Wednesday, November 13, 1963, JFK convened the first major planning session for the 1964 campaign in the Cabinet Room at the White House.[685] The meeting included White House staff advisors, the chairman of the DNC, and a few trusted political advisors. Not invited was Vice President Lyndon Baines Johnson or any member of his staff. The main subject of the meeting, Caro reported, was JFK's chances in the South in 1964, along with a broader discussion of the future of the South in Democratic Party plans. Already evident was the voter realignment that would ultimately materialize as the "moral majority," which 1968 presidential candidate Richard Nixon molded into a "Southern strategy." The meeting also included intense speculation over whether LBJ would be on the ticket since the primary reason he had been chosen in 1960 was that he would be influential in winning southern states and Texas. The intense Democratic Party infighting in Texas, a primary reason JFK scheduled the upcoming trip to Dallas, brought into question whether LBJ could be as effective in 1964 as he had been in 1960. Even with LBJ on the ticket in 1960, Jack Kennedy won Texas by fewer than forty-eight thousand votes of the approximately 1.3 million votes cast.

None less than Arthur Schlesinger Jr. dismissed the notion that dumping LBJ was seriously considered at the campaign strategy meeting. "Johnson's absence stimulated a curious story that the Kennedys intended," Schlesinger wrote in *A Thousand Days*. "These stories were wholly fanciful. Kennedy knew and understood Johnson's moodiness in the Vice-Presidency, but he considered him able and loyal. In addition, if Goldwater were to be the Republican candidate, the Democrats needed every possible asset in the South." Schlesinger wrote to leave no doubt the November strategy meeting convened at the White House "assumed John's renomination as part of the convention schedule."[686]

Clearly, what Schlesinger wrote was the official line. Robert Caro, however, saw it differently. Caro pointed out that even in 1960, there had been no serious discussion about putting LBJ on the ticket, not even with Robert Kennedy, until Jack Kennedy "suddenly announced, to the astonishment of everyone, that he was doing so."[687] Caro reported that the morning after the November strategy meeting, JFK's secretary Evelyn Lincoln was reviewing material from the meeting when JFK came over to her desk. She commented that the 1964 Democratic convention would not be as exciting as the 1960 convention had been "because everyone knows what's coming." According to Lincoln JFK responded, "Oh, I don't know, there might be a change in the ticket." She also reported that about a week later, when JFK was sitting in a chair in her office, he commented that his running mate in 1964 would probably be a moderate southerner, maybe even the young governor of North Carolina, Terry Sanford, but it would not be LBJ.[688] LBJ loyalists dismissed these recollections, insisting JFK never seriously considered dumping LBJ. But Caro was not so sure. He wrote that in his conversation with Evelyn Lincoln, she repeated the conversation, explaining she wrote down word-for-word in her diary what Jack said about LBJ and that she used those notes when writing her 1968 book, *Kennedy and Johnson*. Caro specifically noted that in his conversation with Evelyn Lincoln, she insisted JFK wanted LBJ off the ticket, explaining JFK had implied "the ammunition to get him off was Bobby Baker."[689]

JFK left the White House for Texas having made two important decisions: first, that he would begin a withdrawal from Vietnam by the end of 1963, and second, that he would find a replacement for LBJ as his 1964 running mate. The Diem decision weighed heavily in JFK's decision to withdraw from Vietnam, given his conclusion that the nation was in such internal turmoil there could be no confidence the people in South Vietnam were sufficiently motivated to fight for and win their own freedom. The decision to dump LBJ was motivated by the Bobby Baker scandal. JFK was concerned that, when *Life* magazine got finished investigating and reporting on LBJ, an unfortunately large segment of the voting public would now see LBJ to be nothing more than a corrupt politician who had enriched himself at public expense. What Kennedy had not yet resolved was how best to explain these decisions to voters across the nation, so as not to give impetus to a Goldwater candidacy from the conservative right.

THE FRENCH CONNECTION

In response to a 1976 Freedom of Information Act request, the CIA released documents 632–796 confirming for the first time that a professional assassin was apprehended in Dallas on November 23, 1963. The CIA memo mentioned Jean Souetre, a.k.a. Michel Roux, a.k.a. Michel Mertz—a world-renowned Corsican hit man with a long history as an accomplished assassin and with ties to the French Connection drug trade stretching from Southeast Asia to Marseilles, France, to New Orleans. The memo, stamped "SECRET" and dated April 1, 1964, read as follows:

> Jean SOUETRE aka Michel Roux aka Michel Mertz—On March 5, Dr. Papich advised that the French had hit the Legal Attaché in Paris and also the SDECE man had queried the Bureau in New York City concerning subject stating that he had been expelled from the U.S. at Fort Worth or Dallas 48 hours after the assassination. He was in Fort Worth on the morning of 22 November and in Dallas in the afternoon. The French believe that he was expelled to either Mexico or Canada. In January he received mail from a dentist named Alderman living at 5803 Birmingham, Houston, Texas. Subject is believed to be identical with a Captain who is a deserter from the French Army and an activist in the OAS. The French are concerned because of de Gaulle's planned visit to Mexico. They would like to know the reason

for his expulsion from the U.S. and his destination. Bureau files are negative and they are checking in Texas and with the INS [U.S. Immigration and Naturalization Service]. They would like a check of our files with indications of what may be passed on to the French. Mr Papich was given a copy of CSCI-3/776,742 previously furnished the Bureau and CSDB-3/655,207 together with a photograph of Captain SOULTRE.[690]

What was a Corsican assassin doing in Dallas on the day JFK was assassinated? The obvious assumption would be that Jean Souetre should have been placed at the top of the list of suspects in the JFK assassination. If not a shooter, the possibility remains this Corsican assassin was in Dallas to observe, oversee, or perhaps even to direct and supervise the shooters hoping to catch JFK in a cross fire. Assassination researchers Brad O'Leary and L. E. Seymour in their 2003 book, *Triangle of Death*, suggest the "Mr. Papich" mentioned in the document may have been a CIA asset working in the legal attaché's office as a surveillance operator, or simply as an employee who served as a liaison for the US embassy.[691] The SDECE is the *Service de Documenation Extérieure et Contre-Espionage*, the French equivalent of the CIA. The OAS, or *Organization de l'Armée Secrétée*, was a right-wing extremist group opposed to French President Charles de Gaulle that engaged in acts of terrorism and assassination and opposed France's policy to grant the African nation of Algeria its independence from French rule.

O'Leary and Seymour argued that finding the CIA document implicated the OAS as one of its members, Jean Rene Souetre, was in Dallas the day JFK was assassinated, only to be captured and deported by US authorities some forty-eight hours later.[692] So, a known assassin was apprehended in Dallas and there is nothing to prove he was even questioned. Moreover, the CIA never shared the information with the Warren Commission. When Mary Ferrell, the renowned archivist of assassination material, found the CIA document in early 1977, she described it as one of the poorest documents she had encountered, virtually looking like a copy of a copy of a faint carbon copy.

Investigative reporter Henry Hunt studying the document concluded it was highly unlikely the CIA officer charged with deciding the release of secret papers in 1967 had "even an inkling of the revelations contained in this document." Hunt further concluded the document would never have come to light had it not fallen "under the sharp eyes of Mary Ferrell."[693] Hurt also determined that the "Souetre" referred to in CIA document 632–796 was not Michel Roux. Hunt found independent documentation that the FBI knew Roux was visiting acquaintances in Fort Worth on November 22, 1963, and left the United States on December 6, 1963, at Laredo, Texas. This Michel Roux had spent three years in the French Army in Algeria before deserting. Because Roux was not deported, Hurt ruled out that Roux was Souetre. Hurt also pointed out that since his earliest days in the Senate, JFK was publicly and passionately in favor of Algerian independence, a fact that made him a natural enemy of the OAS.[694]

Henry Hurt traced Dr. Alderson mentioned in the CIA document to Dr. Lawrence Alderson, a respected dentist and longtime resident of Houston who insisted the FBI began trailing him immediately after the assassination and followed him for several weeks. Finally, the FBI asked for an interview to discuss his relationship with Jean Souetre. Alderson explained to the FBI that as a first lieutenant in the U.S. Army stationed in France, he met Souetre, then a captain in the French Air Force. Alderson remembered Souetre as "a political activist of the neo-Nazi persuasion."[695] They became friends and for the next ten years the two corresponded annually around Christmastime. Alderson told Hurt the FBI said agents "had traced Souetre to Dallas a day before the assassination and then lost him," adding the FBI was certain either Souetre killed JFK or knew who had done it.[696]

In 1999, Brad O'Leary located and interviewed Souetre who was then working as public relations director at the Casino de Divonne in Divonne les Bains, France. Souetre explained he and Mertz were both parachute captains in the French Army and that Mertz, some ten years older than Souetre, was in the *maquis* [the Resistance] during World War II. Souetre argued that it was Mertz, using Souetre's name, who was in the United States at the time of the Kennedy assassination. "What I find strange is the fact that [Mertz] was there in Dallas the day of the crime and under my identity," Souetre said. "What was he doing there that day? It is obvious that he knew that something was going to happen and that by implicating Captain Souetre he could blame the CNR [*Comité* Natinale de la Résistance, the later name of the OAS]."[697] Souetre claimed that when U.S. authorities approached him, he proved he was not in Dallas on the day JFK was assassinated and that he had never been to the United States at any time, for any reason.[698]

So what was Mertz doing in Dallas on that fateful day in 1963?

THE DIEM HEROIN DYNASTY IN SOUTH VIETNAM

Souetre claimed the reason Mertz was let go and deported from the United States was because Mertz, when he was apprehended in Dallas, worked at the same time both for the Marseille heroin crime syndicate and for SDECE, French intelligence service. Souetre explained that at that time, the US Mafia, and particularly crime bosses Carlos Marcello, Sam Giancana, and Santo Trafficante, all of whom ran vast heroin distribution networks in the United States, got their product from Antoine Guerini and his Marseille-based heroin enterprise. "We know that Mertz worked directly for that same enterprise," O'Leary and Seymour wrote. "Kennedy's attack on U.S. Mob bosses threatened the stability of Guerini's Marseille heroin market. Almost all of the heroin bought by U.S. addicts came from Marseille after it was processed from the opium base provided by Nhu [brother of South Vietnamese President Diem]. Hence, Guerini and his syndicate had a lot to lose if Kennedy was allowed to maintain his war on the mob."[699]

O'Brien and Seymour argued the reason organized crime wanted JFK dead was that JFK threatened the mob's number-one cash cow, the security of their multi-billion dollar heroin enterprise.[700] Nhu's deal with the Guerini syndicate turned the local South Vietnamese heroin market into an enormous profit machine. The murder of Diem in the coup d'état staged by General Minh with the help and encouragement of the CIA was widely attributed to a decision made by JFK, even though JFK had given explicit orders that Diem was not to be killed. O'Leary and Seymour concluded the JFK assassination was "a premeditated conspiracy between the U.S. Mafia, the Marseille Mafia, and the highest echelons of the South Vietnamese government" in order to protect their heroin trade.[701]

Support for the O'Leary/Seymour argument can be found in history professor Alfred W. McCoy's 1972 study, *The Politics of Heroin: CIA Complicity in the Global Drug Trade*.[702] Noting that Diem, a pious

Catholic, first launched a determined anti-opium campaign when he came into power in May 1955, he documents the policy was reversed three years later by Diem's brother Nhu, seeking additional revenue to fund an expanded network of anti-Communist secret police. Nhu imported opium into Vietnam from the Laotian poppy fields, with assistance from *Air Laos Commerciale*, a small charter airline managed by Indochina's Corsican gangster Bonaventure "Rock" Francisci. According to Lucien Conein, a former high-ranking CIA official in Saigon who helped engineer the Diem coup in 1963, the relationship between Nhu and the Corsican gangsters began in 1958 when Francisci made a deal with Nhu to smuggle Laotian opium into South Vietnam.[703] Most of the narcotics exported from South Vietnam were shipped from Saigon's port on oceangoing freighters.[704] As the Vietnam War progressed, the Corsican mobsters operating in Saigon designated Marseille as the preferred European port of entry. Conein, by the way, was widely reported to have carried forty-two thousand dollars in cash as a means of encouragement for the South Vietnamese generals planning the Diem overthrow.

In an important observation, McCoy noted there is a natural attraction between intelligence agencies and criminal syndicates. "Both are practitioners of what one retired CIA operative has called the 'clandestine arts'—the basic skill of operating outside the normal channels of civil society," McCoy wrote in *The Politics of Heroin*. Among all the institutions of modern society, intelligence agencies and criminal syndicates alone maintain large organizations capable of carrying out covert operations without fear of detection."[705] McCoy scoffed at the interdiction of weaker US drug enforcement agencies, noting that when the US Bureau of Narcotics first opened its office in Bangkok with three agents in the late 1960s, the CIA's "massive covert apparatus" operated in the opium highlands of Southeast Asia with the very drug lords the US narcotics agents were trying to apprehend.[706] While the CIA in Southeast Asia in the 1950s and 1960s operated with vast sums of cash, the CIA had no reason to handle heroin, preferring instead to provide its drug-lord allies with transportation for their drugs, arms, and political protection. "In sum," McCoy wrote, "the CIA's role in the Southeast Asian heroin trade involved indirect complicity rather than direct culpability."[707] This was a perfect model for a CIA that had been molded around the theme of "plausible deniability."

CUI BONO? (WHO STOOD TO GAIN?)

Granted, Lyndon Johnson, Richard Nixon, and the US military industrial complex all had the motive to see JFK forcibly removed from office, even if that meant assassinating him. So, too, organized crime—and especially Carlos Marcello, Sam Giancana, and Santo Trafficante—along with the CIA had their own motives for seeing JFK dead.

This equation had the makings of a good coup d'état, aimed at putting LBJ in office, escalating the Vietnam War, and ramping up the Southeast Asian heroin trade. LBJ and Richard Nixon would permanently put an end to the career of a hated rival who already had bettered both of them. Organized crime stood to make billions not only in operating the French Connection drug trade with impunity, but also on the expectation Robert Kennedy would have to back off the Justice Department's war on organized crime the moment Jack Kennedy was no longer in the White House. The military industrial complex stood to make billions producing the new generation of weapons required to fight a prolonged ground war in Vietnam, as generals giving out contracts prepared for their industry homes in retirement.

What LBJ, Richard Nixon, and the military industrial complex lacked was the operational capabilities to pull off a covert plan as audacious as a coup d'état effected by assassinating the president of the United States without detection. What LBJ, Richard Nixon, and the military industrial complex lacked in operational capabilities, the CIA and organized crime made up for in spades. Moreover, the CIA and organized crime could look to the politicians and the military industrial complex for funds to pull off the operation. LBJ and Richard Nixon had never pulled off an operation, but when it came to funding a political campaign, both were experts.

What putting LBJ in the White House before he left Dallas required was the field implementation of a complex criminal plot by a top team of experienced CIA and organized crime operatives that had successfully worked together before and could be counted upon to do so again. The prototype had been developed in Guatemala in 1954 and 1957. Granted, that E. Howard Hunt put LBJ at the top of his deathbed organizational chart for the JFK assassination, but that did not mean LBJ wrote the operational plan for the covert action. To put the organizational plan of the coup d'état together, the CIA mobilized the Cuban exiles who had worked with the CIA since the Bay of Pigs was first being planned under the Eisenhower administration. That a trained assassin such as Michel Mertz was walking the streets of Dallas the day JFK was murdered can hardly be taken as coincidental. Even if Mertz pulled no triggers that day, the coordination of a complicated crossfire required expert management. Mertz qualified for the job, given a *curriculum vitae* that stretched back to his days picking off Nazis for the French Resistance.

LBJ, the military industrial complex, and Richard Nixon were not necessarily relegated to the role of "benchwarmer," as E. Howard Hunt in his deathbed confession so humbly characterized his own role in the JFK assassination. Nixon was in Dallas when JFK was killed, meeting with his financial ties to industry and his campaign financiers based in Texas. In Dallas, Nixon reconnected with Howard Hughes, the eccentric multimillionaire whose fortune also traced back to the Texas and the Houston Tool Company. In 1957, it was Howard Hughes who lent Donald Nixon, Richard's brother, some two hundred thousand dollars to bail out his failed hamburger "drive-in" joint in Whittier, California. Bobby Baker had extensive tentacles into Texas, too, having finagled along with LBJ the lucrative award of the F-111 fighter plane to General Dynamics, a company headquartered between Dallas and Fort Worth. Before he left Texas on November 22, 1963, Nixon knew that those who financed his presidential run in 1960 would finance him again, as soon as the time was right. Like LBJ, Nixon too was a winner with JFK assassinated.

Even if LBJ was not the "mastermind" of the JFK assassination, the point of the coup d'état was to put LBJ in office. The campaign by investigative journalists like William Lambert and *Life* magazine to expose the rampant corruption at the core of Bobby Baker and LBJ's politics eased off as soon as JFK was pronounced dead at Parkland Hospital and LBJ took the oath of office from his longstanding friend and judge Sarah T. Hughes aboard Air Force One. At 2:38 p.m. Eastern Time on November 22, 1963, LBJ could stop worrying that JFK might replace him and start worrying about picking his own 1964 vice presidential running mate. Despite Jackie Kennedy standing on LBJ's left side in her bloodstained dress as he took the office, the occasion of the JFK assassination was not a sad one for LBJ. Though his head was turned from the camera, LBJ most surely did not miss the wink of the eye captured on film that Congressman Albert Thomas gave LBJ the moment he lowered his right hand from just having taken the oath of office. With a grieving Jackie still at his side, LBJ perfected the *coup d'état* by being sworn in as president before Air Force One lifted off to return to Washington.

The military industrial complex also gained from JFK's death. From his first Vietnam War planning session as president even before JFK's body was placed to rest at Arlington Cemetery, LBJ had signaled to the Pentagon there was no need to worry about the withdrawal of one thousand US military advisors. With LBJ likely to win a landslide victory in 1964 as the successor to a martyred president, the military industrial complex felt comfortable waiting until 1965 before LBJ ramped up the Vietnam War to provide the hundreds of thousands of troops the Pentagon truly felt would be needed to beat the North Vietnamese. Organized crime could continue the lucrative heroin trade from Southeast Asia, with the tacit approval and assistance of the CIA. With LBJ in the White House, the military and the CIA had the receptive ear they never had with JFK.

Everything was fine, as long as the nation concluded Lee Harvey Oswald as the lone-gun nutcase assassin had acted alone.

THE JFK ASSASSINATION AND THE NEW WORLD ORDER

"Under the direction of Allen Dulles, the CIA interpreted 'plausible deniability,' as a green light to assassinate local leaders, overthrow governments, and lie to cover up any trace of accountability—all for the sake of promoting U.S. interests and maintaining our nuclear-backed dominance over the Soviets and other nations."

—James W. Douglass, *JFK and the Unspeakable*, 2008[708]

"A cover-up is like a magic trick. Once you understand how it was accomplished, you can never be fooled by it again."

—Lisa Pease, co-editor of *The Assassinations,* 2012[709]

JFK, LIKE HIS FATHER BEFORE HIM and his brother Robert after him, had an uncanny ability to cause almost irrational anger and hatred in very powerful men that should never have been enemies in the first place. The Kennedy family lived an outrageous lifestyle of social privilege despite the lack of a storied pedigree. Family patriarch Joseph P. Kennedy made a fortune in a series of fast and fortunate deals that years later would be outlawed. But instead of being arrested for stock fraud, President Franklin D. Roosevelt appointed Joseph Kennedy to be the first head of the Securities and Exchange Commission. Perhaps a crook made the best cop, but when Joseph Kennedy became incapacitated, the patriarch's ability to keep his sons out of trouble came to an end. Even Johnny Roselli, the mobster who introduced Joseph Kennedy to Hollywood and assisted John and Robert Kennedy in their attempt to eliminate Castro, ultimately turned on the brothers.

John F. Kennedy made two fatal mistakes: first, he allowed his father, Joseph P. Kennedy, to take on a decades-old grudge match with the predominately Italian and Jewish eastern mob through the offices of his brother, Attorney General Robert F. Kennedy; second, he threatened to break the CIA up into a thousand little pieces. Declaring war on organized crime and on the CIA at the same time had disastrous repercussions, especially because JFK failed to achieve his objectives in each.

Had Robert F. Kennedy broken the back of organized crime in the United States, imprisoned mobsters would have had a much harder time planning revenge. Had JFK closed down the CIA and fired all its employees, embittered intelligence operatives would have had a much more difficult time undertaking an assassination plot. Organized crime felt betrayed, believing JFK owed his 1960 presidential victory to fraudulent votes delivered in Chicago in part by the Giancana organization. The CIA felt the Bay of Pigs invasion would have succeeded if only JFK had resolved to commit the US military to save the Cuban exiles being slaughtered on the beach.

The unfortunate truth is that by leaving in place dangerous mobsters who felt betrayed and an ever-treacherous CIA that felt endangered, JFK left relatively undamaged the two enemies most capable of developing and funding an operational plan to bring about his demise. Having worked together since the Guatemala coup d'état in the 1950s, organized crime and the CIA needed no outside assistance to pull off a presidential assassination for which neither would be blamed. With the patina of Kennedy charm running thin for men such as Allen Dulles, a key member of a family that had helped world leaders achieve prominence since before Hitler, scores were about to be evened.

THE JFK ASSASSINATION: A COUP D'ÉTAT

As we saw in chapter 7 LBJ, Richard Nixon, Allen Dulles, and the military industrial complex each had their motives for killing JFK. While not capable of playing operational roles in the JFK assassination, each of these JFK enemies—LBJ, Richard Nixon, Allen Dulles, and the military industrial complex—could provide the financial support for a CIA/mob plan. Each had access to Texas oil millionaires and other financiers on the political right willing to provide the funds needed to carry out such an operation. LBJ, Richard Nixon, and the military industrial complex wanted to send troops to Vietnam.

The day JFK removed Allen Dulles from directing the CIA was the day JFK signed his death warrant. Even removed from the CIA, Dulles was more than capable of organizing the coup d'état from behind the scenes, the place where Dulles was truly most comfortable. It should come as no surprise that LBJ appointed Allen Dulles to the Warren Commission. This completed the circle, positioning Dulles so he could make sure the Warren Commission assigned all the blame for JFK's assassination to Lee Harvey Oswald, the operative chosen by the CIA to play the role of patsy.

Allen Dulles had a deep motive to see JFK killed that stemmed not simply from revenge, but more importantly from ideology. Truly, Allen Dulles came to hate everything JFK represented, as did Richard Nixon. Dulles and Nixon were Cold War warriors who embraced the idea the United States needed to maintain a large, well-funded, clandestine intelligence agency capable of covert operations abroad to ensure our freedom at home. They agreed that this agency, formed as the CIA at the end of World War II, needed the authority to plan invasions of foreign countries, launch *coups d'etat*, and even assassinate foreign leaders as needed to contain the spread of Communism. Because the missions were covert, the CIA had to lie to the American public that funded it.

In the Eisenhower years, the CIA had a green light. By appointing John Foster Dulles as secretary of state and Allen Dulles as CIA director, Dwight D. Eisenhower had turned over the key components of US foreign policy to a team of brothers with a sordid history. The Dulles brothers were presented to the nation as loyal and patriotic Americans, with a compliant press never probing the key role the Dulles family played in assisting Hitler to come to power. Instead of being prosecuted as war criminals after the war, the Dulles family continued to make sure Nazi intelligence assets were employed by the United States and Western Europe. In this clandestine history of the United States, the Bush family also rose to prominence.

Thus, at the roots of the JFK assassination were key players whose life experiences and attitudes toward US national security where shaped before World War II. Psychologist E. Martin Schotz interpreted Isaac Don Levine's 1959 book, *Mind of an Assassin*, which analyzed the motivates of Communist Ramon Mercader for assassinating Marxist revolutionary Leon Trotsky. Schotz suggested that in Levine's book, Kennedy could be substituted for Trotsky and Dulles could be substituted for Mercader. Doing so, Schotz came up with the following brilliant formulation: "The key to Dulles, who typifies the modern political assassin, is to be found in the special character of the organization in which he has enlisted for life. The American power is an amalgam of a temporal state and a political religion. It is in the nature of a military order in which the government authorities and the anti-communist party priesthood are one supreme source of faith and strength. Dulles became an assassin both as a servant of that government and as a missionary of its anti-Communist faith, and is beyond redemption."[710]

As we shall see next, prior to World War II, the grandfathers of President George H. W. Bush and the Dulles brothers were among a small group of Americans working hard to finance Hitler's rise to power in Germany.

FINANCING HITLER

In 1931, Brown Brothers Harriman & Co. was formed as a Wall Street investment firm by merging three predecessor investment banking firms: Brown Brothers & Co., Harriman Brothers & Co., and W. A. Harriman & Co.

The history of Prescott Bush and George Herbert Walker, the grandfathers of George H. W. Bush, traces back to these investment banking firms founded in the 1920s, and specifically to the Harriman family. W. Averell Harriman, the son of the investment firm founder, was a Republican politician and diplomat who followed Thomas E. Dewey as the

48th governor of New York, serving from 1955 through 1958. In 1920, George Herbert Walker became president of W. A. Harriman & Co. In 1924, Prescott Bush succeeded George Herbert Walker as president of W. A. Harriman & Co. This was convenient because George Herbert Walker was Prescott Bush's father-in-law when on August 6, 1921, Prescott Bush married George Herbert Walker's daughter, Dorothy Walker. The second son of Prescott and Dorothy Bush, born in 1924, was named George H. W. Bush, the future 41st President of the United States. In 1931, Brown Brothers Harriman & Co. was formed from three-predecessor Wall Street investment banking firms: Brown Brothers & Co., Harriman Brothers & Co., and W. A. Harriman & Co. The point is that President George H. W. Bush and his son, President George W. Bush, date back to a prominent Wall Street investment firm where the patriarch grandfathers of the family worked together.

Born in 1888, Secretary of State John Foster Dulles, after graduating from Princeton University in 1908 and getting his law degree at George Washington Law School, joined the prominent New York law firm Sullivan & Cromwell, where he specialized in international law. Born in 1893, the younger brother, Allen Dulles, also graduated from Princeton University. Allen Dulles, however, spent five years in the US diplomatic corps before earning a law degree from George Washington Law School in 1926. Allen then joined Sullivan & Cromwell where his older brother was already a partner.

Political commentator and former Republican Party strategist Kevin Phillips, in his 2004 book, *American Dynasty: Aristocracy, Fortune, and the Politics of Deceit in the House of Bush*, wrote that among the most prominent Wall Street principles turning their attention to Germany in the 1930s were Averell Harriman, George Herbert Walker, and the Dulles Brothers.[711] "In 1941, the *New York Herald Tribune* had featured a front-page story headlined 'Hitler's Angel Has $3 Million in U.S. Bank,' reporting that steel baron Fritz Thyssen had channeled the money into the Union Banking Corporation, possibly to be held for 'Nazi bigwigs,'" Phillips noted. "UBC was the bank, nominally owned by a Dutch intermediary that Brown Brothers Harriman ran for the German Thyssen steel family. Prescott Bush was a director."[712] Since the 1930s, Brown Brothers Harriman was one of the two most notable active investors in a rapidly re-arming Germany that came under Nazi control when Hitler became Chancellor in 1933.

President Franklin D. Roosevelt ordered Union Bank closed after the Japanese attack on Pearl Harbor and the subsequent declaration of war by Nazi Germany on the United States. Going back to the 1930s, one of Sullivan & Cromwell's most notorious Nazi connections was the legal work the firm did for the German chemical firm I. G. Farben, the manufacturer during World War II of the Zyklon-B gas the Nazis used to kill Jews in the concentration camps. John Foster Dulles, the chief legal contact at Sullivan & Cromwell for I. G. Farben signed "Heil Hitler" on the correspondence he wrote to the German chemical firm before World War II.

Political commentator Kevin Phillips drew the conclusion that the men who managed most of the high-level financial and corporate relations between the United States and Nazi Germany in the pre-war period from 1933 to 1941 developed "an unusual kind of information and expertise that made them important to the war effort in general and the U.S. intelligence community in particular." After World War II, with the Soviet Union rapidly becoming the major Cold War enemy of the United States and Western Germany transforming into a major US ally, "the new American national security state formed a new establishment in which Prescott Bush and many of his friends were prominent and honored members."[713] Included in this group were the Dulles brothers.

ALLEN DULLES AND REINHARD GEHLEN

In 1945, at the end of World War II, attorney Allen Dulles, then serving as chief of the OSS Berlin office under OSS founder and director General William Donovan, rescued out of a prison camp Nazi intelligence director Reinhard Gehlen. Under Hitler, Gehlen had been responsible for Nazi military intelligence on the Eastern Front, including the Soviet Union. Gehlen fit perfectly into the plan Dulles had developed to decline prosecuting Nazi intelligence assets so they could be employed by the United States. Dulles wanted Gehlen and the Nazis to advise the newly forming CIA and to be re-employed as the backbone around which an anti-Soviet, anti-Communist intelligence network headquartered in what emerged as Western Germany could be formed to work undercover throughout Eastern Europe.

"By the summer of 1945, Dulles had finished his negotiations with Gehlen," wrote assassination researcher James DiEugenio in his 2012 book, *Destiny Betrayed: JFK, Cuba, and the Garrison Case*. DiEugenio reported that by September 1945, Gehlen and six of his aides were flown to Washington by Eisenhower's chief of staff, Gen. Walter Bedell Smith. As a result of high-level discussions in Washington, Gehlen's Nazi intelligence organization was transferred under his control to work in Eastern Europe until Germany was reorganized.

In 1949 Gehlen signed a contract to work for the CIA for five million dollars a year. In 1950 High Commissioner of Germany John McCloy appointed Gehlen as advisor to the German chancellor on intelligence. Ultimately Gehlen became intelligence chief of the Federal Republic of Germany, better known simply as West Germany.[714] This was quite a reward for a Nazi responsible for torturing, starving, and murdering some four million Soviet prisoners of war. "From the ruins of defeat, the virtual head of Hitler's intelligence became the chief of one of the largest intelligence agencies in the postwar era," DiEugenio wrote. "A man who should have been imprisoned and prosecuted for war crimes became a wealthy and respected official of the new Germany."[715]

Note that Allen Dulles followed Gen. Walter Bedell Smith as CIA Director. Note also that Allen Dulles and John McCloy both ended up being appointed to the Warren Commission.

INDOCHINA AND THE CIA

DiEugenio has argued that the absorption of the Gehlen organization into the CIA was symptomatic of a postwar world shaped by the Dulles brothers leading to a Cold War that became "about American versus Russian dominance in the resource rich Third World," with the CIA standing for U.S. corporate interests in which morals played on part of the CIA's operation in pursuit of these goals.[716]

The Guatemalan plots of 1954 and 1957, extensively discussed in previous chapters as having set a model both for the Bay of Pigs invasion and the JFK assassination, were but two of a series of CIA actions aimed at dominating resources in the Third World for US business interests. In 1953 President Eisenhower authorized Operation AJAX to overthrow

Prime Minister Mohammad Mossadegh in Iran after Mossadegh moved to nationalize Iranian oil interests. In a coup d'état staged by the CIA, Mossadegh was deposed, the oil interests were returned to the disposal of US and British petroleum corporations, and the Shah was returned to power.

Still, nothing better illustrates the chasm between the way the Dulles brothers saw the postwar world and JFK's vision than Indonesia, where the threat of Communism drew CIA attention and intervention from 1957 through JFK's thousand days in office and until the CIA was finally successful in engineering a *coup* in 1965. Despite a CIA attempt to assassinate Indonesia's President Sukarno in 1957, JFK invited Sukarno to the White House on April 24, 1961, and again on September 12, 1961.[717] Kennedy saw the potential of working with Sukarno to position him in a leadership position among the "non-aligned nations" of the Third World.

In 1965 the CIA engineered another *coup* and placed President Sukarno under house arrest. In the aftermath of the coup, the Indonesian army, under the control of CIA-backed General Suharto, engaged in a massacre in which tens of thousands of cadre and supporters of the Communist Party of Indonesia, known as the PKI, were murdered. Estimates are that as many as five hundred thousand Indonesians were killed in the massacre, political violence that took on a religious dimension in that Suharto and the vast majority of his supporters were Muslim and many of those slaughtered were Christian. The CIA assisted Suharto by handing over to the Indonesian army detailed death lists of PKI members targeted for killing.[718]

This CIA effort to exterminate Communists in Indonesia was successful. "Suharto's attack on the Communists and the usurpation of the presidency resulted in a complete reversal of the US fortunes in the country," wrote historian John Roosa in his 2006 book, *Pretext for Mass Murder: The September 30th Movement and Suharto's* Coup d'état *in Indonesia*. "Almost overnight the Indonesian government went from being a fierce voice for Cold War neutrality and anti-imperialism to a quiet, compliant partner of the U.S. world order."[719] Roosa also pointed out how the 1965 Indonesian coup and massacre of Communists was a precondition to LBJ being able to ramp up the US military in Vietnam. "The ground troops that started to arrive in Vietnam in March 1965 would be superfluous if the Communists won a victory in a much larger, more strategic country," Roosa commented. "A PKI takeover in Indonesia would render the intervention in Vietnam futile. U.S. troops were busy fighting at the gate while the enemy was already inside, about to occupy the palace and raid the storehouses."[720] CIA estimates prepared before the Suharto *coup* gave doomsday predictions that Indonesia's government under Sukarno was within two years of coming under PKI dominance.[721]

DiEugenio argued that one of JFK's largest splits within the Eastern Establishment was that JFK was for Third World nationalism. In contrast, the predominant worldview pursued by the Dulles brothers involved globalism "or the One World free trade doctrine" that DiEugenio described as "the idea American companies can take advantage of 'free trade' in order to develop business connections overseas that allow them to exploit foreign workers at low prices, and then bring the profits back to corporate headquarters."[722] Turning back to Guatemala in the 1950s, Eisenhower's concern stemmed from the possibility the Arbenz government might continue nationalizing land to the detriment of the United Fruit Company and its banana business in the United States. As noted in chapter 5, JFK's father, Joseph P. Kennedy, the patriarch of the Kennedy clan, was never accepted by the largely Catholic and Jewish eastern mob. So too, Joseph P. Kennedy's pacifism as US ambassador to Great Britain in the years prior to the start of World War II put him at odds with US financial interests supporting the Nazis as enemies of the Soviet Communists.

As his first term progressed, JFK was moving away from a confrontational model of how he wanted to wage the continuing Cold War. He learned in the Bay of Pigs not to trust the CIA and the military industrial complex. He learned in the Cuban Missile Crisis that he could reach out to Khrushchev in the Kremlin to resolve a crisis that could easily have escalated to a thermonuclear conflict. Kennedy refused to use the US military in both Laos and Vietnam, seemingly rejecting the Eisenhower-era notion of the "domino" theory that a victory for the Communists in any Third World country would inevitably spread Communism around the globe. Kennedy understood that no country could experience freedom unless the people of that country were willing to fight for themselves. He also understood that Communism in Laos or Vietnam would be different than Communism in China, as Communism in China was different than Communism in Russia. Even if all these nations were Communist, nationalism in each country would still be the dominant characteristic.

JFK could deal with Sukarno as a Third World nationalist seeking to free itself from the shackles of European colonialism. JFK's nemesis, Allen Dulles, could only see Communism in terms of black and white. Fundamentally, Dulles and those of his era—including Eisenhower and Nixon—were comfortable building the CIA around Nazis like Reinhard Gehlen. JFK, in sharp contrast, seriously questioned whether the United States needed the CIA at all. Where Eisenhower, Nixon, and Dulles saw covert action as a natural extension of foreign policy, JFK was distrustful—as distrustful of the CIA as he was of the military industrial complex in its totality. In foreign policy, LBJ made a natural Cold War warrior, anxious to exert American might and will into the Third World in a determination to roll back Communism wherever it popped up. When you have them by the private parts, their hearts and minds will follow, LJB liked to say. This quotation would have made JFK uncomfortable, both for its statement of force and its denial of the principle that no people can be free unless that people exerts a right to self-determination, an extension of the statehood politics JFK understood as an essential condition of freedom.

WHERE WAS GEORGE H. W. BUSH ON NOVEMBER 22, 1963?

In recent years, strong documentary evidence is that George H. W. Bush was in the CIA decades before he became CIA director under the presidency of Gerald R. Ford in 1976. Strong documentary evidence has also come to light suggesting George H. W. Bush was in Dallas on November 22, 1963, despite his claims to the contrary.

On Wednesday, November 20, 1963, an advertisement under "Club Activities" was printed in the *Dallas Morning News*, stating that George Bush, president of Zapata Off-Shore Co., would be speaking for the American Association of Oilwell Drilling contractors on Thursday, November 21, 1963, at the Sheraton-Dallas Hotel. A photograph widely circulated on the Internet shows a man standing with his hands in his pocket that bears a striking resemblance to George H. W. Bush, on the street by the front doorway of the Texas School Book Depository in the immediate aftermath of the JFK shooting.[723]

An FBI memo written by J. Edgar Hoover on November 29, 1963, advised that the FBI office in Miami, Florida, warned the Department of State on November 23, 1963, one day after the assassination, that "some misguided anti-Castro group might capitalize on the present situation and undertake an unauthorized raid against Cuba, believing that the assassination of President John F. Kennedy might herald a change in U.S. policy, which is not true."[724] In the last paragraph, Hoover noted that Mr. George Bush of the CIA furnished the background information contained in the report. Spokespersons for Bush suggested the reference might be to a different George Bush. A George William Bush was subsequently identified as a CIA employee. However, this George William Bush submitted a signed statement to the US District Court for the District of Columbia saying he had carefully reviewed the FBI memorandum written by the FBI Director, dated November 29, 1963, and he did not recognize the contents of the memorandum as information furnished to him orally or otherwise while he was at the CIA. Thus, he concluded, he was not the George Bush of the CIA referred to in the memo.[725]

When the memo surfaced, the *New York Times* questioned Stephen Hart, then a spokesman for then-Vice President Bush, and asked when George H. W. Bush first joined the CIA. Hart replied that Vice President Bush denied any involvement with the CIA before President Ford named him CIA Director in 1975. The newspaper also reported that Bill Divine, a CIA spokesman, declined to comment on the possibility that George H. W. Bush, or anyone else with that name, ever worked for the CIA. Devine told the *New York Times*, "We never confirm nor deny."[726]

A second recently disclosed memo supports the same conclusion. FBI Special Agent Graham Kitchel wrote a memo to the FBI's Houston bureau, dated November 22, 1963, the day of the assassination. The memo reads: "At 1:45 p.m. Mr. GEORGE H. W. BUSH, President of the Zapata Off-Shore Drilling Company, Houston, Texas, residence 5525 Briar, Houston, telephonically furnished this following information to writer by a long distance telephone call from Tyler, Texas." Tyler is a small town about one hundred miles to the southeast of Dallas. The memo went on to say that "Bush stated that he wanted to be kept confidential but wanted to furnish hearsay that he recalled hearing in recent weeks, the day and source unknown." Graham then relates how Bush suspected James Parrott, a student at the University of Texas, had been talking of assassinating JFK, when JFK came to Houston. The lead turned out to be inconsequential. But in the last paragraph Graham confirmed that Bush was *going* to be at the Sheraton-Dallas Hotel in Dallas on the day of the assassination, returning to his residence in Houston on Saturday, November 23, 1963.[727]

Others, noting the discrepancy that the *Dallas Morning News* claimed Bush would be at the Sheraton-Dallas on Thursday night, November 21, 1963, while the Kitchel memo suggests Bush would be at the hotel on the night of the assassination, have claimed Bush made the call to Kitchel to establish an alibi. Russ Baker, author of the 2009 book, *Family of Secrets*, argued the real point of the call was "to establish for the record, if anyone asked, that Poppy Bush was not in Dallas when Kennedy was shot. By pointing to a seemingly harmless man who lived with his mother, Bush appeared to establish his own Pollyannaish ignorance of the larger plot."[728] Baker argued the truth was Bush had already stayed at the Sheraton in Dallas, on Thursday, as the *Dallas Morning News* printed. By telling the FBI in a phone call that he was *planning* to go there, he created a misleading paper trail suggesting that his stay in Dallas was many hours after the assassination, rather than the night before, since the phone call incoming to the FBI could have originated from anywhere.

Typically, George H. W. Bush has been vague about where he was when he first learned JFK had been shot, a moment virtually every American old enough to remember has fixed distinctly in their mind. When asked where he was when Kennedy was shot, George H. W. Bush has said vaguely that he was "somewhere in Texas."[729]

THE NEW WORLD ORDER

There are over fifty-eight thousand names carved into black granite walls of the Vietnam Veterans Memorial in Washington, D.C. Lyndon Johnson and Richard Nixon both made the Vietnam War a centerpiece of their presidential administrations, continuing the conflict until the fall of Saigon on April 30, 1975. In retrospect, JFK was right. The Vietnam War was not a war the United States could win, if fought the way the military industrial complex wanted the war to be fought.

On August 2, 1990, some one hundred thousand Iraqi troops invaded Kuwait, starting what became known as the Gulf War. On September 11,

1991, President George H. W. Bush addressed a joint session of Congress, proclaiming the allied forces that came together represented a "new world order." Here is the key passage of that speech:

> We stand today at a unique and extraordinary moment. The crisis in the Persian Gulf, as grave as it is, also offers a rare opportunity to move toward an historic period of cooperation. Out of these troubled times, our fifth objective—a new world order—can emerge: a new era—freer from the threat of terror, stronger in the pursuit of justice, and more secure in the quest for peace. An era in which the nations of the world, East and West, North and South, can prosper and live in harmony. A hundred generations have searched for this elusive path to peace, while a thousand wars raged across the span of human endeavor.
>
> Today that new world is struggling to be born, a world quite different from the one we've known. A world where the rule of law supplants the rule of the jungle. A world in which nations recognize the shared responsibility for freedom and justice. A world where the strong respect the rights of the weak. This is the vision that I shared with President Gorbachev in Helsinki. He and other leaders from Europe, the Gulf, and around the world understand that how we manage this crisis today could shape the future for generations to come.[730]

President George W. Bush, in response to the terrorist attacks on the World Trade Center and the Pentagon on September 11, 2001, launched a US military invasion of Afghanistan, followed by an invasion of Iraq. In so utilizing US military force in major foreign entanglements, President George H. W. Bush and his son, President George W. Bush, have followed in the footsteps of LBJ and Richard Nixon.

Truthfully, millions of Americans who were politically aware when JFK was assassinated mark that day as a turning point in the history of this nation. Gone was the idealism that America stood for righteousness. The protests of the Vietnam War and the resistance to the draft radicalized a generation of Americans. Baby Boomers raised in the Eisenhower era came of age during the presidencies of LBJ and Nixon. With Nixon, Watergate, and the subsequent disclosures of the Church Committee, we now see that much that has transpired since World War II needs to be written in a secret history of the United States. At the heart of this secret history are the clandestine activities undertaken by the CIA, creating what White House counsel John Dean characterized in the darkest days of Watergate as "a cancer on the presidency."

Truthfully, Robert Kennedy understood this. In a recently released classified evaluation of the Taylor Committee Investigation of the Bay of Pigs established by JFK under the direction of Gen. Maxwell Taylor, CIA historian Jack B. Pfeiffer was particularly critical of CIA Director Allen Dulles. Pfeiffer noted in blunt language after Dulles appeared before the Taylor Committee, that he was "headed for the elephants' burial ground," thanks to Robert Kennedy's denigration of him and the CIA, and due in no small part to the "abysmal performance" of Dulles as a witness. "With the conclusion of the Taylor investigation, there was a period of mistrust of both the CIA and the JCS [Joint Chiefs of Staff] by the new President; and [JFK] turned to his inner circle for guidance which previously would have been sought from the Agency or the Department of Defense," Pfeiffer wrote. "General Taylor performed in such acceptable fashion that he was recalled to active duty and into the elite inner circle to become President Kennedy's military adviser and subsequent Chairman of the JCS."[731]

Before concluding, we need to add one more footnote to the story of the 1954 CIA-engineered coup d'état in Guatemala. After Hitler's rise to power, Allen Dulles, as a partner in the New York law firm Sullivan and Cromwell, remained a director of the New York branch of the J. Henry Schroeder Bank, becoming ultimately Schroeder's general counsel. The Schroeder investment banking houses in London and New York remained tied with the Schroeder family in Germany, including Baron Kurt von Schroeder, who was known as Heinrich Himmler's special agent.[732] The J. Henry Schroeder Banking Corporation and the Schroeder Trust functioned in the 1950s and 1960s to be depositories for CIA money, long after the New York branch had formally been reabsorbed by the London-based J. Henry Schroeder and Company, Limited.[733] With Dulles as head of the CIA, this secret depository became a fifty-million-dollar contingency fund held by Schroeder and personally controlled by Dulles.[734]

In 1936 the Dulles brothers, then both lawyers at Sullivan and Cromwell, intervened in a power play on behalf of their Boston-based client, United Fruit Company, and their operations in Guatemala. The Dulles brothers concocted a scheme where the Schroeder Banking Corporation, with brother Allen Dulles acting as general counsel and a member of the board, financed United Fruit to take control of the International Railways of Central America, or IRCA, the owner of most of the existing railroad tracks in the region that United Fruit relied upon in order to ship Guatemalan bananas to market in the United States. The president of the Schroeder bank remained a member of the IRCA board through 1954. IRCA also owned outright Guatemala's only harbor on the Atlantic, Puerto Barrios, from where United Fruit freighters, known as the "Great White Fleet," engaged in the banana trade.[735] In 1954, with Allen Dulles at the head of the CIA, the CIA-engineered coup d'état masterminded by E. Howard Hunt could easily be interpreted as Allen Dulles protecting the business interests of one of his law firm clients.

But the story does not end there. In 1956 the J. Henry Schroeder Banking Corporation financed the opening in Switzerland of a company known as Permindex, standing for the more formal name of the trade group, the Permanent Industrial Exposition.[736] Permindex was closely allied with an Italian trade group, *Centro-Mondiale Commercial*, or World Trade Center, an Italian subsidiary of the World Trade Corporation and reputedly a CIA front. New Orleans district attorney Jim Garrison entered Permindex into his JFK assassination investigation when he established that Clay Shaw, also known as Clay Bertrand, was a member of the boards of both Permindex and *Centro-Mondiale Commercial*. Clay Shaw was head of the International Trade Mart in New Orleans; coincidentally, the speech JFK never gave was at a luncheon scheduled to be held at the Dallas Trade Mart.

Allegations published in an Italian newspaper in Rome, *Paese Sera*, on April 23, 1961, charged that Permindex was used by the CIA to shuffle funds covertly to fund assassinations, including funneling money to the French OAS to pay Corsican assassins like Michel Mertz to assassinate French president Charles de Gaulle. All this may seem farfetched, except that, as we say in chapter 7, an authentic declassified CIA document verifies that Mertz had been in Dallas on November 22, 1963, and that he was apprehended and deported by US authorities. The document indicated French intelligence wanted to know the whereabouts of Mertz because Mertz was a professional assassin with ties to the OAS. The French were worried about the security of de Gualle. The CIA, by the way, has dismissed all the speculation about Permindex as Soviet disinformation propaganda.[737]

Assassination researcher James DiEugenio, after studying documents released over the past few years by the Assassinations Records Review Board, or AARB, has concluded that Clay Shaw, too, was a CIA asset. DiEugenio argued one of Kennedy's largest splits with the Eastern Establishment was that he was a proponent of Third World nationalism. This, Eugenio contrasted to Clay Shaw, arguing that Shaw's two agencies, the International Trade Mart and its sister organization, International House, were early advocates of globalism. International House was founded by the Rockefeller Foundation and spread worldwide. Both David and William Rockefeller III served as trustees of International House, and David served as chairman of the executive committee. John McCloy, formally president of the World Bank, was chairman of the board of International House in the 1950s and 1960s. Once again, recall that John McCloy, along with Allen Dulles, served on the Warren Commission. Although examining Garrison's prosecution of Clay Shaw is beyond the scope of this book, suffice it to note DiEugenio believed Clay Shaw was very close to cracking the JFK assassination case wide open.

The point here is that the "deep politics" background of the JFK assassination cannot be explained fully by a book whose scope, like this one, is limited to answering the question: Who really killed JFK? When the answer turns out to be "all of the above," as it is here, the inquiry turns from an identification of the players to an investigation of the political context in which these players worked together. In other words, it is not enough to conclude the operational plot to assassinate JFK involved the CIA working in concert with organized crime. So, too, it is important but not sufficient to note LBJ, Richard Nixon, and the military industrial complex all had motives for seeing a coup d'état carried out in the United States.

What is important is that all these actors shared a common belief in clandestine government operations. In the postwar world, the Dulles brothers exemplified the intermixture of law, investment banking, foreign policy, and covert intelligence operations. The shared principle was that foreign policy covert operations conducted by intelligence agencies under the principle of "plausible deniability" were justified, as long as the result was to create a "New World Order," even if creating that new world order meant lying to the American people, now for a half century, and probably longer. The innovation represented by the JFK assassination was to apply the covert operations model, initially designed as a foreign policy tool, into a tool that could be applied equally in domestic politics, causing a coup d'état in the United States rather than simply overthrowing an inconvenient foreign government.

WHO REALLY KILLED KENNEDY?

JFK probably would have survived into a second term in office had only he agreed to go along. All it would have taken would have been to green light the US military to send in the air force and possibly the marines to invade Cuba at the Bay of Pigs, with the operation justified in the cause of saving the brave Cuban exile "freedom fighters" who were trying to recover their country and restore freedom to Cuba.

Or, what would have been wrong with JFK just deciding to send in a few thousand US troops to Vietnam in the fall of 1963? Instead of giving a speech in Dallas on November 22, 1963, focused on the US military assistance program, JFK could have planned to explain to the world how his decision to commit US troops to Vietnam was fulfilling the promise he made in his First Inaugural Address to defend freedom around the globe because no price for freedom was too great to pay.

The CIA shared a belief with LBJ, Richard Nixon, and the military industrial complex that even if US military action failed in Cuba or in Vietnam, as it had in Korea, the military intervention would be good for business and the US economy. Besides, in Korea the conflict ended with a partition of the country, a solution the CIA and the military would have accepted in Vietnam, and possibly even Cuba (provided the U.S.A. got Havana). Again, the point is that the New World Order view was comfortable employing the US military to preserve US business interests, as had been done when overthrowing Mossadegh in Iran and Arbenz in Guatemala. George H. W. Bush did not blink when waging war with Iraq, fully realizing US oil interests in Kuwait were being preserved. Under the ideologies of nationalism and self-determination JFK used to analyze Cuba, Laos, and Vietnam, it was clear he felt US military involvement was required in none of these conflicts. JFK cared about US business interests, but not necessarily to the point of going to war.

What George H. W. Bush made clear with his "New World Order" speech to Congress on September 11, 1990, was that the use of US military to protect US business interests was especially justified when backed by an international coalition. Today, US policy makers increasingly look to international organizations such as the United Nations, the World Bank, and the International Monetary Fund, when formulating US policies. While JFK respected international organizations, he did not spend much time worrying about going first to the United Nations before deciding whether or not to commit US troops to Laos or Vietnam. Somehow, ironically, the internationalization of US policy has proceeded apace, despite the obvious conclusion that by 1974, it was clear JFK was right about Vietnam, while nearly every calculation made by LBJ, Richard Nixon, and the military industrial complex turned out to be wrong.

In the final analysis, JFK was killed because he saw US military action in shades of gray, where the Dulles brothers saw only black and white. Still, despite this, JFK might yet have lived into a second term, but once he called out organized crime and the CIA, threatening to destroy both, he needed to succeed. LBJ and Richard Nixon, the two politicians who stood the most to gain from a JFK assassination, may have resented JFK, but they could do nothing about that resentment without the operational capabilities offered by equally resentful CIA leaders and organized crime bosses.

The one who appreciated this the most may have been Robert Kennedy. Before he was finished, Robert Kennedy fired every member of the Dulles family he could find working in the federal government. When Robert Kennedy found out that Allen Dulles's sister Eleanor worked for Dean Rusk at the State Department, he insisted Rusk had to fire her too because "he didn't want any more of the Dulles family around."[738] In Robert Kennedy's answer to the question "Who really killed JFK?" a prime suspect appears to have been Allen Dulles.

At the top level, E. Howard Hunt, Richard Nixon, and George H. W. Bush are also suspect, if only because all three equivocated when asked where they were when they first heard JFK had been shot. Not providing a forthright answer to this question is a sign of a guilty conscious at a minimum, topped with a desire to hide the truth. What did they have to hide? E. Howard Hunt, lacking a cover story for explaining why he might have been in Dallas on November 22, 1963, denied until the end of his life that he was there. In Dallas, Richard Nixon had the opportunity to confer and possibly meet privately with one or more of the co-conspirators, as well as to meet with those wealthy individuals who had helped finance his political career. George H. W. Bush appears to have been in Dallas in some sort of coordination with the CIA.

The evidence suggests the shooters were selected from a combination of Cuban exiles and mob hit men. Top suspects for having participated as shooters would include Frank Sturgis, Roscoe White, and Sergio Arcaha Smith. Most likely, E. Howard Hunt, who played a direct role in both the Guatemala coup d'état in the 1950s and in the Bay of Pigs invasion, both under Eisenhower and Kennedy, was involved in planning the operation. Corsican assassin Michel Mertz was in Dallas on November 22, 1963, most likely with a mission to oversee and manage the shooters. When it came to coordinating mob involvement in the JFK assassination, Johnny Roselli was in charge.

After fifty years of US government misinformation and deliberate stonewalling, researchers are just at the edge of discovering the truth about how and why JFK was assassinated in one of the greatest crimes in US history—a coup d'état in which rogue groups, including the highest intelligence services in the land, conspired to remove JFK from the presidency and to place LBJ in the White House. The consequences of this conspiracy are immeasurable, if only because a group of traitors successfully flouted the constitution and got away with it.

After fifty years of abuse, those who have suspected JFK's assassination was a conspiracy are about to be proven right. History will need to be rewritten to condemn those responsible as traitorous criminals. While prosecutions may no longer be possible simply because so many of the involved parties have already died, justice can be served by setting the historical record straight. At this late date, any attempt by the US government to withhold from the public documents pertaining to the JFK assassination should be deemed by Congress to be a continuation of the traitorous acts that killed JFK.

If we do not want to see this history repeated, all Americans have a responsibility to demand the full truth from the US government now. To do less would be to further dishonor the memory of John Fitzgerald Kennedy, the 35th President of the United States.

NOTES

PREFACE: **THE END OF CAMELOT**

1 Warren Commission Executive Session, Jan. 27, 1964, page 171, http://www.maryferrell.org/ mffweb/archive/viewer/showDoc.do?docId=1328&relPageId=47.

2 Testimony of M.N. McDonald, Warren Commission Hearings, Vol. III, March 25, 1964, pages 295–304, at 300–301.

3 "Warren Commission," Mary Ferrell Foundation, http://www.maryferrell.org/wiki/index.php/ Warren_Commission. See also: "Warren Commission Executive Session Transcripts," History Matters, http://www.history-matters.com/archive/contents/wc/contents_wcexec.htm.

4 Donald E. Wilkes Jr., "Russell Disagreed with JFK Death Report," Popular Media, Georgia Law, Paper 132, Nov. 9, 1989, http://digitalcommons.law.uga.edu/cgi/viewcontent. cgi?article=1136&context=fac_pm.

5 Ibid.

6 "Americans: Kennedy Assassination a Conspiracy," Gallup, Nov. 21, 2003, http://www.gallup. com/poll/9751/Americans-Kennedy-Assassination-Conspiracy.aspx.

ONE: **THE SINGLE-BULLET THEORY**

7 Josiah Thompson, *Six Seconds in Dallas: A Micro-Study of the Kennedy Assassination Proving that Three Gunmen Murdered the President* (Published by Bernard Geis Associates, Distributed by Random House, New York, 1967), page 9.

8 LBJ Tapes, Recorded conversation with J. Edgar Hoover, Nov. 29, 1963. Shirley Jahad, "JFK assassination anniversary: A Private conversation between LBJ and J. Edgar Hoover," Southern California Public Radio, Nov. 22, 2011, http://www.scpr.org/news/2011/11/22/30001/ jfk-assassination-anniversary-private-conversation/. The tapes can be heard at: "LBJ Tapes: Kennedy Assassination, J. Edgar Hoover," YouTube.com, Part 1 at http://www.youtube.com/ watch?feature=player_embedded&v=4ZWERQevzms, and Part 2 at http://www.youtube. com/watch?v=IwmwSEZmgPg.

9 Paul Mandel, "End to Nagging Rumors: The Six Critical Seconds," *Life*, Dec. 6, 1963, page 52F.

10 "The Assassination of President Kennedy," *Life*, Memorial Issue, Nov. 29, 1963, pages 22-32c, with still photographs from the Zapruder film published in a sub-section of this article entitled, Split Second Horror as the Sniper's Bullets Struck.

11 Mandel, "End to Nagging Rumors."

12 Testimony of James Thomas Tague, Warren Commission: Hearings Before the President's Commission on the Assassination of President Kennedy, July 23, 1964, Vol. VII, pages 552–558, at page 553.

13 Testimony of Eddy Raymond Walthers, Warren Commission: Hearings Before the President's Commission on the Assassination of President Kennedy, July 23, 1964, Vol. VII, pages 544–552, at page 546.

14 Warren Commission, *Report of the President's Commission on the Assassination of President John F. Kennedy* (Washington, D.C.: United States Government Printing Office, 1964), page 117.

15 Richard H. Popkin, "The Second Oswald: The Case for a Conspiracy Theory," *New York Review of Books*, July 28, 1966, pages 11–22.

16 Testimony of Darrell C. Tomlinson, Warren Commission: Hearings Before the President's Commission on the Assassination of President Kennedy, March 20, 1964, Vol. VI, pages 128–134, at page 131.

17 Ibid., page 132.

18 Ibid., page 134.

19 Commission Exhibit 1024, no title, Warren Commission: Hearings Before the President's Commission on the Assassination of President Kennedy, Vol. XVIII, page 800.

20 Commission Exhibit 2011, FBI report dated July 7, 1963, Dallas, Texas, Warren Commission: Hearings Before the President's Commission on the Assassination of President Kennedy, Vol. XXIV, pages 410–428, at page 412.

21 Gary Aguilar and Josiah Thompson, "The Magic Bullet: Even More Magical Than We Knew," archived on MaryFerrell.org, http://www.maryferrell.org/mffweb/archive/viewer/showDoc. do?docId=367.

22 Ibid.

23 Thompson, *Six Seconds in Dallas*, page 175.

24 Ibid., pages 158–159.

25 Warren Commission, page 81.

26 Jerry McKnight, "Tracking CE 399: The 'Stretcher Bullet' and the Case for a Dallas Conspiracy," Kennedy Assassination Chronicles, Vol. 7, Issue 3, 2001, pages 22–26, at page 24.

27 Special Agent Andrew E. Berger, White House Detail, Memorandum, "Activities of this Special Agent in Dallas, Texas, on Friday, November 22, 1963, Commission Exhibit 1024, Warren Commission: Hearings Before the President's Commission on the Assassination of President Kennedy, Vol. XVIII, pages 795–796, at page 795.

28 Thompson, *Six Seconds in Dallas*, page 166.

29 Testimony of Seth Kantor, Warren Commission: Hearings Before the President's Commission on the Assassination of President Kennedy, June 2, 1964, Vol. XV, pages 71–96, at page 80.

30 FBI Memo to the File, June 27, 1964, Commission Exhibit 2290, Warren Commission: Hearings Before the President's Commission on the Assassination of President Kennedy, Vol. XXV, pages 216–218, at pages 216–217.

31 Thompson, *Six Seconds in Dallas*, page 166.

32 Testimony of Dr. Robert Roeder Shaw, Warren Commission: Hearings Before the President's Commission on the Assassination of President Kennedy, April 21, 1964, Vol. IV, pages 101–117, at page 114.

33 Dr. Milton Helpern, formerly Chief Medical Examiner of New York City, quoted in: Anthony Summers, *Conspiracy: The Definitive Book on the J.F.K. Assassination—Dramatic New Evidence* (New York: Paragon House, Updated and expanded edition, 1989), pages 35–36.

34 Testimony of Dr. Robert Roeder Shaw, Warren Commission: Hearings Before the President's Commission on the Assassination of President Kennedy, page 113.

35 Testimony of Comdr. James J. Humes, Warren Commission: Hearings Before the President's Commission on the Assassination of President Kennedy, March 16, 1964, Vol. II, pages 348–376, at pages 374–375.

36 Ibid., page 376.

37 Testimony of Lt. Col. Pierre A. Finck, Physician, U.S. Army, Warren Commission: Hearings Before the President's Commission on the Assassination of President Kennedy, March 16, 1964, Vol. II, pages 377–384, at page 382.

38 Testimony of Robert A. Frazier, Warren Commission: Hearings Before the President's Commission on the Assassination of President Kennedy, May 13, 1964, Vol. V, pages 58–74, at page 72.

39 Harrison Edward Livingstone, *High Treason 2. The Great Cover-Up: The Assassination of John F. Kennedy* (New York: Carroll & Graf Publishers, Inc., 1992), page 304.

40 Charles A. Crenshaw, with Jens Hensen and Gary Shaw, *JFK: Conspiracy of Silence* (New York: Penguin Books, 1992), page 123.

41 Russell Kent, "The Wounding of John Connally—Burying the Single-bullet theory," 2005, reprinted at Spartacus.schoolnet.co.uk, at http://www.spartacus.schoolnet.co.uk/KENT-connally.htm.

42 "Connally Buried, Bullet Pieces Intact," *Washington Post*, June 18, 1993.

43 Summers, *Conspiracy*, 1989 edition, page 34.

44 Ronald F. White, "Postscript: Apologists and Critics of the Lone Gunman Theory: Assassination Science and Experts in Post Modern America," in James H. Fetzer, Ph.D., editor, *Assassination Science: Experts Speak Out on the Death of JFK*, pages 377–412, at pages 391–393.

45 Thompson, *Six Seconds in Dallas*, page 151.

46 Ibid.

47 Ibid., page 152.

48 Ibid., pages 152–153.

49 Ibid., page 153.

50 Testimony of Dr. Vincent P. Guinn, House Select Committee on Assassinations, Sept. 8, 1978, Vol. I, pages 491–567, at page 494.

51 Kent, "The Wounding of John Connally."

52 Appendix B, House Select Committee on Assassinations, Vol. II, page 538.

53 Ronald F. White, "Postscript: Apologists and Critics of the Lone Gunman Theory: Assassination Science and Experts in Post-Modern America."

54 Sylvia Meagher, *Accessories After the Fact: The Warren Commission, the Authorities, and the Report* (New York: The Bobbs-Merrill Company, Inc., 1967), pages 112–113.

55 Warren Commission, page 646.

56 Gerald Posner, *Case Closed: Lee Harvey Oswald and the Assassination of JFK* (New York: Random House, 1993), pages 335–342, and especially 335–339; and Vincent Bugliosi, *Reclaiming History: The Assassination of President John F. Kennedy*, (New York: W. W. Norton & Company, 2007), pages 805–815, and especially 809–811.

57 Ronald F. White, "Postscript: Apologists and Critics of the Lone Gunman Theory: Assassination Science and Experts in Post-Modern America," loc.cit, page 394. Bracketed parentheses inserted for clarity; rounded parentheses in original.

58 Gary L. Agilar, MD and Kathy Cunningham, "How Five Investigations Into JFK's Medical/ Autopsy Evidence Got It Wrong," May 2003, http://www.history-matters.com/essays/jfkmed/ How5Investigations/How5InvestigationsGotItWrong_1b.htm; verbatim transcript of press conference interviews with Drs. Malcolm Perry and Kemp Clark, from LBJ Library, obtained by Kathy Cunningham; also, reproduced in Assassination Records Review Board, Master Set of Medical Exhibits, http://www.history-matters.com/archive/jfk/arrb/master_med_set/ md41/html/Image0.htm.

59 Tom Wicker, "Kennedy Is Killed By Sniper As He Rides In Car In Dallas; Johnson Sworn In On Plane," *New York Times*, Nov. 23, 1963, http://www.nytimes.com/books/98/04/12/specials/johnson-kennedy.html. Parentheses added for clarity.

60 Meagher, *Accessories After the Fact*, page 134.

61 Testimony of Dr. Charles James Carrico, Warren Commission: Hearings Before the President's Commission on the Assassination of President Kennedy, Vol III, pages 357–366, at page 361.

62 Letter from James J. Rowley, U.S. Secret Service, to J. Lee Rankin, General Counsel, Warren Commission, May 14, 1964, plus notes written by Secret Service Special Agent Glen A. Bennett, Warren Commission: Hearings Before the President's Commission on the Assassination of President Kennedy, Vol XXIV, Commission Exhibit 2112, pages 541–542.

63 Testimony of Roy H. Kellerman, Special Agent, Secret Service, Resumed, Warren Commission: Hearings Before the President's Commission on the Assassination of President Kennedy, Vol II, March 9, 1964, pages 101–112, at page 103.

64 Thompson, *Six Seconds in Dallas*, page 167.

65 Report by FBI Special Agents Francis X. O'Neill, Jr. and James W. Sibert, "Autopsy of Body of President John Fitzgerald Kennedy," Bethesda, Md., dated Nov. 26, 1963, "Gemberling Version," Assassination Records Review Board, Medical Exhibits, MD 44, also known as "Warren Commission Document No. 7," http://www.maryferrell.org/mffweb/archive/viewer/showDoc.do?docId=625.

66 Testimony of Lt. Col. Pierre A. Finck, Physician, U.S. Army, Warren Commission Hearings, Vol. II, March 16, 1964, pages 377-384.

67 *State of Louisiana vs. Clay L. Shaw*, Criminal District Court, Parish of Orleans, State of Louisiana, 198–059 1426(30), Testimony of Dr. Finck, Feb. 25, 1969, part 1, pages 51-52, http://www.maryferrell.org/mffweb/archive/viewer/showDoc.do?docId=1299.

68 *State of Louisiana vs. Clay L. Shaw*, Criminal District Court, Parish of Orleans, State of Louisiana, 198–059 1426(30), Testimony of Dr. Finck, Feb. 25, 1969, part 2, pages 114-118, http://www.maryferrell.org/mffweb/archive/viewer/showDoc.do?docId=1300.

69 Testimony of Dr. J. Thornton Boswell to the Assassination Records Review Board, Feb. 26, 1996, pages 208-211, http://www.maryferrell.org/mffweb/archive/viewer/showDoc.do?docId=786.

70 Silbert and O'Neill's FBI report is quoted in Meagher, *Accessories After the Fact*, pages 145–146.

71 Jerry McKnight, "Tracking CE 399: The 'Stretcher Bullet' and the Case for a Dallas Conspiracy," page 23.

72 Meagher, *Accessories After the Fact*, page 146.

73 Transcript available at: "Connally Interview with Martin Agronsky, November 27, 1963," Texas State Library and Archives Commission," https://www.tsl.state.tx.us/governors/modern/connally-agronsky-1.html. A video of the Agronsky interview with Connally can be seen at: "John Connally's first interview after 11/22/63," YouTube.com, posted Dec. 27, 2007, http://www.youtube.com/watch?v=cP04_IGjkO0

74 Testimony of Gov. John Bowden Connally, Jr., Warren Commission Hearings, April 21, 1964, Vol. IV, pages 129–146, at pages 132–133.

75 Ibid., page 136.

76 Ibid., pages 138–139.

77 Ibid., page 144.

78 Testimony of Mrs. John Bowden Connally, Jr., Warren Commission Hearings, April 21, 1964, Vol. IV, pages 146–149, at page 147.

79 Ibid.

80 "A Matter of Reasonable Doubt: Amid Heightening Controversy about the Warren Report, Governor Connally Examines for 'Life' the Assassination Film," *Life Magazine*, Nov. 25, 1966, pages 38–53.

81 Ibid., pages 40–43.

82 Ibid., page 48.

83 Ibid.

84 Warren Commission, page 112.

85 Ibid.

86 Testimony of Comdr. James J. Humes, Comdr. J. Thornton Boswell, and Lt. Col. Pierre A. Finck, Warren Commission Hearings, March 16, 1964, Vol. II, pages 347–384, at page 376.

87 Warren Commission, pages 114–115.

88 Meagher, *Accessories After the Fact*, pages 28–29.

89 Richard B. Trask, *Pictures of the Pain: Photography and the Assassination of President Kennedy* (Danvers, Massachusetts: Yeoman Press, 1994), "A Firecracker Going Off," pages 159–166, at pages 160–162.

90 Willis Exhibit No. 1, "Continued (Slide #5)," Warren Commission Hearings, Vol. XXI, page 770.

91 Trask, *Pictures of the Pain*, pages 167–182, at pages 171–172.

92 "Gerald Ford's Terrible Fiction: Moving the Back Wound and the Single-bullet theory," JFKLancer.com, http://www.jfklancer.com/Ford-Rankin.html. See also: Michael J. Sniffen, Associated Press, "Former President Ford confided to FBI about panel's doubts over JFK assassination," *Minneapolis Star Tribune*, Aug. 9, 2008, http://www.startribune.com/templates/Print_This_Story?sid=26469829.

93 Commission Exhibit 903, on title, Photograph of Arlen Specter, in a reconstruction of the JFK assassination, May 24, 1964, Warren Commission Hearings, Vol. XVIII, page 96.

94 Testimony of Robert A. Frazier Resumed, Warren Commission Hearings, June 4, 1964, Vol. V, pages 165–175, at pages 171–172.

TWO: **THE GRASSY KNOLL**

95 Craig Roberts, *Kill Zone: A Sniper Looks at Dealey Plaza* (Tulsa, Oklahoma: Typhoon Press, 1994), page 5.

96 Ibid.

97 Ibid., page 6.

98 Ibid.

99 Ibid., pages 6–7.

100 Ibid., page 9.

101 Description of Dealey Plaza, Commission Exhibit 877, Warren Commission: Hearings Before the President's Commission on the Assassination of President Kennedy, Vol. XVII, pages 897–898.

102 Roberts, *Kill Zone*, page 9. The italics are part of the original title.

103 Ibid., page 11. The italics are part of the original text.

104 Finn Nielsen, "The Mannlicher-Carcano," Surplusrifle.com, http://www.surplusrifle.com/shooting/mannlichercarcano/index.asp; and, Finn Nielsen, biography, Finn Nielsen Consultant Inc., March 7, 1943–July 30, 2008, http://www.finnnielsen.com/.

105 "Probability of competing in athletics beyond high school," NCAA, Sept. 17, 2012, http://www.ncaa.org/wps/wcm/connect/public/ncaa/pdfs/2012/estimated+probability+of+competing+in+athletics+beyond+the+high+school+interscholastic+level.

106 Bill Wall, "The Cognitive Psychology of Chess," Chess.com, June 21, 2010, http://www.chess.com/article/view/the-cognitive-psychology-of-chess.

107 Thompson, *Six Seconds in Dallas*, pages 190–191.

108 Donald E. Wilkes, Professor of Law, University of Georgia School of Law, "Oddities of the JFK Assassination," *Athens Human Rights Festival*, May 8 and 9, 1993, page 8, http://www.law.uga.edu/dwilkes_more/jfk_10oddities.html; mentioned also by Jim Marrs, *Crossfire: The Plot that Killed Kennedy* (New York: Carroll & Graf, Inc., Publishers, 1989), pages 12–15, 35, and 244–245; also, Robert J. Groden and Harrison Edward Livingstone, *High Treason: The Assassination of John F. Kennedy, What Really Happened* (New York: The Conservatory Press, 1989), pages 15–16.

109 Mark Lane, *Rush to Judgment. A critique of the Warren Commission's inquiry into the murders of President John F. Kennedy, Officer J. D. Tippit and Lee Harvey Oswald* (New York: Holt, Rinehart & Winston, 1966), page 32.

110 Testimony of Lee E. Bowers, Jr., Warren Commission: Hearings Before the President's Commission on the Assassination of President Kennedy, April 2, 1964, Vol. VI, pages 284–289.

111 Ibid., page 285.

112 Ibid., page 287.

113 Ibid.

114 Ibid., page 288.

115 Lane, *Rush to Judgment*, page 32.

116 Testimony of Lee E. Bowers, Jr., Warren Commission: Hearings Before the President's Commission on the Assassination of President Kennedy, page 287.

117 Ibid.

118 Bugliosi, *Reclaiming History*, pages 847–848.

119 Posner, *Case Closed*, page 238.

120 Testimony of S. M. Holland, Warren Commission: Hearings Before the President's Commission on the Assassination of President Kennedy, April 8, 1964, Vol. VI, pages 239–248, at 243–244.

121 Ibid., pages 245–246.

122 Ibid., page 246.

123 Ibid., page 247.

124 Thompson, *Six Seconds in Dallas*, pages 103–104.

125 Dallas Police Department, "Investigation of the Assassination of the President," Commission Exhibit 2003, no date, Warren Commission: Hearings Before the President's Commission on the Assassination of President Kennedy, Vol. XXIV, pages 195–404, at page 219.

126 Testimony of Howard Leslie Brennan, Warren Commission: Hearings Before the President's Commission on the Assassination of President Kennedy, March 24, 1964, Vol. III, pages 140–161.

127 Ibid., page 144.

128 Warren Commission, pages 63–64, and 143–146, at page 144.

129 Ibid., page 143.

130 Ibid.

131 Ibid., pages 143–144.

132 Special Agent Robert C. Dish, Memorandum, "Subject: UNSUB: Assassination of President JOHN F. KENNEDY," dated Nov. 22, 1963, filed in Dallas, Texas.

133 Testimony of Howard Leslie Brennan, pages 147–148.

134 Ibid., page 148.

135 Dallas Police Department, "Investigation of the Assassination of the President," Commission Exhibit 2003, no date, Warren Commission: Hearings Before the President's Commission on the Assassination of President Kennedy, Vol. XXIV, pages 195–404.

136 Testimony of Howard Leslie Brennan, page 140.

137 Bugliosi, *Reclaiming History*, pages 951–969, at pages 956–957.

138 Posner, *Case Closed*, pages 248–250, at 249.

139 Gerald McKnight, *Breach of Trust: How the Warren Commission Failed and Why* (Lawrence, Kansas: University of Kansas Press, 2005), page 398.

140 Testimony of J. Herbert Sawyer, Warren Commission: Hearings Before the President's Commission on the Assassination of President Kennedy, April 8, 1964, Vol. VI, pages 315–325, at 317.

141 Ibid., page 322.

142 Ibid., page 320.

143 Meagher, *Accessories After the Fact*, page 10.

144 Testimony of Howard Leslie Brennan, pages 145–146; and, Testimony of Forrest V. Sorrels, Warren Commission: Hearings Before the President's Commission on the Assassination of President Kennedy, May 7, 1964, Vol. VII, pages 332–360, at 348–349.

145 Commission Exhibit 479, Zapruder Film Frame 188, Warren Commission: Hearings Before the President's Commission on the Assassination of President Kennedy, Vol. XVII, page 198.

146 Testimony of Howard Leslie Brennan, page 144.

147 Ibid.

148 Commission Exhibit 486, no title, no date, Warren Commission: Hearings Before the President's Commission on the Assassination of President Kennedy, Vol. XVII, page 708.

149 Commission Exhibit 887, no title, no date, Warren Commission: Hearings Before the President's Commission on the Assassination of President Kennedy, Vol. XVII, page 86.

150 Commission Exhibit 1310, 1311, 1312, no title, no date, Warren Commission: Hearings Before the President's Commission on the Assassination of President Kennedy, Vol. XXII, pages 484–485.

151 Testimony of Seymour Weitzman, Warren Commission: Hearings Before the President's Commission on the Assassination of President Kennedy, April 1, 1964, Vol. VII, pages 105–109.

152 Ibid., page 108.

153 Testimony of D.V. Harkness, Warren Commission: Hearings Before the President's Commission on the Assassination of President Kennedy, April 9, 1964, Vol. VI, pages 308–315, at 312.

154 Testimony of Joe Marshall Smith, Warren Commission: Hearings Before the President's Commission on the Assassination of President Kennedy, July 23, 1964, Vol. VII, pages 531–539, at 535.

155 Meagher, *Accessories After the Fact*, page 26.

156 Testimony of James Thomas Tague, Warren Commission: Hearings Before the President's Commission on the Assassination of President Kennedy, at page 558.

157 Thompson, *Six Seconds in Dallas*, pages 82–111, at page 111.

158 Josiah Thompson's post on educationforum.ipbhost.com on March 30, 2011, at 7:34 pm, http://educationforum.ipbhost.com/index.php?showtopic=17516&page=17#entry222451.

159 David S. Lifton, *Best Evidence: Disguise and Deception in the Assassination of John F. Kennedy* (New York: Macmillan Publishing Co., Inc, 1980).

160 Ibid., page 692.

161 Ibid., pages 692–693.

162 Ibid., page 598.

163 Ibid., page 598.

164 Report by FBI Special Agents Francis X. O'Neill, Jr. and James W. Sibert, "Autopsy of Body of President John Fitzgerald Kennedy," page 3 of the original report.

165 Lifton, *Best Evidence,* pages 601-602.

166 Testimony of J.C. Day, Warren Commission Hearings, Vol. IV, April 22, 1964, pages 249-279; and, Affidavit of Lt. J.C. Day, dated May 7, 1964, Warren Commission Hearings, Vol VII, pages 401-402; and, Affidavit of Lt. J. C. Day, dated June 23, 1964, Warren Commission Hearings, Vol. VII, page 402.

167 Ibid.

168 "O'Connor, Paul K.," in Michael Benson, *Who's Who in the JFK Assassination: An A-to-Z Encyclopedia* (New York: Citadel Press, 1993), pages 319-320, at page 320.

169 For a YouTube presentation of Frame 464 of the Zapruder film, see: GerdaDunckel, "dead JFK rising from his seat ... (?)" uploaded Jan. 9, 2012, http://www.youtube.com/watch?v=lDCJ3Ndvz9M.

170 Testimony of Mrs. John F. Kennedy, Warren Commission Hearings, June 5, 1964, Vol. 5, pages 178-181, at 180-181.

171 Clint Hill, *Mrs. Kennedy and Me* (New York: Gallery Books, 2012), pages 290-291.

172 Press Conference, Parkland Memorial Hospital, Dallas, Texas, Nov. 22, 1963, 2:16 p.m. CST, transcript, http://mcadams.posc.mu.edu/press.htm.

173 Testimony of Dr. Charles James Carrico, Warren Commission Hearings, March 30, 1964, Vol. III, pages 357-366, at page 361

174 Ibid.

175 Testimony of Dr. Robert Nelson McClelland, Warren Commission Hearings, March 25, 1964, Vol. VI, pages 30-39, at 33.

176 Ibid., page 35.

177 Affidavit, signed by Seymour Weitzman, Nov. 23, 1963, in Dallas Police Department, "Investigation of the Assassination of the President," page 63, Commission Exhibit 2003, no date, Warren Commission: Hearings Before the President's Commission on the Assassination of President Kennedy, Vol. XXIV, pages 195–404, at page 228.

178 Testimony of Seymour Weitzman, Warren Commission: Hearings Before the President's Commission on the Assassination of President Kennedy, April 1, 1964, Vol. VII, pages 105–109, at page 109.

179 E. L. Boone, #240, Dallas Sheriff's Office, "Presidential Assassination," Supplementary Investigation Report, Nov. 22, 1963, 2 pages, published as Decker Exhibit No. 5323, Warren Commission: Hearings Before the President's Commission on the Assassination of President Kennedy, Vol. XIX, pages 508–509.

180 Testimony of Eugene Boone, Warren Commission: Hearings Before the President's Commission on the Assassination of President Kennedy, March 25, 1964, Vol. III, pages 291–295, at 295.

181 Press Conference of District Attorney Wade in Assembly Room, Dallas Police and Courts Building, Saturday, Nov. 23, 1963, 12:30 a.m., Commission Exhibit 2169, in Warren Commission: Hearings Before the President's Commission on the Assassination of President Kennedy, Vol. XXIV, pages 829–841, at 831.

182 Testimony of Mark Lane, Warren Commission Hearings Before the President's Commission on the Assassination of President Kennedy, March 4, 1964, Vol. II, pages 32–61, at 46.

183 Ibid., page 47.

184 G. Ray Hall and Maurice J White, FBI Special Agents, investigative report dated Dec. 5, 1963, Commission Exhibit 2086, Hearings Before the President's Commission on the Assassination of President Kennedy, Vol. XXIV, page 522.

185 Testimony of Amos Lee Euins, Warren Commission: Hearings Before the President's Commission on the Assassination of President Kennedy, March 10, 1964, Vol. II, pages 201–210; and, Testimony of Forrest V. Sorrels, Warren Commission: Hearings Before the President's Commission on the Assassination of President Kennedy, May 7, 1964, Vol. VII, pages 332–360, at 349.

186 Warren Commission, page 147.

187 Testimony of Marrion L. Baker, Warren Commission: Hearings Before the President's Commission on the Assassination of President Kennedy, March 25, 1964, Vol. III, pages 242–281, at 246–247.

188 Ibid., page 250.

189 Ibid., page 252.

190 Testimony of Roy Sansom Truly, Warren Commission: Hearings Before the President's Commission on the Assassination of President Kennedy, March 24, 1964, Vol. III, pages 212–241, at page 213.

191 Testimony of Mrs. Robert A. Reid, Warren Commission: Hearings Before the President's Commission on the Assassination of President Kennedy, March 25, 1964, Vol. III, pages 270–281, at page 274.

192 Ibid., page 279.

193 Secret Service Special Agent Rowley, Memorandum, Feb. 5, 1964, with copies of Reports. Commission Document 354, National Archives, http://www.maryferrell.org/mffweb/archive/viewer/showDoc.do?docId=10755&relPageId=4.

194 William Manchester, *The Death of a President: November 20–November 25, 1963* (New York: Harper & Row, Publishers, 1967), page 279.

195 Robert MacNeill, "Covering the JFK Assassination," as told on the documentary, "JFK: Day that Changed America," MSNBC on NBC News, updated Dec. 29, 2003, http://www.nbcnews.com/id/3476061/ns/msnbc_tv-jfk_the_day_that_changed_america/t/covering-jfk-assassination/#.UTYuznxAR4E.

196 Testimony of Miss Victoria Elizabeth Adams, Warren Commission: Hearings Before the President's Commission on the Assassination of President Kennedy, March 25, 1964, Vol. VI, pages 386–393.

197 Barry Ernest, *The Girl on the Stairs: The Search for a Missing Witness to the JFK Assassination* (Gretna, LA: Pelican Publishing Company, 2013).

198 Ibid., page 241.

199 Ibid., page 256.

200 Ibid., page 257.

201 Warren Commission, page 154.

THREE: **OSWALD, TIPPIT, AND RUBY**

202 President Lyndon Baines Johnson, quoted in: "The American Assassins: Part II, Lee Harvey Oswald and John F. Kennedy," CBS Reports Inquiry, as broadcast over the CBS Television Network, Wed., Nov. 26, 1975, 10:00–11:00 PM, EST, with NBC News Correspondent Dan Rather, Produced by CBS News, http://jfk.hood.edu/Collection/Weisberg%20Subject%20 Index%20Files/C%20Disk/CBS-TV%20News%20Special%20American%20Assassins/ Item%2002.pdf.

203 Warren Commission, page 369.

204 Ibid., page 165.

205 Ibid., pages 17–18.

206 Ibid., page 22.

207 John J. Johnson, "Earlene Roberts and 'Tippit as an Accomplice,'" The Dealey Plaza Echo, Vol. 5, No. 2, July 2001, http://www.maryferrell.org/mffweb/archive/viewer/showDoc. do?docId=16245&relPageId=26.

208 Ibid., pages 160–163.

209 Ibid., page 163.

210 Testimony of Mrs. Earlene Roberts, Warren Commission: Hearings Before the President's Commission on the Assassination of President Kennedy, April 9, 1964, Vol. VI, pages 434–444, at page 440.

211 Ibid., page 442.

212 Joachim Joesten, *Oswald: Assassin or Fall Guy?* (New York: Marzani & Munsell Publishers Inc., 1964), page 103, italics in original.

213 Ibid., page 104, italics in original.

214 Testimony of Mrs. Earlene Roberts, Warren Commission, page 443.

215 Earlene Roberts, affidavit executed Dec. 5, 1963, Warren Commission: Hearings Before the President's Commission on the Assassination of President Kennedy, Vol. VII, page 439.

216 Henry Hurt, Reasonable Doubt: An Investigation Into the Assassination of John F. Kennedy (New York: Holt, Rinehart and Winston, 1985), page 141.

217 Joesten, Oswald: Assassin, page 107.

218 Michael Benson, Who's Who in the JFK Assassination: An A to Z Encyclopedia (New York: Citadel Press, 1993), "Grant, Eva," page 158; Joesten, Oswald: Assassin, page 111.

219 Testimony of Mrs. Eva Grant, Warren Commission: Hearings Before the President's Commission on the Assassination of President Kennedy, May 28, 1964, Vol. XIV, pages 429–487, at page 486.

220 Joesten, Oswald: Assassin, page 112.

221 Warren Commission, page 651.

222 FBI Special Agent James W. Swinford, FBI Memorandum, Dallas Texas, July 28, 1964, Commission Exhibit 3001, Warren Commission: Hearings Before the President's Commission on the Assassination of President Kennedy, Vol. XXVI, pages 515–520, at page 516.

223 Meagher, Accessories After the Fact, page 270.

224 Thomas G. Buchanan, Who Killed Kennedy? (New York: G. P. Putnam's Sons, 1964), pages 130–131.

225 Ibid.

226 Ibid., page 133.

227 Ibid., page 135.

228 Ibid., page 137.

229 Lane, Rush to Judgment, page 171.

230 Ibid.

231 Affidavit of T. F. Bowley, Dec. 2, 1963, Dallas Police Department, "Investigation of the Assassination of the President," Commission Exhibit 2003, Warren Commission: Hearings Before the President's Commission on the Assassination of President Kennedy, Vol. XXIV, pages 195–404, at page 202.

232 Lane, Rush to Judgment, pages 171–172.

233 Warren Commission, page 369.

234 Testimony of Domingo Benavides, Warren Commission: Hearings Before the President's Commission on the Assassination of President Kennedy, April 2, 1964, Vol. VI, pages 444–454, at page 448.

235 Ibid., page 449.

236 Lane, *Rush to Judgment*, pages 172–173.

237 Meagher, *Accessories After the Fact*, page 255. The parentheses are part of the original text.

238 Mentioned in testimony of William W. Whaley, Warren Commission: Hearings Before the President's Commission on the Assassination of President Kennedy, April 8, 1964, Vol. VI, pages 428–434, at page 434.

239 Meagher, *Accessories After the Fact*, page 255.

240 Testimony of Domingo Benavides, Warren Commission, pages 449–450.

241 Meagher, *Accessories After the Fact*, page 256.

242 Testimony of Mrs. Helen Markham, Warren Commission: Hearings Before the President's Commission on the Assassination of President Kennedy, March 26, 1964, Vol. III, pages 305–322, at pages 310–311.

243 Meagher, *Accessories After the Fact*, page 256.

244 Warren Commission, page 167.

245 Affidavit of Helen Louise Markham, Nov. 22, 1963, Dallas Police Department, "Investigation of the Assassination of the President," Commission Exhibit 2003, Warren Commission: Hearings Before the President's Commission on the Assassination of President Kennedy, Vol. XXIV, pages 195–404, at page 215.

246 Testimony of Mark Lane, Warren Commission Hearings Before the President's Commission on the Assassination of President Kennedy, March 4, 1964, Vol. II, pages 32–61, at 51; Testimony of Helen Markham, Warren Commission: Hearings Before the President's Commission on the Assassination of President Kennedy, July 23, 1964, Vol. VII, pages 499–506.

247 Testimony of Mark Lane Resumed, Warren Commission: Hearings Before the President's Commission on the Assassination of President Kennedy, July 2, 1964, Vol. V, pages 546–561, at pages 550–551.

248 Testimony of William W. Scoggins, Warren Commission: Hearings Before the President's Commission on the Assassination of President Kennedy, March 26, 1964, Vol. III, pages 322–340, at 327.

249 Testimony of William Wayne Whaley, Warren Commission: Hearings Before the President's Commission on the Assassination of President Kennedy, March 12, 1964, Vol. II, pages 253–262, at 260–261.

250 Ibid., page 256.

251 The Aquilla Clemons and Frank Wright witness accounts are drawn from: Anthony Summers, *Conspiracy* (New York: Paragon House, Updated and Expanded Edition, 1989), pages 90–91.

252 Ibid., page 95.

253 Dale K. Myers, *With Malice: Lee Harvey Oswald and the Murder of J. D. Tippit* (Milford, Michigan: Oak Cliff Press, 1998), pages 304–311, at page 307.

254 Ibid., pages 307–308.

255 John Armstrong, "Harvey, Lee and Tippit: A New Look at the Tippit Shooting," *Probe*, January–February, 1998, Vol. 5, No. 2.

256 Matthew Smith, *JFK: The Second Plot* (Edinburgh and London: Mainstream Publishing, 1992), page 95.

257 Armstrong, "Harvey, Lee and Tippit: A New Look at the Tippit Shooting," and Myers ,*With Malice*, pages 56–57.

258 Warren Commission, page 131.

259 Myers, *With Malice*, pages 56–57.

260 FBI report, Dallas Police Department radio transmissions from Channel 1 and Channel 2 covering the period from approximately 10:00 a.m., Nov. 22, 1963, to 6:00 p.m., Nov. 24, 1963, Commission Exhibit 1974, Warren Commission: Hearings Before the President's Commission on the Assassination of President Kennedy, Vol. XXIII, pages 832–938, at pages 850 and 853.

261 Myers, *With Malice*, page 55.

262 Ibid., pages 857–858.

263 Warren Commission, page 168.

264 Myers, *With Malice*, Dallas Police Department Crime Lab Photo #10, Negative #91-001/024b, Dallas Municipal Archives and Records Center, City of Dallas, Texas, page 123.

265 Warren Commission, page 176.

266 Ibid., page 175.

267 Testimony of William Arthur Smith, Warren Commission: Hearings Before the President's Commission on the Assassination of President Kennedy, April 2, 1964, Vol. VII, pages 82–85, at page 85.

268 Gil Jesus, "Was Lee Harvey Oswald REALLY Guilty? An Examination of the Evidence in the Case Against Oswald," giljesus.com, no date, "The White Jacket," http://www.giljesus.com/Tippit/jacket.htm.

269 Warren Commission, page 175.

270 Testimony of Capt. W. R. Westbrook, Warren Commission: Hearings Before the President's Commission on the Assassination of President Kennedy, April 6, 1964, Vol. VII, pages 109–118, at page 115.

271 Ibid., page 117.

272 Ibid., page 118.

273 Jesus, "Was Oswald REALLY Guilty?

274 Meagher, Accessories After the Fact, pages 280.

275 Warren Commission, page 559.

276 Meagher, Accessories After the Fact, pages 280–281.

277 Ibid., page 281.

278 Myers, With Malice, page 265.

279 Ibid., page 176.

280 Ibid., page 289.

281 Ibid.

282 James P. Hosty, Jr. Assignment: Oswald (New York: Arcade Publishing, 1995), page 62.

283 Myers, With Malice, pages 287–304, at pages 298–299.

284 Ibid., pages 299–300.

285 Ibid., page 297.

286 Testimony of Julia Postal, Warren Commission Hearings, Vol. VII, April 2, 1964, pages 8–14.

287 Ibid.

288 Quoted in Myers, With Malice, page 178.

289 Press Conference of District Attorney Wade in Assembly Room, Dallas Police and Courts Building, Saturday, November 23, 1963–12:30 a.m., Commission Exhibit 2169, Warren Commission: Hearings Before the President's Commission on the Assassination of President Kennedy, Vol. XXIV, pages 829–841, at pages 830–831.

290 Beverly Oliver with Coke Buchanan, *Nightmare in Dallas* (Lancaster, PA: Starburst Publishers, 1994), page 94.

291 Ibid.

292 Ibid., page 134.

293 Letter from Dallas attorney Carroll Jarnagin to FBI Director J. Edgar Hoover; FBI Special Agents Ralph E. Rawlings and Bardwell D. Odum, Investigative Report, dated Dec. 10, 1963, Commission Exhibit 2821, Warren Commission: Hearings Before the President's Commission on the Assassination of President Kennedy, Vol. XXVI, pages 254–259, at page 255.

294 Affidavit of Julia Ann Mercer, given at Sheriff's Department, County of Dallas, Texas, Nov. 22, 1963, Decker Exhibit 5323, Warren Commission: Hearings Before the President's Commission on the Assassination of President Kennedy, Vol. XIX, pages 483–484.

295 Hurt, *Reasonable Doubt*, pages 114–116, at 114–115.

296 Ibid., page 116.

297 Final Report of the Select Committee on Assassinations, U.S. House of Representatives, "Summary of Findings and Recommendations," U.S. Government Printing Office, Jan. 2, 1979, page 180.

298 Lamar Waldron with Thom Hartman, *Ultimate Sacrifice: John and Robert Kennedy, the Plan for a Coup in Cuba, and the Murder of JFK* (New York: Carroll & Graf, Publishers, 2005), page 704–707, at page 705.

299 Patricia Orr, Researcher, "Rose Cheramie," Staff Report of the Select Committee on Assassinations, U.S. House of Representatives, March 1979, Hearings Before the President's Commission on the Assassination of President Kennedy, Vol. X, pages 198–204, page 200.

300 James DiEugenio, "Rose Cheramie: How She Predicted the JFK Assassination," in James DiEugenio and Lisa Pease, editors, *The Assassinations: Probe Magazine on JFK, MLK, RFK, and Malcolm X* (Los Angeles, CA: Feral House, 2003), pages 225–237, at page 225.

301 Patricia Orr, Researcher, page 201.

302 Ibid.

303 Ibid., page 202.

304 Ibid., page 237.

305 DiEugenio, "Rose Cheramie: How She Predicted," page 226.

306 Ibid.

307 John Armstrong, "Harvey and Lee: The Case for Two Oswalds, Part 1," in DiEugenio and Pease, eds, *The Assassinations*, pages 91–112, at page 92.

308 Ibid., pages 99–100.

309 John Armstrong, *Harvey & Lee: How the CIA Framed Oswald,* page Introduction, concluding paragraphs, no pagination given.

310 John Armstrong, "Harvey and Lee – Just the Facts, Please," Acorn.net, *Fair Play Magazine,* Issue #25, Nov.-Dec.-1988, http://spot.acorn.net/jfkplace/09/fp.back_issues/25th_Issue/facts.html.

311 John Armstrong, "Harvey and Lee: The Case for Two Oswalds, Part 2," in DiEugenio and Pease, eds, *The Assassinations,* pages 113–135, at page 123.

312 Armstrong, *Harvey & Lee: How the CIA Framed Oswald.*

313 Testimony of Roger D. Craig, Warren Commission: Hearings Before the President's Commission on the Assassination of President Kennedy, April 1, 1964, Vol. VI, pages 260–273, at page 266.

314 Officer Roger Craig, Dallas County Deputy Sheriff, Supplementary Investigation Report, Assassination of President Kennedy, Nov. 23, 1963, http://jfkassassination.net/russ/testimony/craig1.htm.

315 Testimony of Roger D. Craig, Warrenn Commission, page 270.

316 Armstrong, "Harvey and Lee: The Case for Two Oswalds, Part 2," page 127.

317 Roger Craig, *When They Kill a President,"* notes to Roger Craig's self-published, spiral-bound manuscript, 1971, http://www.ratical.org/ratville/JFK/WTKaP.html.

318 Ibid.

FOUR: OSWALD, THE KGB, AND THE PLOTS TO ASSASSINATE JFK IN CHICAGO AND TAMPA

319 Ronald Reagan, "Conspiracy," Radio Broadcast, Feb. 13, 1979, in: Kiron K. Skinner, Annelise Anderson, and Martin Anderson, editors (New York: The Free Press, 2001), pages 234–235, at page 234.

320 Testimony of Mrs. Marguerite Oswald, Warren Commission: Hearings Before the President's Commission on the Assassination of President Kennedy, February 10, 1964, Vol. I, pages 126–186, at page 162.

321 Deputy Attorney General Nicholas deB. Katzenbach, "Memorandum for Mr. Moyers," Nov. 25, 1963, http://history-matters.com/archive/jfk/fbi/105-82555/124-10010-10135/html/124-10010-10135_0002a.htm.

322 Ion Mihai Pacepa, *Programmed to Kill: Lee Harvey Oswald, the Soviet KGB, and the Kennedy Assassination* (Chicago: Ivan R. Dee, 2007).

323 Email with author, dated Jan. 13, 2013.

324 Pacepa, *Programmed*, page xiv.

325 Edward Jay Epstein, *Legend: The Secret World of Lee Harvey Oswald* (New York: Reader's Digest/McGraw-Hill Book Company, 1978), pages 69–72, at page 71.

326 Email with author, dated Jan. 13, 2013.

327 Ibid.

328 Ibid.

329 Epstein, *Legend*, page 120.

330 Pacepa, *Programmed*, page 53.

331 Ibid.

332 Ibid., page 57.

333 Jack R. Swike, *The Missing Chapter: Lee Harvey Oswald in the Far East* (CreateSpace Independent Publishing Platform, 2008), page 77.

334 Gordon H. Chang, "JFK, China, and the Bomb," *Journal of American History*, March 1988, Vol. 74, No. 4, pages 1287-1310, at page 1287.

335 Ibid., page 1292.

336 Ibid., page 1299.

337 Ibid., page 1304.

338 Mary-Alice Waters, "Maoism in the U.S.: A Critical History of the Progressive Labor Party," Marxists.org, at http://www.marxists.org/history/erol/1960-1970/waters-pl/chapter4.htm.

339 Ibid.

340 Testimony of Vincent T. Lee, Warren Commission Hearings, Vol. X, April 17, 1964, pages 86-95.

341 "Affidavit of Vincent T. Lee," dated May 20, 1964, Warren Commission Hearings, Vol. XI, page 208.

342 Allen Dulles questioning/commenting, in Testimony of Abram Chayes, Warren Commission Hearings, Vol. V, June 9, 1964, pages 307-318, at page 318.

343 Jerry D. Rose, "The Loyal American Underground," The Fourth Decade, Vol. 1, Number 5, July 1994, pages 28-31, http://www.maryferrell.org/mffweb/archive/viewer/showDoc.do?docId=48682&relPageId=28.

344 Ibid., The memo from FBI agent W. R. Wannell, addressed to William C. Sullivan.

345 Ibid.

346 Ibid.

347 Email with author, dated Jan. 13, 2013.

348 Ibid.

349 Ibid. Also, see: Pacepa, *Programmed*, page 186.

350 Pacepa, *Programmed*, page 99.

351 Ibid., page 120.

352 Epstein, *Legend*, pages 177–178.

353 Testimony of George S. DeMohrenschildt, Warren Commission: Hearings Before the President's Commission on the Assassination of President Kennedy, April 22, 1964, Vol. IX, pages 166–284, at page 225.

354 Testimony of Jeanne DeMohrenschildt, Warren Commission: Hearings Before the President's Commission on the Assassination of President Kennedy, April 23, 1964, Vol. IX, pages 285–331, at page 307.

355 Bill Simpich, "The JFK Case: The Twelve Who Built the Oswald Legend (Part 6: White Russians Keep an Eye on Oswald in Dallas," Nov. 22, 2011, http://www.opednews.com/articles/THE-JFK-CASE--OSWALD-AND-by-Bill-Simpich-110814-415.html.

356 James DiEugenio, *Destiny Betrayed: JFK, Cuba, and the Garrison Case* (New York: Skyhorse Publishing, Second Edition, 2012), pages 153 and 194.

357 Edward Jay Epstein, "Epilogue IV: The Man Who Really Knew Too Much (1992)" *The Assassination Chronicles: Inquest, Counterplot, and Legend* (New York: Carroll & Graf, 1992), page 558.

358 Jim Garrison's *Playboy* Interview, Vol. 14, No. 10, October 1967, http://www.jfklancer.com/Garrison2.html.

359 Testimony of Ruth Hyde Paine, Warren Commission: Hearings Before the President's Commission on the Assassination of President Kennedy, July 23, 1964, Vol. XI, pages 389–398, at page 396.

360 Edward Jay Epstein, "George DeMohrenschildt: The Man Who Knew Too Much," March 29, 1977, http://www.edwardjayepstein.com/diary/dem.htm.

361 Epstein, *Legend*, pages 208–214.

362 Testimony of George S. DeMohrenschildt, Warren Commission: Hearings Before the President's Commission on the Assassination of President Kennedy, page 249.

363 Pacepa, *Programmed*, page 139.

364 Email with author, dated Jan. 13, 2013. Also see: Pacepa, *Programmed*, page 147.

365 Pacepa, *Programmed*, pages 142–143.

366 Warren Commission, page 406.

367 Ibid.

368 Testimony of George S. DeMohrenschildt, page 237.

369 Ibid.

370 Ibid., page 258.

371 Testimony of Jeanne DeMohrenschildt, page 311.

372 Ibid., pages 311 and 323.

373 Ibid., page 325.

374 Ibid., pages xiv–xv.

375 Pacepa, *Programmed*, page 172–173.

376 Ibid., page 144.

377 Ibid., page 207.

378 Email with author, dated Jan. 13, 2013.

379 Ibid.

380 Dan Hardway and Edwin Lopez, House Select Committee on Assassinations, *Oswald, the CIA, and Mexico City: The Lopez-Hardway Report*, 2003 Release (Ipswich, MA: Mary Ferrell Foundation Press, 2006), pages vi-vii.

381 Ibid., page vii. Taped telephone call between President Lyndon Johnson and Sen. Richard Russell, Nov. 29, 2963, 8:55 p.m.

382 Warren Commission, page 413.

383 Commission Exhibit 237, "Photograph of Unidentified Man," Warren Commission: Hearings Before the President's Commission on the Assassination of President Kennedy, Vol. XVI, page 638.

384 Hardway and Lopez, *Oswald, the CIA, and Mexico City*, page vi.

385 Ibid., page viii. Memo from FBI Director Hoover to White House and Chief of Secret Service, Nov. 23, 1963.

386 Email with author, dated January 13, 2013; see also Pacepa, *Programmed*, page 222.

387 Email with author, dated Jan. 13, 2013.

388 Ibid., see also Pacepa, *Programmed*, page 223.

389 Email with author, dated Jan. 13, 2013.

390 Ibid.

391 Waldron and Hartmann, *Ultimate Sacrifice*, pages 224–225.

392 Ibid., page 623.

393 Ibid., page 633.

394 James W. Douglass, *JFK and the Unspeakable: Why He Died & Why It Matters*, (Maryknoll, NY: Orbis Books, 2008), pages 205–206

395 Final Report of the House Select Committee on Assassinations, "Summary of Findings and Recommendations, Washington, D.C., U.S. Government Printing Office, Jan. 2, 1979, page 231, http://www.history-matters.com/archive/jfk/hsca/report/html/HSCA_Report_0001a.htm.

396 Waldron and Hartmann, *Ultimate Sacrifice*, page 635.

397 Ibid.

398 Douglass, *JFK and the Unspeakable*, page 202.

399 Ibid., page 205.

400 Rob Kaufman, "JFK & Hampton murders linked," People's World, April 11, 1970; and, Ed McCarthy, An Odyssey for Truth and Justice," HVPress.net, May 14, 2008, http://www.hvpress.net/news/138/ARTICLE/4293/2008-05-14.html.

401 Douglass, *JFK and the Unspeakable*, page 203.

402 House Select Committee on Assassinations, page 231.

403 Ibid.

404 Waldron and Hartmann, *Ultimate Sacrifice*, page 687.

405 Ibid., page 689.

406 Ibid., page 684.

407 Ibid., page 688.

408 Ibid., page 691.

409 Ibid., pages 479–480.

410 Ibid., pages 480–481, quote at 481.

411 Ibid., page 482.

412 Cable Re Analysis of Valerly Vladimirovich Kostikov's Activities, Oswald's CIA "201" File, Mary-Ferrell.org, http://www.maryferrell.org/mffweb/archive/viewer/showDoc.do?docId=109870.

413 Cable Re Traces on Gilberto P. Lopez, Oswald's CIA "201" File, MaryFerrell.org, http://www.maryferrell.org/mffweb/archive/viewer/showDoc.do?docId=98709&relPageId=3.

414 Dispatch of Copies of Photo of Gilberto Lopez at Mexico City Airport, Oswald's CIA "201" File, MaryFerrell.org, http://www.maryferrell.org/mffweb/archive/viewer/showDoc.do?docId=98689&relPageId=2.

415 Hurt, *Reasonable Doubt*, pages 421–423.

416 Cable Re Identification of Miguel Casas Saez, AKA Miguelita, Jan. 25, 1964, Oswald's CIA "201" File, MaryFerrell.org, NARA Record Number 104-19921-10030, http://www.maryferrell.org/mffweb/archive/viewer/showDoc.do?docId=109927&relPageId=3.

417 Information Possibly Connected with the Assassination of JFK, Nov. 2, 1964, Oswald's CIA "201" File, MaryFerrell.org, NARA Record Number 1993.06.28.08:42:08:180410, https://www.maryferrell.org/mffweb/archive/viewer/showDoc.do?docId=98783&relPageId=3.

418 Pacepa, *Programmed*, pages 11–12.

419 Ibid., page 14.

420 Ibid., page 15.

421 Ibid., pages 16–17.

422 Email with author, dated Jan. 13, 2013.

423 Christopher Andrew and Vasili Mitrokhin, *The Sword and the Shield: The Mitrokhin Archive and the Secret History of the KGB* (New York: Basic Books, 1999), pages 225–230.

424 Email with author, dated Jan. 13, 2013.

425 David Miller, *The JFK Conspiracy* (New York: Writers Club Press, 2002), pages 239–240.

426 "C. D. Jackson," biography written by John Simkin, Spartacus Educational, dated September 1997-June 2013, http://www.spartacus.schoolnet.co.uk/USAjacksonCD.htm.

427 Carl Bernstein, "The CIA and the Media," *Rolling Stone, Oct. 20, 1977,* http://www.carlbernstein.com/magazine_cia_and_media.php. Quoted in: Peter Dale Scott, *Deep Politics and the Death of JFK* (Berkeley, CA: University of California Press, 1993), page 55.

428 Jerry D. Rose, "Plain Talk About Isaac Don Levine," The Fourth Decade, Vol. 2, Issue 2, January 1995, pages 35-41, http://www.maryferrell.org/mffweb/archive/viewer/showDoc.do?docId=48685&relPageId=35.

429 Ibid., page 36, http://www.maryferrell.org/mffweb/archive/viewer/showDoc.do?docId=48685&relPageId=36.

430 Ibid., page 38, http://www.maryferrell.org/mffweb/archive/viewer/showDoc.do?docId=48685&relPageId=38.

431 Ibid.

432 Testimony of Mrs. Marguerite Oswald, Vol. I, pages 126–186, at page 133.

FIVE: THE ROOTS OF THE JFK ASSASSINATION— A BANANA REPUBLIC, THE CIA, AND THE MOB

433 President John F. Kennedy, in Fort Worth, Texas, Morning, November 22, 1963, as quoted in: Jim Bishop, *The Day Kennedy Was Shot: An Uncensored Minute-by-Minute Account of November 22, 1963* (New York: Funk & Wagnalls, 1968), page 23.

434 E. Howard Hunt, *Under-Cover: Memoirs of an American Secret Agent* (New York: Berkeley Publishing Company; distributed by G. P. Putnam's Sons, 1974), page 101. In the book, the second sentence is a footnote, referenced by an asterisk and placed at the bottom of the page in smaller type.

435 Testimony of Kenneth P. O'Donnell, Warren Commission: Hearings Before the President's Commission on the Assassination of President Kennedy, May 18, 1964, Vol. VII, pages 440–457, at page 456.

436 Bishop, *The Day Kennedy Was Shot*, pages x–xi.

437 Alan Cowell, "Ireland Knew of Threats to Kennedy in 1963 Trip," *New York Times*, Dec. 29, 2006, http://www.nytimes.com/2006/12/29/world/europe/29kennedy.html?_r=0.

438 Transcript of Milteer-Somersett conversation, November 9, 1963, House Select Committee on Assassinations, Vol. 3, pages 447-450, http://www.history-matters.com/archive/jfk/hsca/reportvols/vol3/html/HSCA_Vol3_0226a.htm.

439 Bugliosi, *Reclaiming History*, pages 1268–1272, at page 1271.

440 Testimony of Forrest V. Sorrels, May 7, 1964, Vol. VII, pages 332–360, at page 338.

441 Miami Police Informant Information on Milteer, Nov. 26, 1963, transcript of an interview with William Somersett conducted by the Intelligence Unit of the Miami Police Department, Miami, Florida, Document 0062e, Cuban Information Archives, http://cuban-exile.com/doc_051-075/doc0062e.html.

442 Final Report of the House Select Committee on Assassinations, "Summary of Findings and Recommendations, Washington, D.C., U.S. Government Printing Office, Jan. 2, 1979, page 232, http://www.history-matters.com/archive/jfk/hsca/report/html/HSCA Report 0131b. htm.

443 Ibid., pages 230–232.

444 Ibid., page 233.

445 Ibid., pages 233–234.

446 Testimony of Forrest V. Sorrels, May 7, 1964, Vol. VII, pages 332–360, at page 341.

447 Ibid., page 342.

448 Don Adams, *From an Office Building with a High-Powered Rifle: A Report to the Public from an FBI Agent Involved in the Official JFK Assassination Investigation* (Chicago: Independent Publishers Group, 2012), page 98.

449 Ibid., pages 96–97.

450 Testimony of Dr. Clyde Collins Snow, Chief of Physical Anthropology Research, Civil Aeromedical Institute, Federal Aviation Administration Aeronautical Center, Oklahoma City, Oklahoma, House Select Committee on Assassinations, Vol. 4, Sept. 25, 1978, pages 380–381; see also, Vincent Bugliosi, *Reclaiming History: The Assassination of President John F. Kennedy*, page 1271.

451 Adams, *From an Office Building*, page 100.

452 Final Report of the House Select Committee on Assassinations, "Summary of Findings and Recommendations, Washington, D.C., U.S. Government Printing Office, Jan. 2, 1979, footnote #3, page 234, http://www.history-matters.com/archive/jfk/hsca/report/html/HSCA_Report_0132b.htm.

453 Robert Groden and Harrison Edward Livingstone, *High Treason: The Assassination of John F. Kennedy, What Really Happened* (New York: The Conservatory Press, 1989), Appendix B, pages 408–410.

454 Adams, *From an Office Building*, caption to a photograph, page 86.

455 Burton Hersh, *The Old Boys: The American Elite and the Origins of the CIA* (New York: Charles Scribner's Sons, 1992), page 52.

456 Edward L. Bernays, *Propaganda: The Public Mind in the Making* (New York: Liveright Publishing Company, 1928).

457 Hunt, *Under-Cover*, page 83.

458 Edward L. Bernays, *Biography of an Idea: Memoirs of Public Relations Counsel Edward L. Bernays* (New York: Simon & Schuster, 1965), page 761.

459 Ibid.

460 Stephen Schlesinger and Stephen Kinzer, *Bitter Fruit: The Untold Story of the American Coup in Guatemala* (New York: Doubleday & Company, Inc., 1982), page 87.

461 E. Howard Hunt, with Greg Aunapu, *American Spy: My Secret History in the CIA, Watergate, and Beyond* (New York: John Wiley & Sons, 2007), page 71.

462 Ibid., page 75.

463 Ibid., page 77.

464 Michael Canfield and Alan J. Weberman, *Coup D'Etat in America: The CIA and the Assassination of John Fitzgerald Kennedy* (Kindle Book: Amazon Digital Services, Inc.).

465 Thomas McCann, *An American Company: The Tragedy of United Fruit* (New York: Random House, 1988), page 62.

466 Hunt, *Under-Cover*, page 101.

467 Canfield and Weberman, *Coup D'Etat*.

468 Ibid.

469 Waldron and Hartmann, *Ultimate Sacrifice,* page 297.

470 Ibid., page 45.

471 Waldron and Hartmann in their book *Legacy of Secrecy* first disclosed CAMTEX undercover FBI operation designed to tape Carlos Marcello in prison conversations at the federal maximum-security prison in Texarkana, Texas. The more complete discussion of CAMTEX can be found in the revised paperback edition of the book: Lamar Waldron with Thom Hartmann, *Legacy of Secrecy: The Long Shadow of the JFK Assassination* (Berkeley, CA: Counterpoint Press, 2009, updated and expanded trade paperback edition), pages 46–50, and 749–760.

472 Ibid., page 50.

473 Ibid.

474 Ibid., page 47.

475 Ibid., page 53. Waldron and Hartmann cite the following source: Seth Kantor, *The Ruby Cover-Up* (New York: Zebra Books, 1992), page 108.

476 John H. Davis, *Mafia Kingfish: Carlos Marcello and the Assassination of John F. Kennedy* (New York: New American Library, a division of Penguin Books, Inc., a Signet paperback book, 1989), pages 142–143, and 484–485.

477 Ibid., page 143.

478 Ibid., pages 156–157.

479 House Select Committee on Assassinations, *Summary of Findings and Recommendations*, Jan. 2, 1979, page 171, http://www.maryferrell.org/mffweb/archive/viewer/showDoc.do?docId=800&relPageId=201.

480 Davis, *Mafia Kingfish*, page 157.

481 Sam Giancana and Chuck Giancana, *Double Cross: The Story of the Man Who Controlled America* (London: MacDonald, 1992).

482 Ibid., page 336.

483 Ibid., page 331.

484 Ibid.

485 Ibid., page 332.

486 Ibid., page 333.

487 Dallas Police Department Personnel Assignments, November 1963, Batchelor Exhibit No. 5002, Warren Commission Hearings, Vol XIX, pages 117-148, at page 148.

488 Ibid., page 335.

489 Armstrong, *Harvey & Lee: How the CIA Framed Oswald*, page 164.

490 Ibid., page 714.

491 See the discussion of Howard Hughes in Giancana and Giancana, *Double Cross*, page 211.

492 Giancana and Giancana, *Double Cross*, pages 227–228.

493 David Talbot, *Brothers: The Hidden History of the Kennedy Years* (New York: Free Press, 2007), pages 139–140, at page 140.

494 Seymour M. Hersh, *The Dark Side of Camelot* (New York: Little, Brown and Company, 1997), page 295.

495 Frank Ragano and Selwyn Raab, *Mob Lawyer: Including the Inside Account of Who Killed Jimmy Hoffa and JFK* (New York: Charles Scribner's Sons, 1994), pages 144–145.

496 Ibid., page 150.

497 Ibid., page 348.

498 Ibid., page 349.

499 Ibid.

500 Ibid., page 357.

501 House Select Committee on Assassinations, *Summary of Findings and Recommendations*, Jan. 2, 1979, page 169, http://www.maryferrell.org/mffweb/archive/viewer/showDoc.do?docId=800&relPageId=199.

502 G. Robert Blakey and Richard N. Billings, *The Plot to Kill the President: Organized Crime Assassinated J.F.K.—The Definitive Story* (New York: New York Times Books, 1981), page 179.

503 "Senators Hear Tales of Scandals," *Life Magazine*, March 11, 1957, Vol. 42, No. 10, pages 31–37, at page 33.

504 Robert F. Kennedy, *The Enemy Within* (New York: Harper & Brothers, Publishers, 1960), page 256.

505 Ibid.

506 Ibid., page 257.

507 Box 2, Pre-administration Personal Files, Christmas Card Correspondence. Card from Elkins Family, postmarked Dec. 17, 1957, from Portland, Oregon, 6 pages. Copies sent by Michael Desmond, Research Assistant, John Fitzgerald Kennedy Library, Columbia Point, Boston, Massachusetts, August 29, 1986.

508 "The Jailbird: He Helped Put Beck on the Spot," *Newsweek*, April 1, 1957, page 28.

509 Clark Mollenhoff, *Tentacles of Power: The Story of Jimmy Hoffa* (Cleveland and New York: The World Publishing Company, 1965), page 155.

510 Eastern Arizona Bureau, "Autopsy puts death blame on car crash," *Arizona Republic*, Saturday, October 12, 1968, page 28.

SIX: **CUBA, NIXON, AND WATERGATE**

511 Warren Hinckle and William Turner, *The Fish Is Red: The Secret War Against Castro* (New York: Harper & Row, Publishers, 1981), page 41.

512 John F. Kennedy Presidential Library and Museum, "JFK in History: The Bay of Pigs," http://www.jfklibrary.org/JFK/JFK-in-History/The-Bay-of-Pigs.aspx.

513 Hunt, *Under-Cover*, pages 128–129.

514 Ibid., page 131.

515 Waldron and Hartmann, *Legacy of Secrecy*, pages 3 and 11.

516 Hunt, *Under-Cover*, pages 130–131, at page 130.

517 Hinckle and Turner, *The Fish Is Red*, page 14.

518 Ibid., page 39.

519 John F. Kennedy, "Speech of Senator John F. Kennedy, Cincinnati, Ohio, Democratic Dinner, Oct. 6, 1960," The American Presidency Project, University of California, Santa Barbara, http://www.presidency.ucsb.edu/ws/index.php?pid=25660.

520 John F. Kennedy, "Statement on Cuba by Senator John F. Kennedy," Oct. 20, 1960, The American Presidency Project, University of California, Santa Barbara, http://www.presidency.ucsb.edu/ws/index.php?pid=74127.

521 The Fourth Kennedy-Nixon Presidential Debate, "October 21, 1960 Debate Transcript," Commission on Presidential Debates, http://www.debates.org/index.php?page=october-21-1960-debate-transcript.

522 Richard M. Nixon, *Six Crises* (New York: Doubleday & Company, 1962), page 353.

523 Ibid., page 354.

524 Hinckle and Turner, *The Fish Is Red*, page 40.

525 Nixon, *Six Crises*, page 352.

526 Ibid., page 354.

527 Ibid., page 355.

528 Robert Dallek, *An Unfinished Life: John F. Kennedy* (New York: Bay Back Books, 2003), pages 356–357.

529 Ibid., page 358.

530 Ibid., page 362.

531 "The Bay of Pigs Invasion," HLRGAZETTE Archives, no date, http://www.hlrgazette.com/2011-articles/145-may-7-2011/1527-the-bay-of-pigs-invasion.html.

532 Richard Reeves, *President Kennedy: Profile of Power* (New York: A Touchstone Book, Simon & Schuster, 1993), page 91.

533 Lamar Waldron, *Watergate: The Hidden History—Nixon, the Mafia, and the CIA* (Berkeley, CA: Counterpoint, 2012), page 6.

534 Len Colodny and Robert Gettlin, *Silent Coup: The Removal of a President* (New York: St. Martin's Press, 1991), pages 126–134.

535 H. R. Haldeman with Joseph DiMona, *The Ends of Power* (New York: New York Times Books, 1978), page 39.

536 "The Smoking Gun Tape," June 23, 1972, Watergate.info, http://watergate.info/1972/06/23/the-smoking-gun-tape.html; also, "The Smoking Gun," Richard Nixon and Bob Haldeman, Oval Office, White House, June 23, 1972, 10:04 a.m.–11:39 a.m., Miller Center, WhiteHouseTapes.net, http://whitehousetapes.net/transcript/nixon/smoking-gun.

537 "He's just got to tell them to lay off," Richard Nixon and Bob Haldeman, Oval Office, White House, Friday, June 23, 1972, 1:04 p.m.–1:13 p.m., Presidential Recordings Program, Miller Center, WhiteHouseTapes.net, http://whitehousetapes.net/transcript/nixon/hes-just-got-tell-them-lay.

538 Stephen E. Ambrose, "Introduction" and "Afterword," to H. R. Haldeman, *The Haldeman Diaries: Inside the Nixon White House* (New York: G. P. Putnam's Sons, 1994).

539 Lalo J. Gastriani, "The Strange Case of Dorothy Hunt," November 1994, http://mtracy9.tripod.com/dorothy_hunt.htm.

540 Don Fulsome, "Richard Nixon's Greatest Cover-Up: His Ties to the Assassination of President Kennedy," http://dirtypolitics.50megs.com/dirty.htm.

541 Marrs, *Crossfire*, page 273.

542 Harrison Edward Livingstone, *High Treason 2: The Great Cover-Up—The Assassination of President John F. Kennedy* (New York: Carroll & Graff Publishers, Inc., 1992), pages 423–433, at page 424.

543 Barboura Morris Freed, "Flight 553: The Watergate Murder?" in Steve Weissman, editor, *Big Brother and the Holding Company: The World Behind Watergate* (Palo Alto, CA: Ramparts Press, 1974), page 130.

544 Harrison Edward Livingstone, *High Treason 2*, page 428.

545 Ibid., pages 429–430.

546 Marita Lorenz, Testimony before the House Select Committee on Assassinations, May 31, 1978, http://www.maryferrell.org/mffweb/archive/viewer/showDoc.do?docId=49347&relPageId=1.

547 Gaeton Fonzi, *The Last Investigation* (New York: Thunder's Mouth Press, 1993), pages 83–107.

548 Marita Lorenz and Ted Schwartz, *Marita: One Woman's Extraordinary Tale of Love and Espionage in the CIA* (New York: Thunder's Mouth Press, 1993), pages 4-5, at page 5.

549 Ibid., pages 4–5.

550 Ibid., page 5.

551 Victor Marchetti and John D. Marks, *The CIA and the Cult of Intelligence* (New York: Alfred A. Knopf, 1974).

552 Mark Lane, *Plausible Denial: Was the CIA Involved in the Assassination of JFK?* (New York: Thunder's Mouth Press, 1991), pages 282–283.

553 Don Fulsome, *Nixon's Darkest Secrets: The Inside Story of America's Most Troubled President* (New York: St. Martin's Press, 2012), page 142.

554 Joe Trento and Jacquie Powers, Staff Correspondents, "Was Howard Hunt in Dallas the Day JFK died?" *Wilmington Sunday News Journal*, Aug. 20, 1978, http://jfk.hood.edu/Collection/Weisberg%20Subject%20Index%20Files/H%20Disk/Hunt%20E%20Howard/Item%2015.pdf.

555 Ibid., page 285.

556 Ibid., page 322.

557 Gaeton Fonzi, "The Odio Incident & The Truth: A Long Time Coming," in DiEugenio and Pease, eds, *The Assassinations*, pages 216–217, at page 217.

558 Testimony of Silvio Odio to the Warren Commission, July 22, 1964, Hearings Before the President's Commission on the Assassination of President Kennedy, Vol. XI, pages 367–389 at pages 372–373.

559 Warren Commission, page 324.

560 Gaeton Fonzi, "The Odio Incident" Hearings Before the House Select Committee on Investigations, Vol. X, pages 16–54.

561 Ibid.

562 Hunt, *American Spy*, page 137.

563 Talbot, *Brothers*, page 197.

564 Ibid., page 198.

565 Ibid., pages 198–199.

566 Ibid., page 199.

567 Ibid., page 200.

568 Hunt, *American Spy*, pages 132–133.

569 Peter Janney, *Mary's Mosaic: The CIA Conspiracy to Murder John F. Kennedy, Mary Pinchot Meyer, and Their Vision for World Peace* (New York: Skyhorse Publishing, 2012), page 133.

570 Ibid., pages 139, 282–283.

571 Ben Bradlee, *A Good Life: Newspapering and Other Adventures* (New York: Simon & Schuster, 1995), pages 267–268.

572 Janney, *Mary's Mosaic*, pages 79–87, at page 85.

573 See here a well-informed note composed under the username "stevenhager420," entitled "The Truth About the JFK Assassination," no date, http://stevenhager420.wordpress.com/2012/08/04/the-truth-about-the-jfk-assassination/.

574 Hunt, *American Spy*, page 134.

575 C. David Heymann, *The Georgetown Ladies' Social Club* (New York: Atria Books, 2004).

576 Talbot, *Brothers*, page 204.

577 Ibid.

578 Final Report of the House Select Committee on Assassinations, "Summary of Findings and Recommendations, Washington, D.C., U.S. Government Printing Office, Jan. 2, 1979, pages 200–201, http://www.maryferrell.org/mffweb/archive/viewer/showDoc.do?absPageId=69268.

579 DiEugenio, *Destiny Betrayed*, page 179.

580 Joan Mellen, "Otto Otepka, Robert F. Kennedy, Walter Sheridan, and Lee Oswald," Mary Ferrell Foundation, http://www.maryferrell.org/wiki/index.php/Essay_-_Otepka_RFK_Sheridan_Oswald.

581 John Newman, *Oswald and the CIA* (New York: Carroll & Graf Publishers, Inc., 1995), at page 171.

582 Mellen, "Otto Otepka."

583 Memo for the Files written by J. Lee Rankin, general counsel, Warren Commission, "Subject: Rumors that Oswald was an undercover agent," January 1964, archived as CIA document 487-195A, Record Copy 201-0289248, http://www.maryferrell.org/mffweb/archive/viewer/showDoc.do?docId=60439. See also: "Was Oswald an FBI Agent?" 22November1963.org.uk., no date, http://22november1963.org.uk/memo-was-oswald-an-fbi-agent. See also: Gerald D. McKnight, *Breach of Trust: How the Warren Commission Failed the Nation and Why* (Lawrence: University of Kansas Press, 2005), pages 128-147.

584 Fonzi, *The Last Investigation*, page 380.

585 Ibid., pages 389–390.

586 Claudia Furiati, *ZR Rifle: The Plot to Kill Kennedy and Castro* (Melbourne, Australia: Ocean Press, Second Edition, 1994), pages 46–47.

587 "William K. Harvey," Spartacus Educational, http://www.spartacus.schoolnet.co.uk/JFKharvey.htm; also, John Simkin, Assassination of John F. Kennedy Encyclopedia, Spartacus Educational e-book, September 2010.

588 Hunt, *American Spy*, pages 134–135.

589 Ibid., page 137.

590 Ibid., page 136.

591 Saint John Hunt, *Bond of Secrecy*, Walterville, OR, Trine Day, 2012) page 135.

592 Hunt, *American Spy*, page 139.

593 "Antnio Veciana," Spartacus Educational, http://www.spartacus.schoolnet.co.uk/JFKveciana.htm ; also, John Simkin, Assassination of John F. Kennedy Encyclopedia, Spartacus Educational e-book, September 2010.

594 Fonzi, *The Last Investigation*, page 142.

595 Ibid., page 408.

596 Ibid, page 409.

597 Ibid.

598 Ibid., page 395.

599 Ibid., page 108.

600 Roberts, *Kill Zone*, page 87.

601 Orville Nix Film, taken in Dealey Plaza, Dallas, Texas, on Nov. 22, 1963. See: Trask, *Pictures of the Pain*, pages 184–188.

602 Commission Exhibit 2582, FBI report dated March 18, 1964, Dallas, Texas, Warren Commission: Hearings Before the President's Commission on the Assassination of President Kennedy, Vol. XXV, pages 853–854, at page 853.

603 Marrs, *Crossfire*, page 38.

604 Commission Exhibit 5323, A. J. Millican, signed statement, on stationary of Bill Decker, Sheriff, Criminal Courts Building, Dallas, Texas, no date, Warren Commission: Hearings Before the President's Commission on the Assassination of President Kennedy, Vol. XIX, page 486.

605 Testimony of Forrest V. Sorrels, May 6, 1964, Vol. XIII, pages 55-83, at pages 67–68.

606 Commission Exhibit, "Sorrels Exhibit No. 1," Secret Service Agent Forrest V. Sorrels, Investigation Report, signed Feb. 3, 1964, Warren Commission: Hearings Before the President's Commission on the Assassination of President Kennedy, Vol. XXI, pages 537–538.

607 Testimony of Patrick Trevore Dean, Warren Commission: Hearings Before the President's Commission on the Assassination of President Kennedy, March 24, 1964, Vol. XII, pages 415–449, at page 432.

608 FBI Report, "Rubin Goldstein," Commission Document 897, FBI Gemberling Report of April 4, 1964, re: Oswald—Russia/Cuba," archived on the Mary Ferrell Foundation website at http://www.maryferrell.org/mffweb/archive/viewer/showDoc.do?docId=11293&relPageId=74.

609 Beverly Oliver, *Nightmare in Dallas* (Lancaster, PA: Starburst, Inc., 1994), pages 122–123.

610 Ibid.

611 Ibid., page 93.

612 Beverly Oliver, emails with the author, dated March 8, 2009, and April 21, 2013.

613 Roberts, *Kill Zone*, pages 85–87.

614 Ibid., page 87.

615 L. Fletcher Prouty, *JFK: The CIA, Vietnam, and the Plot to Assassinate John F. Kennedy* (New York: Carol Publishing Group, 1992), pages 119–120.

616 Bishop, *The Day Kennedy Was Shot*, pages 178–179.

617 "Where Was Richard Nixon on the Evening of November 21, 1963," selections quoted from the *Dallas Times Herald*, Friday, November 22, 1963, Page A25, http://dperry1943.com/nixon.html.

618 L. Fletcher Prouty, "The Secret, Illegal, and Powerful Control of the United States Government by the Military-Industrial Establishment," People and the PURSUIT of Truth, published by Harold Weisberg, May 1975, http://www.yumpu.com/en/document/fullscreen/3952617/people-and-the-pursuit-of-truth-the-harold-weisberg-archive/4 and http://www.prouty.org/nixon.html.

619 Fulsome, "Nixon's Greatest Cover-Up."

620 Ibid.

621 Giancana and Giancana, *Double Cross*, page 334.

622 Ibid., pages 334–335.

SEVEN: VIETNAM, DIEM, THE FRENCH CONNECTION, AND LBJ

623 Peter Dale Scott, Paul L. Hoch, and Russell Stetler, editors, *The Assassinations: Dallas and Beyond: A Guide to Cover-Ups and Investigations* (New York: Random House, Inc., 1976), pages 379–380.

624 Douglass, *JFK and the Unspeakable*, page 223.

625 Ibid., page 225.

626 Robert Dallek, "The Medical Ordeals of JFK," *The Atlantic*, December 2002, http://www.theatlantic.com/magazine/archive/2002/12/the-medical-ordeals-of-jfk/305572/.

627 Reported in Dallek, *An Unfinished Life*, page 683.

628 Ibid.

629 Arthur M. Schlesinger, Jr., *A Thousand Days: John F. Kennedy in the White House* (New York: Greenwich House, distributed by Crown Publishers, Inc., 1965), page 997.

630 Dallek, *An Unfinished Life*, page 684.

631 Thomas L. Ahern, Jr., CIA and the House of NGO: Covert Action in South Vietnam, 1954–63, Center for the Study of Intelligence, SECRET, Approved for Release on Feb. 19, 2009, http://www.gwu.edu/~nsarchiv/NSAEBB/NSAEBB284/2-CIA_AND_THE_HOUSE_OF_NGO.pdf.

632 Ibid., page 5.

633 Ibid., page 4.

634 Ibid., page 8.

635 John Prados, "JFK and the Diem Coup," The National Security Archive, George Washington University, Nov. 5, 2003, http://www.gwu.edu/~nsarchiv/NSAEBB/NSAEBB101/.

636 "Cops Seize Gun-Toting Kennedy Foe," *Chicago American*, Dec. 3, 1963; and "Quiz North Sider on Weapons Count," *Chicago Daily News*, Dec. 3, 1963.

637 Douglass, *JFK and the Unspeakable*, pages 217–218.

638 Ibid., page 218.

639 Ibid.

640 Ibid.

641 Haldeman, *Ends of Power*, page 218.

642 Testimony of E. Howard Hunt, Sept. 24, 1973, Senate Watergate Hearings, Book 9 of Presidential Campaign Activities of 1972, Watergate and Related Activities, Phase I: Watergate Investigation, page 3672, http://www.maryferrell.org/mffweb/archive/viewer/showDoc.do?docId=145092&relPageId=276.

643 Ibid., page 3670, http://www.maryferrell.org/mffweb/archive/viewer/showDoc.do?docId=145092&relPageId=274 .

644 Testimony of L. Patrick Gray, Aug. 3, 1973, Senate Watergate Hearings, Book 9 of Presidential Campaign Activities of 1972, Watergate and Related Activities, Phase I: Watergate Investigation, page 3467, http://www.maryferrell.org/mffweb/archive/viewer/showDoc.do?docId=145092&relPageId=71.

645 Ibid., page 3468, http://www.maryferrell.org/mffweb/archive/viewer/showDoc. do?docId=145092&relPageId=72.

646 "'Deep Throat's' Ex-Boss Shocked by Revelation," ABC This Week, June 26, 2005, http:// abcnews.go.com/ThisWeek/Politics/story?id=883440&page=1#.UXlOiitAR4E.

647 JFK, News Conference, March 23, 1961, transcript, JFKlink.net, http://www.jfklink.com/ speeches/jfk/publicpapers/1961/jfk92_61.html.

648 Schlesinger, Jr., *A Thousand Days,* page 337.

649 Ibid., page 339.

650 Ibid., page 337.

651 "The Unspoken Speech: Text," Remarks prepared for delivery at the Dallas Trade Mart by President John F. Kennedy, November 22, 1963, The JFK Assassination, SMU, http://smu. edu/smunews/jfk/speechtext.asp.

652 Schlesinger, Jr., *A Thousand Days,* page 338.

653 William J. Lederer and Eugene Burdick, *The Ugly American* (New York: W. W. Norton & Company, Inc., 1958).

654 DiEugenio, *Destiny Betrayed,* page 31.

655 Robert Dallek, "JFK's Second Term," *The Atlantic,* June 2003, http://www.theatlantic.com/ magazine/archive/2003/06/jfks-second-term/302734/.

656 Douglass, *JFK and the Unspeakable,* pages 125–126.

657 President John F. Kennedy, "Transcript of Broadcast with Walter Cronkite Inaugurating a CBS Television News Program," Sept. 2, 1963, The American Presidency Project, University of California at Santa Barbara, http://www.presidency.ucsb.edu/ws/index. php?pid=9388&st=&st1=.

658 Douglass, *JFK and the Unspeakable,* page 190.

659 Ibid.

660 "White House Statement Following the Return of a Special Mission to South Viet-Nam," Oct. 2, 1963, The American Presidency Project, University of California at Santa Barbara, http:// www.presidency.ucsb.edu/ws/index.php?pid=9452&st=&st1=.

661 John M. Newman, *JFK and Vietnam: Deception, Intrigue, and the Struggle for Power* (New York: Warner Books, 1992), page 424.

662 National Security Action Memorandum 263, White House, Oct. 11, 1963, JFK Library Presidential Library and Museum, http://www.jfklibrary.org/Asset-Viewer/w6LJoSnW4Ue-hkaH9Ip5IAA.aspx.

663 DiEugenio, *Destiny Betrayed*, page 370.

664 Newman, *JFK and Vietnam*, page 442.

665 Ibid., page 453.

666 Ibid.

667 Ibid., page 459.

668 Ibid.

669 Madeleine Duncan Brown, *Texas in the Morning: The Love Story of Madeleine Brown and President Lyndon Baines Johnson* (Baltimore: The Conservatory Press, 1997), page 166.

670 Ibid.

671 William Manchester, *The Death of a President: November 20–November 25, 1963* (New York: Harper & Row, Publishers, 1967), pages 84–89.

672 Vasilios Vazakas with Seamus Coogan and Phil Dragoo, "Evaluating the Case against Lyndon Johnson," Citizens for Truth about the Kennedy Assassination (CTKA), http://www.ctka.net/2012/Evaluating_the_Case_against_Lyndon_Johnson.html.

673 "That High-Living Baker Boy Scandalizes the Capital," *Life Magazine*, Nov. 8, 1963, pages 32–37, at page 32.

674 Ibid., page 33.

675 Ibid., pages 336–337.

676 Robert A. Caro, *The Passage of Power* (New York: Alfred A. Knopf, 2012), pages 275-299, at page 298.

677 Ibid.

678 Keith Wheeler, "Scandal Grows and Grows in Washington," *Life Magazine*, Nov. 22, 1963, pages 40–40B and 92A–98.

679 Ibid., page 40B.

680 Ibid., page 92B.

681 Ibid., page 40.

682 Caro, *Passage of Power*, pages 298–299.

683 Ibid., page 297.

684 John F. Kennedy, *Profiles in Courage* (New York: Harper & Brothers, 1956).

685 Ibid., pages 294–296, at page 294.

686 Schlesinger, Jr., *A Thousand Days*, page 1018.

687 Caro, *Passage of Power*, pages 294–295, at page 295.

688 Ibid., page 295.

689 Ibid., pages 295–296, at page 296.

690 CIA Document #632–796, stamped "Secret" and dated April 1, 1964.

691 Brad O'Leary and L. E. Seymour, *Triangle of Death: The Shocking Truth about the Role of South Vietnam and the French Mafia in the Assassination of JFK* (Nashville, TN.: WND Books, 2003), page 63.

692 Ibid., pages 58–65, at page 61.

693 Hurt, *Reasonable Doubt*, pages 414–415.

694 Ibid, page 417.

695 Ibid., page 418.

696 Ibid.

697 O'Leary and Seymour, *Triangle of Death*, page 133.

698 Ibid., page 135.

699 Ibid., page 128.

700 Ibid., page 117.

701 Ibid., page 151.

702 Alfred W. McCoy, *The Politics of Heroin: CIA Complicity in the Global Drug Trade* (Brooklyn, New York: Lawrence Hill Books, revised and expanded edition, 1991).

703 Ibid., pages 203–204.

704 Ibid., page 215.

705 Ibid., page 15.

706 Ibid., pages 15–16.

707 Ibid., page 385.

CONCLUSION: THE JFK ASSASSINATION AND THE NEW WORLD ORDER

708 Douglass, *JFK and the Unspeakable*, page xvi.

709 Lisa Pease, in James DiEugenio, *Destiny Betrayed*, page iii.

710 Ibid. See also Issac Don Levine, *The Mind of an Assassin: The Man Who Killed Trotsky* (New York: Farrar, Straus and Cudahy, 1959).

711 Kevin Phillips, *American Dynasty: Aristocracy, Fortune, and the Politics of Deceit in the House of Bush* (New York: Viking, 2004), page 37.

712 Ibid., page 39

713 Ibid., page 199.

714 DiEugenio, *Destiny Betrayed*, pages 3–5, at page 4.

715 Ibid.

716 Ibid., page 6.

717 Kenneth Conboy, *Feet to the Fire: CIA Covert Operations in Indonesia, 1957–1958* (Annapolis, MD: U.S. Naval Institute Press, 1999).

718 Kathy Kadane, States News Service, "Ex-agents say CIA compiled death lists for Indonesians," *Herald Journal*, Spartanburg, May 19, 1990. Also published in the *San Francisco Examiner* on May 20, 1990, and the *Washington Post* on May 21, 1990, as well as the *Boston Globe* on May 23, 1990, http://www.namebase.org/kadane.html.

719 John Roosa, *Pretext for Mass Murder: The September 30th Movement and Suharto's Coup d'Etat in Indonesia* (Madison, WI: University of Wisconsin Press, 2006), page 13.

720 Ibid., page 15.

721 Ibid., page 14.

722 DiEugenio, *Destiny Betrayed*, page 383.

723 Tom Flocco, "FBI memo, photo link Bush Sr to JFK Dallas murder scene, TomFlocco.com, http://tomflocco.com/fs/FbiMemoPhotoLinkBushJfk.htm.

724 J. Edgar Hoover, Director, FBI, Memorandum, Subject: "Anti-Castro Activities," Nov. 29, 1963. House Select Committee on Assassinations Record Number: HSCA 180-10006-10365. House Select Committee on Assassinations File Number: 62-109060-1396.

725 United States District Court for the District of Columbia, Civil Action 88-2600 GHR, Archives and Research Center v. Central Intelligence Agency, Affidavit of George William Bush, Sept. 21, 1988, http://www.aarclibrary.org/notices/Affidavit_of_George_William_Bush_880921.pdf.

726 "'63 F.B.I. Memo Ties Bush to Intelligence Agency," *New York Times*, July 11, 1988.

727 FBI Special Agent Graham Kitchel, Memorandum, Subject: "Unknown Subject; Assassination of President John F. Kennedy, date Nov. 22, 1963, U.S. National Archives.

728 Russ Baker, *Family of Secrets: The Bush Dynasty, the Powerful Forces that Put It in the White House, and What Their Influence Means for America* (New York: Bloomsbury Press, 2009), pages 64–65.

729 Kitty Kelly, *The Family: The Real Story of the Bush Dynasty* (New York: Doubleday, 2004), page 213.

730 President George H. W. Bush, "Address Before a Joint Session of the Congress on the Persian Gulf Crisis and the Federal Budget Deficit," Sept. 11, 1990, George W. Bush Presidential Library and Museum, http://bushlibrary.tamu.edu/research/public_papers. php?id=2217&year=1990&month=9.

731 Jack B. Pfeiffer, "The Taylor Committee Investigation of the Bay of Pigs," CIA, unclassified as of December 1984, http://www.foia.cia.gov/sites/default/files/document_conversions/4186/ bop-vol4.pdf.

732 Hersh, *The Old Boys*, page 73.

733 Ibid., page 368.

734 Warren Hinckle and William Turner, *Deadly Secrets: The CIA-MAFIA War Against Castro and the Assassination of J.F.K.* (New York: Thunders' Mouth Press, 1992), page 83.

735 Hersh, *The Old Boys*, page 336.

736 DiEugenio, *Destiny Betrayed*, page 385.

737 Max Holand, "The Lie that Linked CIA to the Kennedy Assassination: The Power of Disinformation," Center for the Study of Intelligence, CSI Publications, Fall-Winter 2001, https:// www.cia.gov/library/center-for-the-study-of-intelligence/csi-publications/csi-studies/studies/ fall_winter_2001/article02.html.

738 Leonard Mosley, *Dulles: A Biography of Eleanor, Allen, and John Foster Dulles and Their Family Network* (London: Hodder & Stoughton, Ltd, 1978), page 473.

INDEX